The Yankee International

The Yankee

The University of North Carolina Press   Chapel Hill and London

TIMOTHY MESSER-KRUSE

International

Marxism and
the American
Reform Tradition,
1848–1876

© 1998 The University
of North Carolina Press
All rights reserved
Designed by April Leidig-Higgins
Set in Monotype Bulmer by
Tseng Information Systems, Inc.
Manufactured in the United States
of America

The paper in this book meets the
guidelines for permanence and
durability of the Committee on
Production Guidelines for Book
Longevity of the Council on
Library Resources.

02 01 00 99 98   5 4 3 2 1

Library of Congress Cataloging-in-Publication Data

Messer-Kruse, Timothy.

The Yankee International: Marxism and the American
reform tradition, 1848–1876 / by Timothy Messer-Kruse.

p. cm. Includes bibliographical references (p.) and index.

ISBN 0-8078-2403-8 (cloth: alk. paper)

ISBN 0-8078-4705-4 (pbk.: alk. paper)

1. International Workingmen's Association — History — 19th
century. 2. Socialism — United States — History — 19th century.
3. Radicalism — United States — History — 19th century.
4. Social reformers — United States — History — 19th century.
I. Title.

HX11.I5M43   1998   97-36875

324.1'7 — dc21   CIP

For Diana,

my wings when
letting life pass by,
my anchor when
too high I fly

CONTENTS

ACKNOWLEDGMENTS

I CERTAINLY COULD NOT have written this work without the generous and patient help of my family, friends, colleagues, and teachers. Thanks to the Department of History at the University of Wisconsin at Madison for providing funding for my research trips. Needed funds and time away from other duties were provided by the University of Toledo Office of Research. A grant from the Schlesinger Library of Radcliffe College afforded me an opportunity to delve into their women's history collection. I am indebted to David Zonderman for inspiring me to focus on this period of history, Paul Boyer, whose historical insight and thoughtful suggestions brought out my best rhetorical and intellectual qualities and reined in my worst, Herbert Hill for his knowledgeable advice and confidence in my work, Linda Gordon for correcting some serious errors of omission early in my work, and Stanley Kutler and Thomas McCormick for their kind help and encouragement. I am very appreciative of the fine editorial work of Mary Caviness, who corrected, polished, and improved the manuscript in innumerable places. Michael Edmunds, James Danky, Harold Miller, and the terrifically knowledgeable and congenial staff of the State Historical Society library, archives, and periodicals departments have helped me in more ways than I can mention. Edward Weber guided me through the wonderful holdings of the Labadie Collection.

Throughout my short career I have leaned heavily on the moral and material support of many members of my family: my wife, Diana, and my sons, Griffin, Emmett, and Connor; Frederick and Ramona Kruse, Alan and Geri Messer, and Lynne and Len Beyfuss. Lastly, I would like to thank Paul Buhle and Carl J. Guarneri for their insightful comments and critiques.

It seems, to look back to these days again, that men and women had blood in their veins, then, and were alive and wide awake to the things that moved the world forward.

— Addie Ballou, in a letter to Victoria Woodhull, reflecting on her days in the Equal Rights Party and the First International thirty-six years before

The Yankee International

T HE International Workingmen's Association was born in England in 1864 and officially died in America twelve years later. Were its place in history to be judged solely by the deeds attributed to it by its enemies, the IWA might simply have been the most militant, far-reaching, and energetic socialist organization of its century. In little more than a decade the First International was credited with orchestrating the revolutionary uprising of the Paris Commune, conspiring to assassinate the crowned heads of Europe, organizing a wave of strikes that paralyzed America's largest city in 1872, and, not least, the IWA was even suspected of burning down the city of Chicago, before accusing fingers pointed to Mrs. O'Leary's cow. Quite a record for a short-lived party that attracted fewer than 5,000 Americans into its ranks.[1]

Such sensational and false accusations aside, the International Workingmen's Association in America was a remarkable organization, not so much for what it accomplished during its flash of notoriety, but for having existed at all. For a fleeting moment in time in the early 1870s, the IWA served as one big tent, sheltering communalists, anarchists, spiritualists, feminists, and land reformers (though few defined themselves so exclusively beneath a solitary rubric), radical groups that had not been united in pursuit of a single cause since their members were joined in the crusade against slavery. The IWA was an organization more characterized by its contradictions than its consistencies; it brought together those recognized as being the intellectual "fathers" of native anarchism with those credited with introducing Marxism to America. It enlisted both ideological atheists and the founders of American spiritualism. Among its members were trade unionists determined to preserve the privileges of America's racially and gendered industrial caste system and the leading champions of the equal rights of women and minorities. Attracting both rich and poor, black and white, native and immigrant, men and women, the IWA stood at the crossroads of American society and American radicalism.

Of all the differences and potential divisions contained within the IWA, it was the deep ideological chasm between a hardening Marxist orthodoxy and the republican ideals of Yankee radicals that proved insurmountable. The diversity of individuals attracted to the IWA flew in the face of the strategy that Marx and his German American cohorts had hammered out for America. Marx had called for organizing a coalition of German and Irish workers who would together radicalize the American proletariat. Such a vision of the IWA as a worker's vanguard capable of organizing and directing America's fledgling industrial proletariat into a sharp tool of class struggle fared badly at attracting American workers. Much to the chagrin of the IWA's class conscious German American leaders, it instead found itself deluged with Yankee radicals who shared a distrust of coercive authority in any guise. By 1870 the American reform element outnumbered the socialist Germans and had a widely circulated newspaper of its own (*Woodhull & Claflin's Weekly*). By the fall of that year the block representing English-language sections threatened to take control and democratize the IWA's American governing body, the Central Committee.

Yankee Internationalists pursued their own broad egalitarian goals from under their new red umbrella. In New York, native American reformers symbolically marched with African American veterans in their foremost ranks. They organized black sections and railed against discrimination of all kinds in their newspapers. They nominated Victoria Woodhull and Frederick Douglass for the highest offices in the land. They worked with the National Woman Suffrage Association to secure women's franchise. From the viewpoint of the German Americans who maintained close ties to Marx in London, such actions were viewed as "unscientific," idealistic, and simply wrongheaded. To them the Yankee radicals stood as the greatest obstacle to the success of their revolutionary strategy, and go they must.

And go they did. In 1871, after but a year of coalition, the German American agents of Marxist orthodoxy in America became convinced that the reputation of their party among bona fide workingmen was in jeopardy because of their partner's pursuit of the "moralistic" and "idealistic" issues of women's rights, municipal ownership of utilities, and democratic reforms. In December of that year, a German American faction, led by Friedrich Sorge, expelled their fellow English-speaking radicals from the party, a move that spelled the end of the International in America and foreshadowed a similar schism and collapse of its parent organization in Europe. With the purge of the Yankee radicals went the historical connection of the newly purified Left with the taproots of American radicalism and its unique commitment to racial egalitarianism, democracy, and individual civil rights. At the turn of the century, when the largest socialist movement in American history would flourish, it would be a party rife with contradictions: condemning the inequality of racial minorities in principle while showing great ambivalence about racism in party discussions, tolerating segregation in its own ranks, and, in the case of some top party leaders such as Victor Berger of Milwaukee, even publicly proclaiming their belief in white supremacy. Women, in spite of the Socialist Party's vocal support for woman suffrage, found themselves subordinated within the party itself. To no small extent the Socialist Party's contradictions were the inheritance of the Marxist leaders of its short-lived predecessor, who, in the end, choose doctrinal purity over a native tradition of universal reform and humanist morality.[2]

This, then, is the story of the collision of the American radical tradition with the vehicle of international socialism that was driven by Karl Marx himself. The focus of this work is upon the English-speaking radicals who joined the International Workingmen's Association and the reform traditions that they represented. Oddly enough, it is their story that has been slighted by historians over the years. Such blindness has been the result of the quick dismissal of Yankee members of the First International as either opportunistic, as "bourgeois," or as "sentimental reformers." This pattern was established in the first years of the twentieth century by Herman Schlüter, whose seminal history of the IWA, *Die Internationale in Amerika*, hailed the purification of the party of the Yankee reformers and all such tendencies that diverted workers from the task of class organization. More recently other scholars of the American Left have mistakenly branded the Yankee radicals as anarchists or laissez-faire individualists.[3]

All of these historians of the IWA in America have one thing in common—they all interpret American radicalism with categories of analysis derived from European history. Their intellectual yardstick measured a simple dichotomy of class: at one pole it equates radicalism, workers, and Marxism, and at the other it lumps conservatism, market liberalism, and the bourgeoisie. However appropriate such a measure is for points in the European experience, attempting to lay such a ruler alongside American society of the mid-nineteenth century is a futile exercise. Its increments fail to contain such typical Americans as the promarket American labor leader, the ex-slave barred from trade unions, the wealthy Christian socialist, or the labor-oriented feminist. Labels such as Marxist, anarchist, and utopian are of dubious analytical utility in a historical context where they had not yet come into use as terms of self-description.

To be a radical in the United States in the mid-nineteenth century was a far-reaching identity. It encompassed a broader measure of endeavor than the liberation and empowerment of class; it meant that one had a sweeping desire to effect progress in every aspect of human society. As Harvey Goldberg and William Appleman Williams observed in their volume on American radicals, the American radical was a difficult creature to pin down, and they themselves settled on a definition that turned on an axis of commitment and scope rather than upon ideology. Goldberg and Williams defined a radical as someone "who refuses to yield up his deeply conceived principles"; they argued that "to be a radical . . . is to be steadfast" and that American "radicalism points to the unattained future, not the once-attained past; . . . radicals belong to the side of progress."[4] The Yankees of the International Workingmen's Association were all of these things, and the activist tradition from which they sprung was indeed a radical one.

When the men and women of the First International are understood within their own experiences, when the temptation of shoving them into the confining intellectual pigeonholes of earlier Marxist analysis is resisted, a world of ideas and American reform history springs into view. The first key to understanding the Yankees who either joined or tacitly supported the IWA is understanding the radical intellectual milieu from which they came. English-speaking American radicals banded together at a unique intellectual intersection that connected the trailing edge of eighteenth-century political thought to a modern radical ideology rising with the tide of industrialism. Before the eventual seating of the trinity of Marx, Engels, and Lenin, theirs was a pantheistic faith: the statuary in their temple began with Tom Paine, Fourier, Owen, Swedenborg, and John Brown and ended with Brisbane, Kellogg, Proudhon, and, of course, Karl Marx.

It has been said of American radicalism that its most unique aspect is its discontinuity.[5] Dr. Martin Luther King Jr. learned his nonresistance from Gandhi rather than William Lloyd Garrison. The revival of American anarchism that occurred in the 1960s likewise found ideological inspiration abroad in the writings of Kropotkin, Tolstoy, and Proudhon rather than those of the equally important American anarchists Josiah Warren, Ezra Heywood, and Benjamin Tucker. Eugene Debs, a man raised in an industrial midwestern town that once had its own chapter of the IWA, did not study socialism until he turned forty in 1894 and did not read Karl Marx until Victor Berger, an urbane Hungarian immigrant, brought him three volumes of *Das Kapital* to read while he served time in federal prison for his part in leading a nationwide railroad strike.[6] Between such gaps in the memory of American radicalism lie people such as those who for a short time placed their hopes in the International Workingmen's Association.

Throughout this work I will refer to any English-speaking member of the IWA in America as a "Yankee." It is far less cumbersome than constantly referring to someone who was "native born" or "English speaking." Moreover, whenever Marx or his German American comrades spoke of English-speaking members of their party, they referred to them as "Yankees." Though this term in Marx's mouth was laden with derision, it is an apt one for this study since it points to the connection between the radicals of the native IWA and the deeper American reform tradition that was heavily centered in the "Yankee" districts of New England, upstate New York, and the Ohio Valley.

This study begins with a survey of the intellectual roots of American radicalism in order to show the logic whereby such diverse strands of reform thought could be knotted together within the International Workingmen's Association. Chapter 2 turns from radicalism in the United States to the founding and operation of the International in England. It argues that the ideological battles that eventually split the party in America had their origins and reflection in the differing historical and political perspectives of the IWA's London leadership. The next three chapters describe the growth and ideology of the Yankee International. Finally, Chapters 6 through 8 examine the forces, events, and disputes that eventually tore the First International in America apart, and where the pieces fell afterward.

CHAPTER ONE

The American Reform Tradition

THE FIRST INTERNATIONAL traveled to America in the steamer trunk of Cesare Orsini, a man whose name was well known on both sides of the Atlantic because of the exploits of his older brother Felice. Felice, a follower of Mazzini, was a veteran of revolutions along the entire length of the Italian peninsula and was eventually captured by the Austrians. He escaped from prison and made a daring attempt on the life of Napoleon III in 1858.[1]

Cesare Orsini set about recruiting Americans into the International soon after he arrived in 1866. He was immediately successful, as he later reported to Karl Marx, in lining up a number of prominent Americans. Among those he mentioned in his report, besides the few émigré socialists living in New York, was the Irish Fenian James Stephens and a number of American radicals of note, including Horace Greeley, Wendell Phillips, and Charles Sumner.[2]

Historians have tended to doubt that Horace Greeley and Charles Sumner were ever actually involved with the International, not because Orsini is a particularly untrustworthy source but because these American reformers have been portrayed as being so far afield ideologically from Marx, and from the labor movement in general, that no common ground was even conceivable to the scholars who have had to confront Orsini's claim. Horace Greeley, while expressing sympathy for the workingman and endorsing the platform of George Henry Evans's National Reformers, even for a time trumpeting the cause of Fourierist Associationism, could also proclaim the harmony of classes under capitalism and deplore "Jacobin ravings . . . against the Rich or the Banks."[3] Charles Sumner, the guiding light of Senate Radical Republicans and long considered a friend of labor by his Massachusetts constituents, has also been portrayed as remaining well within the boundaries of his party's capitalist "free labor" ideology. Indeed, by the end of the war, the ideology of leading Republicans was rapidly falling out of step with a resurgent labor movement, and Sumner himself raised the ire of workers around the nation when he voted against a federal eight-hour bill in 1868. From what has been written of these two men, none would seem a likely representative of the socialist movement in America.[4] Orsini's success in gaining a sympathetic ear among several of the scions of abolitionism suggests that the attitude of many American reformers toward the labor movement, capitalism, and the working class in general was far more complex than has heretofore been recognized.

Upon closer examination, Orsini's early recruitment of this trio of American reformers, though surprising, was not exceptional. In the years after the Civil War, many of the seasoned veterans of a plethora of antebellum reform movements publicly supported the aims, programs, and actions of the International. The breadth of support for the IWA is evident in the variety of reform journals that supported it. The longest running abolitionist journal, the *National Anti-Slavery Standard*, edited by A. M. Powell, opened its columns to the International and by the 1870s editorially endorsed it as well, as did its kindred reform sheet *The Golden Age*. Spiritualist newspapers such as *The Banner of Light*, *The American Spiritualist*, and *Hull's Crucible* sympathetically reported on the International. So did the *Bond of Peace*, the organ of the Universal Peace Society, and freethought papers such as Boston's *Investigator*. *The Revolution*, Susan B. Anthony's monthly devoted to women's rights gave it good notice, and the more strident (and more widely circulated) *Woodhull & Claflin's Weekly* was the American IWA's official organ in the English language.

Phillips, Sumner, and Greeley's interest in the International was no fluke or misunderstanding. By the end of the Civil War, radicals who had devoted decades to a variety of antebellum reform movements were gaining a new-found concern for the "labor question." In the 1860s and 1870s, many of the same faces that had been regularly arrayed on abolitionist, suffragist, pacifistic, and spiritualist daises of years before now occupied the same chairs under the auspices of the newly formed "labor reform" leagues and "eight-hour" associations. Of all the postwar labor reform organizations, none attracted the attention or recruited as many veteran American radicals as did the International Workingmen's Association. By the early 1870s, the IWA had emerged as a vibrant continuation of the American reform tradition.

The appeal of the IWA to American radicals, who were the glue that held together its diverse constituency, and the ideas that ultimately proved intolerable to its immigrant Marxist partners are all found in the ideological foundations of the American radical tradition. A close examination of this tradition and its connections to the development of American radical movements is necessary to understand the deeper linkages between the diverse nineteenth-century reform movements whose programs on the surface appear so different and even contradictory.

American radicals by the middle of the nineteenth century were the products of two interconnected lines of ideological descent: the revolutionary legacy of the eighteenth century and the dissenting and evangelical religious traditions that had been present since the establishment of the earliest English colonies. In a sense, nineteenth-century radicals were the true inheritors of one major thrust of the American intellectual tradition.

The radical inheritance derived from the Revolutionary era is the more obvious and the more direct of the two ideological legacies. At the beginning of the movement for independence from Britain, a strong radical tendency was apparent within committees and other constituent bodies organized to carry forward the anti-imperial protest. Thomas Jefferson's Declaration of Independence and Thomas Paine's *Common Sense* were not merely protests against King George's autocratic impositions or Parliament's infringements of colonial rights; they were also clarion calls for the recognition of the Enlightenment ideas of natural rights, the social contract, the power of reason to remake the world, and their mutual corollary, the right of revolution.[5]

With the success of the American Revolution, such radical principles became the property of the artisanal and yeoman farmer classes, since they were no longer useful to those of higher station, who now mostly wished to govern and consolidate their control over a fledgling national economy. Many artisans and other workers combined their republicanism with ancient cultural traditions that stubbornly refused to accept that prices and wages were to be free from community regulation and that upheld a "moral economy" against the juggernaut of the market society. At its extreme, this tradition nourished the working-class intellectual movements that produced the first extended critiques of capitalism and fed others who kept alive Paine's resistance to clericalism. By the 1840s, the tradition of artisan republicanism would reappear with renewed vigor in the movements for land reform, "individual sovereignty," producer cooperatives, and the formation of a new "labor brotherhood." By the 1870s, the declarations of the English-speaking branches of the International Workingmen's Association rang with republican rhetoric and revolved around a twin commitment to the principles that all wealth is the product of labor and that justice demands that all workers have an equal voice in government.

The first Yankee radicals to join the International were men and women whose long and deep experience in American reform movements bridged the worlds of the artisan and the industrial worker. They were older veterans of a succession of interrelated reform movements stretching back to the land reform and workingmen's parties of the 1830s.[6] The oldest of these, men such as John Commerford and Gilbert Vale, could boast of having drawn their radicalism from the source, having once worked alongside the great republican freethinker Thomas Paine.[7]

However, the other, deeper root of American radicalism that connects to the International is religious in origin. Long before Thomas Paine took up his quill and assaulted both throne and pulpit, a sectarian movement within English and American Protestantism had established a firm base upon which to rationalize disobedience to earthly authority. So threatening were these ideas to the power of ecclesiastical and colonial elites, who preached long and hard that worldly governments were divinely sanctioned, that advocating them was, for much of the seventeenth century, a harshly punished offense.[8]

These simply iconoclastic ideas grew up from the ontological seed sown by the Reformation that God, who created the world, was sovereign over it. The idea of God as sovereign, so seemingly benign, contained within it a powerful challenge to earthly authority. When this idea was carried over from a strictly religious doctrine to the secular sphere of politics, as it was by dissenting English sects during the English religious wars of the seventeenth century, it led to the defense of the individual conscience against either king or covenant.[9] For if, as it was claimed, God's law was the supreme law of human society, and God, as part of his perfect plan, had placed within every heart an intuitive moral sense and in every will the power to follow his straight and narrow path, then the evil that existed in the world was of human rather than divine cause, and its eradication was possible, even necessary. For dissenters, the clearest expression of such evil was the institution of slavery, a form of human government that completely smothered the soul of the African and corrupted the government of the European. This doctrine, termed "the inner light" among the Quakers, who were the dissenting sect most influential to American radicalism, and God's "Kingdom on Earth" by the evangelicals, who led a religious revolution across New England, Ohio, and western New York in the early nineteenth century, proved a powerful rationale for resistance to the upheavals and expropriations caused by the march of capitalism.[10]

By the 1820s, such ideas had spread across the "burned-over" district, that swath of passionate evangelism that cut across the North, and many Protestants were caught up in the revivals of itinerant ministers, most notably Charles Grandison Finney, who broke with the cold Calvinistic theology of predetermination and preached the doctrine of the kingdom of God, of the inner light, and of Christian free will, which called its adherents to benevolent action and self-improvement. The "Second Great Awakening," as this outpouring of religious revivalism was called, emphasized the perfectibility of mankind on earth. Its theology led to the dangerous belief that the devout should not only work to reform society but also to bring it into complete harmony with natural and divine law. In this sense, reform became less a pragmatic philosophy than a form of millennialism.

The idea of the perfectibility of man and society was open-ended; radical adherents to this idea came to believe that wherever an evil was perceived there was some immediate human remedy for it. Out of the perfectionist doctrine came the idea of universal social reform, a sweeping commitment to all initiatives and ideas that promised to alleviate suffering or improve the morality of society.[11] This conception of reform was all-encompassing in its scope; its goal was to probe every institution and challenge all found wanting. "What is abolition?" asked one midcentury abolitionist. Do you "think it is bounded by chattel slavery?" The answer to this rhetorical question offered a pure distillation of the widely held universal ideal of reform:

No sir — abolition, true abolition, runs the circle of the RIGHTS OF MAN. Overleaping all geographical boundaries, it plants its footsteps on the great universal platform of our common humanity; and its watchword is — "One Country, One Language, One Brotherhood." Man was not made for institutions, but institutions for man. Down with all institutions, be they Church or State, whose existence depends on temporal or spiritual debasement of a single human being. This . . . is the creed that I learned in the abolition school.[12]

One of the distinguishing characteristics of antebellum reform movements in general was their comprehensiveness. Midcentury reformers dabbled in everything from abolitionism to women's rights. No proposal for social improvement seemed to have escaped their attention, whether it involved mainstream reforms such as temperance or uncommon enthusiasms such as phrenology, Spiritualism, free love, Fourierism, or vegetarian diets. Abolitionism was the sun around which all these diverse planets of reform orbited. The pages of the *Liberator* were filled with discussions of the latest findings of pseudoscience and of reports of séances held to gain the advice of long-dead martyrs for the antislavery cause. The universalistic philosophy of reform even took institutional form: in 1840, a group of Boston radicals, chaired by Brownson Alcott, gathered and founded a new reform organization called the "Friends of Universal Reform."[13]

Even more important than the scope of the radical vision that emerged out of perfectionist thinking was the intermingling of this universal concern with the idea of divine sovereignty. The theology of the sovereignty of God paralleled the Enlightenment notion of natural rights: both doctrines preached that some human liberties, especially those connected with the free expression of conscience, were inviolate by any human agency. By itself, the idea that laws made by men were subordinate to the laws of God was subversive, but when wedded to its logical corollary, that the righteous must not respect human law or human rule that blasphemes the will of the divine, it carried its radical potential into action. These beliefs, in the hands of antebellum radicals, justified civil disobedience and resistance to all manner of human institutions. Abolitionists called upon the righteous to abide by the biblical injunction to "come out from her, my people, that ye receive not of her plagues" and leave those churches that refused to condemn the sin of slavery. Many did, and "come-outer" sects proliferated in the 1840s and 1850s.[14]

William Lloyd Garrison and other radical abolitionists institutionalized these beliefs and even carried them close to a form of anarchism when they founded the New England Non-Resistance Society in September of 1838. The Non-Resistants condemned all forms of violence and coercion as sinful, and they specifically rejected their fealty to a government that harbored slavery. Garrison once dramatized this position by burning a copy of the U.S. Constitution. "The kingdoms of this world . . . are all to be supplanted, whether they are called despotic, monarchical, or republican," Garrison wrote. "The kingdom of God is to be established in all the earth, and it shall never be destroyed, but it shall break in pieces and consume all others."[15] Such totalizing moral judgments and a willingness to challenge long-standing institutions—together the hallmark of the radical mind—were nurtured within the ranks of radical abolitionists. It was only natural, then, that they would later be unleashed against other evils. As the problems of industrial society mounted with the ongoing market revolution of the antebellum era, these radical concepts were easily extended to critique the evil of economic exploitation, an evil that the radical abolitionists only had begun to understand in the last years of their crusade.

By the end of the first third of the nineteenth century, the intellectual architecture of a native American radicalism was well established. Its pillars included religious precepts such as perfectionism and the moral imperative to "come-out" from, to reject, human institutions that oppressed or blocked the path to righteousness, as well as the more famous secular ideas of republicanism, natural rights, and freethought. By the end of the 1840s, American radicalism would strike out in new directions, a movement that has often been misinterpreted as a fragmentation of radical ranks. Indeed, on the surface the American reform tradition that was once primarily interested in abolition and communalism does appear to have emerged from that decade having frayed into a thick fringe of unrelated reform hobbies. But if one looks past the eclectic agendas of these reform strands to the people who championed them, the heavy overlap between them becomes immediately apparent. Radicals did not so much abandon their old reform allegiances for new ones; rather, they heaped more commitments upon their already overflowing perfectionist plates.

The year 1848 was a watershed one in the history of American radicalism. It marked the beginning of the most important intellectual and social movements that would culminate in the forming of the Yankee International twenty years later. The events of 1848 must have tapped the reserves of even the most eclectically minded American radical, for within a very short period of time, the modern women's rights movement, the most radical elements of which embarked on a daring critique of marriage itself, was launched; thousands of European radical refugees arrived in Eastern cities; and to top it all off, a new radical religion, or better yet, a religion of radicalism known as Spiritualism, swept the country.

In 1848, the first women's rights convention was held at Seneca Falls, New York. Its declarations rang with the ideals of perfectionism: "Being invested by the Creator with the same capabilities, and the same consciousness of responsibility for their exercise, it is demonstrably the right and duty of woman . . . to promote every righteous cause." As means to this end the radical sisterhood echoed the come-outer's creed: "All laws which prevent woman from occupying such a station in society as her conscience shall dictate . . . are contrary to the great precept of nature, and therefore of no force or validity." [16] Given these declarations, the leap women made from the rejection of patriarchal government in law to a rejection of its patriarchal economic underpinnings was not too great. Decades later, several of those who attended that landmark convention, including Elizabeth Cady Stanton, Amy Post, and Isabella Hooker, were delegates to a "People's Convention" of "Internationals and Woman Suffragists," which supported the socialist program of the time and nominated the IWA publicist Victoria Woodhull for president.[17]

Simultaneously, with the emergence of the mainstream movement for women's rights, a more radical demand for women's liberation was voiced in 1848, as a few militant feminists attacked the legal institutions of marriage as tantamount to legal prostitution and a barrier to morality and virtue. At the Seneca Falls Convention, the demand for legal and political equality was accompanied by a critique of marriage. Seneca Falls's final declaration formally attacked the legal fetters of marriage, which, participants charged, made the husband woman's "master" and gave him "power to deprive her of liberty and to administer chastisement." For the next twenty years the "free love" movement, as this rally against the legal trappings of marriage was called, would be closely intertwined with the general women's movement, until its increasing notoriety in the years after the Civil War drove all but the most radical feminists to distance themselves from it. Out of the "free love" tendency within the women's rights movement came the most enthusiastic supporters for the International.[18]

In the spring of 1848, down the road from Seneca Falls, in Rochester, New York, a pair of teenage girls astonished onlookers with their seeming ability to communicate with the spirits of the dead by means of mysteriously ethereal knocking sounds. The "Rochester rappings," as they were known, were a phenomenon that merely popularized a philosophical movement quietly overtaking much of the intelligentsia of the old "burned-over district." This new faith, Spiritualism, was a curious but historically unsurprising mixture of mysticism, perfectionism, come-outerism, and the scientific method.

Spiritualism is easily dismissed for the air of charlatanism that clings to it. Rapping hands, disembodied trumpets, spirit dials, and the parlor séance were certainly mainstays of Spiritualist practice. Despite such easily parodied trappings, Spiritualists represented a serious intellectual rebellion against what they perceived as the hollowness and the hypocrisy of the various midcentury Christian denominations. The chain of revolt against the strictures of Calvinism, which in New England can be traced from the revolt of the Unitarians to their own repudiation by the Universalists, found its ultimate expression in Spiritualism.

Spiritualism sprung from sources on both sides of the Atlantic. Its European roots can be traced to the evolution of the idea first proposed by the eighteenth-century French theorist Anton Mesmer that a single cosmic medium, "animal magnetism" he called it, interpenetrated and interconnected all material objects. Mesmer's protégés embellished his postulate by claiming that this "magnetism" was not only universal in the material realm but flowed throughout the spiritual dimension as well, thus allowing for communication between the two by means of the subconscious mind. Farther east, the testimonials of the mystic Emanuel Swedenborg (1688–1772), who recorded his transcendent journeys to heaven, hell, and points beyond, captured the imagination of many unhappy Lutherans. Swedenborg's revelations that men were but spirits draped in temporal garments and that therefore one's innate character and personality were unchanged by death made the afterlife a more certain and appealing prospect.[19]

Spiritualism's American roots are thrust deep into the same fertile burned-over soil of upstate New York from which sprung so much of the reform momentum of the antebellum period. Formally founded in 1848, the year of European revolution and the birth of the modern women's movement, the Spiritualist movement likewise expressed a radical and iconoclastic nature. Like the Christian perfectionist thought that underlay the reform impulse as a whole, Spiritualists believed in the essential goodness of all humans and in the possibility of the creation of a heavenly society on earth. Like the Universalists, Spiritualists rejected any notion of Christian hell and upheld the essential goodness of human nature.

Spiritualism was closely related to the Transcendentalist philosophical movement associated with Ralph Waldo Emerson and Henry David Thoreau. Both movements were offsprings of Swedenborgian mysticism and German idealism. In practice, Spiritualists took the Transcendentalist's assertion of the ultimate divinity of every human and made it literal. Like Emerson and others of his school, Spiritualists looked upon all creation, especially upon nature, as being harmonious and invested with spiritual truth. What distinguished Spiritualism from all such other liberal strains of thought was its adherents' belief that the existence of the supernatural in the natural world, like all other natural phenomenon, could be discerned, investigated, and understood through the methods of science.[20]

Unlike participants in other religious movements, Spiritualists believed that their practice did not rest upon faith; indeed, they renounced faith as blind superstition. The bedrock of their belief was empiricism—Spiritualism was toted as the "science" of the metaphysical. Its devotees fancied themselves as critical investigators gathering material evidence of the reality of a supernatural world. In fact, in the early nineteenth century, when such inventions as electricity and the telegraph were associated with the supernatural, and the investigation of perpetual motion, phrenology, and alchemy still passed for science, Spiritualism did not seem so unscientific as it does in our modern age. Spiritualists did not worship their spirits; they worshiped the principles of reason and empiricism, whose power, they believed, had allowed them to glimpse the eternal. As one Spiritualist lecturer claimed, "To me, Spiritualism is a science—the science of religion. It comes with objective facts, and through reason demonstrates that our life is continued beyond this moral." Spiritualism served as a religious bridge for those doubters unreconciled to the world of Calvin and Wesley and confronted with that of Darwin and Marx.[21]

Spiritualism grew rapidly, especially among women, for whom the practice of mediumship allowed them a leadership role and a public voice that most religions had denied to them. Spiritualism gained credence as a philosophical movement with the publication of Andrew Jackson Davis's book *The Principles of Nature, Her Divine Revelations and a Voice to Mankind*, a work that synthesized the many religious antecedents of Spiritualism and added on top a large dollop of Charles Fourier's utopian socialism. Davis's work quickly went through numerous printings and succeeded in shifting the discussion of Spiritualism from table rappings to a more complex Spiritualist cosmology. By the mid-1850s, there were at least fifty Spiritualist periodicals published at any one time; many were small and ephemeral, but a few were more successful. For example, the *Banner of Light* achieved a circulation of 25,000 and was professionally edited by the *Boston Post*'s own editor, William Colby. It was estimated at that time that there were 40,000 practicing Spiritualists in the New York City area alone. Several contemporary estimates of national Spiritualist numbers ran into the millions, though the noninstitutional nature of Spiritualism makes it impossible to verify such claims. The best modern historical estimates peg the number of practicing Spiritualists in the hundreds of thousands. Whatever their numbers, Spiritualists enjoyed a high profile in mid-nineteenth-century society. In Washington, D.C., for example, séances were popular with the Capitol Hill crowd, and one congressman from upstate New York, A. P. Hascall, declared himself a medium.[22]

Like the radical side of perfectionist religion, philosophical Spiritualism was intimately bound up with the goal of earthly reform. Among Spiritualism's most cherished beliefs was its view that all of nature, and, indeed, all creation, was harmonious. Human suffering and injustice, therefore, was the effect of the operation of human institutions or customs that subverted the natural order. This belief in the fundamental harmony and unity of nature moved the possibility of reforming society from a wild dream to a practical reality. Reform would not be the uphill battle to create harmony where none had been before, as the cynical and the "pragmatic" public held it to be, but a process of uprooting the impediments to the natural operation of the universal spirit of harmony—a process of releasing the harmony inherent in nature. Spiritualists believed that the fundamental forces of the universe were on their side.[23]

The earliest Spiritualist societies proclaimed spiritual investigation as but one aspect of their general reform crusade. Philadelphia's first Spiritualist society, the Harmonial Benevolent Association, stated in the preamble of its constitution that "voices from the spiritland" were "cheering us on in the work of human elevation and redemption in our spiritual, intellectual and social natures." The purpose of the association was both "the spiritual cultivation of man" and "the alleviation of some of the many woes by which he is so sadly burthened." The Philadelphia harmonialists armed themselves with the same belief in the supremacy of divine law over governmental authority that charged the radicalism of Garrison and his fellow nonresistants. "With no master but God," they declared, "and no creed but humanity, do we enter the field of our labors, recognizing in man the latent germ of a divine nature, which, when duly cultivated, is the highest rule of right in human action."[24]

Such concern for the universal progress of humanity was so common within Spiritualist ranks that they even claimed that the spirits themselves were organizing for the reform of human civilization. In 1853, John Murray Spear, a Universalist minister who later became one of the founders of an IWA chapter in San Francisco, announced that he had received a message from the spirit world informing him that the spirits had themselves formed a union. The reformers of the hereafter called their organization the Association of Beneficents and pledged to do all they could to end human injustice and misery.[25]

In their affirmation of the divinity of each individual and the existence of a universal and natural harmony against which all human institutions must be measured, Spiritualists took the practice of come-outerism to new heights. Spiritualists were absolutist when it came to giving free reign to individual conscience and were therefore fiercely opposed to all forms of religious orthodoxy. They never established a clergy, formed a church, or codified their doctrines, and they generally shunned hierarchy of all kinds. So libertarian were they in their approach to belief, even Spiritualist belief, that freethinking atheists came to regard them as their allies. Spiritualists were considered "loyal and practical Secularists" by George E. MacDonald, one of the leaders of freethought in America. MacDonald estimated that a quarter of the readers of the leading freethought journal *The Truth Seeker* were Spiritualists and that 90 percent of the Spiritualists in the country supported the program of the National Liberal League, the institutional expression of freethought in America for the last half of the nineteenth century.[26]

Spiritualism attracted many people whose radical activities had already placed them beyond the pale of mainstream society. Spiritualists could readily be found among the partisans of abolitionism and feminism, in Owenite communities and Fourierist phalanxes. In 1859, Gerrit Smith noted that "the Spiritualists I met on my tours through the State last fall, were nearly all reformers. . . . I have no doubt that, in proportion to their numbers, Spiritualists cast tenfold as many votes for Abolition and Temperance tickets as did others." Nearly the entire leadership of the abolitionist movement espoused Spiritualism at some point in their careers. While the same cannot be said for the women's rights movement, Elizabeth Cady Stanton and Susan B. Anthony observed in *History of Woman Suffrage* that "the only religious sect in the world . . . that has recognized the equality of women is the Spiritualists." Until the mid-1850s, the ties between Spiritualism and Fourierist socialism were equally close. A. J. Davis was much influenced by the writings of Charles Fourier, and séances were a regular event at Fourierist colonies, or so-called phalanxes, across the country.[27]

These beginnings, though important in the history of American reform movements, have long been overshadowed by events in Europe. In 1848, across the breadth of Europe, peasants and workers, ethnic minorities, and an emergent liberal middle class rebelled against monarchical and imperial rule. The German states, France, Italy, and the Austro-Hungarian empire all witnessed powerful revolutionary civil wars. In the midst of this upheaval, the *Communist Manifesto*, the most famous work in all socialist history, was published in London by Karl Marx and Friedrich Engels, inaugurating a

European socialist tradition that explicitly rejected as "utopian" and "bourgeois" the philosophies, programs, and practices of radicalism in America.

One by one, popular uprisings were crushed, and Europe's defeated revolutionaries took flight to America to escape the wave of persecutions that followed. Most of those who made it to the United States were refugees from the German states who had joined hundreds of thousands of their countrymen rushing to the land where they believed "nobody need be poor, because everybody is free."[28] Radical "Forty-Eighters," as they were called, were a diverse lot. Most were liberal democrats, though a small socialist contingent brought with them a disciplined intellectual focus whose faith in the predictive power of social theory was alien to the universalist, experimental, and moralistic character of the American radical tradition. Socialist Forty-Eighters such as Friedrich Sorge and Joseph Weydemeyer brought Marxism to America and laboriously built up a succession of small socialist parties, only to see them fail, one after another, until the relative success of the International Workingmen's Association.

While new forms of radicalism appeared and spread in the late 1840s, the older radicalism of immediate abolitionism also moved steadily toward a new understanding of the labor question. At the dawn of the antebellum abolitionist movement, some of its leadership displayed a harsh classical economic outlook that denied that workers faced any sort of collective oppression. In the very first issue of the *Liberator*, Garrison denounced Boston's first labor party, the New England Association of Farmers, Mechanics, and other Workingmen, which was then being organized by Seth Luther, for attempting "to inflame the minds of our working classes against the more opulent, and to persuade men that they are being contemned and oppressed by a wealthy aristocracy."[29] Garrison refused to accept the claim of workers that they faced such systematic economic oppression. To Garrison and other early abolitionists, oppression was a strictly political category. As Garrison explained in the next issue of the *Liberator*, "In a republican Government, where hereditary distinctions are obsolete, . . . the avenues of wealth, distinction and supremacy are open to all."[30]

Such attitudes were shaped by a complex mixture of ideological and social factors. Early abolitionists were, for the most part, a privileged generation—many were college educated, and upper class. Wendell Phillips came from one of the foremost families of Boston. Much of the early New York abolitionist movement was sponsored by the brothers Arthur and Lewis Tappan, wealthy merchants and publishers of the *Journal of Commerce*. Garrison, while not born into such heights, had been a propagandist for

Henry Clay's "American System" before he met Benjamin Lundy and enlisted in the abolitionist crusade. In 1828, Garrison wrote, "We wish to see a manufactory by the side of every suitable stream. . . . Every day's experience teaches this whole people that their interests are best promoted by the erection of *national houses of industry*."[31] But by the 1840s, such rigid views of the "labor question" were becoming increasingly rare within the reform community, and a general willingness to champion the reforms advocated by workers themselves grew.

There were many forces at work pulling abolitionists and other antebellum radicals into a closer alliance with labor in the 1840s and 1850s. Industrial conditions gradually changed, usually for the worse from the point of view of the artisan, and many abolitionists grew alarmed at these worsening labor conditions and the spread of the factory system. The Panic of 1837, which had reduced many New England artisans to beggary, shook the comfortably dismissive attitude of many Northerners toward poverty. Abolitionists used the occasion to heap another charge upon slavery—that it drained away Northern capital and was the cause of the nation's economic troubles. Joshua Leavitt, one of the founders of the Liberty Party, interwove moral arguments for emancipation with just such an economic analysis of slavery when stumping for his party in the presidential election of 1840.[32]

Political events rapidly narrowed the ground between Northern labor and abolitionists. A coalition of interests was formed between workers, whose own desire for land reform collided with the slave interest's demand for the extension of slavery into the Western territories, and abolitionists, who saw containment of slavery as the first step toward its elimination. This agreement proved to be the foundation for both the Liberty and Free-Soil Party coalitions of the 1840s and 1850s.

As the question of the status of the conquered Mexican lands exploded into the Wilmot Proviso crisis of 1846–48, workers found a basis for opposing slavery that did not require that they accept the principle of racial equality, or even mention slaves at all. For the first time, much of the labor press raised their pens against the slave power, though they remained far from allying themselves with abolition. Said the Cincinnati *Daily Unionist*, "We are no abolitionists in the popular sense of the term, but we would belie our convictions of democracy did we not oppose slavery's extension over new lands." With a labor movement largely united in opposition to the extension of slavery, abolitionists found it much more comfortable to support labor's cause.[33]

Abolitionist leaders began to recognize the crucial position of the working-class electorate and its potential power, and they attempted to bring it aboard by emphasizing that the problems of workers were actually created by slave labor. In 1848, English abolitionist Edward West analyzed the political realities of the abolitionist movement in a letter to his "respected friend" Garrison. While the abolitionist movement had made great progress, noted West, slavery was still strong and the day of emancipation remained distant. Abolitionists had to find "some more substantial force than has yet been tried" to overcome slavery. The question was what power this was to be. West's answer was unequivocal: "Bring the question to a settlement by the moral force of public opinion, a power to which all questions of political importance must ultimately yield[;] it must be shown to the Commercial and Working Classes of America, not only that slavery is unjust, and inconsistent with the Christian Dispensation, but also how their private interest is really injured by slavery. Only prove to those powerful classes, that their private interest is so affected, and the days of slavery will soon be numbered." [34]

Abolitionists appealed directly to workers by arguing that slavery degraded free labor by both underbidding it and fostering a climate in which manual labor was viewed as disreputable. Some abolitionists also pointed to the South's role in perpetuating high tariffs that retarded Northern commerce. Most simply warned that slavery would drag free labor down to its level. [35]

In the course of tailoring their arguments to the great "bone and sinew" of society, abolitionists took stock of the condition of the Northern worker. The 1840s were a decade of labor's rise from the ashes of the depression of 1837. As prosperity returned to the country by 1842, workers' organizations begin to reappear and resist the encroachments of the changing industrial order. Throughout the Northeast, mechanics' associations sprung up, modeled closely on the previous generation of workingmen's associations. As local labor organizations grew, they quickly called for the formation of regional and even national bodies that could both coordinate their efforts and represent them with one unified voice in the political arena. In late 1844, the first initiative toward creating such a regional organization since the devastating depression of 1837 was taken when workers gathered in Boston's Faneuil Hall and began the task of rebuilding the defunct New England Workingmen's Association (NEWA).

In the spring of 1845, the dream of a regional network of labor organizations came closer to fruition with a massive convention in Lowell, Massachusetts, which attracted several thousand delegates who succeeded in hammering out a constitution for the new NEWA. Widely hailed in the reform press as departing significantly from the exhausted and narrow agenda of previous labor bodies, the Lowell convention attracted the attention of many reformers. One correspondent to Greeley's *New York Daily Tribune* described how the convention's "proceedings were characterized by a spirit of Universality, a degree of Intelligence and an insight into the real causes of the Evils which oppress the Laboring Classes that promise well for the success of this important movement." The reporter praised the Lowell convention for considering an agenda "broader and more universal than any I remember to have seen taken by the Producing Classes," a plan that was unlike those of the old labor unions, who "assumed a narrow, selfish and exclusive basis" and only "proposed trifling and one-sided measures . . . and these only for this or that class of Laborers." All of this must have been encouraging to many reformers, especially to abolitionists, for whom this gathering promised a reconciliation and an attractive opening for recruitment.[36]

Such must have been the case, judging by the range of reformers who flocked to the NEWA after the convention at Lowell. The first formal meeting of the NEWA followed several months later and was unique in the breadth of personalities that it attracted. Gathering that May in Boston were not only the ubiquitous faces of labor reform of this era, including George Henry Evans, the associationists, represented by Horace Greeley and Robert Owen, and a strong contingent from the Transcendentalist and Fourierist Brook Farm, including L. W. Ryckman, George Ripley, and Charles Dana, but a strong showing of abolitionists as well. William Lloyd Garrison, Wendell Phillips, Theodore Parker, W. H. Channing, Marcus Morton, and Frederick Robinson also attended. Only a decade earlier Garrison had denounced a similar gathering in no uncertain terms: "This is not reform, which in removing one evil threatens to inflict a thousand others."[37]

While no mention was made of the first NEWA meeting in the pages of the *Liberator*, Garrison did post a sympathetic announcement of the next NEWA meeting in several issues under the headline "MASS MEETING":

We see the demonstrations they have made, on former occasions, of self-sacrifice to their cause. If we are not as multitudinous as they, is that a reason why we should not do what we can? Come all who may. . . . The rights of labor demand that not one be missing when the roll is called. . . . Editors who are interested in the elevation of the producing classes and industrial reform, and the extinction of slavery and servitude in all their forms, are invited to give the above an insertion in their papers and also to be present at the meeting.[38]

And for the issue that appeared the week that the NEWA meeting was scheduled to convene, Garrison allotted a full column on the editorial page for an article written by NEWA's president, L. W. Ryckman, entitled "To The Workingmen of New England." That Garrison placed Ryckman's appeal on page two constituted something of an endorsement, since the *Liberator* already reserved the "Reformatory" column on page four for the sundry musings of kindred reformers. Ryckman reviewed the progress that had been made toward forming a coalition "of the distinguished members of the various reform movements which now agitate the country" who were to assemble to "waive the discussion of points upon which they differ, and to adopt such a Constitution as will serve as a basis of action for the attainment of the ascendancy of those principles, upon which they all agree." Among these principles was one that revealed a complex relationship with the idea of a free-market society: the "guarantee to all men, women, and children, education and employment as matters of rights, inherent and inalienable; and social position based upon character, and not upon wealth and other accidental circumstances."[39]

Although Garrison and other leading abolitionists did not attend subsequent industrial congresses, they must have been cheered by the tone of resolutions these assemblies cranked out. At the next congress, held in New York, the Industrial Convention proclaimed that "Life, Liberty, and the Pursuit of Happiness" were "sacred rights . . . universal throughout the world, and to each individual without regard to size, strength, country or color." While not a ringing endorsement of abolition, this plank was clearly aimed at the peculiar institution.[40]

At the same time, a growing empathy for labor's demands was voiced in the proclamations of the antislavery societies. In 1849, the Massachusetts Anti-Slavery Society passed a resolution that exhorted Northern workers to rally around their standard and acknowledged that workers had their own unique grievances:

> Whereas, the rights of the laborer at the North are identified with those of the Southern slave and cannot be obtained as long as chattel slavery rears its hydra head in our land; and whereas, the same arguments which apply to the situation of the crushed slave, are also in force in reference to the condition of the Northern laborer—although in a less degree; therefore
> Resolved, That it is equally incumbent upon the working-man of the

North to espouse the cause of the emancipation of the slave and upon Abolitionists to advocate the claims of the free laborer.[41]

In spite of the progress that had been made in allying abolition and labor, cultural and class antagonisms persisted. At a large meeting of the Mechanics' Association attended by both abolitionists and workers, one Epes Sargent read a poem satirizing elite reformers. To the great discomfort of the abolitionists in the audience Sargent's verses ridiculed a wide array of reformers and philanthropists, from temperance and peace advocates to abolitionists. As one "old member" of the Anti-Slavery Society who witnessed the affair put it, "When any smart thing was said, as many were, — true or false, — the moderate drinkers and sustainers of intemperance, of slavery, of war, of prisons and the gallows, made most delightful manifestations with their heels, and their broad grins and loud laugh at the witticisms of the speaker." [42]

Several years later another abolitionist wrote to Garrison describing a similar encounter he had upon leaving the hall where the Massachusetts Anti-Slavery Society had been holding their annual meeting. "As I was coming out of the Melodeon with the crowd . . . I heard a man, who had apparently been listening to the speeches, say, with a good deal of dissatisfaction, 'These abolitionists never say a word about the oppression of the Northern laborer, who has to toil his life out for a bare subsistence.' " This correspondent went on to note that laborers often charged that the abolitionist movement was led by men who had "always lived upon fortunes, which they never lifted a finger to accumulate." [43]

At a convention of the New England Anti-Slavery Society in 1850, one of the speakers decried the refusal of abolitionists to champion the cause of labor and took a decidedly more critical tone toward the industrial system than had those of the Garrisonian stripe. The famous Unitarian minister William H. Channing rose to explain why Northern workers had failed to lend their wholehearted support to the cause of abolition. He concluded that it was because of the failure of abolitionists to recognize the kindred struggle of labor: "I believe that one reason why the working classes of the whole country have not come up by instinct and in masses, to the support of Freedom, is, that our Anti-Slavery friends have not gone far enough in showing that man is man everywhere." Channing went on to denounce the "power of combined Capital and Party Organization, working upon the cupidity of Northern politicians" to "oppress the poor." "The thorough Emancipation of Work alone corresponds to the Ideal of our Nation," he declared. In spite of the errors of the past there was still hope; were the New England Anti-Slavery Society to broaden their principles to encompass the concerns of Northern labor, then "would all just men be with you." In later years Channing was hailed as a "stout opponent of the wages system" and became an active member of the New England Labor Reform League.[44]

Although tensions persisted, some sympathy for the underdogs of industry grew, even from among those who had before taken the most conservative stance on the labor question. Garrison had apparently warmed to the working class when, in private remarks to a friend in 1848, he decried the excessive toil of the Northern worker and agreed that there should be a reduction in working hours.[45] But in his public statements Garrison still resisted making any specific reform appeal to labor interests out of the belief that any deviation from the single great issue of slavery would only impair a movement "already staggering under the load of responsibilities connected with what we deem to be, for the time being, the most radical movement on the American soil."[46] Likewise, Lydia Maria Child, the editor of the *National Anti-Slavery Standard*, confided in a letter to some friends in 1849, "There are instants, when the sight of rags and starvation make me almost ready to smash thro [sic] the plate-glass of the rich, and seize their treasures of silver and gold."[47] Elizur Wright, the first secretary of the New York Anti-Slavery Society, wrote in 1848 that "slavery is only a species under a genus of wrong and oppression," and he called for "the union of all that work, whether bond or free, to throw off the yoke together."[48]

Cooperation between labor and capital represented the central goal of utilitarian reform. In its pursuit, reformers understood the workers' discontents and to a degree championed the cause of workingmen. Thus Daniel R. Goodloe, editor of the abolitionist *National Era* and a writer on matters of political economy, supported the Shoemakers' strike of 1860. "We sincerely wish success to the journeymen," Goodloe wrote in the *Era*. "The great defect of the social system," he continued, "is the necessity which constrains the laboring class to work at such prices as capitalists choose to accord them and the great desideratum is the discovery of some remedy for the evil."[49]

The voice of labor at the time offered still other solutions—legal limitation of hours, outlawing prison labor, land reform, the state recognition of trade unions, etc.—but these were not universal solutions to the problems of poverty and dislocation that concerned most reformers. Rather, they were viewed as privileges sought by a narrow group of artisans who themselves occupied a social station above that of the destitute and did not share their interests. By the 1840s, then, leading reformers could be just as critical in their understanding of the exploitative nature of the American economic order as any labor radical or utopian socialist, but they still distanced themselves from labor organizations because they viewed their solutions as particular privileges and not general reforms.

Nevertheless, the increasing strength of the coalition between abolition and labor was reflected in a change in the rhetoric of slavery's apologists by the mid-1850s. In earlier years, when the tensions between abolitionists and labor leaders still ran high, slavery's defenders freely drew parallels between the condition of free workers in the North and slaves in the South. "I hold," proclaimed Calhoun on the Senate floor in 1837, "that there never has yet existed a wealthy and civilized society in which one portion of the community did not, in point of fact, live on the labor of the other." Slavery was upheld as the superior institution, for "in few countries so much is left to the share of the laborer, and so little exacted from him, or where there is more kind attention paid to him in sickness or infirmities of age." Labor leaders approved of such sentiments simply because they endorsed their own assertion that the labor question command the top position on the reform agenda. But as the movements for emancipation and labor reform grew together over the next decade, Southern apologists increasingly attacked Northern labor itself, rather than its predicament, and warned of the danger of Northern radicalism. James Henry Hammond's famous Senate "Mud-Sill" speech of 1858 was widely denounced in the labor press for insulting workers in the claim that every society "has a class to do the menial duties, to perform the drudgery of life, . . . a class requiring but a low order of intellect and but little skill." But Hammond also warned his fellow senators from the North against the dangers of a class revolt: "Our slaves do not vote. We give them no political power. Yours do vote, and, being the majority, they are the depositories of all your political power. If they knew the tremendous secret, that the ballot-box is stronger than 'an army with banners,' and could combine, where would you be? Your society would be reconstructed, your government overthrown, your property divided." [50]

And while Northern elites were being warned of the threat of class conflicts brewing on their own doorstep, abolitionists were accused of being agents of anarchism and socialism. Senator Jefferson Davis warned his Northern counterparts of the increasing sympathy among abolitionists for the problems of the worker under capitalism: "The European Socialists, who in wild radicalism, are the correspondents of the American abolitionists, maintain the same doctrine as to all property, that the abolitionists do as to slave property. . . . The same precise theories of attack at the North on the slave property of the South would, if carried out to their legitimate and necessary logical consequences, and will, if successful in this, their first stage of action, superinduce attacks on all property, North and South."[51]

Some of slavery's most influential and systematic apologists began to denounce abolitionist leaders as being "communists." Southern propagandist George Fitzhugh actually wrote to Garrison in 1856, notifying him of the impending release of his new book *Cannibals All!: or Slaves Without Masters*, another in the genre of proslavery critiques of Northern capitalism, and giving Garrison a taste of one of its themes: "I shall in effect say, in the course of my argument, that every theoretical Abolitionist at the North is a Socialist or Communist, and proposes or approves radical changes in the organization of society."[52]

While Fitzhugh and Davis's characterization of abolitionists as communists may have been exaggerated, there is evidence that there was some interchange between the two groups by the late 1850s. In 1858, a group of European refugees and self-proclaimed "cosmopolitan revolutionists," including the illustrious German socialist and Forty-Eighter Dr. Adolph Douai, gathered at Turner Hall in Boston to honor the memory of Felice Orsini, who had recently been beheaded in France for attempting to assassinate Napoleon III. Raising their glasses that night to toast the revolutionary martyr was a polyglot collection of Germans, Frenchmen, and Italians. Many resolutions were read, including several that would have warmed the heart of many abolitionists: "We declare our devotion to the great cause of liberty and justice wherever the battle against despotism is yet to be fought; that in this movement, we recognize no predilections for nationality or race, for caste or condition, for complexion or sex; that our aim is nothing less than the conciliation of all human interests, the freedom and happiness of all mankind, the realization of social justice and harmony everywhere."

At the conclusion of their long toasts and proclamations, one of their number rose to read a letter. The writer of the letter expressed his regret at not being able to attend that evening's ceremony in person. "I deeply sympathize with your gathering, this evening, because it is a heartfelt protest against the cowardly, perfidious, blood-stained usurper who has crushed the liberties of France." He went on to explain that though he was a pacifist in philosophy and couldn't condone killing any man, "not even so great a monster as Louis Napoleon":

Nevertheless, judging from the stand-point of patriotism as manifested at Bunker Hill and at Yorktown, at Bannockburn and Thermopylae, and during the famous "three days" in Paris, when the Republic was in-augurated, with "Liberty, Equality, Fraternity," for its watchwords, I am bound to say . . . that Orsini was not assassin in spirit or purpose, but a brave man, true to his convictions of duty, his hatred of oppression, and his desire for the reign of freedom throughout Europe; and that it was the wholesale murderer Louis Napoleon who deserved to be beheaded, rather than Orsini. . . . Defiance and resistance to despots, come what may, and success to treason as against bloody usurpation!

The letter was signed, "Yours to break every yoke, Wm. Lloyd Garrison." When the reading was finished the room erupted into "frequent and spir-ited demonstrations of approval."[53]

Garrison's endorsement of Orsini is interesting on a number of levels. Except for the brief disclaimer of Orsini's attempt on the life of Napoleon III buried in his endorsement, Garrison's remarks swerved widely from his doctrine of pacifism and nonresistance. But beyond these obvious contra-dictions in tone, Garrison's involvement with the Orsini commemoration indicates also the familiarity of the name Orsini in abolition and other reform circles at this time. By the time the brother of the martyred Orsini arrived in the United States a few years later, the name Orsini had already become fa-mous and carried with it the cachet of radical republicanism and resistance to tyranny. It may only have been respect for Orsini's brother's reputation that granted this representative of the International Workingmen's Asso-ciation entrance to the well-appointed parlors of Wendell Phillips, Charles Sumner, and Horace Greeley.

On the eve of the Civil War, the hostile relationship between abolition-ism and labor had warmed considerably as many abolitionists took a more critical stance toward the emerging Northern industrial order and as others made conscious attempts to build coalitions between the two reform com-munities. The war itself cemented their relationship, since emancipation decisively altered the agenda of abolitionism and moved many reformers to rethink the nature of slavery and oppression. The historical stream of the labor movement and a significant branch of the river of abolitionism ran ever more closely together as the Civil War approached.

Emancipation, ironically, provoked both celebration and dissension within abolitionist ranks. Soon after Lincoln read his Emancipation Procla-mation in 1863, William Lloyd Garrison announced that the American Anti-Slavery Society had served its historic purpose and should soon disband. Garrison's call to dissolve the AAS brought into the open the philosophical terrain of abolitionism on the questions of labor and economics, which had become widely diversified by the time of the Civil War. The idea of closing shop on the abolitionist crusade was seamlessly consistent with the understanding of slavery, oppression, and justice held by most of the Anti-Slavery Society's partisans in its years of infancy. Slavery, according to this logic, defined as a legally sanctioned institution, had been eradicated in the rebellious lands. The fact that a war still had to be won in order for the proclamation to have real impact on the lives of Southern blacks was but a technicality — and the AAS, soaked as it was in pacifist rhetoric, could not do anything about it. Therefore, dissolution was the only appropriate course.

Garrison's proposal quickly ran into the fierce and eloquent opposition of Wendell Phillips. Phillips countered that at no time more than the present did the nation need the AAS. For emancipation to have any meaning, argued Phillips, for slaves to be freed in deed as well as in word, abolitionists must keep their pressure upon the government and upon the nation. He was rapidly moving toward a radical critique of economic inequality as an aspect of servitude. In the winter of 1863, he corresponded with William West, a labor radical who had traveled to Washington to reclaim the body of Benjamin Price, a fellow land reformer who had fallen on one of the many battlefields of northern Virginia. Phillips had recently given a speech advocating land reform as a condition of emancipation, and West urged him on: "Insist that the government shall divide the landed property, not exclusively among negroes & the soldiers who fight our country's battles, but equally among all loyal citizens, and your work will be done and well done. But let me warn you that you will incur all manner of calumny, obloquy, and reproach. 'Agrarian' will be found to be a word of far more horrid import than that of 'fanatic.' "[54] Less than a decade later, William West became a leader of the International Workingmen's Association in New York City.

The distance that had grown between Phillips and Garrison was aired publicly during a meeting of the Massachusetts Anti-Slavery Society in early 1864. Wendell Phillips introduced a resolution that would condemn Lincoln for neglecting the social needs of the Southern blacks by conspiring to restore whites to the Southern statehouses and black labor to the fields. Garrison jumped to his feet in defense of Lincoln. When the vote was called, Garrison came up the loser. Later that year the AAS convened in New York and again passed Phillips's resolution condemning Lincoln and recommending against his reelection. Before the year was over, Garrison's faction had walked out of the AAS. In 1865, Garrison folded the *Liberator*.[55]

Garrison and Phillips's conflict over the continuation of the AAS was more than a debate over strategy and tactics. Their public dispute revealed that over decades of struggle a large segment of the abolitionist community had undergone a philosophical evolution. Slavery, freedom, and justice — categories that had not significantly shifted over time in Garrisonian ideology — had come to mean different things to Phillips and his supporters. While over the decades both groups had reached some degree of sympathy for the plight of labor, Phillips and his circle had to a greater extent incorporated the idea of economic exploitation into their understanding of slavery. Phillips, by the time of the war, had come to understand that physical deprivation could render meaningless formal political rights. To a far greater extent than Garrison did, he understood that newly emancipated slaves, for whom neither formal rights nor material needs were secure, had traveled but a short distance down the road of freedom.

This view of slavery, freedom, and the task of abolitionists was reinforced after Appomattox. With the end of the war and the beginning of the national debate over the terms of Reconstruction, the abolitionists who remained within the AAS retooled their rhetoric and began to explicitly include "social" concerns into their definition of slavery. In particular, Phillips's analysis of the problem of Reconstruction became more explicitly focused on economic issues over the next few years. At the thirty-fifth annual meeting of the AAS, Phillips delivered a keynote address that forcefully argued that Reconstruction "is to-day, mainly an industrial question." Wealth was what was needed for the promised freedom of Southern blacks to become a reality. "Here is the black race. It is a sensible race; it is a shrewd race, its brains have been worked, trained into education. Making its own living has skilled it. But the black man has no capital."[56] Moreover, echoing a traditional theme of republicanism, Phillips argued that the edifice of democracy could only survive upon a foundation of economically independent workers. Taking this eighteenth-century idea and standing it on its head, Phillips proclaimed that independent workers were by nature more fit for democracy than were the better-educated elite who held the reins of state. Said Phillips, "I am fully of the faith that the masses of this land, educated by want and toil, are a safer and wiser class to exercise political power than the class which claims to be educated; mere bookworms, ignorant of what bread is made of, and powerless to earn it."

Phillips and the other abolitionists' faith in the ballot box to carry forward Reconstruction did not last long. By the end of the 1860s, it was becoming clear to many that the Fourteenth and Fifteenth Amendments were proving to be but paper tigers. In an editorial published in the *National Anti-Slavery*

Standard entitled "Land," Phillips argued that the ballot alone was not enough. Even in the North, where voting rights were secure for working men, they "dare not use it," for they are "too poor, landless and dependent." The ballot could only go so far, argued Phillips, who chose as an example what was at that time an extreme illustration: "Of what practical use would the ballot be to six million English workingmen who never know what it is fully to satisfy their hunger?" Abolitionists had to work to place "land, education, and employment" alongside the ballot so as to make the ballot meaningful. As in the controversy with Garrison that blew up after Emancipation, Phillips called upon his fellow abolitionists not to settle for formal rights in the face of suffering but to continue to struggle toward new vistas: "We regard the XVth Amendment as only opening a door; furnishing an opportunity — and the moment it is sure and safe, we must push forward our lines." [57]

Such a broadening of the abolitionist agenda soon became the official policy of the AAS. In 1869, the executive committee of the AAS considered a resolution that read: "Resolved: That as in a Government like ours everything rests on public opinion, and as the vitally important social rights of the negro will never be granted him . . . until an enlightened and Christian public opinion permeates and rules the Nation, we remind all Abolitionists that their work is not done until public opinion . . . protects all the rights of human beings." The resolution drew fire from Philadelphian Mary Grew, who objected that it would commit the abolitionists to all sorts of crusades, ranging from the issue of women's rights to the "labor question." In spite of this protest, the resolution passed with only minor amendments. [58] A week later, at a convention of the New England Anti-Slavery Society, the question of the necessity of land to liberty was discussed. At the conclusion of this debate the group approved a resolution, introduced by Stephen S. Foster and "received with much applause," that declared that "land for a homestead is the natural, inherent, and inalienable right of every human being" and called for Congress to immediately expropriate Southern "monopolies" and distribute the land in parcels to freedmen. [59]

A few in the abolitionist movement carried this line of thinking far beyond the problem of black emancipation and toward a general principle of labor exploitation. At the annual meeting of the Pennsylvania Anti-Slavery Association one delegate took the floor to caution the group against resting on their laurels. Damon Kilgore warned that their work "would not be done in a few months, and then [be] . . . wound up by a grand jollification. . . . There are other kinds of slavery in the United States beside that of four millions of colored men." "After the Fifteenth Amendment is passed," Kilgore concluded, "the country will soon need a Sixteenth."[60]

Abolitionism's newfound concern for class issues prompted a debate over the future of its flagship journal, the *National Anti-Slavery Standard*, in 1869. While some argued for discontinuing the paper as soon as the Fifteenth Amendment to the Constitution was ratified, others believed it should persevere in advocacy of other reforms. Wendell Phillips eloquently presented the case for continuing it, arguing that the "prudent general does not let his regiments melt away, like a Scotch raid from the Highlands, the moment one battle is gained. With his troops, trained by work, and emboldened by success, he presses on to new and greater efforts." For Phillips and others the next logical step after emancipation of slavery was the emancipation of labor. The Republican Party, having emancipated slaves, predicted Phillips, "will now turn its forces, well-drilled ranks, buoyant with success, to the elevation and protection of all labor, white and black."[61]

With land, employment, and liberty on the agenda of abolitionism, the intellectual obstacles to a full coalition with labor were now leveled. Both movements recognized the benefits that such a partnership would bring to each. Abolitionists saw that the success of Reconstruction depended upon the votes of Northern laborers, while the labor movement, which was recovering from the disruption brought by the Civil War, looked to abolitionists for their organizational experience, resources, and political connections. The possibility of a true union between those whose long fight against slavery had instilled in them the most egalitarian view of race and sex of their time and those whose resistance to the coming industrial order had shaped a native radical labor ideology promised to create a new powerful synthesis of reform ideas. And its impact upon American society surely would be significant. In the abolitionists' cherished ideals of human equality lay the antidote to the trade union movement's growing racial, ethnic, and sexual exclusiveness. At the same time, the labor movement's producer ideology provided the solution to the obvious inadequacies of a purely political approach to achieving the social and civil equality abolitionists aimed for.

By the late 1860s, nearly every surviving abolitionist leader had endorsed the labor movement's central demand: the legislated reduction of hours in the working day. By the fall of 1866, the list of major contributors to the eight-hour campaign swelled with the names of former middle-class abolitionists. Gerrit Smith wrote to Ira Steward, the "father" of the eight-hour day, objecting that his idea did not go far enough, since an eight-hour law was only a "temporary" expedient. Smith believed that six hours should be the proper standard of the working day. He enclosed twenty dollars toward the cause all the same, a gesture he continued annually for many years. Other prominent abolitionists, such as Benjamin Butler, Rev. Edward Everett Hale, Dr. Dio Lewis, Josiah Abbott, Rufus Wyman, Ezra Heywood, and William Lloyd Garrison, also offered their support to the eight-hour campaign.[62]

Within a few years some abolitionists took an even more active role in the movement: Rev. John T. Sargent, William Channing, and Aaron Powell were all elected vice presidents of the Eight Hour League. John Sargent probably spoke for many of these reformers when he explained how he turned his attention to labor and how he came to the conclusion that the abolitionist crusade was "only an argument, in another form, for the rights of labor at the South: essentially the same question as is now engaging and concerning us here at the North."[63] Not long afterward, Eight Hour League president George McNeill "congratulated the workingmen upon the espousal of their cause by so many veterans of the anti-slavery movement."[64] Garrison publicly expressed his support of the eight-hour campaign and the league behind it. He sent a letter explaining his endorsement of the campaign along with his contribution. "The same principle which has led me to abhor and oppose the unequaled oppression of the black laborers of the South," Garrison observed in typically universalist terms, "instinctively leads me to feel an interest in whatever is proposed to be done to improve the condition and abridge the toil of the white laborers of the North — or, rather, of all over-tasked working classes."[65]

Garrison qualified his endorsement of the Eight Hour League with a veiled warning, one that demonstrated the lingering suspicions that still caused many middle-class radicals to regard the labor movement warily. Expressing his wish that his donation could be larger, Garrison added that even this amount he could not have contributed "if I did not believe that, in the prosecution of its noble enterprise, the League will give no countenance to the spirit of complexional caste in regard to any of the working classes." Likewise, Rev. J. T. Sargent qualified his support for the labor movement by stating that his endorsement was not unconditional; he held its participants up to the measure of the color-blind abolitionist yardstick that he was accustomed to. Sargent warned that workers held themselves back only by allowing themselves to be divided and weakened by a "spirit of caste and exclusiveness," and to prove his point, he cited the case of recent strike of painters, whose only demand was that a recently hired black man be fired and the color line of their trade maintained.[66]

Garrison's and Sargent's warnings and criticisms are a reminder that middle-class radicals were not enticed easily onto the labor-reform bandwagon. Publicly offering their support to the labor movement was something of a leap of faith for reformers who had in the past been very critical of labor unions on many grounds. Advocates for women's equality were critical of the labor movement for failing to take up the cause of working women and for excluding them from their own trades and organizations. Former abolitionists had long known that many trade unions had turned America's racial caste system to its own economic benefit and limited access to their trades on the basis of race, sex, religion, and ethnicity. The New York *Independent*, a longtime voice of abolitionism, published an editorial cartoon that summed up well how these egalitarian-minded reformers viewed the labor movement. According to common journalistic prejudice of the day, the workers in this cartoon were caricatured with pugnacious noses and Celtic beards. These stereotypical Irish workers were labeled with the words "labor reform," "Tammany," and "California," and they were shown attempting to block the path of a long line of women, African Americans, Chinese, and American Indians on their march to "universal suffrage" and "democracy." Given the exceptional efforts of labor reformers such as William Sylvis and Richard Trevellick and a few labor reform journals such as the *Boston Daily Evening Voice* that loudly called for their labor brethren to welcome women and racial minorities into the labor movement, the *Independent*'s political cartoon was hardly an accurate depiction of labor as a whole. Nevertheless, because of the consistently exclusionary policies of many trade unions, the middle-class Yankees' prejudices against the Irish, and the extremely complex nature of ethnic and class phenomena such as Boss Tweed's New York "Tammany Hall" political machine, it took some effort for middle-class reformers to overcome their suspicions and embrace the new labor reform movement.[67]

In spite of the labor movement's having secured the confidence of many important leaders of the abolitionist movement, middle-class reformers' lingering skepticisms of its inclusiveness remained an obstacle to the Eight Hour League's advance. An important test of the eight-hour movement's appeal came in the spring of 1866, when Ira Steward and Wendell Phillips attended an Equal Rights Convention in Boston. Steward, "who seemed of energy and directness 'all compact,'" presented to the women's group a series of proposals dealing with hours and wages but was rebuffed. The convention voted down his resolutions in spite of Phillips's reassurance that they "were not foreign to the purpose of an 'Equal Rights' Convention."

Still, there were those in attendance who were swayed by Steward's pitch. The Boston correspondent of the *National Anti-Slavery Standard* criticized the convention's actions, thinking it strange that an "Equal-Rights-For-All party" would "give them no welcome."[68]

Mary Steward, a tireless worker behind the scenes of the eight-hour campaign, had more luck with the Social Science Association of Boston, who endorsed the eight-hour day in the strongest terms. The SSA's statement declared that it was concerned with "all . . . departments of general reform," but it "regard[ed] all others as secondary" to labor reform. In a letter to Senator Wilson, which was drafted by Mary Steward and others on behalf of the SSA to thank Wilson for his efforts to pass an eight-hour bill, the principle of labor reform was broadened to encompass the issues of Reconstruction as well: "To remove poverty involves . . . the inference that the essential principle of Slavery consists in a monopoly of the means of living, and hence that the emancipation of the people, and the exaltation of Republican institutions lies in the direction of a more equal distribution of wealth." The full text of the letter was published in the *Standard*, so it certainly reached a wide audience of abolitionist reformers.[69]

The *National Anti-Slavery Standard* quickly adopted an editorial stance favoring an eight-hour law. It ran on page one a letter from Senator Henry Wilson to Secretary of War John A. Rawlings, in which he complained that government officers were in violation of the federal eight-hour law, along with a history of the law. After President Grant issued an executive order mandating the eight-hour day for federal employees, the *NASS* editorialized, "See how common sense justice clears away legal cobwebs."[70] By the end of the 1860s, abolitionist participation in labor reform was widely recognized. *Woodhull & Claflin's Weekly* observed that it was "Mr. Wendell Phillips and his late anti-slavery coadjutors" who were giving their attention to the eight-hour law. Theodore Tilton's reform paper, the *Independent*, reflecting on the legacy of abolitionism, noted that abolitionists, "in digging at the root of the slavery question, . . . mellowed the soil for a score of other great reforms," among which he counted "the hours of labor." The *Independent* noted that postwar reform movements such as labor reform and women's rights followed directly from the logic of antislavery. Abolitionists, the writer asserted, "could hardly shape an appeal for the negro's emancipation which was not in itself a polyglot argument for all other reforms," including that which promised to have "the operative better paid in the factory."[71]

Through the late 1860s, the *National Anti-Slavery Standard*, the most important abolitionist publication to continue publishing after the war, increasingly reported on the progress of labor reform organizations.[72] The *Standard* paid particular attention to two related issues pertaining to the labor movement: the racial policies of trade unions and larger labor associations and the progress of the black labor movement. Readers of the *Standard* had many occasions to applaud the apparent progress the labor movement was making toward racial equality within its ranks. In 1868, the *Standard* reported that the proprietor of an iron works in Harrisburg threw a dinner for his employees and provided separate tables for his black and white workers. The white workers, learning of the segregated seating arrangement, unanimously protested and forced their boss to integrate the tables, and the dinner was then enjoyed in a spirit of racial equality. The *Standard* also cheered news of the admission of black delegates to the National Labor Congress for the first time in 1869. On another occasion, the *Standard* took editorial notice of the *Workingman's Advocate*, the leading labor newspaper, praising articles that it had recently featured "repudiating all caste distinctions in the cases of laborers." [73]

By the summer of 1871, the *Standard*'s broadening agenda of reform prompted a change of name. The *National Anti-Slavery Standard* was rechristened the *National Standard*, and it was launched in a new numbered series, in a new format, and with a fresh statement of purpose. The change was necessary, the editors explained, not because slavery was dead but that injustice was to be found in many places and the scope of reform similarly had to be broadened. "Chattel slavery has been overthrown," it noted, "but other duties summon forth to service thoughtful, conscientious men and women. . . . Monopolies, other than chattel slavery grind the poor and encroach upon the public welfare." Just as the readership of the *Standard*, "the nucleus of the morally grand, the historic Anti-Slavery movement," was now branching out into a whole circle of reforms, so must its voice, the *Standard*, be changed to reflect the new struggles being fought. The rights of women, labor, freedmen, Chinese, and Indians, and the issues of temperance, education, and religious freedom, all would find a place in the new *Standard*'s pages. And the new Standard kept its promises, at least as far as labor was concerned. Throughout the next year, scarcely an issue went by that did not feature several articles, announcements, and notices of the progress of the labor movement.[74]

In 1871, under similar circumstances, the National Anti-Slavery Society met in convention in New York under a new name. The year before, in a gesture meant to inaugurate the dawn of a new era of reform work, the society changed its name to the Reform League. High on the list of new crusades it pledged to embark upon was the "labor question." The reform-minded New York *Independent* bemoaned the loss of the institution that had accomplished so much but looked to the Reform League's future hopefully and observed that "in digging at the root of the slavery question, [the abolitionists] mellowed the soil for a core of other great reforms," including "the possession of land," and "the hours of labor." [75]

Aaron Powell, the secretary of the Reform League, set the tone for the convention in his reading of the annual report. The purpose of the league had grown beyond its mission of crushing slavery in all its forms, he reported. It had turned its attention to "all the existing great wrongs," from the oppression of women to the "securing of justice to oppressed working-men and women." According to one reporter, Powell went on to denounce in "unmeasured terms" the "growing oligarchy of railroad, financial, and land monopoly" and recommended "the agitation of the labor movement . . . as a protection against their power." Although other parts of Powell's report were debated, his sentiments on labor went unchallenged. [76]

Old-line abolitionists may have been the most prominent converts to the labor movement, but they were not the only antebellum reform movement radicals to turn their attention from chattel slavery to wage slavery in the Reconstruction years. Other elements of the antebellum reform community also discovered the "labor question" and offered their support to the strengthening cross-class coalitions working for the eight-hour day and other labor reforms. By the end of the Civil War, movements that had previously been focused upon women's suffrage, pacifism, and Spiritualism, all developed new understandings and sympathy for the labor movement. For a significant radical minority of each of these movements, sympathy steadily led to participation in labor reform activities and in the International Workingmen's Association.

The crisis of the Civil War awakened the consciousness of many women's rights activists to the problems of workers. Thousands of women were drawn into the industrial labor force during the war, particularly in the needle trades, and many others. They lived at the margins of survival at the best of times and were viciously squeezed by rapid inflation and the departure or death of family breadwinners. Thousands of other women, particularly middle-class women who had taken part in antebellum campaigns for women's rights, volunteered in the U.S. Sanitary Commission and other public relief agencies and there witnessed firsthand the daily plight of the working poor. After the war, women, even elite women's rights activists, focused their attention on economic issues, particularly the situation of women workers.[77]

Labor issues were among the first discussed in the elite parlors of the New England Women's Club, America's first women's club, founded in Boston in 1868. It attracted prominent reformers such as Lydia Maria Child, former editor of the *National Anti-Slavery Standard*, writers Julia Ward Howe and Louisa May Alcott, and well-known women's suffrage advocates such as Lucy Stone and Mary Livermore, who was editor of the Boston *Woman's Journal*.[78] At one of its first meetings these outspoken women discussed a number of "circulars" that had recently arrived from Europe. Madame Pinoff's "Plan for Women's Industrial Unions," a scheme based on the "co-operative principle of work," was translated and read by one of the members. They discussed the women's movement in Germany, where "the efforts of women were more directed to education and industry than to gaining their political rights." Finally, the club discussed "the International Congress of Working men held at Brussels" the previous month, finding particularly compelling the fact that the European workingmen had demanded the reform of education, including the introduction of the German kindergarten, for both sexes. The congress in question was none other than the Third Congress of the International Workingmen's Association. In the coming months, the New England Women's Club established a series of seven committees, all but one, the "committee on literature and its difficulties," devoted to the needs and problems of women workers. Among them were the committees on "needlewomen," "laundries," "public nurseries," "labor schools," "co-operative kitchens," and "Raising Money by application to Rich Women."[79]

These elite women's concerns exemplified reformers' general interest in labor questions after the war. But for the women of the New England Women's Club, this did not mean that they agreed with the more radical answers to them. The committee on cooperative kitchens eventually issued a report that was critical of labor unions, and one of its members even complained of "the spirit of combination [i.e., an interest in unionism] among servant girls at the present time." A detailed and historically valuable survey of needlewomen in Boston was completed by the committee on needlewomen, but its recommendations failed to go beyond the establishment of more respectable boarding houses for single female workers, the founding of more industrial schools, and the support of Emigrant Aid societies that could relocate young women to the healthful air and boundless opportunities of the American West. Dominating attitudes among the club women were summed up well by Harriet Hanson Robinson, a woman whose own class background — she was raised in the spinning rooms of the Lowell mills — made her an exception among the ladies of the NEWC. "I hate this talk of rich and poor, labor and capital as if one class in this country should be pitted against another," Robinson confided to her diary. "The sons of these very working men will be the capitalists of the next generation." Nevertheless, beyond the social realm of the women's clubs, more radically minded women activists had fewer doubts and set about addressing the distress of working women in the spirit of the Garrisonian abolitionists who refused to settle for half solutions to full problems.[80]

Suffragists like Susan B. Anthony and Elizabeth Cady Stanton were attracted to the more radical aspects of the labor movement. Among the demands they trumpeted in the inaugural issue of their reform journal, the *Revolution*, was that for the eight-hour day. The *Revolution* was but a few months old when the two suffragists praised in its columns the growing labor reform movement and heralded it as "the dawn of brighter days." Stanton and Anthony steered into a particularly close alliance with the National Labor Union, the umbrella organization of labor reformers and trade unionists that stood on a broad platform of economic, political, and social reform. In 1868, both Stanton and Anthony and two other suffragists on the staff of the *Revolution* were seated at the NLU convention in New York in spite of the fierce opposition of a solid block of delegates from the building trades. That convention further resolved to support the organization of women's labor unions and to demand state and federal laws that would mandate equal pay for equal work in government jobs.[81]

Ultimately, however, the conservative trade unionists prevailed and the NLU voted to exclude Anthony at its next year's convention in 1869. Even after this setback, the two suffragists did not give up on the labor movement. A few months after their defeat at the NLU convention, Stanton wrote in the *Revolution* that "the question of Capital and labor must be more thoroughly discussed in our paper." Continuing in echoes of the arguments that workers used to describe their own plight before the war, Stanton wrote, "Verily, the slavery of the white masses in our factories, garrets, and cellars was never surpassed on southern plantations." In 1871, Stanton and Anthony attended the convention of the American Labor Reform League, another labor reform coalition. There, Stanton delivered a roundly praised speech in which she argued that all capital was the product of labor and that strikes were fully justified. Afterward, the convention voted to honor both women by electing them as vice presidents of the league. Commenting on the convention later in the *Revolution*, Stanton and Anthony optimistically asserted that the American Labor Reform League was "an organization fifty thousand strong—the apparent formation of a day, but in reality the growth of years." Now, they proclaimed, "labor and women suffrage are the twin issues of the hour." [82]

Other women's rights activists swung even further toward giving labor issues priority, an arc that ultimately lodged them in councils of the International. For example, Carrie Sylvester Burnham, a woman whose pursuit of equality in professional life led her through two careers that blazed new trails for women in medicine (she was one of the first women allowed to practice medicine at Bellevue Hospital in New York City) and law (she was also the first woman accepted to the University of Pennsylvania Law School and the first to be admitted to the bar of the Supreme Court of that state), became one of the leaders of the IWA in Philadelphia. Just one month before Burnham enrolled as a charter member of IWA Section 26, she successfully fought to have herself duly registered as a voter by the Philadelphia Board of Election Canvassers, though the ballot she cast was later disqualified. [83] And Belva Lockwood, the vice president of the Universal Franchise Association and later the first woman to plead a case before the Supreme Court of the United States, lectured under the auspices of the IWA, demanding from the rostrum that "business now managed by corporations should be controlled by government for public good." [84]

Along with earning the support of several influential leaders of the women's suffrage campaign, the labor question attracted another antebellum reform movement whose fervent egalitarianism had grown from the same radical sources as had abolitionism itself: pacifism. Pacifists weathered the test of their faith in the Civil War badly. Peace organizations emerged from the Civil War sullied and splintered, their forces diminished, the many years of war having forced their supporters to compromise their ideals and rationalize the brutal conflict. The American Peace Society, once the standard bearer of principled nonresistance to violence, was moribund by 1868. The society had limited its program to restraining governments from making war, and when the bloody guns roared across the nation, they compromised even this principle by distinguishing between unconscionable war and the acceptable police action of suppressing rebellion. Those few pacifists who refused to follow along with such rationalizations, weathering a storm of abuse and persecution for their principled stand, collected themselves after the war into an even more radical and strident organization, the Universal Peace Union. They broadened their definition of peace far beyond what the older APS had been willing to consider.

Caroline Burnham Kilgore, member of IWA Section 26, Philadelphia
(The University of Pennsylvania Archives)

The UPU, led by Alfred Love, a shy and unbending Quaker merchant who refused to fill government contracts and resisted the draft during the war, quickly attracted a few hundred members, over a third of them women, and eventually claimed over 10,000 adherents. Love, along with many other defeated pacifists, believed that the American Peace Society, and pacifism in general, had failed because it had neglected to understand and redress the causes of war. The Universal Peace Union was committed to abolishing war by removing "the causes and the conditions of war," and it understood that among these causes was inequality in the political, social, and economic spheres.[85] Not surprisingly, the UPU supported women's suffrage, temperance, an end to settler and governmental conquest of Indian territories, and full civil rights for African Americans, causes endorsed by practically the full panoply of antebellum reformers. But the UPU went further, placing labor issues at the head of its list of the causes of war. The UPU recognized that "among the primary causes of war [was] the systematic and legalized oppression of the masses of the people everywhere . . . [and that] among the first conditions of enduring peace [was] a more just and equitable distribution of labor and capital."[86]

Such commitment to the cause of labor was not just rhetorical. The Universal Peace Union attracted a number of noted labor leaders, including Ira Steward, the president of the Machinists and Blacksmiths International Union and the most famous propagandist for the eight-hour day. The pages of the UPU's newspapers featured articles on the need to redistribute land to the poor, columns from the labor press, and critiques of the industrial system. By the 1870s, the membership of UPU chapters in Philadelphia, Boston, and New York substantially overlapped with that of the International Workingmen's Association and labor reform organizations.[87]

In keeping with their traditional support of radical individualism against all oppressive systems, labor reform and socialist ideas were also never far from the goals of Spiritualist ranks. Albert Brisbane, the most famous publicist of Fourier's socialism in America, was an early Spiritualist and was present at many of the trance sessions where Andrew Jackson Davis "telegraphed" his revelations from the spirit world, which would later be compiled into the seminal Spiritualist manifesto, *The Principles of Nature*. Davis's work brimmed with Fourieristic ideas and analysis of the labor issue. His *Univercoelum*, the first Spiritualist newspaper, attracted to its staff of writers Joshua K. Ingalls, an ardent labor and land reformer who became one of the founders of the Yankee International. Among the early enthusiastic converts to Spiritualism was George Lippard, a labor activist and founder of The Brotherhood, a fraternal labor union and forerunner of the Knights of Labor.[88]

At their seventh annual convention, held in 1870, the Spiritualists of America publicly committed themselves to the eight-hour day. The *Banner of Light*, the Spiritualist newspaper with the largest national circulation, regularly editorialized in favor of "a juster distribution of the proceeds and profits of industry," and gave its "unqualified sympathy with the efforts of the working classes to organize their forces so as to stand a fair chance with capital." Even the more conservative *Religio-Philosophical Journal*, the voice of Chicago's Spiritualists, featured a series of articles criticizing reformers who devoted themselves to solving the problems of political and social corruption, crime, and intemperance for only "working on the surface." The paper argued that instead "we have got to probe to the very core, to strike at the foundation and remove the cause" of economic injustices. *The Optimist and Kingdom of Heaven*, a Spiritualist paper published in Berlin Heights, Ohio, changed its name to the *Trade Union, or Scientific Socialist* soon after the war. And when the Pennsylvania State Labor Convention resolved to draft an address to the various labor organizations in the state, the group of sober trade unionists ordered that it be printed in three newspapers: the *Pennsylvanian*, the *Anthracite Monitor*, and the *Medium*, a Spiritualist organ.[89]

But most revealing of the extent that Spiritualists were involved in the labor reform movement was an incident that occurred at a convention of the New England Labor Reform League. One speaker surprised many in the audience when he launched an attack upon Spiritualists and the "thinness and feebleness" of their philosophy. Implying that Spiritualists did not care about the labor movement, the speaker asked rhetorically, "Where are the Spiritualists?" and from all about the meeting hall delegates shouted "Here! Here!" and, embarrassed, he stuttered a hasty retreat. The following year the Spiritualists repaid the favor when the annual Spiritualists' convention in Boston welcomed into its fold "all associations of workingmen and women, Crispins, Internationals, trade unions, and other labor organizations as our fellows."[90]

As the 1870s dawned, the problems of industrial society, of workers, and of economic equality had become a part of the consciousness of American reformers and had risen to the top of the agenda of the American radical tradition. Men and women who had devoted decades of their lives to struggling against the evils of slavery, political inequality, and social immorality now turned their considerable organizational experience and willingness to confront authority and convention to the task of elevating the working class.

These American radicals brought to the "labor question" the tactics, values, and conception of revolutionary change itself that they had learned over their years of work in the trenches of antebellum reform. Drawing from their earlier activist experiences and from the body of American radical thought that was their inheritance, they applied the principles of radical democracy and universal equality to this new field of reform. They relied most upon moral principles and a keen sense of justice to guide them, just as they did in their earlier crusades. They approached the problems of labor with a clearer sense of what was wrong with the mushrooming industrial order than of what particular remedies and strategies would work to counter these evils. Of course, some within their ranks rode their own particular hobbies. There were those who had spent the past thirty years advocating the redistribution of land, claiming that this measure alone would tear away the very foundations of capitalist exploitation; and there were others who believed the solution to all economic and social injustice would be remedied with the spread of worker cooperatives. But the majority of the American radicals who came to support the IWA rejected all such attempts to impose a single strategy upon the organization. If they had learned anything from their years of activist experience it was that the paths to progress were even more numerous than the social ills that needed cures.

In the tradition of deliberative democracy, American radicals were tolerant of dissent and pragmatic in their approach to movement tactics. They had complete faith in their hearts' capacity to recognize evil but were less confident of their minds' ability to formulate a solution. Unlike their Internationalist immigrant Marxist comrades, who, because they had complete faith in the efficacy of Marxist theory to comprehend and analyze any given social-political-economic moment, tended to believe that there was but one true line of socialist progress, these descendants of the native radical tradition believed that all reform proposals represented different means to similar ends. This attitude was reinforced by their shared commitment to democratic institutions. Politics, being based on the ability to forge majorities and build coalitions, encouraged native radicals to pitch their tent stakes as widely as possible so as to accommodate as many "true reformers" as possible beneath its folds. This is why American radicals hardly gave it a second thought when their IWA meeting halls were filled with a bewildering assortment of suffragists, Spiritualists, trade unionists, land reformers, greenbackers, cooperationists, communists, and even proto-anarchists; indeed, given the scope of most everyone's radical activities, it was difficult to pin a label on anyone. Lewis Masquerier, one of the founders of the Yankee

International, called for an "ecumenical convention of the world's political and religious reformers" to meet in New York City in 1870. "Never was there such an urgency as now for all kinds of reformers to counsel together as to what must be done to remedy the growing evils of poor humanity," Masquerier declared. Cyrenus Osborne Ward, another radical seasoned through a series of reform movements, in urging others to join the IWA revealed that he viewed the world as being divided into "reformers" and "enemies": "All individuals desiring reform must, on the merit of the principles they strive for, place themselves on this platform, while those not favoring reform will naturally rally on the other side."[91]

When Ira B. Davis, one of the most active members in the New York International, died in 1872, a fellow member published an obituary that emphasized his achievements and noble marks of character. "Mr. Davis was a quiet, earnest man of clearly defined and strong convictions, who had more deeds than words for any reform," his comrade wrote. "His house . . . offered shelter to fugitives from all sorts of oppression, hospitality to opinions of every shade, and a home to which reformers were always welcome." Davis, a "socialist of the Communist school" who advocated women's rights, Spiritualism, land reform, and water cures, a not unusual range of reform ideas, was remembered and lauded in death for his tolerance. What mattered to the Yankee radicals was not the particular course these different reformers advocated but that, when specific campaigns and actions presented themselves, everyone pulled at their own oars in unison and rowed their socialist ship onward. This was the American radical model, one followed in the labor movement by the Knights of Labor, but one that ceased to be a fixture of the American Left after the Yankee International collapsed.

The origins of this collapse and the severing of American socialism from its native legacy are to be found far from the meeting halls of Boston, Philadelphia, and New York. They originate within the ideological divisions that existed from the beginning of the organization, even before it made its transAtlantic passage to the United States. Just what these rifts were is revealed in the political development of the IWA in its early years in London and in the tentative and circuitous means by which its revolutionary dreams traveled to America.

CHAPTER TWO

Marx and the Republican Tradition of the First International

A T AROUND THE same time abolitionists first clasped hands with labor reformers and embarked upon a new crusade in America, an even more diverse coterie of European radicals united under one banner in London, that of the International Workingmen's Association. Like its American labor reform counterparts, the IWA gathered together a mixture of ideologies and historical tendencies on the common ground of republican ideals, whose lineage stretched back to the Enlightenment. Ironically, the First International, the institutional and ideological model for the Marxist revolutionary parties of the nineteenth and twentieth centuries, was launched upon eighteenth-century rhetoric. Only after a period of maneuver and struggle and of steadily marginalizing all those who continued to espouse the deeply rooted British radical tradition of Chartist republicanism did Karl Marx remake the IWA according to his own vision: the vanguard party of the proletarian revolution.

Were it not for the importance of the timing and manner of the International's crossing to America and the complete hegemony of Marx in the end, describing the detailed taxonomy of its roots would be little more than an exercise in radical antiquarianism. Had the International simply arrived in the United States as the full-blown revolutionary party that Marx had originally intended it to be, its defeated ideological tendencies would not rank more than an obscure footnote in socialist history. However, the IWA did not simply appear in the United States, it trickled in. It came in several small waves, each bearing a slightly different ideological line, depending on its timing. The earliest, arriving with the heaviest baggage of pre-Marxist republicanism, was received most enthusiastically in the parlors of America's republican radicals like Wendell Phillips, Horace Greeley, and Charles Sumner. The last wave carried with it a Marxist orthodoxy that was the negation of what came before. It is necessary, then, to explore the ideological struggles taking place within the London headquarters of the First International in order to comprehend the plurality of its articulation in America.

It was not even a labor issue, in the strict sense, that was the impetus behind the First International; rather, it was founded at an antiwar rally. In the fall of 1864, reformers from around Europe who were concerned by the growing threat of European war, by Russia's crushing of Polish nationalism, by the increasing international tensions brought on by Prussian militarism, French imperialism, and the American Civil War, and, of course, by the intensifying exploitation of the working class, assembled and announced the formation of the International Workingmen's Association. Although economic reform and class solidarity were strong themes from the start of the organization, these goals were initially overshadowed by a higher concern for liberty, democracy, national self-determination, and international peace.

London's large expatriate working-class community was well represented that September night in the crowd of over two thousand packed into St. Martin's Hall. Professor E. S. Beesly, the moderator, read resolutions denouncing the imperial rivalries and intrigues of the Great Powers from Hong Kong to Gibraltar. The shoemaker and trade union leader George Odger, one of the English organizers of the meeting, spoke of workers' unique opportunity to mold a foreign policy based on morality and justice. After the German workingmen's choir had sung several songs, the assembly's honored guests, a delegation of three Paris workingmen—a metal carver, a weaver, and a bronze worker—rose and delivered their memorial with the help of a translator. The Parisians took up the theme of democratic rights and personal liberty crushed under the heel of European despotism: "The feeling which brings us together is the sure indicator of a better future for the affranchisement [sic] of the peoples. We must have no more Caesars, with their forehead stained with a crown covered with blood, dividing among themselves peoples despoiled by the repines of the great, and countries devastated by savage wars. . . . One single people oppressed puts the liberty of all other peoples in danger."[1] Despotism came in two forms, they asserted: "tyranny in the political order" and "monopoly in the order of social economy." Economic monopoly was the child of science and the relentless division of labor that engendered "industrial serfdom more implacable and more fatal to humanity than that which our fathers overthrew in those great days of the Revolution." The Parisians concluded by reading an address "on liberty and equality" written by the French labor leader Henri Lefort.

This French history lesson was not lost on the many veterans of British Chartism and the recently revived London trades union movement in the audience who had also come to believe that the working class could only gain its freedom by aiming its blows simultaneously at both these arms of oppression. Union organization alone, these Englishmen had come to realize, would not by itself overcome the combined opposition of business and government. This lesson was learned the hard way just three years before, when the British government lent its troops to crush a strike of Chelsea brickmakers. On that occasion, Benjamin Lucraft, a furniture-maker and longtime Chartist who was one of the St. Martin's Hall meeting's organizers, had scolded the brickmakers for their myopic "New Model" economism. "I should hope," Lucraft had declared, "that the operative builders are by this time convinced that political power has something to do with the social conditions of the people." And Lucraft was not alone. Increasingly, London's workers had begun to move from simple wage demands to a broader social agenda of political reform and the nine-hour day. Uppermost among Lucraft and other labor leaders political goals was the old Chartist demand for electoral reform in Parliament, a cause they worked for through their recently founded Working Men's Suffrage and Ballot Association.[2]

Prior to the St. Martin's Hall meeting, a committee of prominent British labor leaders had drafted an address to the "liberty-loving French people," inviting their participation in forming "a grand fraternity of peoples." The purpose of such an alliance was to check the capricious and despotic powers of governments—regimes that had grown corrupt under "unscrupulous ministers," "affluent arrogance," and "the vices of voluptuous courts":

As a means then to check the existing abuse of power, we echo your call for a fraternity of peoples. Let there be a gathering together of representatives from France, Italy, Germany, Poland, England, and all countries, where there exists a will to co-operate for the good of mankind. Let us have our congresses; let us discuss the great questions on which the peace of nations depends; let us bring our reason and moral right to bear with becoming dignity against the cajolery and brute force of the so-called rulers; and our conviction is that the power of despots will be weakened.[3]

Beyond advocating ideals of morality, justice, and liberty, the address offered a more immediate reason for workers to cooperate across their borders, namely, to advance the cause of labor. The manifest recounted British labor's bitter experience of having been continually forced to acquiesce to the demands of their employers over issues of hours and wages because of their employers having imported European strikebreakers. Rather than resort to easy jingoistic demands for exclusion or discrimination, the British workers sought an egalitarian solution to this industrial problem. Their principle was to "bring up the wages of the ill-paid to as near a level as possible with that of those who are better remunerated, and not to allow our employers to play us off one against the other."

After the meeting, a large group of English trade unionists treated the French delegation at a nearby Soho café, the Henry Bolleter Inn, where the toasts and speeches lasted far into the night. Republican ideals, personal liberty, peace, justice, and class advancement had become inseparably held goals for most of the honored guests on stage at St. Martin's Hall, with one notable exception: the liberal tone of that evening's speeches rendered Karl Marx uncharacteristically stoic that night.

Indeed, it was only by chance that Karl Marx attended at all. For several years Marx had ceased all political activity to devote himself to finishing his life's work, *Das Kapital*, and thereby, as he put it, "deal the bourgeoisie a theoretical blow from which it will never recover." But his goal had been painfully hampered by his chronic liver disease and recurring outbreaks of carbuncles and furuncles.[4] Although in these years Marx rarely ventured beyond the reading room of the British Museum and his sickbed, the twin poles of his existence, he was still famous within London's international community. A few days before the St. Martin's Hall meeting, when its English organizers found themselves without a German speaker, they contacted Marx—not to speak himself, for he was not a workingman, but to solicit the name of a suitable German worker. Marx suggested his friend Johann Georg Eccarius, an expatriate German tailor who had lived for many years in London and whose impeccable English made him an obvious choice to deliver the speech. It was not until the day of the meeting that an invitation for Marx himself arrived at his home.[5]

In spite of his tender carbuncles and the snub he received from the meeting's British organizers, Marx shook off his political lethargy and attended. What distinguished this gathering from the many others he had declined to attend over the years was that it had brought together, under one international banner, many of the most influential labor leaders in England, the "people who really count," as Marx put it. The elements coalescing there, Marx believed, would offer him a chance to participate in a genuine movement of workers, and, more importantly, to channel its energies in the directions required by his own maturing theories of history, capitalism, and revolution. Indeed, Marx's collaborator, Friedrich Engels, later said of him that at this time he had come to believe that England was the only country where the "inevitable social revolution might be effected entirely by peaceful and legal means."[6] In Marx's eyes, the purpose of the IWA was not to free the worker's ballot, raise his wages, lower his hours, cultivate his mind, or restrain his warmongering government from sending him to die on a distant battlefield. Rather, the IWA would be the historical instrument with which the workers would seize the reins of state power from the bourgeoisie.

Although he had been a recluse, the author of the 1848 *Communist Manifesto* was well known by both English and expatriate workers of London as a leader of the radical Germans and as a philosopher. And knitting together this assortment of dissenters on a unified platform required both talents. Marx was immediately elected to the IWA's newly organized General Council. But just as Marx prepared to take the reins of this fledgling radical organization, his health took a turn for the worse and he found himself unable to attend the crucial founding meetings of the Council. With Marx in his bed laying arsenic poultices on his skin lesions, the job of drafting the founding documents fell to a subcommittee.

Two draft constitutions for the International were introduced at the subcommittee's first meetings. One was presented by the former Chartist John Weston and the other by the representative of the Italian workers on the Council, Luigi Wolff, a former adjutant to Mazzini and a major in his army. Weston's address has been lost to history, but its principles must have been those expounded upon at the IWA's founding meeting—international solidarity to resist tyranny, peace, liberty, and the social, political, and economic elevation of all workers. Although members of the Council had some substantive criticisms of Weston's draft, including that it was too long, it was accepted as a working paper and referred back to the committee for revision. Wolff submitted his own English translation of Mazzini's "Brotherly Agreement between the Associations of Italian Workers" as an alternate model for the Council to consider. Delighted with Wolff's work, the committee unanimously agreed to present the work to the full Council and passed a resolution laying out a number of principles that should guide the drafting committee in its work. These guidelines echoed the goals set forth in the "Brotherly Agreement": "This Committee suggests as the basis of its operations the promotion of the moral, intellectual, and economical progress of the working classes of Europe by coming to an understanding with the various working men's associations all over Europe in order to obtain unity of purpose and unity of action, the two great means of arriving at the above-named results."[7]

To the British members of the committee this must have been seen as but another vague, general, and harmless statement of labor's goals, but to Marx and his allies, it amounted to surrender before the battle's opening salvo. Marx's close friend Eccarius was the first to hear of the committee's actions. He immediately dispatched a frantic letter to Marx, alerting him to the idealist danger and telling him of the "absolute necessity" of his attending the next meeting. Without the quick intervention of Marx's rapine rhetoric and analysis, he feared, all would be lost. "You must absolutely impress the stamp of your terseness, full of content upon the first-born child of the European workmen's organization," he urged.[8]

Many elements in Weston's and Wolff's draft papers alarmed Marx and his followers. Eccarius dismissed Weston's address as a "sack of chaff [that] contained a handful of grains, themselves of no character, . . . a sentimental declamatory editorial on the matter, not the matter itself." He complained to Marx that Weston "is an old Owenite, who confines the sentimental doctrine of the old school to the workmen, to be sure, and hates the oppressors instinctively, but seems to know no other basis for labour movements than the hackneyed phrase, truth and justice." The review of Wolff's submission was no better. "I saw the stuff later," Marx wrote to Engels. "It was evidently a concoction of Mazzini's, and that tells you in advance in what spirit and phraseology the real question, the labour question, was dealt with." Marx complained that it proposed little more than to turn the IWA into a "benefit society" whose aim was "really something quite impossible, a sort of central government of the European working classes (with Mazzini in the background, of course)."[9]

It is not surprising that Marx frowned on the idealistic ideology upon which the IWA was founded and that appeared to be on the brink of becoming forever enshrined in the association's constitutional documents. To Marx, all such theorizing committed the most unforgivable logical and philosophical error: it was not grounded in history. This was the crux of Marx's departure from the democratic and egalitarian tradition of eighteenth-century liberalism. Through his deeply rigorous critique of "idealism" in philosophy, liberalism in politics, and the then-current categories of economic thought, Marx had come to reject those reform hopes and schemes that were not based on a dispassionate, "scientific" analysis of the historical moment. As he put it in his famous phrase from *The Eighteenth Burmaire of Louis Bonaparte*, "Men make their own history, but they do not make it just as they please; they do not make it under circumstances chosen by themselves, but under circumstances directly encountered, given and transmitted from the past." Clearly, Marx believed that the International needed to be founded upon something more substantial than a sentimental proclamation of humanitarian ideals.[10]

Marx heeded Eccarius's warning and made a point of attending the next meeting. He was "really shocked" when he heard the draft program read aloud. It was, he reported, "fearfully cliché-ridden, badly written and totally unpolished . . . with Mazzini showing through the whole thing from beneath a crust of the most insubstantial scraps of French socialism." Marx vowed that "not one single line of the stuff should be allowed to stand if I could help it." He didn't like it. Realizing quickly that the momentum of the Council was against him, Marx, as clever a politician as he was a philosopher, chose to protest mildly rather than attempt to stonewall the solidifying consensus of the group. Marx seconded the proposal to accept the draft and cultivated the appearance of having acceded to the will of the majority. Meanwhile, Eccarius offered a friendly amendment to refer the whole draft back to the subcommittee for further editing, so as to "put it into a definite form."[11]

Marx's parliamentary dodge was only half a victory. Marx knew his chances of making substantive changes were better in the smaller committee than in the General Council. Hoping to make his triumph complete, Marx arranged for the next meeting of the drafting committee to be at his own home. William Cremer, a leader of London's carpenters, Giuseppe Fontana, an Italian labor organizer (who sat in for Wolff), and Le Lubez, representing the French, gathered in Marx's drawing room. Marx's ploy was to drag out the discussions until his guests had tired to the point where they would entrust the whole mess to him. "To gain time," Marx wrote to Engels, "I proposed that before we 'edited' . . . we ought to 'discuss' the rules. This was done. It was 1 o'clock in the morning before the first of 40 rules was adopted. Cremer said (*and that was my whole aim*): we have nothing to put before the committee. . . . [In the end,] the 'papers' were 'bequeathed' to me for my perusal."[12]

When the committee next assembled, Marx presented his own "Inaugural Address" as a fait accompli. Many in the Council were surprised by what they heard, or rather, what they didn't hear, and the room fell dead silent. Cremer, Le Lubez, and Fontana had left Marx's house the week before believing that they were near completion of three founding documents, the "Preamble," the "Declaration of Principles," and a set of "Rules." Marx had abridged the "Rules" from forty down to just ten, completely changing the principles and character of the organization. He totally rewrote Le Lubez's "Preamble," and threw out Weston's "Declaration of Principles" altogether. For all of his cavalier editing, however, Marx did rein in his penchant for runaway theorizing and inflammatory language. Ever savvy to the climate and possibilities of the time, he knew that the IWA's members would not march to the beat of the *Communist Manifesto*. Rather than bang that old drum, Marx slowly and deliberately prepared to fashion a new one. As he cautioned Engels, "It will take time before the revival of the movement allows the old boldness of language to be used. We must be *fortiter in re, suaviter in modo* [bold in matter, but mild in manner]."[13]

Marx's strategy of presenting a patient, conciliatory face to his adversaries while quietly manipulating the organization toward his own ends prevailed only because of the ideological inclusiveness of the English members. All were opposed to the narrow economistic direction of the "New Model" trades unions and were committed to the proposition that unions must act politically as well as industrially to secure for workers their equality, rights, and just rewards. Capturing this general republican principle in their constitution was enough for them at this moment. Marx later complained that the drafting committee had forced him "to insert two sentences about 'duty' and 'right,' and ditto about 'truth, morality and justice' in the preamble to the rules," but, he explained, "these are so placed that they can do no harm."[14]

Marx either did not accept or did not understand that the men who had publicly proclaimed such republican and moral rhetoric from the stage of St. Martin's Hall saw no contradiction between their commitment to individual liberty, morality, and democracy and their conception of a class-based workers movement. Leaders such as Odger and Cremer had devoted their lives to the struggles of their class. Having moved from Chartism through New Model Unionism and on into mass movements against war, they had developed a certain ecumenical pragmatism toward theory that allowed them to both enthusiastically endorse Marx's "Inaugural Address" and hold on to their membership cards in the League of Peace and Freedom and the Reform League. Eccarius later recalled how these men's eyes had brightened when Marx read the last part of his address, a section that brilliantly fused together their twin commitments to republicanism and trade unionism: "The lords of land and the lords of capital will always use their political privileges for the defence and perpetuation of their economical monopolies; they will continue to lay every possible impediment in the way of the emancipation of labor. To conquer political power has therefore become the great duty of the working classes."[15] No wonder, then, that in spite of Marx's constitutional coup, the General Council enthusiastically ratified all of his papers.[16]

Such pragmatism on the part of the English was unbearable to Marx who viewed such broad-mindedness as a sign of immaturity. It was clear to Marx and his German comrades from the start that their ideological offensive would have to be directed against the English members of the General Council. Engels, after reading Marx's description of the character of the Council, presciently wrote, "I suspect that there will very soon be a split in this new association between those who are bourgeois in their thinking and those who are proletarian, the moment the issues become a little more specific."[17] It mattered little that most of the English members were bona fide members, and indeed leaders, of Britain's working class; Engels had for many years complained about the "bourgeoisification" of English labor. The English proletariat, Engels observed in 1858, "is actually becoming more and more bourgeois, so that this most bourgeois of all nations is apparently aiming ultimately at the possession of a bourgeois aristocracy and a bourgeois proletariat *as well as* a bourgeoisie." English radicalism had been hopelessly blunted by England's relative prosperity. Engels's prescription for this malaise was one that only a man in comfortable circumstances could hope for: "The only thing that would help here would be a few thoroughly bad years." Prior to the founding of the IWA, Marx held the English working class in similarly low esteem. He described England as possessing a "sheepish" proletariat afflicted with a "bourgeois infection," whose "workers by their Christian, slavish nature" discredited themselves before the world.[18]

In the end, the ideological distance between the English Internationalist's republicanism and Marx's own historical materialism was readily papered over in Britain, where issues of political equality were truly inseparable from issues of class. There, where the franchise was systematically denied to workers, Marx could see in the movement toward claiming the ballot the seeds of a genuine workers' movement and the first step toward the self-consciousness of the proletariat. But elsewhere, where the issues of class and political rights were not so intimately combined, the differing perspectives of Marx and his English republican allies had deeply contradictory implications. When Marx and his English comrades turned their attention from

Britain to the United States, where many workingmen wielded the ballot, the contrasting consequences of their differing ideological frameworks were thrown into high relief.

From the start, Marx and the English members of the General Council viewed American history through different lenses. English leaders such as Weston, Cremer, and Odger saw the American Civil War in moral terms; to them it was a struggle to vindicate certain democratic and humanitarian ideals of justice. But Marx, who dismissed such reasoning as sentimental and idealistic, judged American social and political developments by their overall relation to the long-term progress and processes of history itself. To Marx, the American Civil War was not a moral crusade to wipe out slavery and vindicate the principles of human brotherhood, natural right, and civil equality — such a formulation was quite alien to a man who had struggled to purge the ahistorical concepts of "morality," "right," and "equality," from his intellectual vocabulary. Rather, when analyzed through his cold lens of historical materialism, the sectional battle was a struggle over the future of America's white working class, the only group upon whose fate he believed that history itself was hinged. Marx articulated these ideas in his famous letter of congratulations to Abraham Lincoln.

At the urging of the General Council, Marx agreed to draft a message of congratulations to Lincoln on the occasion of his second election to the presidency. At first he did not consider the subject all that important and only reluctantly turned his rhetorical skills to America. He complained to Engels what a bother the letter was and how this sort of writing was more difficult than composing "a proper work." The problem was how to write the thing so that it was "distinguishable from vulgar-democratic phraseology" of the sort his English counterparts would have produced on their own. As was his strategy within the ideologically diverse General Council, Marx carefully crafted his statements so as not to offend the sentiments of any of the other members of the Council, while strenuously avoiding any hint of their idealism. Marx split these hairs by concentrating only on the impact of slavery upon America's historical progress. Marx held that the historical development of America was dependent upon the organization and self-consciousness of the industrial proletariat — a class that was predominately Northern and white. In Marx's view, slavery had to be destroyed in order to allow for the historical advancement of the white working class and for the evolution of history itself.[19]

Marx began his letter by noting that Lincoln's election signified the redirection of the war from "resistance to the slave power" to the "death of slavery." He went on to argue that Europe's workers recognized the significance of the American war because they "felt instinctively that the star-spangled banner carried the destiny of their class." For them it was quite clear that this was a war to decide whether the "virgin soil of immense tracts should be wedded to the labour of the emigrant or prostituted by the tramp of the slave-driver." (While this last sentence condemned slavery, it can also be read as an implicit endorsement of white immigration over black migration.)

Europe's working classes, the letter continued, recognized that "the slave-holders' rebellion was to sound the tocsin for a general holy crusade of property against labour," and that their "hopes for the future" and their "past conquests" were dependent upon a Union victory. Slavery had lowered the expectations and blocked the progress of the "white-skinned" laborers of the North because, relative to the slave, white workers had counted themselves lucky to have the privilege "to choose his own master." Again, the concern here was for the overarching historical progress of the white working class, not for the condition of black workers, slave or free.

The letter's final lines have been repeated often by historians: "The working men of Europe feel sure that, as the American War of Independence initiated a new era of ascendancy for the middle class, so the American Anti-Slavery War will do for the working classes. They consider it an earnest of the epoch to come that it fell to the lot of Abraham Lincoln, the single-minded son of the working class, to lead his country through the matchless struggle for the rescue of an enchained race and the reconstruction of a social world." Once more, the reason that blacks should be "rescued" was that the institution of slavery constituted a great barricade on the highway of history being traveled by Northern (white) workers and their European counterparts. Marx made it clear in letters to Engels that he did not include the Southern white or the freed black in his definition of the American "working class." "I think the mean whites [meaning the poor whites of the South] will gradually die out," observed Marx, while "the niggers will probably turn into small squatters as in Jamaica." Neither group, then, was a good candidate to turn the wheels of history in Marx's book. Marx later reworked this idea into a more elegant equation in *Capital* a few years later: "Labour cannot emancipate itself in white skin where in the black it is branded." In the final analysis, all of the reasons for supporting Lincoln and emancipation that Marx presented were based on the self-interest of white workers.[20]

Compared to how the English faction on the General Council expressed its ideas on the significance of the American Civil War, Marx was truly successful at avoiding what he termed "vulgar-democratic phraseology."

For the occasion of the International's first anniversary, a soiree was planned. At first it was intended to be simply a celebration of the founding of the International and a reception for the continental delegates who were arriving to attend the London Conference, the first general gathering of delegates of the association. But William Cremer proposed that the soiree also "celebrate the triumph of the federal cause and congratulate the American people on the abolition of slavery." Cremer's motion was carried, though not unanimously.[21]

Cremer drafted an address, entitled "To the People of the United States of America," to be read at the now-combined soiree and emancipation celebration. Its salutation alone reveals the republican tone of the entire work. It hailed the "Citizens of the Great Republic!," a republic that rested on "principles of universal justice," its mission being "the cause of our common humanity." It went on to congratulate the American people in their great victory over slavery, "that dark spot on your otherwise fair escutcheon." Never again "shall the salesman's hammer barter human flesh and blood in your market places." The IWA, Cremer asserted, was "firmly attached to, and believing in those principles of equality and common brotherhood for which you drew the sword." Finally, Cremer took the liberty of offering the Americans some advice:

> As injustice to a section of your people has produced such direful results, let that cease. Let your citizens of to-day be declared free and equal, without reserve.
>
> If you fail to give them citizen's rights, while you demand citizens' duties, there will yet remain a struggle for the future which may again stain your country with your people's blood. . . . We warn you then, as brothers in the common cause, to remove every shackle from freedom's limb, and your victory will be complete.[22]

Undoubtedly, Marx was far more in step with the popular attitude of white working-class Americans than was Cremer. The majority of white Union soldiers did not brave the enemies' cannon shot and musket ball to vindicate what Cremer called "principles of equality and common brotherhood," but to put down the rebellion, save the union, and secure their freedom and future as white farmers and workingmen by eliminating the competition of slave labor. Fewer still would have conceived of what Marx called a "new era of the emancipation of labour," though most would have seen their battles as being waged in their own interests, not in the interests of slaves or abstract principles of justice and equality.

The same ideological basis that underlay this sharp disjunction in principle between Karl Marx's and the English labor-republicans' views also led them to disagreements over many other vital social questions of the day. For example, many of the English labor leaders who sat across the table from Karl Marx at the General Council's meetings were ardent champions of women's suffrage and equal rights. Odger and Cremer were credited with "keeping the woman question open, and in public meetings pledged their aid in finding female work, and also . . . female votes."[23] John Hales, the first president of the IWA, courageously stood up for the right of women to work at his trade of elastic web-weaving. His defense of the rights of women workers nearly cost him his position as secretary of his London union when a faction that was determined to rid the trade of women attempted to oust him by accusing him of graft. Only after an extensive investigation were the charges proved groundless and Hales reinstated. Hales and other British members of the International who had been influenced by the thinking of Owenite socialism retained much of Owenism's utopian vision of sexual equality. But to Marx, the question of women's equality, like that of racial equality, seemed premature. Marx characterized the liberal demand for women's political rights as the "false emancipation of women."[24]

The fact that the two major factions within the General Council of London, that of English tradesmen and of the continental exiles who followed Karl Marx, viewed the world from different ideological frames of reference was of little consequence at the time. Both groups worked well together as long as Marx was circumspect in his language and relied on his powers of persuasion to get his way, and as long as the English deferred to the expatriates in matters of policy. Although these differences remained muted in London, they were soon exported to America, where they grew far beyond the bounds of their European origins.

Engels was absolutely correct in his prophetic prediction that the disjunction between the opinions of Marx and those of his English comrades would only become exacerbated over time. But what he could not have predicted was the even more profound effect this division would have on the offshoots of the IWA. Although the first American branch of the IWA would not be formally organized for three more years, in 1870, in some ways its fate was already sealed. The conflict between Marx's focused revolutionary direction and the extremely broad reform agenda of the English labor leaders, which for the most part was muted successfully within the General Council itself, would later explode in the New World.

THE International Workingmen's Association dispatched two copies of itself to the New World. From the beginning of the IWA, both Marx and the English members of the Council had maintained their own channels of communication and recruitment in America. By 1871, when the IWA reached the peak of its influence in America, it was in reality two organizations: one that reflected the thinking and social agenda of the English members of the General Council, and the other that was tied by ideology, ethnicity, and personal relationships to Marx himself.

The General Council did not intend for the International to travel to America in two separate boats. But the two groups were a natural outgrowth of the ideological rifts within the IWA and the state of transatlantic communication in that era. Lacking a quick, efficient, and convenient method of communication and transportation between the continents, the IWA was forced to rely on the individual initiative of its members to spread its program across the seas. Personal contacts were what mattered, and no one showed greater initiative in cultivating intercontinental friendships than did Karl Marx. At the same time, the General Council established the office of American Corresponding Secretary. This officeholder had the sole responsibility for establishing links to Americans and exporting the International to the United States. Marx was never interested in holding this office, so it went instead to a succession of Englishmen. In the end, two channels of communication were established between London and the New World: one directed by Marx himself and the other by a chain of English corresponding secretaries. Each faction succeeded in recreating itself in America.

Karl Marx and Frederick Engels were the first to show interest in propagating the International across the Atlantic. Marx had established many contacts in the States during the 1850s, when he was active in the Communist League, a secret international communist society. But his many correspondents had fallen silent while America was engulfed by the Civil War. This did not concern Marx at the time, since he then was devoting all his energies to writing *Das Kapital* and living as a political recluse.

By coincidence, one month after the meeting at St. Martin's Hall, Marx received a letter from his old friend Joseph Weydemeyer, a German immigrant to the United States whom Marx had known from the days of the revolutions of 1848 and who was now a colonel in the U.S. Army. Since his arrival in America in 1851, Weydemeyer had been the most active voice for communism in the German-speaking community through his two newspapers, *Die Revolution* and *Die Reform*. While Weydemeyer and Engels exchanged notes on military strategy, Marx took advantage of the opportunity to fire off several copies of his newly minted "Inaugural Address" to America. Weydemeyer quickly arranged for it to be printed in his local St. Louis labor newspaper, the *Daily Press*, thereby giving the International its first mention in the United States.[25]

Marx's private channel to the United States improved with the surprise arrival on his doorstep of Karl Klings, another old German friend who had been active in the General Association of German Workers in Berlin. As it turned out, Klings was emigrating to America, and Marx seized this opportunity to add to his coterie of correspondents and recruiters abroad. It was agreed that Klings would "organize everything in America with Weydemeyer and the others."[26] Siegfried Meyer, another Berliner and veteran of the General Association of German Workers, pulled up stakes and immigrated to America in 1866. Marx wrote him and implored his like-minded ally to "form as many branches as possible in America" and to write him about his progress and general conditions in the States.[27]

At this time, Marx was using his American contacts to spread drafts of *Das Kapital*. He sent a copy of his draft preface to Siegfried Meyer and asked him to get it printed in as many German American newspapers as he could. The German American Forty-Eighter Hermann Meyer was also enlisted in this effort.[28] Engels impressed upon him the importance of bringing *Das Kapital* to the Americans: "With the 8-hour agitation that is in progress in America now, this book with its chapter on the working day will come at just the right time for you over there, and, in other respects too, it is likely to clarify peoples' minds on a variety of issues. The future of the party in America will be greatly beholden to you for any step you can take in that direction."[29]

By the summer of 1867, Marx's efforts bore fruit. The Communist Club of New York, a group formed in 1857 that renounced "all religion and every [doctrine] not founded upon the perception of concrete objects" and vowed to work to "abolish the bourgeois property system," voted to affiliate as Section 1.[30] A kindred club in Hoboken, New Jersey, led by a German American music teacher named Friedrich Sorge, also applied for membership. In his letter announcing these developments, Sorge informed Marx that the International was enjoying increasing success in America, though only among German American workers. Sorge hoped that the International's propaganda could be carried as well to the native-born, English-speaking population and asked Marx for English-language copies of the International's documents.

By this time Marx was not only cultivating his American correspondents, he was assuming the powers of the General Council, which were not technically his. For example, Marx was so taken with Sorge that he took it upon himself to send him an "official credential" of the IWA. It read: "We recommend Mr. Sorge to all the friends of the International Workingmen's Association and, at the same time, empower him to act in the name and on behalf of that Association—By the order of the General Council of the International Workingmen's Association, Karl Marx, Secretary for Germany."[31] There is no record that the General Council ever considered the question of Sorge's credentials, however; nor does such a resolution appear anywhere in the otherwise detailed minutes of the organization.

This was not the first time that Marx had loosely construed his official prerogatives in his capacity as Corresponding Secretary for Germany. Prior to the IWA's first congress in Geneva, Marx wanted to ensure that a large block of German socialists would attend and thereby serve as a balance to his French and English opponents. Toward this end, he prepaid for a block of membership cards and sent them to his friends Siegfried Meyer and August Vogt in Berlin and Wilhelm Liebknecht in Leipzig, with the instructions to "give them away. . . . The principal thing is to get up members, individual or societies, in Germany."[32]

While Marx was establishing his own lines of communication to German Americans, the General Council, in its official capacity, began to reach out to America. In its first year the General Council elected Leon Lewis to the newly created office of Corresponding Secretary for America. Lewis was an American journalist who would later employ his talents in defense of the labor leaders on trial for the Chicago Haymarket bombing in 1886.[33] His name was originally put forward for membership in the General Council by John Weston, a man who was impressed by his liberal writings, particularly a piece he had published entitled "A Requiem for Abraham Lincoln." Lewis was at the time in the process of starting up a labor paper in England that he proposed to call "The Commoner" and that he had offered to place at the disposal of the IWA.[34]

Marx disliked Lewis, whom he described to Engels as a "Yankee," a "worthless" fellow who "has plenty of money and even more ambition." In this case, for all of Lewis's good intentions, Marx's assessment may not have struck too far from the mark. He attended only one meeting of the General Council, apparently never made any attempt to establish an official correspondence with America, and even failed to get his newspaper off the ground.[35] Meanwhile, the Council busied itself with other matters and allowed the problem of the absentee Lewis to drag on for many months before they acted upon it. It was not until May of 1866 that the General Council finally got around to replacing him.

In his place the General Council tapped Peter André Fox, an English journalist and one of the publishers of the freethinking journal the *National Reformer*. Unlike his predecessor, Peter Fox threw himself into his new labors and made his office one of the most active in the Council. From the start, Fox began building his bridges to America in a more systematic way than had ever been done before. Up to this time, all of the Council's official attempts to spread word of the International to America had been haphazard. Lacking a proper secretary, the Council had relied on travelers who offered to carry IWA propaganda across the Atlantic. In 1865 four hundred membership cards were entrusted to a friend of Council member Eugene Dupont who was bound for the States, but nothing was ever heard from him again.[36] Several months later the Italian patriot Césare Orsini passed through London on his way to America and similarly found his luggage stuffed with IWA rule books and pamphlets.[37]

Rather than relying upon such occasional voyages of the International's supporters to recruit members retail, Fox endeavored to sign them up wholesale. Hearing of the efforts of American trade unions to unite in a single national labor congress, Fox initiated correspondence with every leader in this effort whose name and address he could obtain. Over the next year Fox exchanged letters with C. W. Gibson, William Sylvis, William Jessup, and J. C. C. Whaley, all men who were then instrumental in building up the fledgling National Labor Union.[38]

By the summer of 1867, Fox's efforts had reaped impressive gains for the IWA in America. William Jessup, vice president of the NLU and president of the New York State Working Men's Assembly, sent Fox word that he believed it "a matter of great importance that the workingmen of both the old and the new countries should be in close communication in relation to the labor movement" and promised to work toward bringing them together in closer union. At its August convention in Chicago, the National Labor Union voted to send a delegate to Europe to investigate labor conditions and to "effect a more perfect understanding as to the workings of the various reform associations in both countries," although it was by then too late for the NLU's delegate to attend the IWA congress at Lausanne, Switzerland. The NLU further resolved to send its sympathy and extend its hand

Col. Richard Josiah Hinton, member of IWA Section 23, Washington, D.C.
(Kansas State Historical Society)

in cooperation to the working classes of Europe in their "struggle against political and social wrongs." In language that the English members of the General Council would have found familiar, the NLU praised the efforts of European workers as being "a gratifying indication of the progress of justice, enlightenment, and of the sentiments of humanity."[39]

Other channels to America were opening up as well. Richard J. Hinton, a man well known in the Boston radical abolitionist community for his service as a Republican journalist in Bloody Kansas, his abortive attempt to free John Brown from prison, and his leadership of a black regiment in the war itself, attended a meeting of the General Council and gave a speech in which he proclaimed that "a close union, not only between the trades' societies, but of the leading social and political spirits of the two countries was necessary," and he pledged to do all in his power upon his return home to bring about just such a union.[40] A week later, word arrived from America that two members of the IWA had been well received at a meeting of New York's delegates to the NLU.[41] By the end of October, Fox was pleased to announce that he was receiving "constant information" about the state of the labor movement in America from Jessup and from J. C. C. Whaley, president of the NLU, and suggested that the Council allocate funds to purchase a number of subscriptions to English labor journals for the purpose of exchanging them with Jessup and Whaley in return for American papers.[42]

But at the very peak of his success, Peter Fox suddenly resigned his post as American secretary. Although he claimed that he was forced to leave the Council because he needed to work at his journalism full time in order to provide for his family, underlying his decision was a long history of friction with Marx's continental faction on the Council, a group Fox denounced as the "German dictatorship."[43]

Although none of the disagreements between Fox and the "German dictatorship" were sufficient in themselves to prompt Fox's resignation, their effect was cumulative in his mind. After the 1867 Geneva Conference, the German members of the Council who were responsible for compensating the General Council's delegates for their travel expenses had pettily short-changed some of the English members. And when Fox attempted to secure credentials for two of his most productive organizers in America, Victor Drury and a man known only as "Izard," he was rebuffed. Drury's revolutionary credentials were impeccable: he had been a young Parisian street fighter in the uprising of 1848 who later embraced Marxist teachings and was one of the French delegates to the founding St. Martin's Hall meeting of the International in 1864.[44] In spite of Drury's impressive record, Marx maneuvered behind the scenes to have his organizing credentials revoked. He told others that he thought Drury was "a fishy customer" and he mistrusted Marie Huleck and William Cremer, two of the more freethinking republicans on the Council who had recommended him.[45]

In September 1867, Marx orchestrated the expulsion of George Odger from the presidency of the International by having the post itself abolished.[46] Later that same autumn, a more serious row erupted when it was learned that Marx's close friend Eccarius had anonymously dispatched reports to the *Times* of London from the International's congress at Lausserne ridiculing the proposals and philosophies of some of the French and English members. Although Marx and Engels attempted to conceal the identity of the author of these attacks, the truth got out. Fox took the floor at the next Council meeting to denounce Eccarius, and he offered a motion censur-

Victor Drury (The Schlesinger Library, Radcliffe College)

ing his actions. James Carter, a founding member of the International, rose saying that it was "the duty of any Council member who had a stigma cast upon him to resign," whereupon he announced his resignation from his post as Italian Corresponding Secretary and from his seat on the Council and stormed from the room.[47]

As the Council meetings became more and more rancorous that autumn of 1867, a short and seemingly innocuous proposal decisively shifted the center of power from the English members to the "continentals." At the end of October, the Council decided that the secretaries of the Council should compose the "standing committee," wherein they would hold the reins of the Council by virtue of their authority to set the agenda for upcoming meetings. Only the year before, the standing committee was composed of three Englishmen: Carter, Matthew Lawrence, the president of London's tailors' union, and a man named Whitehead.[48] No proposal could come to the floor without having been approved by the standing committee. Moreover, the final drafts of rules, resolutions, and public declarations of all sorts were subject to its editing. Since all the secretaries but one were European exiles, the establishment of the committee signaled the exclusion of the English members from the day-to-day control of the International. Marx's own firm grip on the standing committee's decisions was well illustrated during the winter of 1869–70 when a bout of prolonged illness kept him in bed and the committee held all important discussions at Marx's home.[49]

Even before Marx and his continental allies seized control of the standing committee, Fox had seen the writing on the wall and came to believe that the English trade union leaders were wasting their time on the Council. In one last desperate attempt to break Marx's grip on the Council, Fox secretly plotted to have the seat of the General Council transferred to Geneva, where Marx's influence was weakest. Marx learned of Fox's plans and exposed them before the Council, thus forcing Fox to abandon his scheme.

Marx returned Fox's animosity when he branded him "the only literary man in the Association"— which was not a compliment.[50] Marx was wary of any middle-class involvement in the IWA, exempting Engels and himself, of course, and he warned on many occasions against their influence. Apparently unaware of the personal irony of his words, Marx cautioned: "One has to be all the more careful the moment men of letters, members of the bourgeoisie or semi-literary people become involved in the movement." In the heat of their battle, Marx flung at Fox the greatest condemnation in his repertoire: he told Engels that the "concept of 'class'" was an "alien" one to Peter Fox.[51]

Marx arranged for the standing committee to appoint Robert Shaw, a poor English housepainter who had more loyalty and enthusiasm than ability, to replace the energetic and dedicated Fox.[52] Shaw was a curious choice for an office so vital to Marx's international strategies. He was chronically absent from the Council's meetings and he apparently never read or sent any American correspondence. Indeed, there is no record of his discussing any matter relating to America during his tenure as American secretary. On June 23, 1868, the Council received a letter from Shaw tendering his resignation.

Surprisingly, Marx urged the Council not to accept Shaw's resignation and suggested instead that the Council appoint Eccarius as temporary American secretary until Shaw could be convinced to return to the fold.[53]

After Shaw returned later that fall, Friedrich Lessner, an old friend of Marx's from the Communist League days of the 1840s, moved that Shaw be reappointed American secretary. Marx seconded the motion, and Shaw continued on in his moribund office for another year.[54]

Marx's support for Shaw was premised on three qualities Shaw possessed in a unique combination: he was an Englishman, he was a trade unionist, and he followed Marx's orders.[55] Since Marx had arranged for the composition of the powerful standing committee to consist of the foreign secretaries and officers of the association, Shaw was a particularly valued ally. With only one other regular English member, the carpenter John Weston, Robert Shaw was oftentimes the standing committee's token Englishman. Yet even Shaw's loyalty would not have been enough to maintain Marx's unflagging support had it not been for the fact that Marx was at this time busily building up the International among German Americans on his own initiative. In many ways, Shaw was a convenient English figurehead for an office that Marx had already made obsolete through his own back-channel efforts. Eccarius later revealed that during this period he had managed the U.S. correspondence himself because he understood that Shaw was only appointed to sign the American membership cards.[56]

In the end, the International's links to the United States remained divided between Eccarius and Marx just as the International in America remained divided between the German-, French-, and English-speaking sections. At the prompting of two key English members, it was finally agreed to dispense with the fiction of an American secretary and recognize this arrangement officially. Now Eccarius was to correspond with the National Labor Union and the few English-speaking sections of the IWA in the United States, Eugene Dupont would handle the French letters from America, and Marx would be in charge of American correspondence in the German language. With this act, the United States of America became the only country within the International's compass that was officially compartmentalized by language and ethnicity.[57]

Thus were the walls of ethnicity, language, and ideology that separated the German Internationalists from their French and native-born associates in America buttressed by the division of authority and communication on the General Council. Lacking a single chain of information, each American group was informed by its own London secretary's peculiar interpretation of the International's ideals, methods, and rules. Marx tutored his German American correspondents to view the International as he did — as an instrument: Marx wrote to Siegfried Meyer and August Vogt and lectured them that "the most important object of the International Workingmen's Association" was "to hasten the social revolution in England."[58] On more than one occasion Marx fertilized the seeds of discord between his German correspondents and the other American Internationals. For example, Marx was deeply suspicious of Victor Drury, one of the most active organizers of the English-language branches in America, and he told his American agents to spy on him. Marx instructed Meyer to "observe the man more closely . . . either [by] yourself or through friends." Likewise, Marx informed his German American comrades about another official IWA organizer in America, General Gustave Cluseret, whom he called "a flighty, superficial, officious, boastful fellow," and encouraged them "to get to know this 'hero,' even if only to sound him out."[59]

English-speaking Internationalists in America, on the other hand, found their own kindred spirits on the Council. American abolitionist Richard J. Hinton was a close friend and admirer of the Council's George Odger. Hinton wrote a profile of Odger for the *National Anti-Slavery Standard*, wherein he hailed him as the leader of the wartime British workers' movement who was most responsible for organizing labor support for the Union cause and for the abolitionist movement as well. He went on to describe him as the "founder" of the IWA. Other American peace advocates who became early Internationalists, such as Cyrenus Osborne Ward, were probably well acquainted with the Council's William Cremer, Robert Applegarth, and Benjamin Lucraft, who were also active in the pacifist International League of Peace and Liberty, as well as the Workingmen's Peace Association. C. O. Ward, a machinist for the Brooklyn naval yard during the war and a teacher and journalist after that, was invited to speak before the General Council when he passed through London on a trip to a peace convention. He claimed later that he paid up his IWA dues for the next twenty years on the spot.[60] Other leaders of America's English-speaking International were old veterans of the land reform movement and had close ties to English land reformers, some of whom, such as Martin Boon and George Harris, now sat on the General Council. But all of these transatlantic contacts were unofficial.[61]

Soon after assuming responsibility for the English-language American correspondence, Johann Eccarius, the German tailor who was one of Marx's oldest comrades in London, drifted out of Marx's orbit. Rather than serving as an instrument of Marx's control of the American International, Eccarius steered an independent course that eventually brought him into direct conflict with his longtime German friends.

Cyrenus Osborne Ward (Special Collections Library, University of Michigan)

Eccarius's trajectory in office is all the more surprising given the animus that existed between him and the English members of the Council. Since Eccarius was the one member of Marx's circle who regularly published articles in the daily press, including routine reports of the International's proceedings, his views were more exposed to criticism. When Peter Fox had complained of a "German dictatorship," Eccarius was one of the primary figures he had in mind. And when tempers flared and accusations flew against Eccarius, more often than not it was Marx himself who intervened on his behalf.

Eccarius's drift away from Marx's camp began sometime after the International's Brussels congress in 1868. Marx and the other European members of the General Council had been extremely displeased with the reports of the congress Eccarius had written for the *Times* of London. Marx was particularly incensed at what he believed to be Eccarius's jealous refusal to mention *Das Kapital* in any of his columns. After this episode, Marx was determined that Eccarius would never again represent the General Council at an International congress.[62]

To some degree, Eccarius's falling out with Marx reflected not only a clash of egos but also some ideological movement on Eccarius's part. One of the complaints made against his reporting from Brussels was that he distorted the resolutions introduced by the German delegates regarding the Franco-Prussian War. Whereas the original resolution was intended to lay the blame for the war at the feet of Russia, Eccarius simply labeled it as a "civil war." He also misattributed to the Germans what Marx called "the Belgian nonsense" of calling for a national strike against the war. Perhaps this mistake reflected Eccarius's own evolving opinions of the war rather than carelessness or malice.[63]

In any event, Eccarius was well on the road to apostasy. Marx began to complain that Eccarius "commits unpleasant tomfooleries from time to time": "I generally take no notice of this. Now and then my patience is exhausted. I give him a brain washing, and all is right again for the time being."[64] The exact reason that Eccarius needed frequent ideological refresher sessions from Marx remains unclear. What is apparent is that over the next few years Eccarius edged closer and closer to the English side of the Council, advocating their political strategy of running workers for Parliamentary seats and of forming broad alliances with "the advanced men of the middle classes." By the time of the International's congress at the Hague, Marx and Eccarius were no longer on speaking terms. Long after the International was dead and buried, Engels still referred to Eccarius as "the traitor to our cause."[65] Little wonder, then, that English-speaking American Internationalists found Eccarius a reliable spokesman for their interests on the Council.

For the next few years, Marx cheered on his correspondents Siegfried Meyer, August Vogt, and Friedrich Sorge as they built up a strong core of German socialists in New York and Chicago. Similarly, Eccarius and the English Internationalists gave their support and encouragement to their own men in America, Richard J. Hinton, Victor Drury, Osborne Ward, and Robert Hume, who shepherded a highly diverse coterie of reformers under one red umbrella. Each transatlantic group cohered around its own unique interpretation of the meaning and purpose of the International. While German Americans steeled themselves to their teleological, revolutionary purpose under the tutelage of the master revolutionary theorist himself, Yankee reformers received a different gospel, one that reinforced their penchant for all-embracing, ecumenical, universal reform—reform that, while condemning capitalism, recognized as its first principles the republican values of popular democracy, liberty, and equality, and that appeared to have historical links to the reform movements with which they were familiar and comfortable, such as abolition, land reform, civil rights, anticapitalism, and pacifism. Much to the surprise and chagrin of Marx and the International's German American leadership, not only did the Yankees' hoped for recruitment of labor reformers, trade unionists, and land reformers materialize, but an unexpected coterie of abolitionists, spiritualists, suffragists, and cultural rebels of numerous stripes also flocked to the International's call. The Yankee International was born.

CHAPTER THREE

The New Democracy

I T TOOK SEVERAL YEARS for either the English-speaking or the German-speaking branches of the International Workingmen's Association in the United States to grow large enough to attract the attention of journalists. Consequently, the record of these early years is spotty. Cesare Orsini had stayed but a few months in the summer of 1866 before returning to Europe—his famous radical recruits abandoned without even an official membership card. The following year Peter Fox began to extend his circle of American correspondents and made progress in enlisting the support of American labor leaders. But with an ocean separating them and without an official representative in America to act as a liaison, except for the exchange of good wishes and statements of solidarity, the relationship between the two remained as distant as the continents.

Between the time the labor reform movement began to enlist the support of many of the veterans of America's antebellum reform crusades and the First International was formally founded in the United States, a small group of radical men and women launched a new reform association in New York, called the "New Democracy," the forerunner of the Yankee International. In 1870, the New Democracy requested admission into the International Workingmen's Association and the first two English-speaking sections of the International in America were organized by former leaders of the New Democracy.

By itself the New Democracy seems historically insignificant: it was a tiny, local, ephemeral organization that never attracted a broad membership or extended itself beyond Manhattan, and whose legacy has been but a small footnote in the history of labor. Its constituency consisted primarily of aging land reformers, most of whom had been active in the Democratic and Free-Soil Parties or had helped found George Henry Evans's National Reform Party in the 1830s. These so-called land reformers were also early adherents to the individualistic, even proto-anarchistic, philosophy of Josiah Warren, a working-class intellectual who rejected both the exploitation of capitalism and the rigidity and depersonalization of Fourierist socialism. Radical Jacksonians who saw the rise of industry and finance as the result of the machinations of a corrupt cabal in the federal government and had fought the Bank of the United States, members of the New Democracy had come to believe that government itself was the fount of economic inequality and were committed to an extreme variant of Jeffersonianism—to creating a freeholder's republic where each man was an economic "sovereign" unto himself.

The New Democracy may not have been significant for what it did during its brief existence, but it is highly important as an ideological enigma. Why did a group of proto-anarchist land reformers found a political party dedicated to state socialism? Because the New Democracy was the ideological proving ground for the future English-speaking International, understanding the relationship between its land reform leadership and its socialistic program is the key to unlocking the complicated ideology of the Yankee International itself. In the New Democracy's principles and proclamations, and in the philosophical evolution of its founders that led to them, can be glimpsed the various ideological elements that were at the core of the future Yankee International's hopes and beliefs.

ALTHOUGH THEY started later, Marx's allies made much more rapid progress than did the General Council's official correspondents in the United States. Marx's agents had the advantage of returning to a land they knew and recruiting among men with whom they had already worked. Upon landing in New York, Siegfried Meyer, Marx's like-minded friend and confidant, discovered that the old Communist Club, which he had helped to found in 1857, was still in existence, though it had dwindled to fewer than twenty members. Even though the German labor reform community had languished from the time that Meyer had left it, there were still some promising signs. A new political party called the Social Party had just been founded by a few of the two-dozen-odd surviving members of the Communist Club, while the trade union movement seemed to be reviving. Meyer quickly took to the New York milieu and undertook an active and vigorous agitation to spread Marxist principles among the predominantly Lassallean German radicals.[1]

Meyer's old connections paid off within a few months when the Communist Club and an offshoot club organized by Friedrich Sorge, a fellow charter member of the Communist Club, affiliated with the International. Each club sent letters announcing their adhesion to London, their tone certainly confirming Marx in his back-channel efforts. The Communist Club wrote that it was founded on the principle that rejected "every [doctrine] not founded upon the perception of concrete objects." Sorge wrote of the "great danger" to American workingmen of the professional politicians of the likes of Radical Republican Senator Benjamin Wade who "were advocating working men's measures to retain their places." Sorge reported that so far the International was being propagated only among the German workers, but he did ask for official documents in English so that native workers could be appealed to as well.[2]

When the Social Party failed at the polls in the fall of 1868, New York's German radicals turned their backs on political strategies and focused on perfecting their labor organizations. A long-standing but moribund German union the *Allgemeiner Deutscher Arbeiterverein*, or General German Labor Union (GGLU), was reinvigorated by Social Party veterans and was purged of its last holdovers of the older Lassallean faith in electoral movements. Sorge and Meyer rapidly ascended to leadership positions in the GGLU, remaking it into something of a school of Marxism for German workers. Sorge later recalled with fondness those days when it "was a real joy to be at union meetings." Gathering weekly in a "low, badly ventilated room in the Tenth Ward Hotel," union members "competed with each other in learning economics, in overcoming the most difficult economic and philosophical problems." So effective was this pressure cooker of Marxist education that Sorge could later boast that "among the hundreds of members who belonged to the union between 1869 and 1874 was hardly one who had not read Marx [*Capital*]."[3]

Meanwhile, the Yankee branch of the International tree had also grown into the labor societies of New York. Victory Drury and his shadowy French companion, Izard, made the rounds of New York's trade unions, promoting cooperative banking and mutual-aid proposals that were popular with workers who saw them as alternatives to the hated wages system. William Jessup and the Workingmen's Union of New York were so impressed by the speeches and Proudhonist schemes of Drury and Izard that they established no less than five separate committees to carry out their plans.[4] In the end such ideas did not take hold, though their brief popularity did associate the International with cooperative schemes in New York and attracted some local radicals to the red standard.

To the immigrant radicals of New York's "Little Germany," who remained intellectually closer to Berlin than to Boston, Drury and Izard's watered-down Proudhonism was derided as "humbug" and such schemes were viewed as hopeless panaceas.[5] But to the Yankee radicals who rejected the wages system but lacked acquaintance with the broader, teleological theories of Marx, Drury and Izard's plan seemed a pragmatic idea that promised immediate relief from the exploitation and deprivations suffered by New York's workers. Veterans of an American reform tradition, whose perfectionist optimism continually tended to push its expectations and claims toward the realm of the utopian, they had little skepticism for yet another idealistic reform plan.

Sometime in 1868, a handful of these Yankee reformers in New York began meeting in one another's homes. After deciding to organize, they gave their new reform movement the name the "New Democracy, or Political Commonwealth." The New Democracy enjoyed a mixed membership that included both professional and working-class members. Its president, Leander Thompson, was a butcher. William West, the New Democracy's corresponding secretary, had worked variously as a tinsmith and a police officer but in his old age had found employment as a clerk. George Allen, the recording secretary, was a housepainter. As for its middle-class members, none even approached the outer circles of New York's elite. Edward Newberry was a dentist, and Esther Andrews (the wife of Stephen Pearl Andrews, the politician) was a physician, though she reportedly "practiced almost wholly among the poor and destitute." J. W. Gregory, or "Grandfather Gregory," as he was known to his radical friends, had been a farmer and an expressman in San Francisco. Ira B. Davis was the proprietor of a bathhouse whose connection to earlier health reform fads is evident in its advertising for its selection of "persian baths, vapor baths, sulphur, mercurial, iodine, electro-magnetic and friction baths."[6] What nearly all of these individuals had in common was that they were among the last surviving partisans of a radical movement known as "land reform," a term that had come not only to encompass land redistribution as a means to end poverty, inequality, and crime but also to imply an early form of native anarchism.

As the New Democracy claimed rightly, it was "the direct successor[,] if not the actual continuator, of the industrial congress and labor and land reform movement of twenty and twenty-five years ago in this country."[7] In membership and outlook it represented the confluence of several generations of native reform ideologies. All of its programs, addresses, and manifestos bore the mark of a half century of American reform thought. Ideologically, the New Democracy connected eighteenth-century Enlightenment republicanism to the proletarian radicalism that flourished at the end of the nineteenth. Indeed, some of its political goals when taken out of context appear more appropriate to the days of Jefferson and his vision of freeholder capitalism than to the dawn of the industrial corporate society of the Gilded Age. In one address, the New Democracy pined for a time when "the people learn[ed] to employ themselves on their own farms [and] in their own workshops," a sentiment any Revolutionary era American liberal would have approved. Taken alone, such a statement makes the New Democrats seem naive and ignorant of the social and economic realities of their own day. Indeed, this superficial reading of the New Democracy's ideology has mislead most recent historians to portray its members as "sentimentalists" and "bourgeois reformers."

Steeped as it was in the language of patriotic republicanism, the New Democracy often has been misunderstood as an echo of Jeffersonian agrarianism or native American anarchism. David Montgomery, in *Beyond Equality*, his classic work on labor reform in this period, sneeringly refers to the entire community of Yankee radicals as "sentimental reformers" and proclaims the founders of the New Democracy to be "thorough anarchists." David Herreshoff would have us believe that "when the Germans spoke of 'class struggle,' the Americans spoke of 'the scientific reconciliation of labor and capital.' " David De Leon, in *The American as Anarchist: Reflections on Indigenous Radicalism*, finds that "the bourgeois philanthropists" of the Yankee IWA and Mikhail Bakunin, the leader of the anarchist movement in Europe, "had something in common: their rejection of central authority."[8]

Others have depicted the New Democracy as being hostile to the very idea of socialist collectivism. According to Samuel Bernstein, whose book *The First International in America* was long considered the definitive work on the American branch of the IWA, the New Democracy was an antisocialist organization that believed that labor enjoyed a basic "compatibility with capital" and its aim was "not the abolition of private property, but its wide distribution." [9] But the New Democrats, at least in terms of their willingness to use the power of the state to appropriate capital, were far closer to Marx than to any anarchist, and Jefferson would have found their views of property repugnant. Interestingly, the first labor historians to study the New Democracy were not so dismissive of its radical thrust. Selig Perlman, in his section of John R. Commons's landmark *History of Labour in the United States*, published in 1918, had no problem in labeling the New Democracy's orientation as "socialist," and he even correctly described their program as advocating "state socialism." [10]

Although members of the New Democracy proclaimed the ideal of "individual sovereignty," a notion that has come to be identified as the rallying cry of the early anarchists, they were clearly not anarchists. In America, the word "anarchist," though used self-descriptively for some time in France by Proudhon, was not used as a general label for a radical individualist until after the demise of the First International. None of the Americans whom historians have claimed as the "fathers of American anarchism" ever referred to themselves as anarchists or to their ideas as anarchism prior to that time. What has been described as anarchism in this period was primarily the revolt against the long line of utopian communitarian schemes that linked Saint-Simon, Charles Fourier, Albert Brisbane, and Robert Owen. It was a revolt against the forms of collectivism that denied private property in labor and mirrored capitalism in its alienation of the worker from the fruits of his or her work. Rather than upholding private property in principle as a countervailing power and realm of freedom against the state, as did classical liberals from John Locke to Adam Smith, American "mutualists," to which they sometimes referred themselves, only considered as property the product of one's own labor. Anything beyond what was justly earned by toil was illegitimate and presumably subject to confiscation for public use. "As all legitimate property is the product of industry, it rightly belongs to the producer" was the first "General Thesis" of one tract published in support of the New Democracy. In this way the ideal of private property in labor as the highest form of property, indeed, the only "sovereign" aspect of property, turned the liberal ideal of property against itself. Property now was a powerful weapon against unimpeded accumulation and against private ownership of capital. [11]

If the laborer was merely the owner of the product of his or her toil, argued William West in a series of 1870 articles for the New Democracy, then capitalists were by definition the possessors of ill-gotten gain. The source of their wealth was not individual pluck and perseverance but a political system of privileges that siphoned value from the toil of workers. Codified in law were systems that allowed the private acquisition of land, the collection of rent, the usury of credit, and the manipulations of currency. While Jefferson and other seminal republicans argued that the answer to such economic oppression was the wider distribution of land and capital among agrarian freeholders, and though the New Democrats viewed land redistribution in near utopic terms, they also went beyond such individualistic solutions and offered a collective alternative.

Warrenite individualism as a feasible strategy for change weakened with the rising scale and complexity of finance and industry in America. In Josiah Warren's day, when most workers still toiled in small shops and corporations were just a blip on the horizon, the idea of a peaceful transition to such a "cost the limit of price" economic order did not yet seem so outlandish. But by the 1870s, the idea that workers simply needed to be free of government interference and support for monopoly, or that workers themselves could just "opt out" of the established system and create their own parallel equitable economy, no longer seemed practical. Ira B. Davis announced to the Labor Reform League in 1872 that he "believed cost should be the limit of price" but that he simply "did not see how that doctrine can be carried out except by getting the whole nation to associate on that principle." In other words, Warren's followers joined the New Democracy, and later the IWA, not because they continued to hold radically anarchist principles of individual sovereignty, but that they had ceased believing that they could be fulfilled without seizure and use of government power itself.[12]

Given the great depth to which this system of exploitation had become rooted in society by their time, the New Democrats believed that the only way to restore workers to their rightful place as sovereigns of their own labor was to "[transform government] from an Aristocracy of Privileged Capitalists to a Democracy of Equal Fellow-Citizens" by making it "the Employer of Labor and the Superintendent of Trade, Commerce, Exchange, Education and Insurance."[13] While Enlightenment liberals were primarily concerned with balancing the liberty of citizens against the oppression of the state, the New Democrats recognized a third player in this equation, the capitalist, who posed an even greater threat to the liberty of the individual by virtue of his stranglehold on the necessities of life. New Democrats believed that the threat to individual liberty posed by government could be offset by constitutionally restricting its power to legislate personal affairs, such as belief, love and marriage, custom and culture, "within the narrowest limits . . . conceded to the utmost verge of social safety." Moreover, once the structures of government were democratized through the introduction of the direct legislative mechanisms of the initiative, referendum, and recall of representatives, then the workers would have effectively seized the state. The final element in restoring to the workers their own sovereignty was to place the largest productive industries in the hands of the workers through their agent, the state. In collectivizing industry under a democratic government rather than extending the ownership of capital in a laissez-faire environment, the New Democracy hoped for every man to "become a producer, every producer a consumer, and every consumer a ruler; in other words, that all men may become their own employers, traders, merchants, bankers, insurers, and consequently possessors of those fruits of their united industries requisite to the exercise of all those powers constituting *sovereignty of the individual*." [14]

The source of confusion surrounding the New Democracy—and its successor, the Yankee International— was its understandable tendency to analyze social problems, proscribe remedies, and frame their vision of a better world in their native radical vocabulary. Separated as they were from the evolving lexicon of Marxist social critique, the men and women of the New Democracy spoke not of capitalism, proletarians, historical stages, modes of production, and surplus value, but of democracy, community, justice, and sovereignty. And though they spoke in a language that was born, to paraphrase Marx, out of the bourgeois revolution against feudal aristocracy, they found it adaptable to their modern industrial situation and they expressed through it many of the same concepts that Marx had formulated far more rigorously and systematically in the manner of a Heidelberg academic.

Moreover, the men and women of the New Democracy, believing as they did that all those who desired the reform of society were their natural allies, were typically tolerant of contrasting views and agendas within their organization. This is not to say that the Yankee IWA lacked a core of shared values, a common set of social concerns, or specific proposals necessary to bring about change. Rather, their belief that the paths to progress were many and their willingness to subsume their individual hobbies to the organization's program allowed for a diverse and yet united membership. For example, Lewis Masquerier, an original land reformer who never abandoned his personal utopian vision of a nation of freeholders whose government was no broader than a township, who published terse criticisms of those "reformers, urging the communitizing and nationalizing principle of rights and property," and who even argued that "labor cannot be communitized without running into abuse and tyranny," continued to describe himself as a member of the International.[15]

Underneath the deceptive liberal-reformist garb of its rhetoric, the New Democracy wore red knickers. When William West's credentials as delegate to the 1869 National Labor Union congress were challenged, West defended himself by explaining that the New Democracy was no less a labor organization for advocating political tactics than were those committed to trade unions, for its ultimate goal was "to make the State the employer and the workingmen the State."[16] In 1870, Cyrenus Osborne Ward published a tract in support of the IWA, called "The New Idea: Universal Co-operation and Theories of Future Government," that summarized the industrial policy of this "new labor party" as advocating "deliver[y] to the state, or rather to the people through the state, the management of business in all its productive and distributive ramifications." Ward called this policy "the plan of collectivity in the commonwealth."[17]

Marx would have also recognized in the New Democracy's ideology a historical perspective that paralleled his own. William West, the leading spokesman for the New Democracy, wrote of society progressing through stages of development, each characterized by its system of labor. He described the current wages system as the step beyond the reins of "chattelism and serfdom," won at the cost of "years of devoted sacrifice and millions of human lives." West did not believe the present mode of labor any more permanent:

> Away then, with the wild phantasy that because King Wealth does rule in the present his reign must be perpetual. As well might it have been said, as indeed it probably was said, in the days when warriors only were kings, and stalwart men hewed their way to the thrones they sat upon through rivers of blood shed by their own red hands, that they and such as they only, could ever reign. Those days have passed. The sword has yielded to the purse. And so, likewise, the reign of King Wealth shall cease, and property be Democratized.[18]

There was nothing "natural" or inevitable about the wages system. One of the New Democrats' most impassioned observations was that modern society increased its productivity, its knowledge, and its technology at an incredible rate while, paradoxically, at the same time it bred ever more dire conditions of poverty. The inevitable result, they predicted, would be a crisis too terrible to contemplate, unless the social and political system was rebuilt. Where they differed most from Marx was on the question of tactics. Marx hoped to rebuild society from the bottom up, through the slow organization of workers aimed toward their eventual seizure of the state and industry; the New Democrats hoped to do so from the top down, by opening the channels of democracy and expanding the state itself.[19]

As true radicals, the partisans of the New Democracy were even prepared to advocate other means of achieving their ends if political and electoral tactics failed. Although they stood in the shadow of militant revolutionaries like John Brown, William West and many of his comrades were not doctrinaire pacifists. They recognized that history had progressed less by reason and argument than by blade and shot:

> The time may come when . . . it may be necessary to resist even by violence the enforcement of any more laws by representative bodies. The people should, therefore, reserve to themselves the SACRED RIGHT OF REBELLION! It is a fact which should not be lost sight of that not one of the rights of labor (so-called) has been accorded by the legislation of the past, without a prolonged struggle to secure it. . . . Possibly, probably, other means besides violent ones to arrest the course of legislative injustice, may be found practicable. But the right to resort to violence, all other means failing, never, never should be abandoned.[20]

The radical thrust of the New Democracy's ideology is made more apparent as the sources of its reform language are uncovered. Many of the New Democracy's ideas were adapted from older reform slogans and refitted to respond to the social and economic problems of workers of its day. To excavate the New Democracy's radical vocabulary is to dig down through layer upon layer of the intellectual history of America's urban working class. Its concern for republican institutions and democracy and its hatred of aristocracy and privilege descend directly from Locke, Jefferson, and the American Revolutionary experience. A remnant of the youthful crusades of the New Democracy's aging land reformers was firmly lodged in demands for the nationalization of land and exclusive settler tenure. In the "Loco-foco" party, which splintered from the Democracy in the 1830s over artisan concerns of the economic manipulations of banks, of the growth of monopolies, and of the schemes of currency speculators, can be found demands for the nationalization of banks and money and the abrogation of all corporate charters. Demands for women's suffrage and racial equality had their own obvious roots in the radical women's and antislavery movements. Rhetorical support for "individual sovereignty" derived from the proto-anarchism of

Josiah Warren that sparked an entire generation of experiments in "equal exchange" schemes and producer cooperatives on both sides of the Atlantic.[21]

But the New Democracy was more than the sum of its historic parts. While the reform ingredients that went into its radical stew are recognizable, they were combined in ways that would have surprised the original chefs. The New Democracy's faith in the premise that all value derives from labor and that labor should reap its own reward would have found congenial support among the likes of Benjamin Franklin and Thomas Jefferson. Likewise, the New Democracy's argument that the worsening maldistribution of wealth was the result of corruption and inequality in the government echoed the American Revolutionaries' view that the usurpations of the British aristocracy were the source of European poverty and of the colonists' own economic oppression. But in combining these two well-worn elements, the radicals of the New Democracy decisively parted company with their Enlightenment predecessors and embarked upon a new radical synthesis.[22]

The ideology of the New Democracy proved durable and enduring among its membership. Sixteen years after the New Democracy was formed, former member Dr. Edward Newberry was called before a Senate committee investigating industrial conditions. Newberry read a statement that recapitulated the principles of his earlier radicalism and revealed much about the nature of the belief system that would animate many of the Yankee radicals who came to join the International Workingmen's Association.

Newberry began with a sweeping definition of the responsibilities of the state that expanded the Lockean idea of the social contract from merely the protection of established rights to the provision of life's necessities. In keeping with the Christian perfectionist roots of the antebellum reform impulse, Newberry argued that government's purpose was not simply to regulate and police the interactions of men but to "have for its object something like the divine motive," namely "the perfectibility of man." Government should organize, tutor, and nurture its citizens so as to further "the strengthening of their weaker faculties" and "the progressive attainment of all truth in its application and uses." Newberry appealed to the skeptical senators to remake government as the center of industry and thereby perfect mankind and establish justice in society:

The true moral government should, in the first place, guarantee to every individual useful employment in the production of all the necessaries of life. . . . Government should also establish justice, and should sell the

results of the guaranteed employment at the cost of production and distribution—superseding all profits of labor, all interest on capital, and all the
means by which the rich rob and oppress and destroy, not only the poor,
but themselves. If we could establish that much, all things else would follow in the natural order.[23]

Next to the nationalization of industry Newberry emphasized the importance of eliminating fraud in government. Cleansing government of fraud
was hardly a radical idea at the time—it was the battle cry of liberal Republicans and reform Democrats in the 1870s long before it became the engine of
the Progressive movement at the turn of the century. But fighting corruption
had a very different meaning for Newberry and his former New Democracy comrades; indeed, in this demand for corruption-free government lies
the key to understanding the reason that these radicals chose to name their
organization the "New Democracy," rather than, say, the "State Socialists"
or the "Government Industry." The radicals of the New Democracy understood the potential tyranny that could follow if government were entrusted
with such sweeping powers and responsibilities before it was institutionally
purged of all its potential for fraud and corruption. Enhancing the democratic nature of the state was but a necessary precursor to the creation of a
workable system of state socialism. "If the Government was rightly constituted" and if the "Government was not a fraud," argued Newberry, "Why,
then, should not everything be owned by the Government?"

> Why should not every man in his capacity, whether as lawyer, as farmer,
> as merchant, or whatever his field may be, be guaranteed the usefulness of
> his faculties in the same way? Why should we have great masses of people
> crowded up into single rooms in the cities, huddled together in centers
> of pestilence and disease? Why should we not have integral homes—
> beautiful hotels, in which people may have ample room and fresh air—in
> which they shall have all that science can contribute to their welfare and
> all that art can contribute to their tastes? This would produce for every
> individual that highest practicable disposition of his powers.

To so restructure society, Newberry told the committee in shades of antebellum millennialism, was part of their Christian duty to perfect mankind:
"It is our duty to perfect each other, not only as individuals, but as nations,
integrally and in harmony with truth and usefulness."

From the beginning, these New Democrats looked across the ocean
to Europe and saw an International Workingmen's Association there that

seemed to them to be their direct counterpart. Little could the New Democrats know, in 1869, as Marx neared his goal of remaking the International into an instrument of proletarian revolution, that the official documents in their hands no longer reflected the controlling ideology of the organization. Having no reason to doubt the sincerity of the official IWA documents available to them, they took them at face value and found in them the gratifying confirmation of their own analysis laced with a familiar republican flavor.

Americans who did not have the benefit of Marx's own correspondence and leadership derived their view of the International from three primary sources: the International's "Inaugural Address" and "Rules" of 1864, the occasional declarations of the General Council in London, and the widely distributed reports in the American press on the IWA's annual congresses. The New Democracy drew inspiration and encouragement from all of these sources.

Much of what was enshrined in the IWA's documents was repeated in the manifestos of the New Democracy. The preamble to the IWA's founding rules begins with a statement that became the rallying cry of the Marxist sections: "The emancipation of the working classes must be conquered by the working classes themselves." The New Democracy stated the same thing, but in a less succinct manner: "when a reform has to be undertaken [to be successful] it must be supported by the people that feel oppressed, and as they are largely in the majority, they have the power to speedily and peacefully change the principles upon which society rests." Similarly, when the First International declared that "the economical subjection of the man of labour to the monopolizer of the means of labour, that is, the sources of life, lies at the bottom of servitude in all its forms," the New Democracy echoed, "The conditions of all classes of people may be directly traced to that state of dependence of labor upon capital."[24]

Perhaps the most popular slogan of the First International in Europe, and one Marx disliked, was "No rights without duties, no duties without rights." It was a motto that found its way onto countless red banners, badges, and membership cards. The New Democracy echoed this sentiment closely with its version: "The party was inaugurated . . . for the purpose of founding a new commonwealth based on principles of perfect equality of rights, and of a corresponding reciprocity of duties."[25]

No doubt the New Democrats, steeped as they were in the principles of radical equality, felt great affinity for an organization that proclaimed that it would "acknowledge truth, justice, and morality, as the basis of their conduct towards each other, and towards all men, without regard to colour, creed, or nationality." Unfortunately, as will be seen, only the Yankee Internationals took these principles to heart and carried them forward as an integral part of their agenda.[26]

The New Democrats closely followed the reports of the First International's yearly congresses. In 1868, when it convened in Brussels, the IWA demanded the establishment of national "banks of exchange" that provided "democratic and equal" access to credit at cost, the nationalization of mines, railways, canals, highways, forests, and telegraphs, and the "converting [of] arable land into the common property of society." The following year the New Democracy placed all three of these demands, in essentially the same form, into its founding platform.[27]

The Brussels Congress called upon the International's sections "to establish courses of public lectures on scientific and economical subjects, and thus to remedy as much as possible the short comings of the education actually received by the working man." Whether the New Democracy took this directive to heart or simply acted coincidentally cannot be known for certain, but in the fall of 1869 the members of the New Democracy founded the New York Social Reform Club, an organization devoted to lectures and free discussion of "questions of social science." Over the next few months the Social Reform Club featured many speakers, most of them New Democrats. At one of its first meetings, Albert Brisbane, the man who had brought Fourierism to America in the 1840s, recounted his own educational experience. Other evenings featured discussions of poverty and wealth, theology and religion, love and marriage, and government and the Constitution. Later, when these groups had become Yankee sections of the International, they kept up their tradition of hosting evening debating and educational forums with the founding of the "Cosmopolitan Conference." Meeting on Sundays, the most convenient time for workers, in a rented hall at the rough corner of Bleeker and Bowery, the Cosmopolitan Conference invited prominent speakers from the labor and reform worlds to present a half hour talk, after which his or her topic was debated. After his or her ideas were thoroughly picked apart, the intrepid visitor was finally allowed fifteen minutes at the close of the hour "to answer objections." This was not a format designed for idle conversation or for the polite reception of orators, but one whose project was the sifting and winnowing of the truth.[28]

But the greatest confirmation of the New Democracy's course came when English members of the IWA General Council founded their own offshoot of the International, the "Land and Labour League," in October 1869, the same month that the New Democrats publicly promulgated their first manifesto.

For years a number of influential English members of the General Council had argued that the Council should charter an English national council of the IWA, a demand that Marx stubbornly opposed, fearing that once left to themselves and beyond his direct control, the republican-minded English would stray from his narrow course and again take up their old Chartist and pacifist enthusiasms. After the old Reform League died in the summer of 1869 and English members of the General Council moved to revive its spirit and agenda by establishing the Land and Labour League, Marx accepted the development as a timely safety valve that could siphon off demands for a separate English national council.[29]

The New Democracy hailed "with great delight" the news of the formation of the Land and Labour League, which it considered the "natural precursor of the advent of true Democracy in the Old World." It noted many points in the Land and Labour League's program that echoed those in its own agenda, including, at the top of the list, the demand for the nationalization of land and the colonization of the urban poor to the countryside. New Democrats also praised the League's demands for free, secular, and compulsory education for all children and equal electoral rights for all citizens as involving the same "principles enunciated in our Declaration of Independence."[30]

By the autumn of 1869, then, the two movements that would comprise the American International had assumed a public form. The future Yankee members of the New York International were issuing their proclamations in the name of the New Democracy and holding their evening forums in their Social Reform Club, while Siegfried Meyer and Friedrich Sorge educated workers in the doctrines of Marxism in the German General Labor Union.

Yet for all their differences in ideology, the New Democracy and Meyer's GGLU shared one common tactic: both groups attempted to steer much larger labor associations toward their own sectarian courses. In each case this meant pushing for a broader agenda than the bread-and-butter issues of narrow trade unionism. Meyer and Sorge hoped that political goals would help to centralize workers' organizations and sharpen their class consciousness, while the Yankees of the New Democracy hoped to place the radical reformation of the American republic at the top of labor's agenda. In 1869, each of these small groups thought big and took aim at the largest labor organization of them all, the National Labor Union, an entity that claimed to represent a half million American workers.

In a hot Philadelphia hall bedecked with patriotic bunting, the rival Yankee and German proto-affiliates of the American International at last found themselves face to face within the same organization.[31] William West from the New Democracy and Siegfried Meyer of the GGLU both took their seats as delegates to the Fourth Congress of the National Labor Union.[32] For the better part of a week, Meyer and West, along with a hundred other representatives of labor and reform organizations, debated the pivotal issues confronting the American worker. On the most divisive issue of the convention — women's suffrage — Meyer and West disagreed. Their differences foreshadowed the growing tensions between the Yankee reform tradition and German American socialism that would eventually destroy the First International in America.

The women's suffrage issue had divided the NLU once before. At the previous year's convention a heated debate had erupted when Elizabeth Cady Stanton submitted her credentials from the Woman Suffrage Association. Angry delegates had denounced women's suffrage and asserted that Stanton should not be seated because she did not represent a bona fide labor organization. Still, by a margin of over two to one, Stanton had been voted a place on the floor. When a number of representatives of building trade unions could not stomach the result and threatened to bolt, the congress passed a resolution distancing itself from Stanton's "peculiar ideas" and renouncing woman suffrage.[33]

In 1869, it was Susan B. Anthony's turn to demand inclusion to the NLU, though this time she came as the representative of the Woman's Typographical Union of New York. While this tactic made it more difficult for her credentials to be challenged on the same grounds Stanton had been opposed, the strategy did not preclude it. Mike Walsh of the Typographical Union of New York led the attack on the WTU, accusing it of working for less than union scales and strikebreaking.[34] Walsh's attempt to clothe his opposition to Anthony in the garb of labor solidarity proved futile as the suffrage issue quickly came to the fore. Someone accused Anthony of coming solely to "attempt to introduce the suffrage question into their deliberations," prompting Boston labor reformer Charles McLean to ascend his soapbox and lecture his fellow delegates on women's rights. "To stop the coming of the suffrage question would be as futile as an attempt to obstruct the cataract of Niagara with a straw," said McLean, and he for one thought that it would be better for the NLU to take up the question of Anthony fairly and squarely before the American people, rather than to hide behind technicalities.

During the ensuing debate, the emerging idea of the "family wage" and the well-established social ideas of woman's "sphere" and proper role in society were aired by representatives of the trade unions. The bellicose Mike

Walsh expressed this ideology quite nakedly. "The lady," he railed, referring to Anthony, "was in favor of taking women from the kitchen. If she does that, who is to go there? Are we or our families?" Walsh stood in favor "of the man doing the work, and marrying and supporting the woman." At another point, Anthony defended herself against the charge of aiding nonunion, or "rat," printers by asking just how many women Walsh's union had trained in the art of typesetting. To this Walsh ham-handedly defended the exclusionary policy of his union: "You might as well ask why we don't send for the colored men or the chinese to learn the trade," he responded. "There are too many in it now." Here, then, was laid bare the resistance of the established and growing trade union movement toward following the lead of the labor reformers and widening their definition of "worker" to include women and people of color. In the end, the three delegates who would later become leaders of the German American faction of the IWA chose to support Walsh and his strategy of exclusion.[35]

Just as Stanton bargained for her acceptance of the NLU's condemnation of women's suffrage in exchange for a place at labor's table at the previous year's convention, Susan B. Anthony offered to resign so as to "save the delegates to the congress the publication in the daily papers of the disgrace they would inflict on themselves by [her] rejection." Though the assembly denied her offer and then narrowly voted to seat her, the debate raged on for yet another day.[36] The following day, August 19, 1869, Walsh laid down his gauntlet in the form of a telegram from his New York Typographical Union ordering him to resign at once from the NLU if Anthony remained. The authors of the telegram could not resist taking a swipe at Anthony's principles as well as her disputed affiliations. "We are opposed to all humbugs," they stated.[37]

Finally, a rare roll-call vote was taken, and by a margin of two to one, Anthony was thrown out of the congress. A reporter for the *New York Tribune* described the struggle over Anthony as a "square fight between the Unionists, and those who strive to give this labor movement a wider and higher scope than the mere question of high wages will admit of." Indeed, the question of the seating of Susan B. Anthony highlighted the division between the more egalitarian labor reformers and the less reform-minded trade unionists, whose entire conception of the labor movement at best allowed women into the margins of industrial society and at worst excluded them altogether. Overwhelmingly, the labor reform delegates defended Anthony to the last motion, but only a few bona fide representatives of trade unions stuck by her in the end.[38]

While even a few trade unionists joined the reformers to defend Anthony and a "wider and higher" vision of the labor movement, those who would in a few years' time be leaders of the German American International did not. Not surprisingly, William West and another future member of the Yankee International, Edward D. Linton, defended Anthony's right to represent women workers. Siegfried Meyer and two of his future comrades in the German American faction of the IWA, Conrad Kuhn and Robert Blissert, voted to expel her.

There is no mistaking Meyer's vote against Anthony as a vote against "rat" labor unions rather than against women's suffrage. Being a representative of the GGLU, Meyer was merely doing his duty to uphold its constitution and principles before the general assembly of labor. The GGLU stood firmly against bourgeois democracy and all of the false hopes they saw in it. Their union statutes declared that "whereas, universal suffrage cannot liberate humans from slavery, the General German Labor Union resolves . . . the granting of the right to vote to women does not concern the interests of workers." [39]

West and the other members of the New Democracy reacted bitterly to their defeat at the Philadelphia Congress. On the heels of the New Democrats' disappointment, the American labor press belatedly published an address from the IWA's General Council to the NLU. Meant as a eulogy for the late NLU president William H. Sylvis, the address lauded the NLU as a leader in the struggle of the "great brotherhood and sisterhood of toil." In a move reflecting both their sympathetic feelings for the IWA and their disgust with the NLU, the leaders of the New Democracy took it as their task to educate the International Workingmen's Association's London leadership as to the true policy and position of the National Labor Union.[40]

"From the general tenor of your address," wrote the members of the New Democracy in an open letter to the London Council of the IWA, "it would seem that the European working men believe that the unions represented in that convention are composed of the more advanced practical advocates of the rights of labor in America. We heartily wish the fact wholly justified that belief." Unlike Susan B. Anthony and Elizabeth Cady Stanton, who after the Philadelphia convention attacked only the trade union movement, the New Democrats argued that labor reformers also fell below the "true standard of opinion on the subject of the rights of labor and practical measures of reform" that prevailed in Europe. After all, both labor reformers and trade unionists were responsible for the recent NLU platform that failed to endorse land reform measures similar to those passed overwhelmingly by the IWA congress, and that rejected the New Democracy's proposal for the introduction of the electoral reform of the national referendum. The NLU's platform, said the members of the New Democracy, fell "more than twenty years behind the public opinion of the most thoughtful and earnest labor reformers of the age."[41]

The General Council's reply confirmed much of what the radicals of the New Democracy believed to be the philosophy and policy of the International. Responding to the New Democracy's charges against the NLU, the General Council refused to take sides, saying that its only duty was "to endeavor to connect and combine the various labour organizations all over the world, independent of any particular views, doctrines, or even shortcomings that may prevail in the advocacy of labour's rights here and there." Eschewing any role in dictating tactics or controlling affiliated organizations, the Council seemed to share a common goal with the Yankees: democratic and decentralized organization. "In appealing to the President of the National Labour Union," the Council asserted, "we invited the working population of America to co-operate with the labouring millions of Europe. By what particular means the Americans choose to advance is no concern of ours. Practice will ever remain behind theory, and the great mass of the population moves but slowly, step by step. Provided it be in the right direction, the goal will be reached."[42] In closing their reply by welcoming the formation of the New Democracy and inviting its leaders to continue their correspondence, the General Council allowed the New Democrats to believe that they were now allied in their thinking. Indeed, the New Democrats and many of the English members of the General Council were of like minds, and much of the conciliatory tone of the Council's letter can be attributed to the fact that it was penned by Johann Georg Eccarius, a man who was increasingly estranged from Marx.

From this point on, the New Democracy considered itself the representative of the International in America, even though it was not chartered as an official section. William West, in discussing the new tide of radical reform, announced the arrival of a new style of "Labor party, calling itself The New Democracy in the United States, and The International Workingmen's Association in Europe."

Most members of the New Democracy probably received their membership cards individually from the General Council's Yankee agent in New York, Robert W. Hume, a Long Island schoolteacher. Hume earned his commission as the IWA's American agent early in 1870, after writing a letter to Eccarius in which he compared the antagonism of the English and

Irish workers in Great Britain to that between black and white workers in America. Hume's apparent sensitivity to the Irish question ingratiated him to Marx, who was at that time formulating a secret strategy for the International that would elevate the emancipation of the Irish above all other goals. However, Hume, who was a longtime correspondent to the *National Anti-Slavery Standard*, was simply trying to impress upon London the particular importance of the race issue in America. Nevertheless, Marx, declaring that "we [always] wanted such a man," arranged for Hume to be appointed as the official correspondent and agent of the IWA in New York.[43]

Later that summer, the General Council directed Hume to establish an "American section as soon as possible," and Hume arranged for the first English-language membership cards in America to be printed. These cards perfectly captured in word and symbol the ethos of the Yankee reformers. Its central figure was a globe topped by a liberty cap. Cascading down one side of the card was the slogan of the French Revolution, "Liberty, Equality, Fraternity," to which was added the word "Solidarity." On the other side of the card were the words "Agitate, Educate, Organize, Unite." Crowning the top was the International's own motto, "No duties without rights; and no rights without duties," while across the bottom were demands that recalled one of Thomas Paine's famous mottoes: "War to the Palace, Peace to the Cottage, Death to Luxurious Idleness."[44]

This development was too much for the orthodox Friedrich Sorge, who wrote to London complaining of Hume's use of a bourgeois republican slogan from the French Revolution. On Sorge's word alone, the General Council rebuked Hume and ordered him to discontinue use of the card. Confused, Hume dutifully obeyed. This was only a preview of the sort of ideological differences that would come to plague the Yankee International. A few years later, Sorge would take up his cudgel again in a vein attempt to suppress the practice common among Yankee Internationals of addressing one another in a republican spirit as "citizen."[45]

But all such differences were momentarily put aside and the national factions of the International displayed their utmost unity to the public in order to condemn the Franco-Prussian War. In the winter of 1870, members of the New Democracy shared the platform at Cooper Institute with Sorge and other leaders of the GGLU to denounce the war then raging across Northern France. After the various speakers and officers of the meeting were introduced, several letters of support from notable individuals were read. Charles Sumner, one of the original Yankees contacted by Cesare Orsini years before, was among these, and he expressed his hope that American workmen would "unite with their brethren in other countries for the overthrow of the intolerable system" of war taxes. Suppressing his more doctrinaire side, Sorge diplomatically appealed to the most basic common sentiments of this mixed assembly of Germans, French, and English speakers and defined the gathering's purpose: the support of "republicanism against royalism." "Above all," he continued successively in all three languages, "we are men born all alike, and hav[e] the same right to the pursuit of happiness, life, and liberty."[46]

That cosmopolitan evening marked the high water mark of the public cooperation between the Yankee radicals and German-speaking Marxists. Over the course of the next year these two factions, divided as much by culture and style as by ideology, remained wedded to each other in their common desire to further the cause of the International, though they differed markedly as to what they understood this to be. As they warily continued to work together, these differences in understanding and temperament became ever more obvious. By December 1872, only one year after their successful antiwar meeting, Friedrich Sorge and his comrades, most of whom were German Americans, unable to tolerate the distinctly American brand of radicalism espoused by their fellow Yankee Internationalists, took the initiative and purged the English-speaking sections from the organization. Sorge's putsch was not a sudden act of desperation but the culmination of the German American socialists' mounting disdain for, what seemed to them, a reformist clique of utopian enthusiasts.

From the beginning, Sorge had tried to exclude the Yankee Internationals from the party. For example, soon after the German, French, and Yankee Internationals had come together to condemn publicly the Franco-Prussian War in the fall of 1870, the French- and German-speaking associations met and agreed to found a "Central Committee" of three delegates, one each from the German, French, and Czech sections of the International, with Sorge himself at its helm. The organizers envisioned the Central Committee as a means of more effectively carrying out propaganda and collecting funds. Veteran activists, such as Sorge and Meyer, certainly were aware that power over any party flowed from control of its mouth and its purse.[47]

The absence of any delegate from the English-language sections was not accidental. Prior to this time, the New Democracy had already formally applied to London for official recognition as a section of the IWA. It had even changed its name to the "New York Labor League" for the occasion, a title with a more proletarian ring to it and one that followed in the footsteps of their English comrades whose "Land and Labour League" had made such an impression upon them.[48] Still, the German American Marxists regarded them scornfully. When the corresponding secretary of the German section wrote to Marx informing him of the creation of the Central Committee, he revealed several reasons that the German American section had viewed these Yankees as undesirable members: "The English speaking trade unionist[s] were for homeopathic remedies, they wanted to cure society by becoming capitalists themselves by means of co-operative societies and other little schemes, they talked of re-elections but there was no such thing, every office was obtained for money, and those who invested money to get an office made up for it when they got it."[49]

Sorge wrote to London in defense of his committee's claim to represent all the Internationalists in America, explaining that his German, Czech, and French members were not merely foreign interlopers in America but full-fledged citizens. More importantly, it was just such men who "form[ed] an important and considerable part of this country's Trades Unions & Labor Societies, being well represented in every one, whilst some of the most powerful and best Trades organizations in the U.S. consist almost exclusively of so-called 'foreigners[,]' viz. the Miners and Laborers Benevolent Association, the Cigarmakers International Union, the Cabinetmakers Societies, the Crispins, etc." Sorge, who believed that it was the foreign-born who made up the backbone of the American labor movement, saw little urgency in recruiting Yankees.[50]

However much Marx shared Sorge's view of Yankee workers and radicals, he and the other members of the General Council thought it odd that the "Central Committee of North America" contained not a single native worker. They immediately voted to instruct the German and French leadership in New York "not [to] presume to represent the Yankee element," though they could if they wished form a committee to represent the interests of their own nationalities.[51]

Marx wrote directly to his old friend and confidant in America Siegfried Meyer, telling him that "the formation of the so-called central committee in New York was absolutely not to my taste." Marx made clear that he could sympathize with Meyer's situation since he faced a similar one in London, where "we work with Englishmen, some of whom are not at all to our liking." Offering Meyer instruction in the art of party manipulation, Marx noted that the disagreeable English members were more useful in the General Council than out of it, for "if we were to withdraw in indignation on their account, we would only give them a power which is at present paralyzed by our presence. And you must act in the same way."[52]

By the spring of 1871, Sorge's Central Committee still lacked London's official designation as the representative of all Internationalists in America. There remained but two options for them in the face of the General Council's criticisms: either follow the Council's advice and claim to lead only the French and German Internationalists, or open their doors to Yankees. Finally, Sorge took Marx's advice that such elements could be better controlled within the organization than without, and in April of 1871 the first representative of an English-speaking section of the International, Theodore Banks of Section 9, a section descended from the New Democracy and the New York Labor League, took his seat on the Central Committee. The participation of the Yankees was tolerable as long as they remained junior partners to the leading German and French sections. At the time that Theodore Banks, a housepainter by trade, was admitted to the Central Committee, the Central Committee's leadership felt secure in its control of the party, since the German sections alone enjoyed a clear majority. And Sorge had no reason to expect that this situation would change anytime soon; he clearly believed that the most fertile fields for recruitment lay in his own German American community. It would be several months before Sorge and his compatriots realized that they had made the mistake of seriously underestimating the ability of the International to attract a wide spectrum of native-born American radicals.

As the first few months of Yankee organizing would reveal, there existed in America much potential for a new reform coalition to recombine the fragments of radicalism that had been scattered by the victorious closing of the abolitionist umbrella. By the early 1870s, the men and women who had participated in antebellum reform crusades found themselves pushed to the margins of politics as both Republicans and Democrats scrambled to control the center of the political spectrum. The appearance of a naturalized International Workingmen's Association, fully imbued with the principles and yet-to-be-fulfilled agenda of the American reform tradition, tapped into this well of alienated and restless Yankee radicalism.

CHAPTER FOUR

The Rise of the Yankee International

I N THE YEAR between the falls of 1870 and 1871, the International Workingmen's Association grew from a tiny clique of activists in New York City to a small but far-flung organization with branches in many major cities across the nation. Much of this growth would be among native-born Americans, many of whom had years of experience in grassroots reform work. During this time the International rose out of obscurity to attain a prominence in the press and public consciousness far beyond its true power of numbers and influence. While the large metropolitan dailies vilified it as the guiding hand of bloody mob rule, the traditional reform journals of abolitionists, feminists, and Spiritualists rallied to its defense, hailing it as the hope for a new era of democracy, justice, and peace. In the rise of the Yankee International, the native reform impulse that had its start in the religious fervor and social dislocations of a half century before was temporarily wedded to the new immigrant revolutionary communist movement.

The veterans of the New Democracy were the first native radicals to form their own section of the International Workingmen's Association. New

Democrats Ira B. Davis, who reformed the health of his customers in his faddish bathhouse, Joshua King Ingalls, one of the old-time land reformers, and Leander Thompson, one-time president of the New Democracy, along with some fiery leaders of a local New York city housepainters' union founded Section 9, the first English-speaking group in the International. These Yankee Internationalists naturally turned to their traditional reform allies to build their ideas into a movement. Several former New Democracy members, including Robert W. Hume, the first Yankee agent of the IWA's General Council, attended meetings of the Universal Peace Union, the institutional expression of Garrisonian nonresistance, and lectured its pacifist members on the principles of the International.

On both an institutional and ideological level, the UPU was a natural ally of the Yankee IWA. Their European affiliates had cooperated for years in the cause of peace, and, had it not been for the stern opposition of Marx to middle-class pacifists in principle, the two would have likely formally affiliated. In 1867 the annual congress of the IWA and the founding meeting of the League of Peace and Freedom were held consecutively near Geneva, Switzerland. Against Marx's wishes and efforts, many of the delegates to the International's conference stayed on and deliberated the question of war and helped found the LPF. The following year Marx's allies succeeded in passing a resolution that called for the disbanding of the LPF and for its members who desired to work for peace to join the IWA. But the uncompromising tone of this pronouncement did little to discourage the pacifists and did even less to restrain the members of the IWA from cooperating with the LPF. Several members of the General Council itself maintained ties to the international peace movement, and the Council's Benjamin Lucraft and William Cremer became treasurer and general secretary of the Workmen's Peace Association of Great Britain and Ireland.[1]

The IWA and the UPU also shared a basically similar analysis of the causes of war. At its congress of 1867, the IWA proclaimed that the root of war was poverty and economic inequality, a sentiment the UPU frequently endorsed. With the outbreak of the Franco-Prussian War, the UPU's journals followed with excitement the antiwar actions of the IWA on both sides of the Atlantic. In 1870, a number of reform journals gleefully reprinted the General Council's address on the Franco-Prussian War. *The Advocate of Peace*, for example, sympathetically explained to its readers that "these workingmen represent the toiling, oppressed masses in Europe, who are beginning to get restive again under the tyranny of their rulers." Later that year, the UPU devoted to the IWA's New York antiwar meeting the space and attention its journal, *The Bond of Peace*, previously gave only to the proceedings of its own conventions.[2] In Philadelphia, the membership of the UPU and the Yankee IWA dovetailed and the ground for a long working relationship between the two organizations was firmly laid after thirty members from Section 26 attended the fifth annual meeting of the Pennsylvania Peace Society, offered their support to the UPU, and received a hearty welcome in return. So closely were the two organizations associated by 1871 that Wendell Phillips publicly described the president of the UPU, Alfred Love, as "an agent" of the IWA; and though Love himself confided to his diary that he thought Phillips had overstated the case, he was nevertheless "inclined to sympathy with the Internationals."[3]

Other future leaders of the nascent Yankee International sought allies among the ranks of the spiritually minded. For example, a number of IWA leaders attended the national conference of Spiritualists held in New York in 1870, and several took the floor. J. W. "Grandfather" Gregory, "a staunch old Communist and Radical whom every demonstration for liberty converts once again into a young man," lectured on the International and the New Democracy. Joshua King Ingalls, the land reformer and advocate of producer cooperatives, was obviously very familiar with this crowd when he spoke more generally on the "Law of Progression, Land Reform and the Laws of Progress." New York's Spiritualists had leased their first permanent meeting place, Dodsworth Hall, in Ingalls's name back in 1853, and Ingalls was a regular speaker there. He later remembered often insisting that Spiritualists "apply our spirituality in equalizing conditions and compensations here, and give the human spirit opportunity of harmonious development in this life." Ira B. Davis also spoke to the Spiritualist throng, arguing that "it was impossible to develop the spiritual in man without laboring for the natural. . . . All men must be made physically comfortable before they will attend much to the higher or spiritual nature." The efforts of the Yankee Internationalists would soon pay off. Within a year, national organizations of Spiritualists, suffragists, and abolitionists would pledge their support for the principles of the International, and many of these movements' old hands would enlist.[4]

Yankee Internationalists found their most receptive audience among the veterans of the antebellum era's reform crusades who had long followed the news of this European movement. Years before the first official American sections of the International were organized, American reformers of many stripes were already discussing the principles of the IWA. In 1867, not long after Cesare Orsini, the pioneer agent of the International, landed in

Joshua King Ingalls, member of IWA Section 9, New York City
(Labadie Collection, Special Collections Library, University of Michigan)

America with an armload of IWA pamphlets, the American Social Science
Association of Boston, an elite reform group that attracted many from the
old abolitionist and women's suffrage fold, gathered to discuss the recent
IWA convention held in Lausanne, Switzerland. The featured speaker of the
evening, after praising the convention for "grappl[ing] in a manly way with
questions of the highest importance," urged the group to support the work
of such labor organizations. As a writer in the abolitionist *NASS* publication
said in his summary of the speech, "Labor is awakening to a consideration
of its rights, its responsibilities and duties. The world seems alive to the discussion of all questions affecting the humanity, improvement and elevation
of men and women, and the speaker could see no reason why religion and
religious people should not take a share in this work."[5]

With the increased attention given to labor issues in the surviving abolitionist press and the increasing sympathy for labor reform evidenced by
many antebellum reform leaders, the rise of the International Workingmen's
Association naturally captured reformers' attention. For those who had ha-

bitually distinguished European despotism from American democratic traditions, the International appeared as the most energetic opponent of tyrannical authority in Europe. More importantly, the International inherited the goodwill of abolitionists who had long appreciated British working-class opposition to the Confederacy. It was commonly said at the time that only the protest of the English working class restrained Britain from extending diplomatic recognition to the Confederacy. It was also commonly believed that this protest movement was organized and directed by the same men who later founded the IWA.

But the truth was, English workers were sharply divided in their opinions of the American Civil War. Before Lincoln's Emancipation Proclamation turned the North's war effort from one of conquest to one of liberation, there was little labor support for it. Even after the Emancipation Proclamation, when working-class support for the Union was galvanized, the attitudes of English workers remained deeply divided. The winter of 1862–63 was something of a turning point for popular opinion. Demonstrations were held throughout England in support of the Union, culminating in a mass meeting at London's St. James Hall that condemned the Confederacy, the British government's American policies, and slavery, in radically uncompromising terms. Some of the organizers of this important meeting were, indeed, founding members of the IWA. And though he was not an organizer of the St. James meeting, Karl Marx was a prominent guest that night.[6]

American abolitionists readily appreciated the importance of English working-class resistance to slavery and the tremendous sacrifice that many workers, especially those employed in the cotton industry, were making for the Union cause. Word of another workers' meeting, this one at Exeter Hall, praising President Lincoln for his Emancipation Proclamation, quickly made its way into the pages of the abolitionist *Liberator*, where it was noted that the English "working classes . . . have proved to be sound to the core" and that workers had been heard to say that "they would rather remain unemployed for twenty years than get cotton from the South at the expense of the slave." When London workers held a meeting in November of 1864 to celebrate Lincoln's re-election, the *National Anti-Slavery Standard* carried the full text of the congratulatory letter to the American president (penned by IWA General Council member William Cremer) on its front page; the letter included the workers' hope for "the restoration of the Union with freedom for the negro, and . . . his ultimately being placed before the law on a perfect equality with the white man." A few weeks later the *Standard* carried a similar letter of congratulations to Lincoln from the recently organized Provisional Central Council of the International Workingmen's Association.[7]

Although the IWA was not the leading force in organizing working-class opposition to American slavery — it had waited until September 1864 to organize as a society — after the war it was viewed in America as the embodiment of earlier English working-class abolitionist sentiment. George Hoar, a radical Republican senator from Massachusetts, reflecting on the IWA in the 1870s, attributed to it the "sublime accomplishment" of preventing the English government from according the Confederacy diplomatic recognition.[8]

Hoar's interpretation of the role of the International was also the one voiced by the *National Anti-Slavery Standard*. In 1868, the *Standard* profiled George Odger, an English shoemaker, trade union leader, and former Chartist seeking to become the first working man in Parliament. Abolitionists were in the debt of Odger and his associates, the article began, for their "arduous and unrequited services on behalf of the Union cause in England." It was Odger and others, the *Standard* asserted, who had led London's working-class opposition to the overtures of Confederate agents and who shouted down pro-Southern resolutions at workers' meetings. It was they, the Standard continued, who established the workers' paper the *Bee-hive*, one of the few anti-Confederate papers in London (this in spite of large bribes dangled before them by Southern agents), and who organized the great meeting at St. James Hall, the meeting at which "John Bright made his most famous speech in defence of this Republic — a speech which killed all further attempts in the British Parliament to recognize the Southern confederacy." Having made clear Odger's abolitionist credentials and contributions, the article went on to detail Odger's labor reform activities. He was "the originator and leading spirit in that most important movement known as the 'International Workingmen's Association,' whose aim is nothing less than the perfect and peaceful Federation of labor in Great Britain and on the continent of Europe." What better introduction could the IWA receive within abolitionist ranks? As this *Standard* article indicates, after the war, the IWA was viewed by some abolitionists as the inheritor of English working-class abolitionism and the chief democratic opponent of European tyranny. Indeed, the article represents the IWA as striving to remake Europe in America's image: "Such men as Odger are the forerunning waves of the incoming tide of genuine Democracy in England. Thank God! It rises higher and higher. By and by, like the famous tidal wave it will overseek the bounds. Out will go that 'blotch of a crown,' down will go the State Church; the

House of Lords will be 'shunted' into oblivion; the feudal land system will be swept away, and from out the ruins will arise a new Federal Republic."[9]

Given the IWA's abolitionist and republican reputation, the *Standard* soon accepted it as a member of the larger reform community of which it kept its readers abreast. In addition to publicizing the upcoming Fourth International Congress of the IWA at Basle, Switzerland, in 1869, the journal's editors provided an outline of the convention's agenda, reported on those Americans who attended the convention, and subsequently published a report of the congress's proceedings.[10]

Interest in the International among American reformers received a tremendous boost when, on March 26, 1871, French workers ran the red flag up the pole atop the Tuileries Palace in celebration of the election of a revolutionary municipal government in Paris. Thus was born the famous Paris Commune. Before the declaration of the Commune there had been little talk of the International Workingmen's Association in the mainstream American press. The year before the Commune the respected journal *The Penn Monthly* featured an article, entitled "A Current Revolution," describing the rising power of radicalism within the labor movement, but it didn't even mention the IWA. In the months after the Paris Commune, nearly every newspaper associated the International with the Commune, and the term "Internationals" fell into common usage. So famous did the IWA become in 1871 that the *American Annual Cyclopedia and Register of Important Events* for 1871 devoted three fact-filled pages to the organization.[11]

The Commune inspired many radicals, and the specter of violent workers' revolution forced all informed observers—even those who weren't so taken with the idea of proletarian revolution—to confront the vexing "labor question" in a new light. Sadly, the Commune was short-lived, and soon a vicious counterrevolution on the part of Napoleon III, aided by Prussian troops, had turned the tide. By May, when the last barricade was overrun by monarchist troops and the Paris revolution was finally drowned in the blood of over 20,000 of its citizens, the question of wages, hours, equity, and poverty were discussed and debated in an atmosphere of public emergency on both sides of the Atlantic. The rise and fall of the Paris Commune jarred the European and American worlds of the late nineteenth century as deeply as did the Bolshevik revolution in the twentieth.

With almost one voice, the established metropolitan presses of America reacted against the establishment of the Paris Commune with a vehemence usually reserved for national enemies in wartime. The workers who declared their independence from the Versailles government were portrayed as rampaging, murderous mobs. The Commune government was held up as tyrannical, capricious, and corrupt. Furthermore, it was under the command of a shadowy organization called the International, whose mastermind, a ruthless German philosopher named Karl Marx, dispatched orders from his hideout in London.[12]

Amidst the tidal swell of denunciation that roared from American presses, the formerly abolitionist journals stood apart in their uncompromising support for the Commune. The *National Anti-Slavery Standard*, for example, featured the Paris dispatches of W. J. Linton, a radical who had cut his teeth in the struggles of Chartism in Britain and who was one of the most outspoken defenders of the Commune in America. Linton's articles explained the Commune not as the anarchic government of a mad rabble bent on looting, but as the rebellion of republicans against dictatorship and aristocracy. Linton provided many a radical with debating points by carefully exposing the distortions and lies of the daily press. The Standard kept its readers abreast of the progress of the trials and sentencing of the Commune leaders. Taking a literary turn, it featured a sympathetic poem on its front page, entitled "A Woman's Execution, Paris, May, '71," which ended with the slogan, "*Vive la Commune!*"[13]

In the eyes of the editors of the *Standard* the IWA was not the terrorist band that the leading dailies made it out to be; rather, it was a group of democratic reformers working toward a peaceful solution to the ever worsening situation of workers in both Europe and America. As industrial conditions deteriorated, the *Standard* predicted, the International would spread in America as it had in Europe. Indeed, its growth in America would be more rapid than in Europe because of the "more general diffusion of intelligence than prevails abroad." In the pages of the *Standard*, the mantle of reform leadership was passed from Garrison to Marx. One editorial, entitled "New And Old Leaders," traced a line of succession from Garrison to the International: "It is the new leaders, in their work-day clothes, frightening kings, — 'making history and a name,' that are hissed, pelted, and snubbed as Garrison was in 1835. Mazzini has almost finished his glorious work. The *Internationals* have the field to-day."[14]

In the spring of 1871, Aaron Powell, the editor of the *Standard*, revealed his own feelings about the International Workingmen's Association when he accepted the invitation of New York's most prominent Internationalists to be the featured speaker at one of their weekly discussion groups. Powell took as his topic the question of "Agitation." Unfortunately, none of the reports of that night's meetings recorded Powell's remarks. The full story of

Powell's relationship to the International and the labor movement in general will probably never be told. Powell died when he was in the midst of writing his memoirs, having only covered the years through the Civil War. He left behind a tantalizing outline that included a heading entitled "Socialism."[15]

Moncure Conway, a Southern abolitionist minister who had moved to Boston before the war and there published the *Commonwealth*, also showed his sympathy for the Commune in both his journal and his personal life. His editorials in the *Commonwealth* defended the Commune and sympathized with the plight of the Communards. While attending a meeting of Commune veterans in London, Conway witnessed a comrade that had been thought killed suddenly enter the room: "Ah, how they shook his hand," he reported. "How they kissed him again and again on both cheeks, and how eyes glistened and grew moist as they beheld the rescued brother. I saw then that the word 'fraternity' was not an idle one as uttered by these men." Conway later corresponded with Karl Marx to help raise money for the Communards living in exile.[16]

Conway's interest in the International predated his defense of the Commune. He discovered the IWA while he was on a European tour in 1870.[17] When Conway was in Switzerland, he found the country in a state of intense anxiety. It was, he recalled, "of the divided condition of Maryland and Kentucky in the civil war." A short time later he was told that class antagonisms lay at the root of the country's tension. "You see sir," he recounted being told by one of the locals, "we Swiss love freedom, . . . so you will find that the working people in Switzerland are not fond of the French dynasty. But our rich men — oh, our rich men make all their money out of France! . . . They are for France." Adding to the tense climate was the recent "congress extraordinaire of the International League of 'Peace and Liberty,' " which was held in Basle and included a sizable delegation from the IWA. At Basle, Conway departed from his traveling companion to seek out the League, because he "took them more seriously than my comrade." Soon he found himself in "the neat little parlor of a Swiss workingman." There he met with the leaders of the Basle branch of the IWA, took notes of their conversation, and was presented with a group photograph taken in front of their club's flag, upon which was emblazoned the motto of the International: "Keine Pflichten ohne Recte — Keine Rechte ohne Pflichten" (No Rights without Duties — No Duties without Rights.) Conway later included in his memoirs one of the Basle section's broadsides, an appeal to all European nations for peace.[18]

Conway's interest in socialism culminated with his publication of an article analyzing socialist principles in *Harper's Monthly*. The *Standard* reviewed Conway's article and reprinted one of the more attractive passages, a definition of socialism quite palatable to the middle-class reformer: "The socialistic principle is very simple and universal. Every man who by riding in a car or omnibus — the common carriage — saves many times what he would pay for a private carriage, or by sending his child to public school pays but a tenth of what he would pay for a family teacher, avails himself of the Communistic principle." [19]

Not surprisingly, the most outspoken partisan of the Commune in America was abolitionist Wendell Phillips. Phillips viewed the Commune as the harbinger of the future and proclaimed, "There is no hope for France but in the Reds." From podium and pen he described its historical importance in the sort of rhetoric that he had previously reserved for the accomplishments of antislavery heroes like Garrison, Lovejoy, or John Brown: "The Commune must bide its time. That is not far off. Men now alive will hear frothy orators ride into favor by proclaiming, in stolen bombast, the difficulty of finding marble white enough and gold pure enough to record the world's gratitude to the Commune." [20] The Commune was, he continued, "the grandest declaration of popular indignation which Paris wrote on the pages of history in fire and blood . . . the vanguard of the Internationals of the world." [21]

Support for the Communards could also be found in the pages of Spiritualist newspapers. The *Banner of Light*, the largest of the Spiritualist weeklies, clarified for its readers what the Parisians meant by the frequently abused term "Commune," a term that differed from the popular idea of communism, which "derived from a knowledge of the writings of Fourier and others of that school." The editor of the *Banner* tamed the image of the bomb-throwing Communards by explaining that the word meant, simply, self-government in the tradition of the original French Revolution. Later that summer, long after the last of the barricades had been cleared from the streets of Paris, the *Banner* even defended the Communards' widely condemned razing of some of Paris's most famous landmarks. Citing the International's "Address on the Civil War in France" (a document that it called a "powerful proclamation" that would "create a profound impression on the civilized world"), it queried: "Was it worse, asks the Commune, for us to destroy brick and mortar than for Frenchmen outside the walls to make havoc of human lives?" Finally, the *Banner* summarized the International's more radical view of the Commune's objectives and revealed its deeper motives: "[The Communards] thought the few had long enough appropriated the products of the many" and were "weary of the servitude that practically accompanies the wages condition, when all exercise of political power is denied it." [22]

The sympathy that many old Yankee radicals felt for the Paris Commune extended to its supposed orchestrator, the International. Lester Frank Ward, the eminent sociologist and editor of the liberal *Iconoclast* of Washington, D.C. (as well as sibling of Cyrenus Osborne Ward of Section 12), noted that "the 'Commune' movement appears to be a general rather than a national one, and is intimately connected with the International Workingmen's Association." Responding to the shrill chorus of denunciation of the "terror" of the Communards and their destruction of some of the landmarks of Paris, Lester Ward observed, "Few great and sudden changes in the organization of human society or government are achieved without sacrifice of life and property." [23]

For some Yankee reformers, like Theodore Tilton, the former abolitionist and "wunderkind" editor of the nation's leading religious newspaper, *The Independent* (whose new reform journal, *The Golden Age*, also trumpeted the causes of racial and sexual equality), the Commune was a radicalizing event that shook loose their settled conservative opinions of labor, replacing them with a newfound sympathy for worker's movements. [24] Initially mislead by the distorted reports of the Commune's "atrocities" that appeared in the daily press, Tilton harshly condemned the Commune and skewered the American labor movement while the red flag still flapped over Paris. In May 1871, when the Commune was only days away from being overrun by Versailles' troops and when New York's coal-heavers struck for higher wages, Tilton blasted both protests as "wrong-headed." A week later, while crowds of Parisians were being cannonaded in the boulevards, Tilton praised the Commune's democratic principles but called them insignificant compared to the "rapine, murder, spoilation of private property" that was "covered by red flag." Weighing the Communists' actions in the balance, Tilton judged them "unjustifiable" and warranting a "vengeance of condemnation." [25]

Given that the Versailles government controlled the telegraphic dispatches from France and that independent reports of sympathetic correspondents such as W. J. Linton, John Russell Young, and George Wilkes had to be smuggled out of the city and did not surface in America until later that summer, Tilton's scornful opinion of the Commune was based on extremely biased information. As the story of the Commune from the Communard's perspective began to be told, Tilton quickly made amends. By the end of June, he referred to the Communards as the "heroes of the barricades" and called on all the world "to witness that Communism on the one hand, and

Republicanism on the other, are, like Liberty itself, not to be charged with the crimes committed in their name." "Justice will be done slowly to the workingmen of Paris," Tilton predicted, "but when it is done it will wash their names as white as the bloodstained hands of their French enemies." As more sympathetic reports reached the States, and as Wendell Phillips, the "golden trumpet" of oratory, raised his voice in defense of the Commune, Tilton's conversion was complete. Rather than the uprising of a blood-thirsty mob, as Tilton earlier described it, the Commune was Europe's shot heard round the world. Paris was Europe's Lexington and Concord and the communists were its Sons of Liberty.[26]

> Communism is another name for Republicanism. If the Republic of America is right, the Commune of Paris was right. The curses which American republicans utter against Communism, might just as well be directed against the genius of their own government. . . . The central idea of communism is the same that George Washington spent seven years in killing his fellow-countrymen to achieve — the same which Alexander Hamilton wrote into a constitution which survives to this day.[27]

Tilton was greatly influenced by Marx's "Address on the Civil War in France," which began to be circulated in America early that fall. After reading it, Tilton understood that the International, whatever its role in organizing the Commune, now clearly stood as its most able defender and ideological inheritor. Seen through his Yankee reform lens, the IWA's agenda seemed remarkably similar to his own: republicanism, abolition of standing armies, settlement of international disputes by arbitration, and the abolition of monopolies. Tilton praised the International's pacifism and called its members "Quakers without drab, . . . conquerors without a sword; they are the peace-makers of the world." Most importantly, Tilton believed that the International shared the racial egalitarianism of the abolitionists and espoused as the fundamental basis of its program the principle that "regards alike the African and the American, European and the Asiatic; that is to say, the fraternity of men, to whatever nation they may belong." In short, the IWA "takes Christian charity and makes it the law of the world's politics."[28]

To Tilton, the International was truly the successor to abolitionism. Observing that the French republic was just as much a mockery of the principle of republicanism under Napoleon III as the American republic had been when it encompassed slavery, he compared the attack of the Communards on the Versailles government to John Brown's raid on Harpers Ferry. The crusade of the International was the same crusade that Tilton and all of his weary fellow antislavery co-agitators had devoted their lives to, though the battlefield had shifted.[29]

> The same logic and sympathy — the same conviction and ardor — which made us an Abolitionist twenty years ago, make us a Communist now. Half a dozen cabinets in Europe send each a representative to a congress of consultation; and these satraps, sitting like a committee of slaveholders, rule the workingmen of Europe. This may not be slavery; but it is tyranny. Hence, the International; in other words, Emancipation. Having been an Emancipationist, why should we not be an Internationalist?[30]

With the International firmly in his embrace, Tilton reexamined his attitude toward the labor movement in his own backyard. Trade unions, because of their conservatism on issues of race and their basic exclusiveness, remained a problematic category for reformers like Tilton, though the ends that they struggled for — the eight-hour day, higher wages, better working conditions — received their support. No such ambivalence existed in Tilton's opinion toward the labor reformers, however. They were, in his words, the natural "offshoot of the International society of Europe; or rather, under a different name, it is the same thing."[31]

The Paris Commune may also have been the radicalizing spark that fired Victoria Woodhull and her sister Tennessee Claflin's interest in the International Workingmen's Association. This pair of enigmatic and remarkable radicals would within a year become the hub of the Yankee International in New York. It was in the pages of their journal, *Woodhull & Claflin's Weekly*, that the myriad movements for Spiritualism, feminism, abolitionism, and of course, labor reform, converged. Begun as an eclectic journal of reform with no particular journalistic interest in the International Association, *Woodhull & Claflin's Weekly* rallied quickly to the side of the Communards and soon afterward remade itself into the English-language organ of the American IWA. By the summer of 1871, it devoted much of its space to official International communiqués and local IWA sections' meeting reports, and it even sported a biography of and interview with Karl Marx. Marx himself sent Woodhull and Claflin his daughter Jenny's firsthand account of her expulsion from France with a note to the sisters thanking them for sending him issues of their "highly-interesting" paper.[32]

Along with showing a journalistic interest in the IWA, Victoria Woodhull and her sister helped to organize the second English-language branch in America. Designated as Number 12, it met at the *Weekly*'s Broad Street offices and counted as members all the office staff and typographers who worked for the paper. Though organized by a number of the original radicals of the New Democracy and led by the venerable constable, tinsmith, land reformer, and abolitionist William West, Section 12 would quickly be dominated by the independent political activities of the sisters, and would, in most minds, be inseparable from them.[33]

Section 12 attracted some of the most eccentric and garrulous personalities to ever call themselves Internationals. For those whose political lives had been shaped by the antebellum crusades of antislavery, feminism, and the anticlerical skepticism of Spiritualism, Section 12 was a beacon of reform. But to those who viewed the IWA as an organization whose primary constituency lay in the established trade unions, Section 12 was an embarrassment and an obstacle to their grandiose vision of proletarian revolution. The battle for the soul of the American International would be waged over Section 12.

Section 12 was filled with eccentrics, though none were as roasted and reviled in the press as were Victoria Woodhull and Tennessee Claflin, and none were ultimately more central to the meteoric rise and fall of the Yankee International. For Woodhull and Claflin, eccentricity came naturally, since they had lived at the margins of society their entire lives. They were born into a poor family of seven children, burdened with the stigma of a father who was reputed to be a gambler and swindler. Their mother became swept up in the Methodist revivals of the time, and her mystical enthusiasm carried over to her young daughters, who quickly gained a reputation for psychic feats of divination. Their formative years were spent in the sleepy hamlet of Homer, Ohio, until their father, who was suspected of arson and insurance fraud, was run out of town.

From that day on they became an itinerant band. Victoria avoided this gypsy life by marrying Dr. Canning Woodhull, an alcoholic physician, at the tender age of fifteen. Tennessee, however, suffered for her precociousness. Her father, always keeping his one unpatched eye peeled for an easy buck, quickly recognized the lucrative potential of the psychic healer business. Not yet an adolescent, Tennessee became the clan's breadwinner. Her parents brewed up "Miss Tennessee's Magnetio Life Elixir for Beautifying the Complexion and Cleansing the Blood," in a cauldron in their backyard, and Tennessee was put to telling fortunes, invoking spirits, and rubbing quack ointments and laying hands on the desperately sick. They moved from town to town, sometimes warned out by the local authorities, sometimes by disappointed customers. On one occasion, in Ottawa, Illinois, the Claflins converted an entire floor of a local hotel into a magnetic healing cancer hospital, and when one of the patients succumbed to the tumor in her breast, local authorities indicted Tennessee on charges of manslaughter. Once more the family hurriedly decamped and set up shop in another state. Seeing how Tennessee—more of a victim than a perpetrator of these frauds—was exploited by her parents, some sympathetic friends in Chicago tried to take her away, but she was a golden goose who was not easily given up.

Meanwhile, Victoria faced her own trials. Canning Woodhull was a drunken philanderer who was too sauced to even attend to Victoria the night she gave birth to her son, Byron. Woodhull's practice eventually failed, and Victoria moved the family to California, hoping that the streets there were truly paved with forty-niner gold. Instead, she found a dreary existence as a cigar girl in a saloon and then as a seamstress, before she landed a few minor roles as an actress. Her short acting career came to a crashing end when she experienced a powerful spiritual vision while she was on stage. Victoria abruptly took her family back around Cape Horn and ended up in Indianapolis, where she advertised her services as a Spiritualist physician. Soon afterward, she rejoined the Claflin brood and took much of the financial burden from Tennessee's shoulders. From then on, there was no more selling of potions and cure-alls, only the shingle outside their door that read, "Tennessee Claflin and Victoria Woodhull, Clairvoyants," and together the pair accumulated a small fortune.

Within a few years Victoria had rid herself of Canning by divorce and in St. Louis wed Col. James Blood, a Union soldier who carried the scars of five rebel bullets and very definite ideas about greenbacks, the value of labor, and republican principles. Another vision told her to move to New York, and her destiny was fulfilled in 1868 when the dozen or so Claflins and Woodhulls and Col. Blood, moved into a large house on Great Jones Street. Tennessee and Victoria's luck changed when they were introduced to the most important client of their lives, Commodore Cornelius Vanderbilt, reputedly the richest man in America at that time.

Befriending, doctoring, and divining for this aged millionaire whose puritanical exterior belied the ruthless businessman beneath, Victoria and Tennessee earned for themselves the patronage that enabled them to forever abandon the spiritual snake oil business and embark on their mission to combat the rampant hypocrisy and injustice they perceived in all walks of nineteenth-century American life, especially the political and social oppression of women. When the first great crash on Wall Street occurred in September of 1869, the Commodore remembered his friends and advised the sisters on how to pluck profit out of the financial rubble. Soon Victoria and Tennessee had accumulated sufficient capital to open their own investment house, with the Commodore's partnership, of course. It was a project that they felt perfectly tied together their own pecuniary needs to provide for the growing clan of relatives, in-laws, friends, hangers-on, and even Victoria's estranged first husband, who all packed into their new spacious brownstone on Thirty-Eighth Street, and to blaze a new trail for women's rights.

Woodhull, Claflin & Co., the first brokerage managed by women, opened shop on Broad Street in 1870 and shocked the financial world. Reporters streamed into their offices and thanked the gods for providing such rich subjects for their adjective-laden prose. When the press discovered that Victoria lived with her ex-husband as well as her current one and that her house had become something of a salon for New York's cultural rebels who were known then as "free lovers," their prose turned from florid to lurid. Later she would explain the pity she had felt for Canning the day she opened her door and saw him there on the stoop, a morphine addict and a broken man. She took him in, and the arrangement worked well, as Canning cared for their son Bryon, who was mentally disabled from a fall he suffered as a toddler.

The public's condemnation of her lifestyle seemed only to harden her resolve to claim her right to conduct her affairs as she saw fit, regardless of conventional strictures on women's roles. That spring Victoria wrote a letter to James Gordon Bennett's *New York Herald*, explaining the political purpose behind her activities: "While others argued the equality of women with men, I proved it by successfully engaging in business; while others sought to show that there was no valid reason why women should be treated, socially and politically, as being inferior to men, I boldly entered the arena . . . of business and exercised the rights I already possessed. I therefore claim the right to speak for the unenfranchised women of the country."[34] She then announced the latest move in her crusade to establish the *existing* equality between men and women: she would run for the presidency of the United States. A few weeks later, with the earnings from Woodhull, Claflin & Co., Victoria launched the *Woodhull & Claflin's Weekly*, a paper devoted to a panoply of reforms and views. Often derided for her sensationalism and even branded as irresponsible, editor Woodhull understood quite clearly that shock and curiosity sell more papers and fill more seats in auditoriums than does dispassionate erudition. As a fellow journalist noted of Woodhull at the time, "She and her associates are no doubt sincere in the social views they advocate so zealously; but they are also alive to the fact that the best way to make their paper pay is to make it sensational, and this they know well how to do."[35]

Her greatest political influence at this time, besides her husband, Col.

Blood, was the charismatic Stephen Pearl Andrews, by all accounts a brilliant man whose colossal ego continually overreached his own considerable abilities. He was a gifted linguist, fluent in classical and modern languages. In his youth he had championed the cause of abolition among the pioneers of Texas, and with characteristic modesty but not without a grain of justification, he claimed that he was personally responsible for setting in motion one link in the chain of events that contributed to the outbreak of the Civil War. His claim to fame was introducing stenography to America, not as a business tool but as a method of eradicating illiteracy. Using his system of "phonography," the unschooled learned to read and write in a very short time, a few days at most, though upon graduation they were still hampered by their inability to decipher standard English.

A fervid individualist and communalist, Andrews was one of the founders of "Modern Times," a communist town located on Long Island where individual freedom and the principle of equal labor exchange ruled. When the Modern Times experiment went bust, Andrews resumed his activities in Manhattan, establishing a lecture society and entertainment club that gained the reputation of being a den of "free lovers" and was eventually raided by the police for being a "disorderly house." The charge was ludicrous, though Andrews was indeed a pioneer advocate of what would later be dubbed "free love" by the press. Hardly a blueprint for casual sexuality, free love was in fact a serious critique of the contemporary institution of marriage as a form of legalized prostitution and one of the pillars of the ongoing oppression of women. For Andrews, the "whole existing marital system is the house of bondage and the slaughterhouse of the female sex." Andrews pointed out the exploitative nature of the law that privileged the husband in marriage and divorce, and asserted that the private relations between individuals should be simply beyond the pale of law. At the very least, a woman should enjoy an equal right with her husband in divorce.[36]

After his lecture and entertainment club was closed down, Andrews established another commune in a row of brownstones on Fourteenth Street, dubbed "Unitary Home," which lasted until the war. Later, Andrews, with his wife, Esther, founded the New Democracy; and when that group had divided to form Sections 9 and 12 of the IWA, Andrews followed William West into Section 12. Andrews was nearing seventy years of age and his life had been a roller-coaster ride of success and failure. He had made and lost several fortunes, and when he met Woodhull he was broke. She invited him and his wife to stay along with everyone else at Thirty-Eighth Street, which he did.[37]

Section 12's party opponents were not incorrect in labeling its members as "extraordinary followers of free love" (though they willfully distorted what the free love program was and opposed the feminist principles that undergirded it). Mary Leland was a crusading suffragist whose frankly sexual columns, written under her maiden name, Mary Chilton, were largely responsible for the charge that the Modern Times community was a hotbed of licentiousness. Leland had good reason to rail against the legal structures of marriage in America, however: her rich, abusive first husband was awarded total custody of her children when she left him. By the 1870s, though, Mary Leland had tempered her free love advocacy and focused instead on the political status of women, creating a stir in New York City by entering polling places and attempting to cast her ballot.[38]

Francis Rose MacKinley was another crusader for women's rights. A young woman "who beamed with the most coquettish light," she lectured across the country on Spiritualism, the International, and "the Poetry of Free Love." MacKinley's poetry, written in chanting phrases similar to Walt Whitman's, attempted to invert Victorian virtue and press it into service for the cause of women's liberation. At a time when women's public speaking was still frowned upon, it took a great deal of pluck and courage for MacKinley to ascend the platform in a public auditorium and recite the following lines:

I would sing the glory of the sexual act,
The most ecstatic bliss of the body;
I would sing the praise of creative copulation,
The act generative of an immortal soul . . .
I would sing of the coming woman,
Moulder of a new race,
Made perfect by her recognition
Of the goodness and purity of nature's laws — [39]

Under the guidance of Esther Andrews, the wife of Stephen Pearl Andrews, MacKinley moved from campaigning for the right of women to vote to demanding women's right to autonomy over her own body. When Andrews died in May of 1871, MacKinley recalled her urging her to go beyond the question of voting: There are plenty of women working for suffrage, Andrews instructed her young apprentice, so "preach the true religion of woman's existence, instead of her political needs, that is, the full possession of herself, her soul, and its affections, her body and its desires."[40]

Experience in the fight against slavery, against the exploitation and political disenfranchisement of women, and against religious establishment and orthodoxy, was the common denominator among the men and women of

Section 12 and the Yankee International in general. Section 12's Robert W. Hume, the first native New Yorker to receive official credentials from the General Council in London, was a longtime correspondent to the *National Anti-Slavery Standard*.[41] Woodhull and Claflin grew up in the Spiritualist milieu, and by the time of their association with the International, they were recognized as national leaders of the women's suffrage movement. Stephen Pearl Andrews, a man of considerable charisma and intense but unfocused intellectual powers, began his long radical crusade while living in the South and was forced to flee for his life from his home in Texas when his abolitionist principles became widely known.[42]

But if the members of Section 12 had anything in common, it was their shared experience of having participated in a wide array of many antebellum reform movements. Theron C. Leland, a law reporter who had years before taught young Theodore Tilton stenography and who applied his skills to the day-to-day needs of Section 12 as its recording secretary, like so many antebellum radicals, came from a rural background and trained for the ministry, graduating with highest honors from Wesleyan Seminary. He was an early and ardent abolitionist, later eulogized as being "an abolitionist associate and friend of Wendell Phillips and Garrison." Like other perfectionist-minded radicals, he was swept up in the wave of Fourierist socialism that rolled over America in the 1840s. After that crest broke, Leland shared the disillusionment of Josiah Warren and adopted his anticapitalist individualist philosophy; but, like other native socialists, he blended it with his communistic ideals. Leland was one of the founders of the Modern Times community, and when the abolitionist Moncure Conway visited the community, he was a guest in Leland's home.[43]

A similar depth of reform experience was found wherever the Yankee International sprang up. The IWA in Boston, the cradle city of antebellum reform movements, was organized by men and women who were well connected to the reform movements of the past and present. Boston's International Section 20, the first English-speaking section outside of New York, was founded in 1871 by Victor Drury, one of the original agents of the General Council in London. The founding meeting took place at the home of Mrs. Elizabeth L. Daniels, a woman who, as much as anyone, epitomized the breadth of the Yankee radicals' reform imagination. Daniels was known as an artist, an inventor, and a lecturer on Spiritualism, though she did not restrict herself to such activities. Her involvement in Boston's labor reform movement was extensive. She was one of the founders of the Boston Working-Women's League, an organization devoted to uplifting working-

class women without the "condescending charity" of "professedly philan-
thropic," "non working-class women." In 1870, Daniels work on behalf of
working women was recognized when she was made the vice president of
the New England Labor Reform League. Indeed, Daniels was a featured
speaker at each of the League's conventions in 1870, 1871, and 1872. She was
active in the struggle for women's suffrage and, along with Victoria Woodhull, testified before Congress in support of the view that the Fifteenth
Amendment had already constitutionally enfranchised women.[44]

Daniels epitomized the Yankee egalitarian ethos of her reform generation.
Within her circle of radicals, the ideals of equality and democracy were of
the utmost importance. Daniels belonged to a secret society based in Massachusetts called the "Order of Equality and Justice." What its activities
were is unclear, but Daniels did once describe how the Order attempted to
create within its own meetings the sort of absolute democracy and equality
that it hoped to see respected everywhere. The Order was concerned that
"the minority shall be heard kindly, tenderly, respectfully, and shall not be
choked down." To prevent the tyranny of the majority, the Order of Equality
invented what is today described as "consensus decision-making": the majority was not allowed to impose its will upon a minority; rather, when an
impasse was reached, the issue continued to be discussed and compromised
until all were satisfied with the final decision.[45]

Boston's IWA soon attracted an odd assortment of "men with hands
hardened with labor and brows contracted by thought," and women who
were not "pink and white, befringed, belaced, flounteced, frilled, frizzled,
ornamented and decorated beauties, but real, true, noble, earnest, bent-on-
a-purpose, determined-to-do-something women." Among them was Eliza
Philbrick, an elderly seamstress whose deceased husband, according to her
obituary in the *Boston Transcript*, was known as "one of the old abolitionists," and whose home had been a station on the Underground Railroad.[46]
Edward Linton, a ship carpenter who was active in the New England Labor
Reform League and was yet another alumnus of the Modern Times utopian
community, was elected secretary. His experience in American radicalism
reportedly was deep—he claimed to have been involved in reform movements since the 1830s. Like other radicals who had been influenced by a
variety of reform theories, he had apparently picked up some eccentricities
along the way—one newspaper reporter lampooned Linton as "a fanatic
who prophecies, sees Christ now and then, and has a horror of soap and
water." He may have been odd, but he was also a loyal friend. When the
health of his old friend Josiah Warren, the father of "individual sovereignty"

and the "labor dollar," failed, Linton took him into his Boston home, where fellow Internationalist Kate Metcalf nursed him through his final months.[47]

When Boston's International outgrew Mrs. Daniels's parlor, Col. William Batchelder Greene, another former Unitarian minister who turned to socialism, put up the money to rent a small backroom hall in Tremont Row. Greene was related by marriage to the "first families" of Boston and had received his education at West Point. Seemingly destined to fulfill his familial legacy and pursue a military career, after his graduation he was commissioned to fight the Seminoles in Florida. Later, Greene declared that the war was "unjust," entered the ministry, and went on to gain a reputation for having "fraternized with abolitionists, Brook Farm enthusiasts and other unfashionable doctrinaires of Eastern Massachusetts." In the 1840s Greene became famous for his essays on banking and credit, which followed in the main the economic thought of Proudhon. His interest in money and banking landed him in the Democratic Party, wherein his advocacy of women's suffrage, abolition, and voting rights for African Americans at the Massachusetts Constitutional Convention of 1853 surely didn't win him many friends. After briefly commanding Massachusetts' Fourteenth Regiment in the Civil War, Greene turned more of his attention to labor issues. Just as he was among the Democrats, Greene was an uncompromising champion of women's equality in labor circles. Greene openly criticized some of his fellow labor reformers whose idea of labor reform considered "men only," as opposed to the International, which was concerned with "all toilers." [48]

Greene was not the only man of the cloth represented among the Boston Internationals. Moses Hull, for example, began "exhorting" the fire and brimstone doctrines of Adventism at prayer meetings in his native Indiana at the young age of sixteen. A voracious reader, Hull spent his money on books and claimed to have finished every book in the township library by the time he was twenty, a burst of learning that led him to the doctrines of Spiritualism.[49] After becoming acquainted with Victoria Woodhull, Hull perceived that "some power had thrust her to the front" and he "hoped that she could be kept there until the cause of moral and social reform would gain such impetus that it would go without her assistance." For a time, he was one of her staunchest defenders in the press.[50]

About the same time, Section 23 in Washington, D.C., was organized by a group of government clerks, journalists, and other professionals. Outraged by the spring tragedy in France, its first public act was to publish the General Council's scathing indictment of European states for their complicity in the crushing of the Paris Commune, an act that it attributed to "the cosmopolitan conspiracy of capital." The pamphlet did not include any reference to its own officers or members because so many of them were government employees who stood to lose their positions if their activities became known. For this reason few hard facts about the activities or membership of Section 23 are known.[51]

A few tantalizing names do surface in the records of the Washington IWA. One of the charter members was William Emmette Coleman, a Richmond native who become an abolitionist and the city's first Republican. Like other social critics of his day, Coleman's vision of reform was a broad one. He championed the rights of women and workers and had developed an interest in Spiritualism. After the war, Coleman served the Reconstruction government of Virginia in a number of posts.[52] Another Washingtonian associated with the International was Belva Lockwood, a woman who ran for president in 1884 and 1888 under the same party label as Victoria Woodhull had in 1872.

Perhaps the most famous member of Washington's International was its secretary, Richard Josiah Hinton, a well-known journalist. As a young man Hinton abandoned his engineering studies at the Columbia School of Mines and traveled to Kansas to report on the outbreak of sectional bushwacking for a New York newspaper. But strict journalistic objectivity was not his priority, and he soon lent his pen to the Free State forces and John Brown. Hinton rose to leadership in the Free State militia and in 1859 was one of the conspirators in the cabal that planned the raid on Harpers Ferry. Volunteering for the Union army when the Civil War began, he led one of its first black regiments, the First Kansas Colored Volunteers, through more than three years of battle. After the war he traveled in Europe, attended the International Congress of Pacifists in Geneva in 1867, toured the famous cooperatives, such as Rochdale, of England, addressed the General Council in London, and remained committed to socialist principles for the rest of his life.[53]

Philadelphia's Yankee International, Section 26, attracted a number of abolitionist veterans who remained active in a wide field of reform. Damon Kilgore, an Internationalist known equally well in the National Labor Union, the women's suffrage movement, and Spiritualist circles, had begun his agitator's life as one of Garrison's footsoldiers, distributing abolitionist tracts when he was not teaching school in Madison, Wisconsin. John Stout, the eldest member of the section was an octogenarian carpenter who worked at his trade until a week before he died. He was eulogized by the other members of the section for his work in the antislavery struggle.[54]

Many of Section 26's members were active Spiritualists, who, for the

INTERNATIONALS

We Seek but Justice to the Producers of Wealth.

A MASS MEETING

OF THE I. W. A. WILL BE HELD AT

Commissioners' Hall, 37th & Market

ON THURSDAY EVENING, MAY 2d,

At 8 o'clock. The citizens of West Philadelphia are invited to hear explained the objects of the organization that is interdicted by despotisms, and hated and feared by the enemies of progress. Workingmen, to the Rescue! **By Order of Section No. 26, I. W. A.**

A poster announcing a mass meeting called by Philadelphia's Section 26 (State Historical Society of Wisconsin, neg. no. WHi[x3]34895)

most part, were of an extremely materialistic bent of mind. One of these, Isaac Rehn, was a lecturer on spiritual matters but was most concerned with combating what he feared was a movement on the part of some states to reestablish official religions. Before the International was established in Philadelphia, Rehn was a leader of the "People's Free Conference," a group dedicated to resisting attempts of orthodox religions to gain state sanction for their creeds. Like other radical Spiritualists, Rehn was attracted by the materialistic aspects of Spiritualism: its apparent use of the scientific method and lack of a metaphysical deity. He created a stir in the Spiritualist press when he wrote several articles on the future of the movement and criticized Spiritualists for leaning too heavily on "inspirational" themes and drifting away from its "scientific" foundations.[55]

Like Woodhull, Claflin, and Andrews's Section 12, Section 26 was a hotbed of women's suffrage advocacy. Among its many women members was Caroline Sylvester Burnham, a schoolteacher who defied the law and registered to vote in Philadelphia. When her ballot was thrown out, Burnham sued the election officials. She eventually argued her own case before the Pennsylvania Supreme Court, ultimately losing before the bar but publicizing the suffrage cause along the way. She later became the first woman to graduate from the University of Pennsylvania Law School.[56]

Jacob and Mary Byrnes, he a government clerk, she a Philadelphia schoolteacher, were equally indefatigable activists for women's rights. Jacob, who had some legal training, found legal precedents to bolster the claim that women's right to vote was already established in federal law. And Mary was not afraid to stand up for her sex during the meetings of the International. During one lengthy discussion on the sovereignty of the individual, she scolded her male comrades, "Does it ever occur to you men that women have rights equal to man . . . ; that there is no inferiority of mind in the female?" She made sure that her local chapter of the International pursued women's rights issues with as much vigor as they did any other question. Though she once complained to Victoria Woodhull that "I don't get much sympathy with my views of things; that is why I write to you," members of Section 26 helped to organize a union of women workers and established a committee on suffrage that, among other things, petitioned the Philadelphia Constitutional Convention to extend the franchise to women when a new state constitution was debated in 1872 and 1873. On one occasion, upon assembling, the members of Section 26 voted to immediately adjourn so that all could go and hear Elizabeth Cady Stanton speak before a constitutional committee.[57]

Some of the Philadelphia section's members were also regular habitués of that city's Reform League, a club described as "an outgrowth of the time-honored American Anti-Slavery Society, and its fellowship of souls." There local abolitionist, women's suffrage, and Spiritualist leaders such as Mary Grew, E. M. Davis, Dr. Henry T. Child, and Sarah Pugh mingled with the Internationals and debated the issues of the day. The walls of the Reform League's hall bore evidence of this collaboration. The room was adorned with the portraits of the members' heroes and guiding lights, each elected for display by popular vote; looking down upon their meetings were not only the expected lithographs of Garrison, Phillips, Douglass, and John Brown but also the likeness of Victoria Woodhull. Befitting such a diverse yet experienced group of radicals, the evening meetings often ran late, as one topic of consideration spilled over into the next. It was reported that in just one night the Reform League discussed "labor reform, woman suffrage, the Internationals, marriage and divorce, science and the bible, psychic force and spirit manifestations, and many other cinders, meteors, and sparks."[58]

Another branch of the Yankee International grew up in the sandy plains of southern New Jersey, in a place dubbed "Vineland" by its boosters. Vineland's pioneer land speculators had a difficult time attracting settlers to its stretches of scrub pine until they began to promote it as a mecca for reformers. This scheme proved successful when more than a few radical teetotalers moved into the area after the town government prohibited the sale of alcohol.

Subsequently, Vineland's moral fiber was promoted in Horace Greeley's *Tribune*. As one old-timer later remembered, so many reformers populated the town that "it did not do to throw stones, for the man whose overalls showed his shoe tops and finished up under a frock coat shaded by a ten cent sundowner hat—he might be a lecturer on political science when not the man with the hoe." Spiritualists were especially numerous, and one visitor noticed immediately that there was "a preponderating element of Spiritualism in the town." Women's rights activists in Vineland made an annual event of marching to the town's polling place on election day and casting their votes in a ballot box of their own. In 1870, 161 votes were cast in this way.[59] The women of Vineland were very independent, and it was not unusual to see a woman walking the streets in her "bloomer," a product of the dress reform of the day. The unconventional independence of women was generally noted, and Vineland women were praised in the reform press for "work[ing] at any calling they please, out-of-doors or indoors."[60] Within a short time Vineland gained a reputation for its "cosmopolitan middle class" and for being "a power for all progressive movements" in "the conservative State of New Jersey." Vineland was so crowded with reformers that the New Jersey state Spiritualist convention was held there in 1870, as was the 1868 New Jersey State Women's Suffrage Society convention.[61]

The formation of Vineland's Section 27 of the International coincided with the convening of a "radicals convention" there in September of 1871. Meeting in their "Hall of the Friends of Progress," Vineland's well-known radical suffragists and Spiritualists mingled with Victoria Woodhull and her husband Col. James Blood. Woodhull delivered the keynote address, a speech on "Constitutional Equality," and a resolution committing the convention to the cause of labor was passed. It stated that "this Convention accepts as true the doctrine that the success of the woman cause and the labor question lies in their coalition."[62]

The day after Vineland's "radicals convention" closed, one of the local participants, Thomas Cairn Edwards, a graduate of Edinburgh University and a leading freethought author, sent a letter to Friedrich Sorge, the corresponding secretary of the Central Committee, requesting the official rules and documents of the IWA and asking whether it would be possible for Internationalists in Vineland to join the organization in New York. A month later Vineland's section was admitted to the International, its representative on the Central Committee being none other than Col. James Blood. Undoubtedly, many of the participants at the "radicals convention" formed the nucleus of the Vineland International. One of those who took an active part in the convention, Ellen Dickenson, secretary of the New Jersey State Association of Spiritualists and Friends of Progress, expressed her support for the IWA and explained that she was prevented from being an active member in the local section only "owing to press of other business, not for want of interest."[63]

FROM THE FALL of 1871 through the spring of 1872, the leaders of New York's Yankee International fanned out among the various reform causes that for decades had been the core of American radicalism. From the middle-class podiums of suffrage and Spiritualist conventions Yankee Internationalists promulgated the socialist creed to an increasingly receptive audience. The moral content of the International's program of purifying the state, establishing true democracy, and uplifting the working masses through state action appealed to many of these American reformers. In May of 1872, the Yankee Internationalists' efforts to build their movement upon a foundation of an older American reform platform reached its apogee at a mass "Equal Rights" convention held in New York, which induced over five hundred delegates from all corners of the antebellum reform tradition to declare their support for the IWA.

Victoria Woodhull boldly sang Internationalism's praises among her fellow Spiritualists and was rewarded with the loyalty of a solid majority who kept her in office as the president of the American Association of Spiritualists for the next two years. In her first speech after being elected leader of America's Spiritualists in September 1871, Woodhull told the attentive audience that she thought of the American Association of Spiritualists as "a Socialistic and Practical Organization." Her highest goal, she proclaimed, was to work toward the "smelting of all the radical elements in one great movement for the reconstruction of society." She hoped to see leading radical groups such as Spiritualists and suffragists join forces with the leading elements of the labor movement, among which she counted "the National Labor Union, the Internationals, the New Democracy, the Working-Women's Association and the like." Toward this end, she declared that "the Communalists and Internationals . . . are already allied directly with me."[64]

Woodhull elaborated more clearly her view of the relationship of Spiritualism and socialism at the following year's Spiritualist convention:

Now to my mind, practical Spiritualism and Internationalism are the two extremes of the same general movement. Internationalism was the first political organization to recognize the material interests of humanity as common, and Spiritualism was the first religious organization to demonstrate the spiritual interests of humanity as common, while the acceptance of either of the tenets of the other would constitute a universal and permanent foundation for a humanitarian organization. . . . I am and was an Internationalist and Spiritualist, desiring Internationalists to become Spiritualists, and Spiritualists Internationalists; but instead of at the expense of either Spiritualism or Internationalism, for the profit of both without regard to mere personal ambition.[65]

Woodhull's attempt to redirect America's Spiritualists onto a more overtly political course met with resistance among some of the faithful, especially those in the West. However, most of those who protested against Woodhull's election, program, and leadership denounced not her advocacy of socialism, but her endorsement of free love. Except for those who objected to Woodhull on puritanical grounds, initially there were few opponents of her plan to lead the nation's Spiritualists in a more socialist direction. Anna Middlebrook, a Spiritualist and reformer from Bridgeport, Connecticut, observed: "I have been astonished to find the public, individually and collectively, inside and outside of the spiritual ranks, so thoroughly alive to these radical reforms. . . . Those persons among the Spiritualists who are afraid of Mrs. Woodhull's views, and who protest against them, after they have really become informed what those views are, are the exception and not the rule, in my experience; while nearly all admit that our social system is corrupt and needs some radical reform."[66] Many Spiritualists shared Woodhull's vision of a convergence of reform crusades that would realize the same sort of success as did the coalescence of antebellum reformers around abolition. "It seems to me," continued Middlebrook, "the masses are more ready now to hear discussed the living subjects of the age, among which are 'Woman Suffrage,' 'The Labor Question,' and the great 'Social Problem,' than they were in 1861 to hear of the emancipation of the negroes."[67]

Even the idea of Spiritualist socialism fired the imagination of many in the movement. One medium in the District of Columbia told of the apparition she witnessed while she listened to Woodhull deliver her speech "The Impending Revolution." She wrote: "While Mrs. Woodhull was speaking I saw a large band of spirits immediately over her head, arrayed·in pure white, each waving a red and white flag; the vision is significant of Liberty for the children of the earth, and equality for all classes."[68]

The inroads made among the Spiritualists by the organizers of the Yankee International soon paid dividends. Over the next six months, five more English-speaking sections, many of them filled with ardent Spiritualist radicals, applied for admission to the Central Committee. Victor Drury was a particularly active organizer. After helping to establish the sections in Boston and Philadelphia, Drury moved on to Baltimore, where numbers warranted the establishment of several English-speaking sections. As he did in other cities, Drury delivered "an able and eloquent" address on the labor principles of the International and was then joined on the dais by his co-agitator Addie Ballou. Mrs. Ballou, a noted artist, a widely acclaimed Spiritualist lecturer, and a freethinker, spoke not on the topics for which she was famed but on labor issues, urging the Baltimore Internationals to send delegates to the upcoming convention of the National Labor Union.[69] Section 40, one of the two Baltimore groups, was composed principally of Spiritualists. Its corresponding secretary was A. Briggs Davis, editor of the *Crucible*, a Spiritualist journal, and a man remembered for his annual ritual of ringing his farm bell on Tom Paine's birthday.[70]

The IWA reached Chicago relatively late, and it was not until the spring of 1872 that that city's radicals debuted their new organization. With a greater degree of interethnic unity than was evident in other parts of the nation, German-, French-, Swedish-, and English-speaking sections held a joint public meeting that attracted several hundred people to the Globe Theater. Beneath a red flag bordered in white fringe, with the inscription "Workingmen of all Nations, be United," speakers addressed the crowd in a succession of languages. The English-speaking Internationals were represented by Thomas Watson, "a staunch spiritualist" and the president of Chicago's alliance of Spiritualists, the Chicago Progressive Lyceum. Condemning a system that enslaved workers and forced them to spend their entire lives "making money to put into the pockets of the few," a system characterized by "a natural antagonism between capital and labor," Watson lectured on the principles of the International and explained its basic purpose as striving "to release the laborer from the bondage imposed on him by capital."[71]

Woodhull, along with a number of the leaders of the New York Yankee International, also attempted to sell the Internationalist idea to the reformers who gathered in Washington, D.C., in early January 1872 for the convention of the National Woman Suffrage Association (NWSA). Woodhull gave one of the opening speeches, in which she described the efforts she had made to persuade the nation's Spiritualists to take up the cause of political reform and work against "all class rule and legislation." Her speech was described by a reporter for the *New York Herald* as a containing "a thousand other radicalisms of the Internationals and other 'reds.'"[72]

Victor Drury was granted time to deliver a speech later that evening. The main point of his remarks was that the principles behind the women's suffrage movement were those of universal application. This idea provided a door through which Drury ushered in the tenets of socialism and the slogans of the First International amidst the suffragists:

> The principle of the woman's platform is the platform of every working man, because by it they could see that there is no freedom when woman is a slave. Upon this platform is discussed the principle of the abolition of all class privileges, and the social and political equality of all people. . . . Our position is this: That labor is entitled to all it creates, and that no one has a right to take advantage of any portion of that labor to enrich himself and crush the laborer. We demand that equality, politically and socially, for woman exists, not only as a right, but as a duty on the part of man to give the right of suffrage. There can be no rights without duties, and no duties without rights.[73]

During the following day's proceedings, the suffragists invited Theodore Banks, who was, as one reporter present described him, "one of the bright, particular stars of the International Society," to the platform. Like Drury, Banks attempted to show the connection between the movement for women's suffrage and the International. He pointed out that the demand for women's suffrage was included in the International's program. "The woman question," he went on, "is a question of human rights and we have got either to have that or to be slaves. The Internationals and the workingmen will rally . . . and the working people of the world will come to the front, for *they* understand this question of human rights a great deal better than the people who sit in Congress do."[74]

Other Internationalists such as Ira Davis and Stephen Pearl Andrews also were granted time to address the convention. Andrews praised the gathering for representing the "first complete fusion of three or four great branches of the great army of reform," namely, the women's rights movement, Spiritualism, and the "industrial-politico-financial" branch that encompassed the labor movement and the Internationals. Finally, the convention voted unanimously to support Victoria Woodhull's candidacy for president and also adopted a resolution declaring: "We rejoice in the rapidly organizing millions of Spiritualists, labor reformers, temperance and educational forces now simultaneously waking to their need of woman's help in the cause of reform." [75]

The idea that the women's suffrage, Spiritualist, and labor reform movements were combining into one confluent radical crusade was seconded in Theodore Tilton's reform journal, the *Golden Age*. Shortly after the Washington NWSA conference, the *Golden Age* applauded the beginnings of this merger of reform around the core of women's rights. "The woman question is assuming importance from the adhesion of the labor reform party and the Internationals, a vast growing power," it declared, and "the Spiritualists also are making woman's equality a cardinal point in their faith." [76]

The idea of a confluence of reform movements also seemed to be spreading among the suffragist grass roots in the winter of 1872. Many leading feminists shared such hopes for the building of an alliance of reform movements. Most of the members of the National Woman's Suffrage Committee, Matilda Joslyn Gage, Isabella Beecher Hooker, Paulina Wright Davis, and Elizabeth Cady Stanton, initially saw Victoria Woodhull's candidacy for the presidency as a way of bringing together the NWSA, the Spiritualists, and the International into a united front. Stanton was especially eager in these months to see the focus of the women's suffrage campaign broadened. In April of 1872, the National Woman's Suffrage Committee issued a call for a "Women's Suffrage Convention" to be held in cooperation with the International in New York. [77]

The call, written by Stanton, marked a decisive break with the suffrage strategies of the past: Stanton proposed "that instead of simply rehearsing the time-worn arguments on suffrage," that the convention debate the great public issues of the day upon which women will, she expected, soon be called upon to cast their ballots. She called on "those women who are prepared for a more revolutionary step" to meet in convention with labor and temperance reformers and "Internationals" to consider a platform for a new "People's Party." Stanton closed her statement on a note of hope and with a warning to those who would dismiss their efforts: "The temperance, labor reform, and International movements, in hearty cooperation with the educated women of the country . . . will influence what politicians most fear — numbers and votes. . . . Let American statesmen thoughtfully review the history of France, and the part women have played in its bloody revolutions, and decide whether in this republic woman shall be an enlightened, recognized power, in establishing peace and prosperity—the true principles of progress—or a blind, inflammable, irresponsible force." [78]

Expectations for this joint suffrage-Spiritualist-Internationalist convention ran high as the appointed day in May approached. *Woodhull & Claflin's Weekly* published column after column filled with hundreds of names of reformers from around the country who had responded to the NWSA's announcement by signing a petition calling for the creation of a "Party of the People to Secure and Maintain Human Rights." Contained in this document were a list of "charges" against the existing government, including Internationalist grievances such as "using and abusing millions of citizens who, by the cunningly devised legislation of the privileged classes, are condemned to lives of continuous servitude and want." It indicted the system wherein the "office-holders, money-lenders, land-grabbers, rings and lobbies" robbed the "mechanic, the farmer, and the laborer" of "all they produce[d]." The alliance of "Labor, Land Peace and Temperance reformers" with "Internationals and Women Suffragists," the petition optimistically proclaimed, heralded the beginning of a movement that would ensure that "the principles of eternal justice and human equity" were carried into the "market-places" as well as the halls of Congress. [79]

If it weren't for the determined opposition of Susan B. Anthony to the idea of expanding the agenda of the women's suffrage movement, this combined convention of radicals may have marked the beginning of a new united reform coalition rather than the climax of the Yankee International. Because Anthony was away on a speaking tour in the West she had not been consulted on the plans for the People's Convention by the other leaders of the NWSA. Anthony complained later that her signature had been placed onto the call for the convention without her knowledge. Hearing of the upcoming convention just weeks before it was to convene, Anthony hurried back to New York to do what she could to keep the suffrage association free from what she saw as diversionary reform demands. With unscrupulous determination, Anthony first attempted to convince the landlord of Steinway Hall to cancel the contract with the People's Convention. The owner of the hall stated that he would not allow his property to be used to nominate candidates for office, but that he did not object to the holding of a suffrage convention. Failing to stop the convention before it began, Anthony next tried to discourage People's Party radicals by arranging for an admission fee of twenty-five cents and some intimidating police officers to be posted at the door. Indeed, according to one eyewitness, many radicals were disgusted by the fee and the police and refused to enter the hall. Anthony appeared at the first day's preliminary session to order all but members of the NWSA from the hall. Shocked at Anthony's "narrow" and "bigoted" behavior, Stanton resigned as president of the NWSA. Later that night, when Woodhull attempted to announce that the People's Convention was reconvening at Apollo Hall, the regular meeting spot for New York's Spiritualists, Anthony ordered the building supervisor to cut off the gas so there would be no light in the hall. Though many of the NWSA's faithful abandoned Anthony for Woodhull and the International, Anthony had succeeded in preventing the NWSA from formally entering into a coalition with the IWA.[80]

In spite of Susan B. Anthony's extraordinary efforts to prevent it, the Apollo Hall People's Convention lived up to most of its organizers' expectations. Between five and six hundred delegates crowded the hall. Reformers of both genders and from a wide spectrum of class backgrounds, religious beliefs, reform experience, and color, including Elizabeth Cady Stanton, Isabel Beecher Hooker, most of the Yankee Internationalists in New York, and many Internationalist delegates from other cities, assembled beneath large banners that proclaimed: "Government Protection and Provision from the Cradle to the Grave"; "Public Employment the Remedy for Strikes"; "Nationalization of Land, Labor, Education, and Insurance"; "I.W.A. and They Had All Things in Common"; "The Products of the Past Should be the Equal Inheritance of the Living Generation"; and "Neither Said Any That What He Possessed Was His Own, But They Had All Things in Common—Acts V:32." A committee of thirty members who were charged with drafting the platform unanimously decided on twenty-three planks, many of which were decidedly socialistic. As they were read, each was greeted with deafening cheers and applause. The fifth and sixth planks demanded that the government revoke all the charters of all private corporations and manage them itself "for the common benefit of the whole country." Another proclaimed that "it is the duty of the government to guarantee employment to all unemployed persons upon equitable principles of time and compensation." Infused in all the sessions of the convention were the racially and sexually egalitarian sentiments and declarations that hearkened back to the movement's roots in radical abolitionism and feminism.[81]

The socialist character of the People's Convention was accepted, even welcomed, by some middle-class reformers who one might have assumed would have shied away from such radicalism. Isabella Beecher Hooker, though less famous than her sister, the author of *Uncle Tom's Cabin*, or her brother, Henry Ward Beecher, the most read clergyman in the nation,

Isabella was one of the principle spokeswomen for the suffrage movement. Hooker praised the Apollo Hall convention, calling it the "true Labor Convention" (as opposed to the labor reform convention held several months earlier under the auspices of the National Labor Union). She wrote Stanton that she thought the convention's socialism was a boon to the cause of women's suffrage: "Now by the absolutely deferential tone of the Press toward Apollo and by the red flags and communistic mottoes there displayed we must recognize the powerful aid that new party brings to suffrage. They will not dare repudiate us, for they want the prestige of our social position and we want the vague shadowy honor that haunts politicians the moment that bloody revolution is threatened by the ignorant, though often good hearted leaders of the oppressed working classes." [82]

Like the members of the newly minted sections of the Yankee International from Boston to San Francisco, the participants at the Apollo Hall convention shared the ideological and historical perspective of the American reform tradition, a commitment to democracy, economic justice, civil equality for men and women regardless of their race, and a willingness to tear down any institution that stood in the way of these goals. All these groups had influential members whose activist lives had begun in their hatred of slavery, the denial of the political rights of women, and the hypocrisy of denominational religion. In their fine-tuned sensitivity for civil rights and their dedication to the ideal of representative government, these radicals stood firmly in the republican spirit upon which the International was founded. Apollo's delegates identified with the martyrs of the Paris Commune whose red flag connoted the same republican trinity of liberty, equality, fraternity, as did their parents' tricolor pennant.

At a time when many former participants of antebellum reform movements were retiring to their studies to write their memoirs, or settling for fighting the corruption gnawing away at the body politic by rallying under the laissez-faire banner of the Liberal Republicans, these Yankee radicals discovered in Victoria Woodhull's campaign, the Equal Rights Party, and the International Workingmen's Association a way to carry on their long crusade of "universal reform." With their participation, the IWA was no longer a foreign transplant but a part of the long-running stream of indigenous American radicalism.

But in spite of its numbers, its buoyant enthusiasm, its splashy coverage in the press, and the sincerity of its partisans, the Apollo Hall People's Convention did not inaugurate the grand coalition of reform that its organizers had dreamed of. Some of the links between suffragists and Internationals forged in these months proved durable—the Woman's Suffrage Club of Hammonton, New York, sent a donation to Philadelphia's IWA later that year to, as Hammonton's suffragists put it, "aid in carrying on the International."[83] But these ties weakened as the International itself declined. Soon after the last gavel fell at the People's Convention, the Yankee International began to crumble under the weight of the concerted attack made upon it by Friedrich Sorge in New York and Karl Marx in London. Rather than beginning a new era in American radicalism, the People's Convention occurred at the beginning of the end of Yankee radicals' commitment to the IWA, and ultimately, of the IWA itself.

Marxism, Civil Rights, and the Sources of Division in the American International

FROM THE START, the relationship between the "Yankees" and their German-speaking Marxist partners in the International Workingmen's Association was a prickly one. Coming between these two radical groups were extremely different complexes of ideology, organizing strategies, and movement cultures that ultimately proved incompatible. The characteristics they shared, a passion for social justice and economic equality, a hatred of capitalism, a vision of a borderless, peaceful world, and a willingness to challenge long-established institutions, proved too weak a glue to hold them together. After less than a year of coalition, Friedrich Sorge moved to centralize the power of his faction and split the American International along intersecting lines of ethnicity and belief.

In defending their coup, Sorge's Marxist faction argued that the International Workingmen's Association had no room for middle-class interlopers, that their action was a defensive measure taken to ensure that the class interests of the workers themselves would not be overwhelmed by the interests of the sentimental elite who could not truly understand the workers' problems or champion their interests. "There is no place in the I.W.A. for a great or small bourgeois, middle-class men and the like," they explained in an appeal to American workers, "since their own class-interest—the necessary result of their social position prevent[s] them from ever comprehending fully the labor movement."[1]

Such a position reflected a crudely mechanical interpretation of the Marxist theory of the material basis of ideology, but it reveals the rigidity of the thinking of this first generation of Marxist ideologues and the conceptual gulf that separated them from the native radicals in the party. Yankee Internationalists, reflecting their long experiences in cross-class coalitions, viewed membership in any cause like an evangelical did—each new member, regardless of his or her background, was a convert to the path of righteousness and moved the great crusade of social salvation one step forward. One member of Philadelphia's English-speaking section criticized the Marxist's exclusivity by pointing to the success of earlier cross-class movements:

> [T]he views taken by those New York Sections [were] too exclusive, by their endeavoring to shut out those who are not always working for wages. . . . [In] the Antislavery movement . . . were to be found men and women of all grades and conditions in life working together for the great object to emancipate the slave from . . . tyranny. . . . In that movement all who came into the field of labor were hailed as coworkers in the task put before them, years of steady unceasing toil rolled on . . . and the result was their efforts were crowned with success.[2]

Yankee radicals did not question the social background of any individual as long as in his statements and actions he demonstrated that he had arrived at a radical understanding of the nature of poverty, inequality, and social exploitation. If such a person was a member of the elite, he was viewed as having been reformed. To Yankee radicals social truth was liberating, and, in the manner of camp preachers, they refused to believe that anyone was beyond redemption.

Over the years much has been made of this basic difference in outlook between the two factions. The multiclass character of the Yankee sections within the IWA has been singled out as dangerous cancer that had to be excised from the body of socialism in order for it to even have had a chance to man the barricades against the bourgeoisie. Until recently, most of the scholarly accounts of the internecine fights of the First International have followed in the main the charges flung against the English-speaking sections of the IWA by Sorge's faction. From Morris Hillquit and John R. Commons early in the twentieth century to Samuel Bernstein, Philip Foner, David Montgomery, and others in more recent times, most historians have argued that social class was the wedge that cleaved the International. According to this theory, the Yankee element, coming mostly from the ranks of the "middle class" itself, had no understanding of the working class, was insensitive to class issues, was accommodating of capitalism, and was impatient with the Marxists' slow, methodical, and laborious road to proletarian revolution. Such an argument echoed the German American Marxists own complaint that the Yankee sections of the International were filled with "middleclassmen, bosses, bankers, etc.," while their own meeting rooms were places "you find none but the men of toil, the workingman, the wages-laborer, bent upon promoting his interest, the interest of the working classes."[3]

There is no question that the English-speaking sections of the International were economically and socially diverse, though not to the extent that many have claimed. A typical socio-economic profile of the seventeen-odd sections of the American International that conducted their meetings in English is probably that found in Section 26 of Philadelphia, the only branch of the Yankee International whose papers have been preserved. Over the course of its three-year existence, Section 26 enrolled a total of seventy-three members. Of these, nearly two-thirds were laborers and tradesmen, evenly divided between the building, garment, shoemaking, printing, and machinist trades. The single largest occupational category in the professional third of the section was physician. Six members of the section described themselves as "manufacturers," and four were merchants.[4]

But occupational categories are not wholly reliable indicators of financial solvency. The census of 1870 affords a glimpse into personal finances of the Philadelphia Internationalists, about a fourth of whom appear on the rolls. The nine professionals in the sample, as expected, were overrepresented among those who owned the most property: they constituted but a third of Section 26, but they made up only half of those who owned property totaling more than $1,000. Still, they were joined in this elite group by two tailors and a carpenter. On the other end of the spectrum, being a "brain worker" did not necessarily ensure wealth, comfort, or security. Two-thirds of Section 26's radicals owned property totaling less than $500, including one of the merchants, S. A. Slocombe, a dealer in the farmers' market, who told the census-taker that his personal worth was only about $200. Half of the Internationalists had so little property, their total worth being less than $100, that the enumerator was instructed to leave the appropriate line on the census form blank. A third of those who were white-collar workers were among these have-nots.[5]

Other branches of the International were also filled with Yankees who worried about where the next month's rent would come from. Section 9 in New York had many members who worked in the housepainting trade. Boston's Yankee International attracted many working-class women. Section 12 was well known for its famous sister stockbrokers, Victoria Woodhull and Tennessee Claflin, but also had a number of typesetters and clerks on its rolls. William West, one of the guiding lights of the Yankee International, wore many hats during his lifetime, from that of clerk to cop, but all of his headgear marked him as a man who lived by manual toil.[6]

The Yankee International had more than its share of professionals. There were quite a few doctors, lawyers, writers, and government officeholders in the English-speaking sections, especially Woodhull's Section 12 and Washington, D.C.'s Section 23. Section 9's Henry Beeny owned a fruit and candy store on the corner of Fourth Avenue and Twenty-First Street in New York City, where the old land reformers occasionally met.[7] But the Yankees were not alone in attracting such elements to their clubs. Sorge's German American sections were far less uniformly proletarian than they claimed. Sorge himself led a comfortable existence teaching music. Besides earning an income from his work, he lived off the rents he collected from a boardinghouse he owned in Hoboken. When Sorge sailed to Europe to attend the International's congress at the Hague in 1872, he did so first class. Even Marx commented on the fact that "Sorge has pecuniary resources."[8]

Other members of Sorge's socialist circle were also well-off. Siegfried Meyer was professionally trained as a mining engineer. Hermann Meyer, an organizer of the St. Louis German-speaking branch that aligned with Sorge, was a merchant. While most of the members of Sorge's Section 1 were artisans in the fields of tailoring, cabinetmaking, and cigarmaking, its two most prominent leaders, Sorge and Siegfried Meyer, were what was popularly known at the time as "brain workers," and the Manhattan hotel in which the group met was owned by one of its members.[9] Furthermore, when the International was in decline and Sorge was interested in recruiting "genuine" working-class Yankees, he had no objections to the membership of Edwin Martin Chamberlin, a man who had run for governor of Massachusetts on the labor ticket in 1871 and had inherited millions from his father, a Boston industrialist.[10]

The Sorgean critique of the elitist nature of the Yankee International not only depended on the class makeup of the sections themselves but also was based on the assumption that there existed a tight correspondence between ideology and class. This presumption breaks down under the weight of anomalous facts. That the relationship between class background and ideology was quite confused within the Yankee IWA was amply demonstrated when the question of supporting the wave of eight-hour-day strikes sweeping New York and elsewhere was taken up by the English-speaking Section 26 in the summer of 1872. Isaac Rehn, a professional lithographer and photographer, expressed his support for the eight-hour movement and a resolution on the floor that declared that the section was "in full sympathy with the eight hours movement and endorse[s] the platform of the Eight Hours League . . . [and] recognizes all efforts looking to the emancipation of the producers of wealth from the dominion of capital." Eighty-year-old John Stout, who still had to rise each morning and face a day's hard toil as a carpenter in order to support himself, opposed Rehn, saying, according to the meeting's secretary, that "he did not concede the wisdom or uses of strikes, he could not conceive of the possibility of them doing any good to the Masses. He thought that Cooperative Labor, by the producers was the only true idea worthy of their adoption and practice." Thomas Carrol, a housepainter by trade, seconded Stout and urged the meeting to table the resolution supporting strikes and the eight-hour movement. Clearly, class and ideology were not inextricably intertwined in this important debate.[11] In the end, class differences were less the cause of the Sorgeans' enmity toward the Yankees than it was the handy rhetorical coinage of their opposition to them.

Other scholars who have analyzed the breakup of the American International Workingmen's Association have concluded that the disagreement arose from the widely divergent reform priorities of the German American Marxists and the Yankee reformers. From this point of view, Sorge's materially grounded Marxists, who understood that all reforms began by resolving the oppression of the worker at the point of production, were the polar opposites of the flighty Yankees, who floated freely amidst a panoply of reforms, advocating any and all panaceas, from women's suffrage to the propagation of a universal language, with equal fervor. This historical explanation also follows one of the charges Sorge's followers leveled against the Yankees: that they were, in Sorge's words, merely "reformers and phantastics" who "tried to force the workingmen to kill their time with idle talk about women's rights and suffrage, universal language, social freedom, (a euphemistic expression for 'free-love' every possible kind of financial and civil reform and the like)."

At bottom, this line of analysis leads one to believe that the Yankee Internationalists were not socialists at all.

Such an argument has the merit of focusing attention on the ideological rather than social differences between the opposing groups, but it suffers from grossly misrepresenting the complexities and underlying coherence of the Yankees' ideology. The Yankee Internationalists did promote an array of seemingly unrelated reforms in comparison to Sorge's narrow agenda of trade unionism. However, Yankee Internationalists, in spite of their personal eclecticism, kept the demands of workers at the fore of their crusade. The Yankees' apparent inability to elevate any reform into a position of priority above any other was actually a misleading legacy of their reform culture.[12]

When all the statements, proclamations, and actions of the two factions are distilled into their elemental principles and laid side by side, it becomes clear that the splitting of the American International was not precipitated by disagreement over any one issue, or even any handful of specific issues. While German American Marxists had little patience for women's suffrage, and outright disdain for Spiritualism and libertarian views of marriage, these issues themselves, though immensely important in precipitating the breakup of the IWA, were but manifestations of a fundamental American reform ideology that broke ranks with Sorge's rigid interpretation of Marxism. In the final analysis, the breakup of the First International in America resulted from the collision of a carload of imported Marxist theories of social change, government, and human nature with the equally heavy freight of fifty years of belief accumulated by successive native reform movements.

The first questions to be asked in any inquiry into a system of beliefs that claims for its name "socialism" must have to do with that ideology's understanding and attitude toward wage labor, economic competition, social class, and the means of achieving an alteration in these relationships. Sorge and his followers enjoyed a far higher degree of unity of understanding of these concepts than did their Yankee counterparts. The German Americans, by virtue of sharing their first language and a direct correspondence with the master theoretician, Karl Marx, himself, had a highly refined and systematic understanding of the concepts of class, capital, history, and struggle. Sorge and his comrades were all graduates of those intense theoretical discussions of *Das Kapital* that had filled the fetid rooms of the Tenth Ward Hotel back in the days of the General German Labor Union. While many Yankee speeches and resolutions were packed with calls for the "abolition of the wages system" and the "abolition of class rule," clearly, Sorge's Marxists had a more precise idea of what they meant when they employed such terms. But though the Yankee Internationalists were less systematic in their thinking, they were no less antagonistic to the principles of capitalism and the accelerating encroachments of its industrial economy upon the lives of the working class, and they too are best described by the ideological label of "socialist."

From outward appearances, the English-speaking sections of the International were a babble of competing reform voices: women suffragists demanding political equality, land reformers advocating homesteads, proto-anarchists proclaiming the "sovereignty of the individual," and Communalists attempting to revive the failed phalansteries of a generation before. Knitting them all together was a shared sense of the injustice of the wage system, of capitalism. At the meetings of the Yankee International, no matter how one had arrived at his or her condemnation of the present social order—whether through the theories of George Henry Evans, Josiah Warren, Proudhon, Fourier, or common sense—the touchstone of affiliation remained anticapitalism. As one leader of the English-speaking Internationals—who was a member of the notorious Section 12 that had so often been accused of introducing personal hobbies into the association—observed, "The whole arm of the I.W.A. acts in the interest of the producing classes and . . . no body such as positivists, communists, Free Lovers, etc., can be affiliated as such."[13] Philadelphia's Section 26 passed a resolution that included this sort of tolerance into its bylaws: "We regard the promotion of the interests of labor to be the chief object for which the I.W.A. was instituted and that its membership should, in so far as they act with the I.W.A. regard all other reforms as secondary to this: but at the same time hold all persons eligible to membership who aim to work with us for the attainment of our end, irrespective of any opinions they may hold on other matters, or of any cooperation they may lend to other *reformatory* movements."[14]

Yankee Internationalists, without exception, supported labor's agenda, from the eight-hour day to the creation of labor bureaus, just as vigorously as did any member of Sorge's camp, though they were occasionally critical of the "narrowness" and exclusiveness of trade unions themselves. But their support for labor was often couched in a reform language that the German Americans either did not understand or they perceived as weak and accommodationist. For every member of the Yankee International who stood up to denounce the wages system, there was another who expressed the same idea by hailing the growth of cooperation or demanding the abolition of all "monopolies."

At their first American congress without their Marxist allies, the Yankees discussed amending the IWA's "Declaration of Principles" and its platform. At the end of the day, the group, in spite of their differences, agreed to let the "Declaration" (which was rewritten and shepherded through the General Council by Karl Marx himself) stand without any substantial alteration, save a clause tacked on at the end reserving the right to conduct their own affairs "without dictation from the General Council at London." The tone of the platform they drafted was hardly less radical than Marx's famous "Preamble" itself. The foremost plank endorsed the "total abolition of class rule and class privileges." As for how to accomplish this goal, the convention was flexible and willing, in the universal reform spirit, to experiment and strike out in a number of directions at once. At the head of their radical economic proposals was the "nationalization of land and of all the instruments of production," a scheme that went far beyond the independent homestead plans long proposed by the former associates of land reform founder George Henry Evans who were a vocal minority within the congress. Along with having the state "assume possession of the lands and labor-saving machinery which have been alienated from the people," the congress urged the "adoption of the principle of associative production, with a view to the complete supercession of the present system of capitalistic production." Beyond endorsement of the eight-hour day, the only other economic measure included in their brief platform was a mild currency reform plank that, in effect, demanded only that private bank notes and commercial paper be made illegal. The rest of the planks were means to these ends: political equality for women and minorities, universal public schooling, the referendum, and an abolition of standing armies—measures that were all aimed at unclogging the calcified arteries of the body politic and making radical social change possible.[15]

Yankee Internationalists, not too far removed from the Christian perfectionist roots of the American reform tradition, often framed their opposition to capitalism in moralistic and even religious metaphors, well sprinkled with a Puritan ethic of temperate behavior and an abhorrence of laziness. "Why is it that *they* ["the rich"] are wasting their lives in debauchery and idleness, while *we* ["the toilers"] are wasting our lives in exhausting our energies, by over work and privation?" asked the English-language IWA paper, *The Worker*. The *Worker*'s Yankee editors blamed the "rich" and the "idle" for having rendered "the whole fabric of society . . . rotten" and for having "demoralized the world." Embedded within the *Worker*'s statement of principles was the biblical admonition: "When no man eats the bread of idleness, none will suffer hunger." Whereas Marx attempted to base his indictment of capitalism upon the unimpeachable grounds of its own historical transitoriness, Yankee socialists constructed their argument upon the ideal of justice. "We go for the abolition of the wages system," the *Worker* asserted in its statement of principles, "because the results of our labor should belong to *us*, and not to a man who has unjustly amassed a large fortune by paying starvation prices to *his* laborers."[16]

The Yankees' moralistic analysis of social problems often led it away from the sorts of analytical abstractions favored by Marx and his German American followers. Indeed, the Yankee Internationalists had a penchant for personifying capitalism—condemning the "wealthy paupers," the "idlers," "monopolies," and "corporations,"—rather than focusing on capitalism's theoretical characteristics. At a mass rally of the unemployed, organized by the Yankee sections of the International in New York in March of 1872, Theodore Banks attacked capitalism in the typical language of his circle of radicals. He denounced "the aristocrats, who enjoy a monopoly of everything that is good and pleasant" and bemoaned the lot of the workingman, "who has not even a guarantee of that whereon to live." Charging that every such "aristocrat" was a "thief and rascal, he demanded that each one should get "out of the way whenever he stood between the poor man and his bread and butter." John Shedden, a member of Section 26 who worked in the needle trades, once described the International as a "movement that is opposed to kingly rule . . . to every form of tyranny that crushes the working class." Other members of Section 26 used the only radical language they knew, which they had inherited from the American reform tradition, to explain their reality. The shoemaker Thomas Phillips used the phrase "speculators in others' toil" interchangeably with "capitalists." In this way, the inherited language of the American reform tradition served to mask the radical thrust of the Yankee Internationalists' view of capitalism.[17]

"Monopoly," a word in common parlance then, was another term of disapprobation frequently used by the Yankee socialists to connote the entire system of industrial capitalism. Like the terms "speculator," "idlers," "corporations," and "aristocracy," the word "monopoly" was one that masked more of Yankee thought than it revealed. In less radical hands, the term "monopoly" not only lacked the encompassing sweep of "capitalism" but also carried a limited critique of business practices. However, the Yankee Internationalists often used the word "monopoly" in place of "capitalism." In attempting to define "capital" for its readers, the short-lived newspaper *The Worker* summed up this common equation: "To the various exponents of the Labor problem: we would again call their attention to the definition

Thomas Phillips, member of IWA Section 26, Philadelpia (State Historical Society of Wisconsin, neg. no. WHi[x3]34895)

of Capital. *Capital is accumulated Labor*. This hackneyed phrase of Capital and Labor would be better explained if the position was taken as *Monopoly and Labor!*"[18] James Mackintosh, a weaver, delivered a lecture before his Philadelphia IWA section one night on the history of labor and there extended the meaning of the word "monopoly" to include both a monopoly of the means of production and a monopoly of political power: "There was one cause that lay at the base of all the ills under which Labor toils, that was the monopoly of the soil, from this all other Monopolies grew, and gave birth to the classification of Society the many producing and the few governing."

Likewise, in the statement of principles published on the front page of each issue of *The Worker* was a similar understanding of monopoly as the control of the historical productions of the masses by a small number of capitalists: "We go for the abolition of ALL monopolies," it declared, "for we think that the results of the collective labor of ages in both the moral, intellectual, and material world, were intended for the happiness of the people at large, and not for the enjoyment of a favored few."[19] The term "monopoly" to the ears of native radicals connoted usurpation and tyranny, and it was in this double meaning, both economic and political, that the Yankee International often found the term more precise to their political view of the world than the term "capital," which to them appeared purely economic.

Another term that loomed large in the Yankee lexicon was "cooperation." It was a term that had gathered many connotations during its long journey down the decades of the American reform tradition. It was favored by the Fourierists, who used it in the 1840s to describe their communities. Josiah Warren, in spite of his total rejection of communal socialism, used it to describe his system of equal labor exchange and his ethics of individualism and producer property. Labor leaders picked it up soon after the war to describe the Rochdale system of factories and stores, whose sole shareholders were the workers and buyers themselves. Pacifists used the term to describe their wish for the relations of nations to be conducted on a basis of arbitration and conciliation instead of ultimatums and war, and to describe a means of social change that did not result in bloodshed. Because of the accumulated experiences of many Yankee radicals in these various movements, the term "cooperation" was tossed about in their discussions in all of its guises. Within the IWA, however, the predominate use of the term was to describe a social order in which capital had been nationalized and the wage relationship abolished. Just as some Yankee radicals casually broadened the word "monopoly" to mean the economic system that concentrated the instruments of production into the hands of a few capitalists, they were also apt to use the word "cooperation" in place of "socialism."

Activists of the Yankee International were quite familiar with the many uses to which the term "cooperation" was put, and they clearly distinguished their more radical meaning. Conservative reformers argued that workers and capitalists should cooperate because their interests were identical, an idea taken to task by Philadelphia International's Isaac Rehn, who declared that "it was needless to talk of harmony between labor and capital unless they were both in one hand."[20] On a different occasion Thomas Phillips of Section 26 was compelled to make clear what he meant by cooperation in a discussion on savings unions and cooperative building associations. Unions and associations, he said, "were used more for capitalist assistance than [for] the producers," and the cooperation he spoke of "proposed to undermine just such institutions and render them unnecessary."[21] When speaking of cooperation in the more limited sense of consumer cooperatives and cooperative stores, Yankee activists advocated them not as ends but as means.

"We must use the same arms to conquer our Independence that Capital has used to subvert us," was a common Yankee socialist view of cooperative commerce.[22]

To Yankee socialists, what *The Worker* called the "associative and emulative principle of industry" was the opposite of the "individual and speculative system of production." To them, "cooperation" expressed their dreams of a future social order that would replace the existing tyranny of economic self-interest, as well as one possible means of reaching such a goal. Theodore Kinget, an IWA physician whose practice in New York's Bowery specialized in venereal disease, sexual problems, and "self-abuse,"[23] expressed such a hope when he wrote that "the cooperative principle properly carried out in all the departments of production and distribution, will . . . abolish the wages system, and give to every man the entire product of his labor, to which he is justly entitled." But unlike their American Fourierist forebears, who believed that the cooperative commonwealth could only be built incrementally through the proliferation and growth of scattered cooperative communities, Yankee socialists did not advocate retreating into utopian isolation. They wanted an answer to the "labor question" that would encompass all workers and the entirety of the republic. Like their German American comrades they saw the working class as the vehicle of revolutionary change (though, as will be seen, they disagreed as to what this class consisted of and what it was to do) and knew the road to their dreams was neither straight nor smooth. As one Yankee poet put it,

Ye who would the vict'ry gain,
Know that first must come the pain,
To succeed you must obtain
    Solidarity.

Happy times when from the world,
Selfish competition is hurl'd
On our banner wide unfurl'd
    Cooperation.[24]

The IWA's Ira B. Davis, the spiritualist and bathhouse proprietor who was described by reporters as wishing "individual property done away with, and all wealth placed in the hands of government for redistribution," stated these same goals in the language one would expect of an aged native radical who had been a reformer since the age of ten: "We must change the whole nation into a co-operative association, making the government the agent of the people." Cooperation was the come-outer's creed for a generation that viewed themselves as the abolitionists of capitalism.[25]

The economic thought of the Yankee International, then, although conveyed through a reform language alien to the German American socialists, expressed as deep a hostility to capitalism and as full a faith in the promise of the socialist reorganization of society as did Sorge's own. As would be true of nearly all the internecine struggles that regularly tore apart the American Left for the remainder of the nineteenth century, the core of the conflict between the Yankee and German American wings of the First International in America was the strategic question of what means would prove most effective in achieving the goal of socialism. In the American context, this question was not, as it was in Europe, colored by the personalities and theories of Bakunin, Marx, and Fourier but was essentially a disagreement over the nature of the American republic, democracy, and civil liberties. The ongoing debate for many years would pit those, such as Sorge, who believed that meaningful social change could only be won by the militant actions of workers outside of the corrupted world of government and politics, against those, such as the Yankee members of the IWA, who aimed to capture the existing political institutions of the republic.

The Yankee members of the International Workingmen's Association were socialists, but socialists within the framework of republican belief. They looked upon the American republic as the unique fruit of generations of radical struggle and sacrifice. Their republican ethos was reflected in their frequent references to the Declaration of Independence, to the republican icon Thomas Paine, and to their preferred mode of salutation—when English-speaking members of the International addressed one another, they called each other "citizen," in the fashion of the French Revolutionaries of 1789.[26]

Yankees looked upon the state as the great lever of social and economic change, and democracy as the tradition that had placed this lever in the hands of the people. They took it as an article of faith that once the blessings of democracy were extended to all, and the people grasped the true nature of their exploitation under the wages system, the government would inevitably fall to the workers. As one anonymous Internationalist put it, "As regards our Republic, when workingmen are fit to rule, they can prove that they are so easily, by capturing Washington at the ballot boxes. That the labor interest does not rule this country is simply a proof that it is not yet fit for the position. When workingmen know their strength the financiers and distributors must give way to the producers and will have to take back seats."[27]

Since those who were oppressed and exploited by the existing system constituted a majority of the nation, the path to victory went in two directions simultaneously. To achieve their ends, the democratic institutions of the nation had to be made as open and free as possible. The first step in this direction was to win the ballot for women. At the same time, the people had to be educated as to the true nature of their oppression. Consequently, Yankee Internationalists saw their primary role as being educational, though they were also committed to aiding workers with whatever moral or material support they could. In this vein, William Emmett Coleman, a prominent member of the Washington, D.C., section, wrote optimistically: "The entire work of the I.W.A. in this country is that of a *propaganda*. What a glorious field! With perfect freedom of speech, freedom of the press, freedom of assembly, on the side of truth and justice, with a naturally intelligent and an oppressed people for an audience, and possessing the right of the ballot, what might not be accomplished with patience and zeal?"[28]

While they displayed a far greater faith in the electoral system than did their Sorgean counterparts, the Yankee radicals' belief in democracy was not unconditional. They did not blindly believe in the efficacy of the ballot box; they tactically judged it a practical means of reform. But while eschewing war and promoting peace, few Yankees were philosophical pacifists; Like Locke, the Yankees reserved their right to take up arms. Victoria Woodhull spoke for many of her fellow Internationalists when she declared at a rally in Thompkin's Square, "Ballots are more powerful in this country, than bullets, but if there should come those who oppose your ballots, why[,] give them bullets instead, and my voice shall ever be heard in your behalf."[29]

Like the New Democracy that came before it, the Yankee International held a radical conception of civil liberties and natural rights. This is most evident in their unflagging support for women's suffrage and social equality. And Section 12, the club of Woodhull, Claflin, Stephen Pearl Andrews, and William West, led the way. They redefined the preamble to Marx's "Rules" — the ringing proclamation that "the economical emancipation of the working classes is . . . the great end to which every political movement ought to be subordinate as a means" — by specifically including women. The Yankees' version read: "The object of the International is, simply, to emancipate the laborer, male and female, by the conquest of political power." Women's rights received prominent attention from the rest of the Yankee International as well. Soon after it was formed, the branch in Vineland, New Jersey, suggested that the IWA change its name to the "International Labor Association" because, it argued, "nothing in its rules or by-laws limited membership to a single sex." Later, when the various English-speaking sections held their own convention and launched their own "American Confederation of the IWA," they included as their second most fundamental principle the "complete political and social equality for all, without distinction of sex, creed, color or condition."[30]

In upholding equal rights as one of the fundaments of reform, the Yankee Internationalists felt assured that they were following the official policies of the organization. After all, the preamble to the IWA's own "General Rules" stated that "the struggle for emancipation of the working classes means not a struggle for class privileges and monopolies, but for equal rights and duties." Moreover, the "Rules" stated that members of the International must "acknowledge truth, justice, and morality, as the basis of their conduct toward each other and towards all men, without regard to colour, creed, or nationality." (This idealistic line about truth, morality, and justice was precisely the one that Marx complained he had been compelled to include to please the more republican-minded Englishmen on the Council.)[31]

While embracing natural rights as an abstract ideal, the Yankee Internationalists had practical reasons for stressing rights and liberties as well. Natural rights and liberties were the rallying cry of political reform. Yankee radicals hoped to conquer the corruption that pervaded the existing political system — the rings, machines, and bosses, the corrupt parties, bought legislatures, and stolen elections — through the inclusion of women in the political process. Believing with the spirit of their age that women occupied a higher moral ground than men, the Yankees fully expected that women would be the first to raise their shovels in the cleansing of the Augean stables of American politics. As Mary Leland of Section 12 warned the men of America, "The many abuses in our government call loudly for the aid of woman to redeem the country from the evils inseparable from a purely male administration. Give us the [franchise] . . . and we pass peacefully into the exercise of the duties and the enjoyment of the privileges of citizenship. Refuse us this, and I speak advisedly when I say the next move will be revolution."[32]

In pinning their hopes of overturning the wages system upon seizure of the state through elections, the Yankee Internationalists were led to an inclusive definition of the working class. Elections, after all, required winning a majority of votes, and not even by the most optimistic calculations was the organized labor movement a majority of the enfranchised electorate. To win elections, allies had to be found among farmers, professionals, and every other aggrieved group regardless of whether they worked by the hour and lived on wages. With the passage of the Fifteenth Amendment and the hoped for Sixteenth (that would grant suffrage to women), Yankee Internationalists looked forward to the support of men and women of all races as well. Theodore Banks, the president of the largest New York painters' union and a leader of Section 9, acknowledged this idea in a letter to the *New York Times*: "We don't unite because we are working men, but because we are the swindled ones. Whoever is not a party to this whole system of legalized fraud is our friend." This inclusive view of their constituency was cemented into the constitution that the Yankee Internationalists drafted for themselves after being expelled from Sorge's Central Committee. It set no occupational or class criteria for membership, and required only that prospective members promise to defend the principles of the IWA and adhere to its rules.[33]

The Yankees believed that an open, decentralized, and democratic party structure was best suited to achieving their goals. All of their organizational blueprints emphasized local control. Decision making was to ascend a pyramid of power that extended from the grass roots to the national committee, rather than the other way around. It was feared that "committees, in whose hands too much power is centralized, are too apt to substitute their own often short-sighted selfish action for the unselfish, intelligent action of their constituents, thus insuring defeat instead of success." To prevent such accumulations of power, the internal structures of the American International were to incorporate the same political safeguards that the Yankees hoped to institute in the national government, namely, the referendum and the initiative.[34]

SORGE AND HIS fellow Marxists' ideology rested upon a view of the state, democracy, and civil liberties entirely contrary to that of their fellow English-speaking Internationals. For them, the American republic was not fundamentally different from the governments of other capitalist countries. From their perspective, whatever differences of form or philosophy the American republic proclaimed for itself against the corrupt European monarchies were superficial compared with the great secret that they all shared: that all real power was wielded by their native capitalist classes. Sorge's brand of Marxism rested upon a fatalistic attitude toward politics; democracy was a sham, and elections were merely a method of diverting the working class from the real arena of economic struggle. As one of his party's circulars put it, "Capital governs the elections, rules the legislature as well as any other thing, consequently the workingmen, who are not the lucky posessors [*sic*] of the mighty dollar, never will gain much by performing his duty on the election day, but will lose his time only. The pure and well engineered rule of Capital in this country does not permit the workingmen to gain anything, but finally forces him to take everything."[35]

Sorge observed many of the political tricks common in his time, though he connected all of them to a single vast conspiracy of capital. "Modern bourgeois society," Sorge maintained, "is *one* and a *unit* in endeavoring to preserve at all cost its political and economical rule over the man of labor." In normal, quiescent times, capital relied upon what Marxists would later come to call "false consciousness" to delude the workers into doing its bidding. The foremost example of this was voting itself, a ritual seen as usually meaningless in its consequences but that served well as a pressure valve in venting popular grievances. When political contests were truly joined by the working class, then the bourgeoisie had to resort to the practices of vote buying, ballot stuffing, voter intimidation, and false counts. In the rarest of circumstances, according to the Sorgean view of American politics, when even these frauds could not overcome the popular will, then the bourgeoisie resorted to its most reliable and insidious weapon of them all: the mystifying distractions of middle-class reformers whose pet issues, temperance, greenbacks, women's suffrage, and the like, served well to sidetrack the labor movement from its true course.[36]

To Sorge and his followers, the bases of the power of the American ruling class were the very same ideals of freedom and liberty that were the mortal enemies of the rulers of Europe. The Americans, Sorge believed, because they sincerely believed in their own rights and liberties, were their own worst enemy. Civil rights were but illusions that only chained workers by allowing even the most wretchedly poor laborer to believe that he actually possessed his own freedom. "When bourgeois-society at its cradle proclaimed charlatan-like 'personal liberty,'" wrote Sorge, "its consequence was a new slavery of the working classes." Sorge had little but contempt for the "emptiness" of the liberal phrases that were so cherished by his Yankee counterparts: "'Freedom, independence,' and the like, are the most misused words in every language and should bring anybody who still uses them today under suspicion. 'Patriotism' and 'universal right to vote' are the next on the list and have served the ruling class of this country well." So deep was the animosity to republicanism among the predominantly German American Marxists that one prominent member of Sorge's group, Robert Blissert, an Irish tailor, made the grave mistake of ridiculing the Fourth of July before a mass meeting of workers. To his surprise he found himself roundly denounced by the same trade unionists who had sponsored his speech.[37]

Sorge and his fellows had not always harbored such disdain for the principles of republicanism. After all, many of these German American Marxists had fought for these very same ideals in the German revolutions of 1848. As a young man, Sorge himself had fought and tasted bitter defeat in the battles for the establishment of a liberal republic in both Saxony and Baden. In 1860, the Communist Club, the first Marxist organization in America and the party of Sorge and the other future German American leaders of the IWA, worked assiduously to convince their fellow New York Germans to vote for Abraham Lincoln. Steadfast Republicans and Unionists, so many members of the Communist Club enlisted when the war began that the club was forced to suspend its activities for the duration. At war's end, when the Communist Club was reestablished under the new banner of the "Social Party," political reform was one of its goals. Among the Social Party's demands were leveling the highly diverse legal requirements for officeholding to that of mere citizenship in every state, and making election-fraud laws more stringent and having them vigorously enforced. Clearly, up to the time of the founding of International Workingmen's Association in America, most German American radicals, however critical they were of its hypocrisies, looked to representative government as one viable avenue of reform.[38]

Sorge's and other German American radicals' rejection of republicanism was not a dramatic ideological transformation accomplished in one fell swoop but was the endpoint of their own long experience of defeat and disappointment. In the span of twenty years, these radical Forty-Eighters went from the youthful shouldering of liberty's musket in the dream of winning a German republic to the cynical economism of their maturity. In between they had witnessed the mainstream of the Republican Party lurch from its original proproducer, Free-Soil policy to a procapital, industrialization ethic. They had witnessed labor's Pyrrhic legislative victories: the child-labor, eight-hour, and factory safety laws that had been passed in several states and then quietly ignored by the authorities. Living in New York, they had seen the complete absorption of the city's political life by the greatest of all political "machines" of the age, boss William Marcy Tweed's Tammany Hall. In light of such experience, it is no wonder that Sorge and his comrades looked upon politics with a jaundiced eye.[39]

Nevertheless, experience is only half of understanding; the other half is the framework of beliefs that organize it into meaning. Yankee radicals had similar political experiences, had lived through the same defeats and disappointments, and knew as well as anyone the political frauds that undermined the will of the majority. Yet they took this as evidence not of the failure of the democratic ideal but as a call to arms for its redemption. For those like Sorge who had spent years contemplating, defending, and propagating Marx's ideas, these experiences confirmed Marxist theories as surely as a discoloration in a chemist's test tube validated his chemical equations. Moreover, cynicism toward republican ideals helped inoculate them against the sting of their own electoral defeats. The mounting number of political outrages were more bearable for Sorge's Marxists than they were for the Yankees; for the former, each new revelation of political fraud confirmed their hard-nosed ideology.

Just as the Yankee International's organizational structure was molded by their understanding of the necessities of struggle, so too was the German American Marxist's ideal of party organization constructed from their understanding of American realities and their long-term strategies for achieving socialism. Sorge and his followers believed that fundamental historical progress could only be brought about by the self-activity of the working class. Their primary duty, then, was to support, strengthen, and educate whatever organizations members of the working class organically created in defense of their own interests. The path was clear to them: build up the trade union movement, work to control and radicalize its agenda, educate the workers through their immediate struggle in the workplace, then, when the working class has reached a high point of awareness and discipline, lead it onward toward conquest of its true enemy, the capitalist ruling class. In Sorge's determinedly instrumentalist vision of social change, his concept of the working class was shrunk to the point where it encompassed little more than the trade union movement. The working class thus distilled, the task at hand was greatly simplified. As Sorge put it, "The principal duty of the members & sections of the IWA shall be: To organize the working people of the industrial centres as well as of the agricultural districts into Trades Unions not only on the narrow basis of obtaining higher wages, but on the broad basis of the complete emancipation of labor." Toward that end, once Sorge gained control of the party, he restricted membership to wage earners only.

It was Sorge and his party allies' belief that their organization, though small in numbers, could influence the policies and ideologies of much larger trade unions, and in this way usher in the revolution. In their own minds it was possible for the communist tail to wag the conservative trade union dog because they were the only ones who firmly grasped the totality of the true historical situation; and by their single-minded pursuit of this truth they would prevail. Secure in their theoretical rectitude, Sorge and his fellows arrived at the quite logical conclusion that what was most important was achieving a unity of purpose within their party. Sorge stated his idea plainly in one of his exhortations to the working class.[40]

> Laboring men of the world! The emancipation of our class must be your own work! To effect it you must organize, you must combine, centralise your forces, — for without centralisation you will never be ready to act & all your isolated efforts will be crushed! . . . Banish the false prophets, cast off the pretending friends, close your ears to their shallow phrases & return to your own deliberate judgment of things & measures, that will certainly lead you to a perfect understanding, to common irresistible action with the workers of the whole civilized world! [41]

German American Marxists viewed the centralization of the party as a necessary evil. It was not a feature of their utopian dreams, and they hoped to rid themselves of it as soon as they had toppled the capitalist order. At their first congress, the German American sections stated this explicitly: "We recognize the profound necessity of strong centralisation, without which we would be powerless in the face of the constantly growing centralisation of the ruling classes, but we believe that, after the abolition of all class rule, the federative system, i.e., independent communal administration, will prevail." [42]

Seen in this light, the ideological battles waged by Sorge and his fellow Marxists against the Yankees were no sideshow to the main revolutionary attraction. Rather, they were central to it. Little did Sorge's faction care whether the achievement of ideological unity was won at the expense of alienating greater numbers of radicals. Numbers, in the end, counted for little if they could not be lined up into ranks and marched off in a common direction. "Fellow-workmen!" cried Sorge. "Keep our standard pure & our ranks clean! Never mind the small number! No great work was ever begun by a majority!" [43]

It was this characteristic of the Sorgean faction, their eagerness to exclude others and winnow their membership, that most alienated Yankee Internationalists. The Yankees' own antebellum experience in the antislavery crusade taught them the practicality of broadening the base of their movement to its widest extent. It was, after all, the successive coalitions of the Liberty and Free-Soil Parties that paved the way for the election of Lincoln. It was Lincoln—a politician who offered only the thinnest thread of antislavery rhetoric as a candidate for high office—who declared the emancipation of the slaves.

These old memories were recalled one night when the Yankee International of Philadelphia debated the question of participating in an upcoming congress sponsored by the Sorgean forces. Jacob Byrnes, a government clerk and ardent women's suffrage advocate, spoke out against cooperating with the German American Internationalists because they were "too exclusive" in their attempts to throw out of the movement all of whom they deemed to be not sufficiently working class:

> [In the] Antislavery movement . . . were to be found men and women of all grades and conditions in life working together for the one great object to emancipate the slave from the tyranny of being held subject to the will of his fellow being. In that movement all who came into the field to Labor were hailed as coworkers in the task put before them, years of steady uncessant toil rolled on . . . and the result was their efforts were crowned with success. Why then should we exclude any who come to aid us in our work for the emancipation of Laborers of the World[?] . . . All who are willing and able to help in this great cause should be freely admitted, *exclusiveness* would retard and hinder the progress of our movement. Therefore it was not proper that any man or woman, or race of men and women should be excluded or restricted in their efforts to change the fearful conditions of society which now exist in the present relations of Capital and Labor.[44]

To those Yankee Internationalists who had cut their radical teeth in the cross-class antebellum American reform milieu, the German American attempt to purify and refine the International into an instrument solely of the working class was both immoral and self-defeating.

Karl Marx himself contributed greatly to the development of this theme of Sorgean revolutionary thought and strategy that was so preoccupied with exclusion and intellectual purity. In many ways, Marx's own intellectual development foreshadowed that of his disciple. In the years before the crushing of the liberal democratic movements in Germany, Marx closely identified democracy with the proletariat. He viewed the historical struggles of 1848 as pitting democracy, which he then believed was man's true being, against aristocracy and religion, which reduced man to an animal state. When, in the midst of the revolutions of 1848, the middle classes of the German states turned on their working-class allies and embraced the protection of their monarchs against what they then saw as a threatening mob, Marx's view of democracy dimmed. After this, Marx began to associate democracy with a traitorous middle class.

However, unlike Sorge, Marx, for all of his denunciations of "democratic simpletons," "democratic jack-asses," and "democratic blackguards," continued to appreciate the occasional historical usefulness of democratic demands in advancing working-class struggles against autocracy. "The first step in the revolution by the working class is to raise the proletariat to the position of the ruling class, to establish democracy," Marx wrote on one of his less invective-filled days, and "the proletariat will use its political power to wrest all capital gradually from the Bourgeoisie." But as an ideal or an end in itself, Marx continued to denounce democracy, the highest particular form of the state under capitalism and liberalism, as the concomitant ideology of the historically mature capitalist ruling class.[45]

More important than the influence of Marx's critique of democracy was his influence on Sorge's views of party strategy and party structure. From the earliest years of German American engagement with the First International, Marx and Engels encouraged Sorge and his comrades to march a narrowly defined line. In the spring of 1870, Marx wrote to Siegfried Meyer and August Vogt, informing them that the General Council had recently issued a "secret circular" that detailed the "attitude the International Association must take towards the Irish question." Outlining its main points for them, Marx described how he had arrived at his conclusion that the first blow of the socialist revolution would be struck in England. England, Marx believed, was the linchpin of the international worker's struggle: "England, as the metropolis of capital, as the power that has hitherto ruled the world market, is for the present the most important country for the workers' revolution and, in addition, the only country where the material conditions for this revolution have developed to a certain state of maturity. Thus, to hasten the social revolution in England is the most important object of the International Workingmen's Association."[46]

The first task in bringing about England's proletarian revolution was toppling its landed aristocracy. This, in turn, hinged upon destroying the aristocracy's material and moral basis of support. Marx believed that the last decayed pillar propping up the anachronistic English aristocracy was its exploitation of Ireland. England's dukes, earls, and lords fattened upon the royalties they wrung out of their vast Irish colonial estates. Moreover, as aristocratic rule over Ireland enriched the English bourgeoisie by flooding the English marketplace with cheap meat and wool, the exploitation of Ireland bonded England's bourgeoisie to its aristocracy. Lastly, the immigration of displaced Irish laborers into the English labor market created divisions in the proletariat that allowed the bourgeoisie to dominate workers through the tactics of "divide and rule" and the fostering of national hatreds and jealousies. As Marx put it, the attitude of the English worker to the Irish "is roughly that of the poor whites to the niggers in the former slave states of the American Union."[47]

Through this reductionist analysis, Marx had convincingly focused world history and the coming of the socialist millennium upon the single point of overthrowing English rule over Ireland. It was therefore the task of Internationals around the world "to bring the conflict between England and Ireland to the forefront everywhere." For Sorge, Meyer, Vogt, and the International in America, this meant working to overcome the national prejudices that separated the Irish from other American workers. Marx instructed his German American correspondents that "a coalition of the German workers with the Irish workers (naturally, also, with the English and American workers who wish to join in) is the greatest thing you could undertake now."[48]

Sorge and his compatriots took this analysis to heart and tailored their long-term strategies accordingly. They placed their highest priority upon the recruitment of Irish workers into the IWA, though this was a daunting task because of the cultural differences between them. As Sorge reported to Marx in August of 1871, "We have made great efforts for inducing the Irish Workingmen of this country to join the I.W.A., but religious and political prejudices and above all—their leaders have to this day withstood all our efforts. . . . Still we do not give it up & hope yet to gain a firm foothold amongst the Irish."[49] Sorge even wrote Engels asking him to send along a good book on the Irish question, written from Marx's perspective, so that he could educate himself on the subject. Engels thought his friend's request humorous since such a book had not yet been written, but he sent him a reading list nonetheless.[50]

By such precise and sure social prescriptions, Dr. Marx transformed his intellectual genius into his own Achilles heel. What supreme confidence he must have had in the scope of his social vision, his grasp of the direction of political economic variables, and the firmness of his final calculations to make such a demand of his little clique. The sophistication of Marx's social analysis towered above his contemporaries and yet paled beside the sheer unbounded possibilities of social being and historical development.

This degree of intellectual self-confidence was not part of the American radical tradition and was not shared by Marx and Sorge's Yankee comrades. Yankee Internationals may have been more diverse in the range of their ideological commitments, but this diversity discouraged them from placing too much stock in any one scheme of reform. The Yankees, given the moral wellsprings of their radical impulse, depended on a sense of rights and conscience to guide their action rather than a "scientific" approach to social change. When particular programs were considered, many Yankee radicals seemed willing to experiment out of a sense of the limitations of human understanding. "As Internationals we are at school in search of knowledge," argued one member of Yankee Section 26 in the midst of a debate over a specific land reform scheme, "and do not in the present attempt to decide what would be the best steps in all cases to take." Stephen Pearl Andrews, a radical who prided himself on his critical faculties and his systematic approach to social issues, expressed the common view of Yankee reformers during a particularly polyglot airing of viewpoints at a convention of the American Labor Reform League. "One mistake people make is to suppose that the truth is simple," he told the diverse crowd, and the "complication of opinions displayed here would be sufficient proof of this." But, Andrews continued, there "is doubtless great truth in the arguments of all reformers who have spoken in this convention, though they may seem to contradict each other." [51]

Such pragmatism, as it turned out, was a needed but absent counterbalance to the hubristic faith in political strategizing that became endemic in the American Left after the Yankee elements were purged from the IWA in 1872. Indeed much of the infighting, the circular firing squads that have been the sad and constant plague of the American Left, has been fueled by the persistence of this unreasonable faith in the proscriptive power of abstract social analysis.[52]

Marx's Irish strategy led to great mischief in America. Because of the rivalries and racial hatreds that had grown up between the Irish and African American communities in New York, it encouraged Sorge and his comrades to turn their backs on their own internationalist principles of human brotherhood and ignore the needs of their potential black constituency. Given the conservatism of many Irish workers on questions of women's suffrage, legal equality, and, especially, divorce, Marx's Irish strategy further deepened the divisions between Sorge's Marxists and the libertarian Yankees.

The strategy of appealing to the Irish was only one of the elements in the German American Marxists' decision to dump the Yankees from the party. Since workers of Irish descent constituted a high proportion of the membership of many trade unions, Marx's Irish strategy mightily reinforced the trade union emphasis of the Sorgean Internationalists. Indeed, on the eve of the splitting of the American International, Marx wrote a confidential letter to Carl Speyer and Friedrich Sorge, telling them that "you must strive to win the support of the Trades Unions at all costs." Many American trade unions were at that moment turning toward a policy of social and political conservatism, as well as a long-term economic strategy of racial and sexual exclusion and job segregation. In this context, Sorge believed that he faced a choice between embarking on a broader crusade of reform, arm in arm with his Yankee comrades, or allying with America's skilled unionists in pursuit of more immediate, bread-and-butter demands. The choice to him was clear: the trade unions must have priority.

Appealing to trade unionists and Irish workers reinforced the German American Marxists' long-held dim view of women's equality. Friedrich Bolte expressed the common sentiments of his comrades when he took the floor at one of Section 1's meetings to denounce Section 12. Section 12, declared Bolte to a flurry of applause, was a "disgrace" to the International. "All this talk of theirs is folly, or worse than folly, and we don't want their foolish notions credited as the views of this society. This nonsense which they talk of, female suffrage and free-love, may do to consider in the future, but the question that interests us as working-men is that of labor and wages." [53]

Bolte's outburst revealed the deep hostility of the German American Marxists to feminism. Women's suffrage and free love were the two most common examples held aloft by the partisans of Section 1 to "prove" the Yankees' deviation from the principles of the International. Section 1's final statement on the issue of women's equality was given in a resolution that connected their hostility to women's rights to their deeper suspicions of republicanism in general: "In recognition, that universal suffrage cannot free humanity from slavery, . . . the gaining of the vote by women is not in the best interests of the workers." [54]

The sources of this hostility to women's equality were complex. On the one hand, the antipathy was fed by the well-established trade union demand for male workers to be paid a "family wage." This wage would allow the man to be the family's breadwinner and his wife to work exclusively in the home. The demand for a family wage was one that went to the heart of workingmen's efforts to redefine their masculinity and preserve patriarchal authority in the face of an industrializing society that battered down some of the ancient barriers separating men's and women's work. Because many of the German American Marxists were skilled artisans who usually could command an income large enough to allow their wives to remain at home, they were especially committed to the family-wage principle. Moreover, these immigrant men cherished their native German culture, which raised the domestic ideal of womanhood to heroic heights. Marx himself was also susceptible to these beliefs: he once observed that "German women should have begun by driving their men to self-emancipation [instead of] seeking emancipation for themselves directly."[55]

Sorge and his fellow Marxists fell into a circular logic when they occasionally publicly professed their belief in women's equality as an abstract ideal but worked against it in practice. They feared that to pursue the issue would only serve to alienate the common workers who were repelled by the idea. Sorge often averred that demands for women's suffrage and equality were opposed by workers and therefore could only set back the International. He blamed the electoral defeat of Massachusetts's Labor Party on its inclusion of a suffrage plank in its platform. The trade unions, Sorge told Marx, "will never connect with organizations tainted by adventurous ideas & action," such as were trumpeted by the Yankees of Section 12. This was especially true of the all-important Irish, whose "religious and political prejudices" disposed them least of all to the Yankee's ideals.[56]

The differences in the Yankee's and German American Marxist's understandings of the issue of the family wage and women's equality were well illustrated when the Central Committee considered the application of the English-speaking section from Vineland, New Jersey. Delegates from Section 1 were surprised to see that half of the names on Vineland's application were women's. They were even more upset when the occupation listed beside many of these names was that of "housekeeper" ("homemaker" in today's vocabulary), hardly what they considered a profession that fell into their definition of "workingmen" or "wage-laborer." In the end, Vineland's delegate, Col. James Blood, was admitted to the Central Committee over the objections of Section 1. So upset were the German Americans of Section 1 that after losing the question of the admission of the Vineland section in the Central Committee, they continued their denunciations at their own meeting later that night.[57]

Although the question of women's suffrage and social equality was one that rendered the most stark contrast between the ideology of the Yankees and that of their erstwhile German American Marxist allies, it was not itself sufficient to cause the breakup of the American International. The issue of women's rights and equality was not a matter of dispute in London, though the republican-minded English members of the General Council split from Marx just as surely as the Yankees did from the Sorge's Marxists. To the German American Marxists, feminism became the defining symbol of what was wrong with their Yankee comrades. Feminism was to them the most egregious example of what really troubled Sorge's Marxists: the Yankees' idealistic worship of democracy, republicanism, civil equality, and their inclusive view of the labor movement itself.

As Sorge's rivalry with the Yankees heated up, Marx continued to throw fuel on the fire. On the eve of the American IWA's final split, Marx wrote to one of Sorge's fellow officers of Section 1, Friedrich Bolte, elaborating upon what he saw as the *true* purpose of the International Workingmen's Association and insisting that the General Council had no time for "bourgeois philanthropists, sectarians, or amateur groups." The International was founded "in order to replace the socialist or semi-socialist sects by a real organization of the working class for the struggle. . . . The history of the International was a continual struggle of the General Council against the sects and attempts by amateurs to assert themselves within the International against the real movement of the working class."[58] While Marx may have had his own troubles with the anarchistic Bakuninists he had in mind in writing this statement, to Bolte, Sorge, and the other leaders of Section 1, Marx's pronouncement perfectly reflected their own feelings about their erstwhile Yankee partners.

In the end, the Sorgean Marxists and the Yankee radicals simply had insufficient ideological common ground upon which to stand. To the German American Marxists, the State was unredeemably the creature of the capitalist class and therefore all of its political guarantees—its democracy, its formal liberties, its system of justice—were but corrupted instruments of capitalist control. For these men, meaningful change required disciplined organization aimed at overturning this sham republic by agitating for a true workers' democracy on the factory floor. The Yankees viewed the state not as the instrument of oppression but as a potential instrument of reform. They, too, saw the *existing* government as corrupted, unrepresentative, and oppressive, and they agreed that the organized power of capital blocked the channels of democracy. But they fervently believed in the principles of representative democracy and were not prepared to abandon what they viewed as the legacy of all the hard-won battles from Bunker Hill to Gettysburg.

Sorge and Marx, either out of their critical rejection of democratic ideals or their disillusioning experience in failed liberal revolutions, were simply out of step with the socio-political geography of American society. By the 1870s a majority of the male working class wielded the ballot, and a significant portion of the black working class was beginning to as well. At this point in time a coalition of white and black workers represented a massive threat to the hegemony of the Republican Party and the electoral strategies of the Democrats. Whatever the actual potential pool of support for such an alliance (and the obstacles to it, given the benefits of racial exclusivity that many white workers enjoyed), the possibilities for its consummation would steadily diminish as the century wore on. Disenfranchisement and Jim Crow in the South and the heightened hurdle immigrants had to leap to become voting citizens combined to make the United States an even less democratic polity by the end of the century than it was in the days of the First International. If ever there was a time when electoral strategies had some purpose, this was it. By the time Eugene Debs rolled his "Red Special" through innumerable whistle-stops across America in pursuit of the presidency for the Socialist Party in 1908, so many workers, white, black, and female, were disenfranchised that the prospects for seizing power through the ballot box on a national level were practically nil.

Moreover, the American working class, for better or worse, looked upon politics as the engine of social change and the fount of reform. Republicanism was the bedrock of American working-class identity in the nineteenth century. Any social movement wishing to enlist the support of the masses had to contend with that reality. The English-speaking sections of the IWA, in their concern for popular democracy and combating the corruption and inequalities inherent in the political system, spoke a language that could have appealed to a great many Americans. Instructing Americans, especially recently minted ones or recently freed ones, to abandon their small but symbolically significant claim to citizenship and "turn their back on the ballot box," as the Sorgean International did, was sheer utopian folly.[59]

Yankee radicals were just as serious about emancipating the worker from the chains of wage labor as the Sorge camp was, but their solution was to redeem the republic, make good on its egalitarian promises, and widen the channels of democracy so the workers would be free to seize the state and wield its power against their capitalist oppressors. For the Sorgean International, revolution was the means to democracy. For the Yankee International, democracy was the means to revolution. For both, revolution was the ultimate goal. That they shared elements of the same social equation, though with reversed numerator and denominator, was the reason they were able to stand publicly for the same ideals. Yankees repeatedly proclaimed that their goal was to "emancipate the laborer," and, occasionally, the German American Marxists stated that "removing all social inequality and injustice" was their aim. Neither was insincere in making such claims, though each side's choice of action ultimately undermined these ideals. The Yankee's dedication to democracy and civil liberties steered it into conflict with the trade unions, who had opted for a policy of racial, ethnic, and sexual exclusion in their own ranks, while the German American Marxists commitment to building up the existing autonomous institutions of workers led them to abandon democratic tactics and even their internationalist ideals of human brotherhood and equality.[60]

CHAPTER SIX

The Marxist
Coup and the
Splitting of the
American
International

RIEDRICH ENGELS once wrote that "a party proves itself a victorious party by the fact that it *splits* and can stand the split." By his own standard, the International Workingmen's Association was many times over a defeated party. By 1872, the IWA was riddled with fissures: in England, British delegates quit the General Council and formed a rival organization; in Geneva, the central council declared its autonomy from London; in Italy, the newly formed Federal Council likewise declared its independence; in Spain, the forces loyal to Marx and those demanding separation from his General Council had fought each other to a stalemate; and in North America, Sorge's German American Marxists declared themselves the sole authority over the International and kicked the Yankees out.

All of this division and dissension came to a head at the International congress at the Hague in September 1872. There, the future of the International was decided. The choices for Marx and Engels in Europe and for Sorge in America were the same: they could either relax their grip upon the organization and allow for local variations in doctrine and practice according to the needs and circumstances in each region, or they could demand fealty to increasingly refined party doctrines and centralized governing structures. Both Marx and Sorge opted for the latter course and steered the First International into its grave.[1]

IN THE SUMMER of 1871, the International's Yankees and German American Marxists had only just begun to plumb the depths of their ideological differences. At first, the new Yankee members had no apparent qualms about working within the German American–dominated Central Committee. Victoria Woodhull expressed the prevailing cooperative spirit by printing and donating to the Central Committee one thousand copies of Marx's pamphlet entitled "The Civil War in France." Little did she know that her contribution annoyed Sorge, who, in all likelihood, resented her action because it indebted the committee to the Yankee reformers and because she had bypassed his own hierarchies of control. A few days later, Sorge fired off a letter to Marx complaining that the gift was Marx's fault for not having shipped a sufficient number of these pamphlets directly to him.[2]

At about the same time, Sorge's desire to centralize and control the American International caused the first rift in the organization. Section 23 of Washington, D.C., had a number of members who preferred to keep their identities secret. There were many reasons for this. Some were probably public figures whose association with the International would not have sat well with a public recently inflamed with images of blood-thirsty Parisian mobs. Others were government employees whose positions depended upon the whim of the political appointees above them. More than any other section in the American International, Section 23 had an interest in keeping the names of its members a secret.[3] In keeping with his vision of the Central Committee as the command center of a centralized organization, Sorge responded to Section 23's application for formal membership by notifying them that they must submit a list of all their members and their occupations. They refused. The members of Section 23 and most other English-speaking members of the American IWA did not see themselves as subordinate units within a hierarchy of control but as autonomous groups bound together by a common purpose and beliefs.

Richard Hinton, Section 23's corresponding secretary, wrote to London instead, stating that his group preferred to correspond with the General Council directly rather than submit to the demands of the Central Committee. The rules of the IWA clearly permitted such action, and the General

Council quickly recognized Washington's independence from Sorge's committee. Marx himself had to tell Sorge that his committee "went too far," that the rules of the IWA expressly granted Washington its right to affiliate directly with London. Marx made clear to Sorge that the only information he could demand of sections seeking affiliation was the size of their membership and the name of their secretaries. But before the General Council's messages had time to steam across the Atlantic, Section 23 had already caved in to Sorge's demands and his assurances of secrecy and reluctantly surrendered its list. Later, when the lapsed correspondence had clarified the situation, Section 23 withdrew again from the Central Committee, though Sorge continued to claim them as active members.[4]

New York's Yankee radicals did not begin to realize the depth of the ideological gulf separating them from their German-speaking allies until they began to take some initiative in the Central Committee. When the Yankees brought their first proposition to the committee, what seemed to them an innocuous proposal in keeping with Internationalist doctrine, it provoked a controversy that soon exposed the ideological fault lines along which the International would soon divide.

The precipitating event behind the Yankee's first Central Committee initiative was the so-called "*Westfield* disaster" of 1871. On July 30, 1871, the steam boiler of the Staten Island ferryboat *Westfield* exploded while taking on passengers at its Battery slip. It was a Sunday afternoon and the boat was filled not with its usual complement of commuters but with families enjoying a summer outing. The explosion tore through the boat with such force that a few of the victims were thrown thirty feet into the air. Hundreds were horribly scalded, and days later, when the last had succumbed to their injuries, a total of eight-two people were counted among the dead.

Victoria Woodhull and Tennessee Claflin wasted no time in pointing out the larger social and political significance of the disaster for their readers. Woodhull and Claflin looked beyond the individual responsibility of the captain and crew of the ship to indict capitalism and class rule. The real cause of the disaster, they fumed, was not a single stuck valve or a rusty plate of iron; rather, it was a system of transportation where "passengers are usually considered as freight—goods, cattle or human—it is all one to the carrier." Worse even than the owner's avaricious disregard of passenger safety was the fact that American law, biased as it was in favor of wealth, would give the robber barons preferential treatment: "A petty theft of a pound of steak would subject the miserable, hungry offender to months of imprisonment; the infamous dereliction of the most solemn civil duty perpetrated by men of intelligence and position in the pursuit of wealth and self-aggrandizement leaves them intact, except to the nominal penalties of commercial insolvency."[5]

Many other New Yorkers must have had similar feelings, for in the wake of the disaster, coroner's juries were impaneled in both New York and Brooklyn. The testimony they heard failed to single out any one cause for the accident, but it clearly revealed the low priority given to safety in the keenly competitive ferry business. In the end, both juries indicted the crews of the steamship and its owner—Jacob Vanderbilt, Cornelius's less famous older brother.[6]

With the sensational prospect of one of the city's wealthiest men going on trial along with his hirelings, the leaders of Section 12 saw their opportunity to turn the tragedy into an object lesson of the consequences of unrestrained capitalism. Under the guise of publicly voicing its approval of the indictments, the lengthy resolution Section 12 introduced to the Central Committee condemned the elitist nature of the judicial system. It denounced the legal system for allowing Vanderbilt to go free pending the outcome of the trial and demanded that he be treated just like any person accused of murder. "As human life is esteemed by such men of less value than dollars," the resolution proclaimed, "their dollars should not save them from the punishment they merit." The resolution concluded with the argument that only the socialist solution of government ownership and control of "all means of public transport and communication" could prevent such slaughters in the future.[7]

To the surprise of the Yankees of Section 12, the resolution was given a chilly reception by the Central Committee. Sorge, still in control of a majority of votes in the committee, effectively tabled Section 12's proposition by remanding it to each constituent section to ratify. William West, Section 12's delegate to the committee, was clearly angered by Sorge's evasion. In his report of the meeting he pointed out that the IWA had already gone on record in favor of the nationalization of transportation and communication at its congresses of 1867 and 1868. He suggested that in shelving the *Westfield* resolution, the committee's officers (a clear reference to Sorge, who was then the Central Committee's corresponding secretary) had placed their own "merely personal objects" above the "business of the sections."

West was not about to take his defeat lightly, and a short time later he turned the tables on his adversary and proposed that the referendum process to which Sorge had subjected the *Westfield* resolution be made a standard procedure of the Central Committee. Having established the precedent for

NEW YORK CITY.—THE INTERNATIONALS IN COUNCIL—THE FEDERAL COMMITTEE OF WORKINGMEN ASSEMBLED AT THEIR HEADQUARTERS, NO. 68 GRAND STREET, TO RECEIVE THE REPORT OF THE DELEGATION TO ALBANY.—SEE PAGE 247.

A meeting of the IWA Central Committee in New York City (North Wind Picture Archives)

the referendum himself, Sorge was placed at a severe disadvantage in this fight, and a few weeks later the Central Committee voted to institute the referendum.[8]

Sorge's foot-dragging opposition to the *Westfield* resolution was but one of his many efforts to retain control of an organization in which he saw with every passing month the addition of another Yankee section and the further stagnation of his own recruitment efforts. He did what he could to hold the line through his position as corresponding secretary of the Central Committee. His responses to inquiries from Yankee sections were cold and even threatening, while those to Irish sections, which Marx had singled out as having the highest strategic importance, were warm and welcoming. When a group of Yankee radicals from Philadelphia first asked him for information on joining the association, Sorge warned them that "it is essential that the Section should be composed of *Workingmen* understanding their position toward Capital and modern society, ready to make a radical change of Society's structure and rebuild it anew on the basis of Labor, men entirely free from present political (bourgeois) affinities and rejecting all compromise." That same week, when William Nicholson applied for admission on behalf of a section of Irishmen from Jersey City, Sorge thanked him for his welcome news. "The formation of more Sections of Irish Workingmen will always be viewed with pleasure," he warmly replied.[9]

Sorge also made a ham-handed attempt to censure *Woodhull & Claflin's Weekly*, the mouthpiece of the Yankee International, which revealed to the Yankee Internationalists Sorge's intention of keeping firm control of the party. Early in September 1871, the *Weekly* had reprinted a profile of Karl Marx from the German journal *Grenzbotem*, which was clearly written from the perspective of someone who viewed the rise of communism with alarm. Woodhull informed her readers that *Grenzbotem* was "a journal hostile to the policy of the International League" and printed the article without further comment. Sorge, Starke, and Bolte, three of the officers of Section 1, were perturbed that their enemies' lies were being spread by their own erstwhile allies, and protested the piece in a meeting with the editors and sent a letter of rebuttal to the *Weekly*. The three declared that they would have preferred to remain silent but for the fact that the *Weekly* was read by "a not inconsiderable number of members and friends of the International." They were worried, they continued, that their readers would look "only at the surface of the treated subject" and be led astray by its half-truths and misrepresentations. After citing a half dozen such distortions, Sorge and his fellow officers tipped their hand by requesting that the *Weekly* not publish anything of the International except its rules, resolutions, congress proceedings, and the declarations of its authorized executive bodies (presumably including their own Central Committee). This demand only served to confirm the suspicions of the Yankee Internationalists that Sorge meant to dictate to them.[10]

In what may have been partly intended as a rebuttal to Section 1, the "Appeal of Section 12" to "the English-speaking citizens of the United States" was published in the same issue of the *Weekly* that carried Sorge's complaints and demands. It was a call for like-minded radicals throughout the nation to form their own sections of the IWA. While never directly alluding to the conflicts that had prompted their independent action and even directing prospective members to send their applications to Sorge, Section 12's "Appeal" included a passage that captured the bitterness and the fears that Sorge's bid for power had raised among the Yankees.[11] Informing prospective sections that they must nominate a delegate who resided in New York to represent them in the Central Committee, the "Appeal" noted that this was only a "temporary representation" as a "single committee will not always be able to transact the entire business of the International." Nor should it:

> Committees, in whose hands too much power is centralized, are apt to substitute their own often short-sighted selfish action for the unselfish, intelligent action of their constituents, thus insuring defeat instead of achieving success. What have been termed the excesses of democratic proletarian revolutions in other countries have been occasioned by just such committees blindly leading where none understandingly followed. The success of similar revolutions in this country must not be hindered nor marred nor disgraced by similar excesses.[12]

Rather than a unitary central body directing the organization from the top, Section 12 envisioned a decentralized party built from the ground up—of municipal councils working at the city level, of state councils operating at the state level, and of a national council lobbying Congress—united by the democratic safeguards of the referendum and popular initiative.

In accordance with the republican thrust of Yankee ideology, Section 12's "Appeal" called for a democratic revolution that would institute a new government "within existing forms." The object of the International, it declared, was to emancipate the laborer, "male and female," through the conquest of political power. Spelling out what they meant by "emancipation," the "Appeal's" authors explained their ultimate goals as being the establishment of "Political Equality and Social Freedom of man and woman alike" and of a government "based primarily on Equality of Rights and Reciprocity of Duties in the matter of the Production and Distribution of Wealth." Along with the cry for abolition of the "anarchical competitive rule of self-seeking capitalists" and the "traffic in land, labor, and money . . . to say nothing of love," the "Appeal" heaped onto its plate generous dollops from many old reformist pots, claiming for the International an agenda that included "the abolition of standing armies, national boundaries, secret diplomacy, class distinctions, religious bigotry and even differences of language."[13]

Section 12's article apparently struck a chord among readers of *Woodhull & Claflin's Weekly*. Within a few weeks West had received so many responses that in answering these requests for information on the International he had exhausted his supply of IWA Rules and other documents. After vainly asking Sorge for more copies, West resorted to publishing a page of IWA rules in the *Weekly*. Section 12 then resolved to print a broadside that included all of the needed information on one sheet for the convenience of their harried corresponding secretary.[14]

Sorge and Section 1 attempted to meet head-on this challenge to its dogma and control but found themselves maddeningly hamstrung by West's referendum procedure. First, it drafted a clarification of what it believed to be the true purposes and goals of the International, and then it submitted a resolution censuring Section 12. Both propositions had to make the rounds of the sections before being finalized, and, ultimately, neither secured the required number of votes. Sorge also sent a report to the General Council, by way of Marx, wherein he described Section 12's action as some sort of a ruling-class conspiracy: "The intention of politicians and others is now pretty clear; to identify the IWA in this country with the Woman Suffrage, Free Love, and other movements[,] and we will have to struggle hard for clearing ourselves from these impostations." And struggle hard they did.[15]

Woodhull & Claflin's Weekly, in the spirit of a fair referendum, published Section 1's condemnation of their "Appeal." Sorge's retort, pointedly addressed "to the workingmen of America," offered a dialectical and historical justification for their conclusion that all political action was folly and the "whole movement" of the working class must instead concentrate on achieving its first objective, namely, the "normal workday." America, this manifesto conceded, was like no other country in the world—not, as the Yankees alleged, because of its democracy but because the crushing of the slaveholder's rebellion had overcome the "last obstacle" to the "complete development" of the bourgeoisie and thus made possible its "absolute control and rule of the United States." The economic control of capital rendered all democratic privileges meaningless: "As long, therefore, as the working classes do not appropriate the means of labor[,] they will, even in the politically freest country, remain in the same state of abject dependence they are in to-day." Meaningful change was not going to be achieved within the forms of government established by the bourgeoisie in their own struggle against the feudal state; history had shown that "ruling classes never surrender voluntarily anything of their privileges, it must be *wrested* from them." The working classes had to conquer the State in order to win their own complete emancipation. This day would only dawn once the working class was "combined and united"—once its rank and file moved toward shared goals.[16]

In an ever-spiraling round of declarations and protests, the following week *Woodhull & Claflin's Weekly* printed Section 12's response. This rebuttal objected to Section 1's attempt to restrict membership in the IWA to "so-called" workingmen, pointing out that there was no provision in any of the official rules, resolutions, or pronouncements of the International to warrant it. The Yankees reminded their critical comrades that "first of all, and above all, working men and women are human beings, before they are either laborers or capitalists." The other primary objection to Section 1's point of view was that it unduly restricted the International's sphere of action. Again, the Yankees returned to their bedrock republicanism: it was "self-evident," they argued, that economic gains, such as the normal work-day, "cannot be attained until politics are made subordinate to the rights of labor by the substitution of the State in the place of the individual, and the power of the Almighty Ballot in the hands of poor men and women, in lieu of the Almighty Dollar in the pockets of rich men and women." Later, in yet another defense of his section's original "Appeal," William West clarified this point even further: "The simple truth is that Political Equality and Social Freedom for all alike, of all races, both sexes, and every condition, are necessary precursors of the more radical reforms demanded by the International."[17]

Unable to secure a vote in the precariously balanced Central Committee in favor of his resolution censuring Section 12, the last attempt having failed by a vote of just ten against eleven, Sorge resorted to making the rounds of the different section meetings in New York in an attempt to use the procedure of popular initiative to secure passage of his resolution over the heads of his Yankee opposition. The balance of power was in the hands of the French, especially the largest section in New York, Section 2. Sorge scored a fleeting victory when Section 2 removed its delegate to the Central Committee, the abolitionist Françoise Jean Baptiste Hubert, for voting with the Yankees. However, William West made a point of attending Section 2's next meeting. West debated the representative of Section 1, who had also showed up that night, and swayed the radical Franco-Americans to his side. West achieved a complete vindication of Section 12's actions when the members of Section 2 voted unanimously to reinstate Hubert.[18]

The situation was now rapidly approaching a crisis. The Central Committee's one-year mandate was due to expire on the first of December, and its members could not reach agreement on the structure or composition of a new one. The last Central Committee meeting was held on November 19, at which time William West proposed that the sections simply elect new delegates within the same committee structure and adopt the old rules. The new body to was to reconvene the first Sunday of the new year. By this time, Sorge could see the handwriting on the wall: he understood that with the gathering speed of Yankee recruitment efforts and the success of Section 12's

"Appeal" among Yankee radicals, the continuation of the present Central Committee structure and rules of membership guaranteed that the Yankees would soon rule the organization. As both West and Sorge had enough strength to block each other's proposals but not enough to pass their own, a stalemate ensued. In the end, both Sorge and West voted to adjourn without having made any provision for the Central Committee's successor, leaving the IWA in America, as one Internationalist put it, "without a head."[19]

In the week following this vote, two groups formed and attempted to fill the vacuum the defunct Central Committee left behind. Sorge rounded up a dozen of his allies on the committee and organized a rump assembly of sections that voted to call itself the "Provisional Federal Council." A few days later the five delegates who had voted against dissolving the committee, Theodore Banks, of New York's English-speaking Section 9, Edward Grosse and Dr. George Stiebling, representing the German-language Sections 6 and 13, and Theodore Millot and "H. Charnier," who spoke for the Francophone Sections 14 and 30, declared that they would continue to meet at the usual time and place as if nothing had happened. Their efforts were thwarted when they arrived at the committee's usual meeting room at the Tenth Ward Hotel and found the landlord, who was a member of Section 1, barring the door.[20]

Section 12 stood aloof from both of these groups and branded their efforts to organize new committees "Anti-Republican and Anti-Democratic." To the cosmopolitan committee composed of Grosse, Banks, Stiebling, Millot, and Charnier, members of Section 12 noted that the dissolution of the Central Committee had been perfectly constitutional, and they branded Sorge's Provisional Federal Council as a "sort of Theirs usurpation," referring to the counterrevolutionary government of France. Revealing a tinge of Yankee nativism, William West described his opponents as having "no higher conception of the qualifications necessary to membership of the I.W.A. other than that the applicant shall be an alien, of the masculine gender, and a slave, at that." In spite of such invective, Section 12 offered hope for some sort of reconciliation when they voted to join any meeting whose intention was to form a new Central Committee that would not discriminate against any previously recognized section.[21]

While the leadership of the International in America fell to pieces, the General Council's ruling that the American branch should remain unified finally reached New York. The General Council had not yet heard of the breakup of the American Central Committee, but was acting instead on a request of Section 12 that it be given permission to organize English-speaking sections—the power that it had already claimed for itself in its "Appeal." The General Council construed Section 12's "Appeal" to mean that it wished to operate independently of the Central Committee—though, in fact, Section 12 had not then reached this point. Replying officially on behalf of the Council, Karl Marx instructed Section 12 to remain within the Central Committee until a general congress of American sections could be called and a new, reorganized Central Committee could be elected. Johann Georg Eccarius, the General Council's corresponding secretary for North America, enclosed a personal note to West along with the Council's official resolutions, offering friendly advice on settling Section 12's differences with Section 1. The best course, Eccarius advised, was for the Yankees to be patient and remain within the Central Committee. Time and circumstances were on their side, he observed; eventually "with the present temper of the public mind," their numbers would grow to the point where they would overcome their causes of complaint and "the prevalence of foreign notions." In "a few months hence," if they stayed the course, "the delegates of the English-speaking sections should become a majority in the committee" and "the delegates representing sections consisting of recent immigrants would have to fall in with the majority."[22]

Eccarius's belief that the Yankee sections would spread most rapidly in America was not commonly held by his fellow General Council officers. But then, through his years of correspondence with Americans from all walks of life, Eccarius had developed a keener understanding of America's social realities. Even Marx was blind to the great potential of the Yankees to adapt the International to their own situation and spread it among experienced American radicals. Marx did not perceive Section 12 as a viable alternative or threat to the well-organized, disciplined Section 1. After all, according to his own theories, Yankees were the least important element of the American working class while the Germans and the Irish were its vanguard. Naturally, then, in Marx's view, the Yankees could hardly threaten to overcome these more vital components of the working class.

After reading Section 12's "Appeal," Marx wrote privately to Sorge, warning him that Section 12 had asked the Council "that it be constituted the leader in America," but assuring him that the Council had acted to put down such "pretensions." By ordering the Yankee section to remain within the Central Committee, Marx believed that he had kept them in their place, where, as he had advised Sorge before, they could be better controlled. Months later, when Marx became aware of how this tactic had blown up in constituents' faces, he as much as conceded that he had acted on a mistaken understanding of the situation in America. "We were by no means duly informed in time about the elements that brought about the breach," he complained to Sorge.[23]

The General Council's ruling that the Central Committee should remain in place until a general congress of American sections could elect a new body hardly satisfied Sorge, who knew all too well that this meant the inevitable takeover of the American International by the advancing ranks of Yankees. Besides, it was now a moot point—Marx's letter and the General Council's resolutions had arrived a day after Sorge had dissolved the Central Committee. Engels was quite upset that Sorge had acted so quickly. "Sorge is a busybody who forgets that correspondence between here and New York takes 3 weeks," Engels complained to his friend Wilhelm Liebknecht. "Had they only waited just 1 day before staging their coup d'etat, they would have had the answer from here, which would have rendered it superfluous." Actually, Sorge knew that he was lucky that the General Council's resolutions did, in fact, arrive belatedly. Had they been received before the fateful November 19 meeting, Sorge probably would have not been able to build support for adjourning the Central Committee sine die.[24]

The leadership crisis in the American International appeared to be over when Sorge's Provisional Federal Council voted to reconvene on December 3 and invited the other sections to send their delegates for the purpose of forming a new "Federal Council." The meeting was scheduled for the customary hour of three o'clock at the usual meeting rooms in the Tenth Ward Hotel, but when the twenty-five delegates representing the majority of the sections in the International entered the room, they discovered a handful of men from Section 1 and the Irish Americans John Devoy and William Nicholson seated around a table already engaged in their deliberations.

The coup had been hatched. Sorge was most candid about his actions in a report to Marx and the General Council. To avoid "a revival of the old Central Committee and a renewal of the struggle with Section 12 & its adherents & supporters," he acknowledged, "we called our meeting at 2 o'clock P.M. with a view of getting some shape of organization,—to obtain which it would have been impossible in an assembly of all the old Delegates." Sorge's nine delegates proceeded to pass the very resolutions that had been blocked in the old Central Committee for the past two months. They moved to bar any section from the International whose membership was composed of less than two-thirds wage laborers, and they elected themselves officers of the new Provisional Federal Council. Just as they concluded nominating a committee to judge delegates' credentials, the majority of delegates arrived.[25]

The newcomers were perplexed at first, then Theodore Millot asked what body was in session. It was, he was told, the Central Committee of the International Workingmen's Association of North America. John Devoy, who had already been appointed chairman, instructed the newly arrived delegates that they could present their credentials to a committee of three that had just been nominated if they desired to take part in the meeting's deliberations. Millot began shouting: "I want somebody to explain how it is that when we come here at three o'clock we find you here already, with the whole business already done—everything cut and dried behind our backs." Devoy, meanwhile, jumped on his chair and attempted to shout Millot down. Others soon joined in the fray. When Sorge moved that the reporters who were present be asked to leave so the delegates could "settle things among our selves," he was hooted down. As curses, threats, and recriminations were hurled across the room, Sorge declared the meeting adjourned and led his forces downstairs to the saloon. Ordered to leave by the proprietor of the hotel (a member of Section 1), the other group moved to the favored bistro of New York's exiled Communards, the "Café Restaurant Internationale."[26]

From that day on, there were two Federal Councils of the International Workingmen's Association in America. Sorge and his forces continued to meet at the Tenth Ward Hotel. The rest set up shop in the spacious rooms of Section 2 on Spring Street. Both Councils stated their terms for reunification, each group's being the negation of the other. Sorge's Tenth Ward Hotel Council set three conditions before they would agree to unite: the International's agenda must be limited to "only the Labor question"; the two-thirds worker rule must be applied to all new sections; and, most importantly, Section 12 and all other sections that were formed on the basis of Section 12's "Appeal" must be expelled from the organization (a condition that would have excluded at least a half dozen sections). For their part, the Spring Street Council demanded only that all sections be admitted on an equal basis.[27]

Sorge, for all his efforts, was left with a shadow of an organization. In his report to the General Council, Sorge claimed the allegiance of twelve sections. Of these, two, Sections 11 and 28, were mere paper organizations set up before the schism to tip the scales in Sorge's favor. Both quickly evaporated as soon as the fight was over. To Sorge's great dismay, the Irish section led by the Fenian exile John Devoy (so strategically vital according to Marx's "Secret Circular") chose to take a neutral position until the General Council ruled definitively on the situation. Another, the Washington, D.C., Section 23 never actually followed Sorge, but its secretiveness and aloofness from the rest of the International enabled him to claim its allegiance nonetheless.

When the dust from his coup had finally cleared, Sorge's Provisional Council consisted in reality of only eight sections, all but one of which conducted their business in German.[28]

The Spring Street Federal Council began its existence in much better shape. In addition to the allegiance of sixteen or so Yankee and Francophone sections, the Yankee International received the support of three German American sections. The most important of these was Section 13, the section composed of the society of German "freethinkers." They published a newspaper, *Die Neue Zeit*, that had the distinction of being the foremost German-language paper in its tenacious defense of women's rights. It even expressed editorial support for Victoria Woodhull. Among the members of this small section of radicals was Augusta Lilienthal, one of the best-known speakers and writers in the cause of women's rights in the German American community. With the *Neue Zeit*, *Woodhull & Claflin's Weekly*, and the French *Socialiste* rallying to their side, the Spring Street Council enjoyed a monopoly on the radical press.[29]

Both Councils publicly claimed to be the sole legitimate representative of the International in America, though both were uncertain of their exact status before the General Council in London. The Yankees, having scoured the rules, regulations, and proceedings of the congresses of the International with a lawyer's eye, felt certain that once London acted upon their case they would be vindicated. For months after the acrimonious confrontation in the Tenth Ward Hotel, *Woodhull & Claflin's Weekly* reprinted column after column of the IWA's official documents to prove their point. It was in support of his section's claims of being true to the spirit and letter of the International that Stephen Pearl Andrews translated Marx's *Communist Manifesto* into English and published it in the *Weekly*—the first American publication of this classic work.[30]

But for all the rules and statutes in their favor, the Yankees lacked an ally on the General Council who could rival Karl Marx at the game of party politics. The Yankees also made the fatal error of sending all of their correspondence to John Hales, the secretary of the Council, rather than to Eccarius, the American secretary. Hales did not pass along their letters to Eccarius, who was their most sympathetic ear in London, but probably gave them to Marx. As a result, while more and more letters arrived from each of the two American factions with each passing week, some to Marx and some to Hales, all bulging with accusations, only those from Sorge's faction were read before the General Council. By the end of February, Engels moved that all the correspondence be referred to the standing subcommittee, chaired by

Eccarius, which was instructed to prepare a report on the matter.[31] However, Karl Marx, suspicious of Eccarius's sympathy toward the Yankees, bypassed the subcommittee altogether and wrote the report himself. He gathered together all of the copies of *Woodhull & Claflin's Weekly* that Sorge had sent him and set about constructing his case against the Yankees. Marx's report, a masterpiece of distortion, had excised all evidence from the record that contradicted his conclusion that Section 12 "almost exclusively consist[ed] of middle-class humbugs and worn-out Yankee swindlers in the Reform business."

Marx began his brief by quoting from Section 12's controversial "Appeal," carefully leaving out anything that alluded to class consciousness, labor, or socialism. Marx jeeringly quoted Section 12 as advocating "the establishment of a Universal Government . . . [and] the abolition of . . . even differences of language." What lay between his ellipses was Section 12's radical proposal for state socialism:

> The proposition involves . . . the establishment of a Universal Government, based primarily on Equality of Rights and Reciprocity of Duties in the matter of Production and Distribution of Wealth, including the abolition of the traffic in land, labor and money—(to say nothing of love, which, if it be made the subject of trade, either with or without the pale of matrimony, is not love, but lust)—and the substitution of the Providential Intervention of the State in place of anarchical competitive rule of self-seeking capitalists. Of course, the abolition of standing armies, national boundaries, secret diplomacy, class distinctions, religious bigotry, and even differences of language are embraced in the program.[32]

Calling Woodhull a "banker's woman, free-lover and general humbug," and the other Yankee sections "riffraff," while accusing the entire Yankee International of existing only for the purpose of "place-hunting," Marx wasted no ammunition in his venomous report. He alleged that Section 12 had claimed the independent right to interpret the rules of the International. Indeed, a resolution had been introduced asserting the right of Section 12 to construe the International's rules however it pleased, but Marx failed to mention that this resolution, proposed by a lone member of Section 12, had been resoundingly voted down.[33]

By drafting the report on Section 12 himself, Marx determined the "facts" with which the rest of the General Council would debate the fate of the Yankees. In short, Marx had already won the battle even before he presented his detailed excoriation of Section 12 to the full Council. The ensuing debate placed the Yankees' defenders, Eccarius and a couple of Englishmen, in the weak position of having to argue for the inclusion of "middle class" sections organized strictly for "electoral purposes" into the IWA. Eccarius took his best shot at Marx and Engels, observing sarcastically that the principle that members must be wage laborers just "might be applied to the General Council." Maltman Barry, a British journalist, also entrapped himself in Marx's "facts" and argued that the International should "absorb such of the middle class that was favourably disposed to our principles."[34]

Marx proposed a series of measures to resolve the situation in America. His first few proposals—that the two Federal Councils in America should reunite until a new central body could be organized at a general congress of American sections and that smaller sections in the same localities should combine—were entirely uncontroversial. Indeed, these proposals were mostly a restatement of the recommendations given to the Americans a few months earlier. But Marx's final set of resolutions, intended to deal with the "problem" of Section 12, provoked opposition on the Council. Repeating his fallacious charge that Section 12 had proclaimed its right to construe the rules of the IWA however it desired and that it "never ceased to make the I.W.A. the vehicle of issues some of which are foreign to, while others are directly opposed to, the aims and purposes of the I.W.A.," Marx recommended that Section 12 be suspended pending action by the upcoming International congress to be held in September of 1872. Moreover, said Marx, as "the social conditions in the United States . . . peculiarly facilitate the intrusion into the International of bogus reformers, middle-class quacks and trading politicians," no new American sections that are not composed of at least two-thirds wage laborers should be allowed to organize. Finally, Marx instructed the Americans not to pursue any "special missions" other than the "common aim" of the International Workingmen's Association, namely, "to emancipate the man of labour from his 'economical subjection to the monopoliser of the means of labour.'"[35]

After these resolutions were passed by a lopsided vote, Eccarius angrily accused Marx of dictatorially bypassing the appropriate committee. Eccarius swore that he would sooner resign as the American secretary than send such resolutions to America. Embittered by Marx's tactics, Eccarius exposed the whole affair to the Yankee Council in New York. He informed them that their reports were never read before the General Council and that others had been "abstracted." At the next meeting of the General Council, Eccarius read a letter from the Yankee Federal Council in America that said that "those who charged [their] Federal Council with using the name of the

Association to propagate extraneous doctrines such as free love, etc., were guilty of misrepresentation."[36]

Marx now concluded that Eccarius, whose loyalty he had begun to question years earlier, had crossed the ideological Rubicon and had now become his foe. Marx knew that he had only to bide his time until the opportunity arose to discipline Eccarius before the Council and thereby remove his most formidable opponent. It took only a month for Marx to receive the evidence he needed from his informants in Section 1. At the General Council's meeting of April 23, 1872, Marx charged Eccarius with refusing to carry out the official decisions of the Council and encouraging rebellion against its authority. Eccarius did not deny the charges, saying only that he had long been dissatisfied in his position as American secretary and wished to resign.

Publicly attacking one of his oldest friends in London was a painful step for Marx and showed the lengths he would go to keep Sorge in charge in America. Engels echoed Marx's position: "Sorge and Co. have . . . made a number of formal blunders, but if the International in America is not to degenerate into a bourgeois tricksters' society pure and simple, they must have our full support." In the end, Marx hoped to clip Eccarius's wings while preserving their friendship. "You must not think that old personal and party friends are or will be less well disposed towards you just because they see it as their duty to oppose your freaks," Marx wrote his old comrade. "Since it is my birthday the day after tomorrow I have absolutely no desire to celebrate it in the unpleasant conviction that I have lost one of my oldest friends and like-minded comrades."[37]

Engels took a harder line and confided to his close friend Wilhelm Liebknecht that he and Marx had come to the conclusion that "Eccarius is mad." Indeed, so blinded were they to the realities of the American situation, that the only comprehensible explanation they could think of for Eccarius's defense of the Yankees was that he had either gone insane or turned completely venal. "You seem to have lost your wits," Marx told Eccarius. Engels proposed an alternative explanation for Eccarius's behavior—greed—and accused him of defending the Yankees because he "had foreseen that the organ of Section 12, *Woodhull & Claflin's Weekly*, might provide him with a new literary refuge." Engels believed they had to act to remove him from office because they could not "stand aside while he turned the International into his own milch cow."[38]

For their part, the Yankees rejected the General Council's resolutions as evidence of Marx's despotism. English-speaking Section 9 drafted a statement denouncing as "extremely arbitrary and contrary to the spirit of justice" the General Council's suspension of Section 12 without giving them an opportunity to respond to the charges. It also condemned the rule mandating that two-thirds of all sections should consist of wage laborers as "a departure from the general rules of the International Workingmen's Association," and they predicted that such a rule would "greatly retard the expansion of the International Workingmen's Association."[39]

Victoria Woodhull accused those who drafted the two-thirds rule of "ignorance . . . regarding our political status." She thought it was absurd to pass a rule that would "exclude almost everybody west of the 'Alleghanies,' as well as fully one half of all laboring people elsewhere in the country, from membership." Woodhull may have derived her figures from the recently published tables of the Census of 1870. Such statistics showed that 48 percent of the population over the age of fifteen had "no recognized occupation for which they receive compensation in the shape of wages or salary, or from which they derive products of a merchantable character." The vast majority of these unrecognized laborers were women engaged in "keeping house." Indeed, so large was this group, by the census's reckoning, that it encompassed one-third of the aggregate adult population. Whereas the total number of adults engaged in all occupations totaled about eleven million, the number of women who kept house totaled nearly seven and one-half million. Given that one-quarter of those who were gainfully employed were farmers and another 5 percent or so were traders and professionals of one sort or another, Woodhull was correct in asserting that the number of women who labored at home roughly equaled the number of men and women who left it each day to work for a wage.[40]

The Yankees' feelings that they had been treated unjustly and that the General Council was being ruled with an iron fist by "Pope" Karl Marx were reinforced by the messages of support they received from Eccarius and John Hales. Hales, who they wrongly believed to be the American secretary, wrote a series of letters in which he confessed that he had voted in the dark: "I must say that I wish I had as deep an insight into your dispute as I have now before the council came to its decision. The report of the Federal council that you belong to has thrown new light upon the subject." In a longer letter, Hales agreed with every one of the Yankees' criticisms of the General Council's actions:

I deeply regret any thing should have arisen to cause divisions. . . . The remarks made about bogus politicians I consider altogether unnecessary, and only calculated to breed ill will. . . . If I understood the platform of the Association, it is quite broad enough to allow a divergence of opinion upon theoretical points, so long as those points are not in antagonism to the general principles. . . . I recognize the right of my fellow-members to be either Atheists or Theists, Spiritualists, Materialists, Free-lovers or Monogamists, as they please, so long as they don't put forward those specialties as doctrines of the International. . . . The general rules say that any person may become a member by declaring adherence to the principles of the Association. Both sexes and all grades are included.[41]

In drafting his resolutions, Marx believed that he was paring the diseased American sections from the healthy core of the organization. But the surgery killed the patient. In suspending Section 12 and alienating the Yankee leadership of the International in America, Marx succeeded only in confirming the worst fears of American radicals. No ideals stood closer to the beating heart of Yankee radicalism than did the broad concepts of liberty and democracy. Marx and the General Council, by summarily condemning Section 12 and unconditionally supporting Sorge's blatant grab for power, had made the London Council appear to be under the thumb of his own dictates and, by implication, the entire International to be tyrannical. These were precisely the charges leveled against the IWA during the Paris Commune by the establishment presses of the world. Now, in many American radicals' eyes, these charges appeared to have been substantiated. William West pointed out the difference between the organization he had joined and worked so hard to build up and the one that had just revealed its darker side: "Yesterday, any Section might take the initiative; speech was free and the press was free. The way to equality was through liberty. To-day nothing must be thought or spoken, or written or printed, and nothing must be done without permission of the power ruling the deliberations of the G.C."[42]

Whereas a year earlier the International's stock had soared among American radicals by its association with the republican spirit of the Paris Commune, it now sank even more rapidly under accusations of despotism and intolerance. Because of the well-publicized fight between the Yankee International and London, the tremendous gains that had been made by the Spring Street Council in recruiting new members came to an abrupt halt. As one reporter observed, "The society at present is like a ship that lost its masts." In the five months after Sorge's coup in December, the English-speaking Federal Council had added over twenty sections to its rolls. After the General Council's censure of the Spring Street Council and Section 12 was publicized in April and May, the growth of the Yankee International was halted in its tracks. Not a single new section was organized between May and August. By the end of the summer of 1872, with their numbers dwindling, the desperate Yankees attempted to replicate the success of their "Appeal" of the previous year by printing up five thousand pamphlets addressed "to the working men and women in the United States." But unlike the earlier "Appeal," whose tone exuded confidence and energy, this one was dispirited and defensive. At one point it stooped to plead: "Let no rumor of divisions existing among us deter any who would otherwise organize from so doing. . . . Whatever divisions there may be in our midst will be transient in their nature and duration." In fact, though it took a few months for the fact to become evident to all, the dispute with the General Council had fatally crippled the Yankee International.[43]

Yankee radicals simply had no good reason to join an organization that was torn by faction and treachery. Dr. A. Orvis, a man who had early in 1872 attempted to organize a section of the Yankee International in his hometown of Rochester, New York, wrote a letter of support to Woodhull after her paper had carried news of Marx's resolutions. "If your branch is suspended because you are prominent in it," Orvis said, "it will be sufficient reason for me to abstain from taking any part" in the International. Orvis then offered a theory of his own to explain London's actions, one that echoed his own native radical commitment to women's equality: "I have not much doubt but the action had at London has been because of your prominence as a woman in it, which, if you had been a man, would have not been noticed." "I do not propose," Orvis declared, "to give any support to any organization which by its action, whether directly or indirectly, strikes at woman." That this reaction was a common one among American radicals more than accounts for the collapse of what was a promising and thriving organization.[44]

By the summer of 1872, the Spring Street Council gave up any hope of moving the General Council to reconsider its resolutions and instead voted to disassociate itself from London. Several "stirring speeches" denouncing the General Council were given in the course of their regular weekly meetings. "The tenor of their remarks," according to one journalist present, "was that, owing to the different forms of governments in Europe, and their manner of doing things in general being quite different from that of this country, it would not be reasonable to suppose that laws framed for the ruling of the association in Europe would at all answer for the people of this country." In a resolution that accused the General Council of having "usurped the power vested in them" and having "disorganized" the IWA in America, the Spring Street Council declared that it no longer recognized its authority.[45]

But the Yankee Council had not yet given up entirely on its European parent. A couple of weeks later it voted to send three delegates to the upcoming International congress at the Hague. Of the three chosen, only one, William West, actually journeyed to Holland and entered the raucous hall where the fate of the International Workingmen's Association was decided.

The International congress at the Hague was the most important convention in the history of the First International. Owing to the upheaval and disarray wreaked by the Franco-Prussian War and the Paris Commune, no official congress had been held in 1871. For two years the disputes and conflicts that had begun to crack apart the organization had gone unresolved. All the various factions looked to the upcoming congress with the highest expectations, and all sides knew that either the ideological conflicts and schisms would be settled at the Hague or the organization would finally fall to pieces.

No one was more aware of the importance of the Hague Congress than Karl Marx. (It was the only IWA congress that he or Engels ever attended.) Marx had spent the last year fighting against his archrival Mikhail Bakunin, the Russian anarchist whose leadership abilities and political skills matched those of Marx himself. While the International grew in France and Germany, Bakunin organized the rival Alliance of Socialist Democracy in Italy, Spain, and Switzerland. In 1869, Bakunin struck a deal with Marx and disbanded the Alliance in exchange for the merger of all of its branches into the IWA. It was not long before both leaders accused each other having broken their promises and of attempting to seize complete control of the International. Both men's suspicions became self-fulfilling prophesies as each took measures to counter the threat of the other: Marx secured a change in the constitution of the International that lent the General Council more power over the branches, while Bakuninist elements, most notably in Switzerland, declared their autonomy from London.[46]

Marx began to consider Bakunin a serious threat when, in 1871 and early 1872, Bakunin's influence, especially in southern Europe, seemed to soar. The leadership of Italy's fast-growing International was strongly influenced by Bakunin's thought. Bakuninists also made great advances within the new International sections that had sprung up in Spain. By the early summer of 1872, Marx was determined to rule or ruin the organization he had devoted eight years to building up. "At this Congress the life or death of the International will be at stake," he wrote Sorge in June.[47]

Marx and Engels used every weapon and trick they could to slant the battlefield of the upcoming congress to their favor. They won the selection of a congress site in Northern Europe so as to make it easier for their partisans to attend and more costly for those in Bakunin's southern strongholds. They did what they could to pack the congress with their own delegates: Engels underwrote the expenses for the loyal delegates from the General Council and Marx secured a fistful of phony credentials from Sorge in New York for his friends in Europe. He instructed his German comrade Kugelmann to send "as many representatives as possible." Together, so as to sow discord among their opponents, Marx and Engels penned a flurry of articles filled with accusations and revelations against their opponents and had them published in loyal journals on the eve of the conference. After finishing one of these, Engels boasted: "We shall be launching a bombshell . . . which will cause no small panic among the Bakuninists." [48]

Marx and Engels knew that the single most important task at the convention was to dominate the committee on credentials. Whoever controlled that committee would carry the day. "Everything depends [upon how] the mandates are scrutinised," Engels confided to his friend Johann Becker. A favorable judgment on the delegates' credentials (mandates) was essential since Marx and Engels had spent months arranging them, both genuine and bogus, for their trustworthy allies around Europe. Sorge was essential in this effort because he claimed to lead over twenty sections, each of which had the right to send a delegate to the congress. Since many of these sections barely functioned and others were fictitious, Sorge simply paid up the dues out of his own pocket and filled out the sections' mandates on Marx's orders. Indeed, when Sorge arrived in London he carried with him three blank mandates, just "in case of need," as he put it. Another leader of Sorge's Section 1, Carl Speyer, also sent Marx bogus mandates. In a letter accompanying these official papers, Speyer confided in Marx: "I admit to you that I did it only by way of precaution. . . . I was and am still today in favour of making out these mandates because I know by experience that the enormous sacrifices a Congress costs can only bear fruit if the German element is sufficiently represented." These services were invaluable to Marx because collecting such open-ended mandates from Europe proved far more difficult. Another of Marx and Engels's agents, Adolf Hepner of Leipzig, tried to secure blank mandates but could not. "It is impossible for me to get blank mandates," he explained, "because when you suggest to people to make them out, they consider the International a 'swindle.' " [49]

Marx and Engels had no intention of allowing the Yankees to be given a seat and a vote at this all-important congress. Engels warned his comrade that three delegates had been sent by the Woodhull faction from America, and, referring to Harriet Burton of Yankee Section 12, added the snide remark that they "includ[ed] a petticoat." Sorge boasted in one of his last letters to Marx before he departed for London, "If our opponents here really do send delegates to the Congress, we shall send them packing."[50]

William West arrived in London with a week to spare before the opening of the congress. He was put up at the home of George Harris, an old Chartist and a member of the General Council since its inception. West accompanied Harris to a meeting of the Council, where he sat quietly and observed the proceedings. After a number of items of business had been dispensed with, another British delegate, Martin Boon (whom West knew as the founder of the Land and Labour League), took the floor and introduced West to the dozen men in the room. It is not recorded who raised the first objection to West's presence (both Marx and Engels were in attendance that night), but once his identity was known, he was summarily expelled from the room.[51] Undeterred, a few days later, West walked across London to Marx's townhouse at 1 Maitland Park Road and knocked at the door. He had the idea that, perhaps, if only he could explain things in person, he could make Marx understand the American situation. But, this was not to be; Karl Marx refused to let him in.[52]

As predicted by all, the Hague Congress proved less a convention of those pursuing a common goal than a contest between irreconcilable enemies. During the five days that the congress was in session, nearly three were devoted to verifying the credentials of the delegates. The very last mandate to be considered was that of William West for Section 12. Speaking in a monotone and pausing occasionally to adjust the monocle that had the annoying habit of slipping from his eye, Marx read the report of the credentials committee. The charges Marx leveled against West were variations on a single theme and revolved around his association with Section 12 and Victoria Woodhull. West's credentials, Marx noted (according to Engels's notes of the meeting), "are signed by Victoria Woodhull, who for years has had an eye on the presidency; she is president of the spiritists, preaches free love, has a banking business, etc." And as if that were not enough, Marx added to Section 12's sins the charge that it was composed of bourgeoisie and "it agitated especially for the women's franchise." He cited Section 12's "Appeal" as the principal evidence of their apostasy: "Among other things in it there was talk of personal liberty, social liberty (free love), dress regulation, women's franchise, universal language, etc." They should be expelled from the International Workingmen's Association, demanded Marx, because "they give precedence to the women's question over the question of labor and take exception to the assumption that the I.W.A. is a workingmen's organization."[53]

West, knowing that his situation was hopeless before Marx's handpicked delegates, used his one opportunity to harangue the congress for nearly an hour and a half. West recounted the underhanded and unjust way his section was suspended by the General Council. He denied that Section 12 ever took up issues foreign to the program of the IWA. "The labor question," railed West, "is also a woman's question." In response to charges that Section 12 advocated Spiritualism and free love, West pointed out that these were not official policies of the section but the private beliefs of some of its members. What right had they to dictate the religious opinions of their members? he asked. "Woodhull and others are spiritists and free lovers! Can you forbid it? . . . [It] is none of your business." [54]

When West was finished, Sorge took his turn, though this time he tellingly broadened his condemnations against Section 12 to encompass Yankees in general. He began by repeating the tired charge that the members of Section 12 were bourgeois, but he felt he needed to explain to everyone why this was especially troublesome in America. According to Eccarius, who reported the proceedings for the London *Times*, Sorge elaborated: "The great bulk of the workpeople in America were Irish; then came the Germans, then the niggers. The natives did not work; they were speculators, making profit out of other people's labour. It was no use combining with them; they formed only a small part of the population. The great point was to get the Irish into the society, and they would not come as long as people of the sort of Section 12 were in the Association." [55]

Once again, Marx's old Irish strategy came to the surface in Sorge's defense of his coup and his exclusion of native-born Americans. Here, in starkest form, Sorge laid bare the myopic view of the American working class that would hobble American socialism for the next fifty years. Particularly tragic and debilitating was his dismissal of African Americans as a valuable working-class constituency. Not until the Great Depression of the 1930s would the American Left begin to rectify this mistake.

Even accepting the logic of his argument, Sorge's figures were hopelessly out of touch with reality. According to the 1870 census, there were 1.8 million native-born Americans working in the manufacturing and mining industries alone, nearly six times the number of foreign-born Germans and nearly seven times the number of foreign-born Irish. Even in the most unskilled categories of "laborer" and "mechanic," the jobs held by the greatest proportion of new immigrants, native-born workers outnumbered the Irish by two and one-half to one and the Germans by six to one. (Such large differences are reduced significantly, though not eliminated, if the native-born children of immigrant parents are included.) As for African Americans, they numbered a million more than the immigrant Germans and Irish put together. The vast majority were agriculturists, but they were an army of the dispossessed: sharecroppers and laborers. The one place in the nation that resembled Sorge's social typography was his own New York. If the Left ever was to have been a national force, Sorge's narrow understanding of the American working class had to have been abandoned.[56]

When the question of West's mandate finally came to a general ballot, there was no contest: West had no supporters left in the room. Eccarius was there, but he chose not to vote on the issue because he remained the subject of the General Council's investigation of his own conduct as American secretary. John Hales, who had written sympathetically to members of the Spring Street Council in the preceding months, had already left the congress in disgust and returned to England, where he organized the breakaway Universal Federal Council of the International Workingmen's Association. Thomas Mottershead, an English weaver and General Council member who was reported to have "not sobered up since he arrived" by a member who encountered him "on a bridge over a canal which he seemed to be trying to fill," could hardly have been expected to find the courage to cast the only dissenting vote. In the end, nine delegates abstained and none voted against expelling the Yankees from the International.[57]

Harriet Law, a British feminist, republican, freethinker, and former member of the General Council, was the one person who might have had the temerity to defend West but for some mysterious reason was unable to attend or was prevented from attending the congress. Law had been elected to represent the Central Section of Working Women of Geneva at the congress, and though she never made it onto the floor of the convention, her mandate was quite explicit and spoke to some of the questions raised by the Yankee International.

Geneva's Internationalist women vigorously opposed the family wage concept that Sorge and his fellow Marxists embraced in America. Arguing that "the working woman's needs are equal to those of the working man [though] . . . the pay for her work is much less," they directed Harriet Law to introduce a resolution demanding that all labor agreements include provisions for "equal advantages" for women. Being in the minority on such issues led these women to call for tolerance within the IWA. As much as West and the Yankees in New York did, the working women of Geneva believed that in diversity there is strength "The more different groups of opinion there are on the ways of achieving the same aim, *the emancipation of labour*," the Swiss women asserted, "the easier it is to generalise the working-class movement without losing any of the forces (even the most widely diverging) to concur in the final result." Toward this end, Law was instructed to work for passage of a rule that echoed West's own defense of his fellow Yankees. They demanded that the General Council should "not have the power to reject any section, whatever particular purpose it proposes, whatever its principles, provided that purpose and principles are not capable of harming those of the [IWA]." Had Law shown up at the Hague Congress, she certainly would have been one of West's staunchest supporters, though she probably would have suffered the same fate. The one representative from Geneva who did attend, the Russian anarchist Nikolai Zhukovsky, was exiled to the observer's balcony by Marx's credentials committee.[58]

West stayed until the bitter end of the Hague Congress—long enough to witness the vote that transferred the seat of the International from London to New York. Marx had a multitude of reasons for wanting to move the party headquarters. Most of the original British members of the General Council had resigned, and a few of the most active, such as Eccarius and Hales, were now organizing a rival party. The Frenchmen in the General Council increasingly challenged Marx's authority, and Marx himself longed to retire from politics and complete the last volumes of *Das Kapital*. Now that he had found a faithful lieutenant in Sorge, a man who had proven his loyalty throughout this crucial congress by securing mandates and fighting dissenters at every turn, he could sleep safely in the knowledge that the IWA, though exiled from its native European soil, would preserve its hard-won ideological purity in the New World.[59]

When the congress adjourned, West began his long journey home. He was nearly penniless, having traveled this far on a one-way steerage ticket and twenty-five dollars. He was, after all, an old, poor man whose life had been spent variously as a tinsmith and street policeman, neither occupation known at the time for its generous remuneration. Section 12's Colonel Blood had promised to send him passage home, but because of the persecution of their newspaper under the federal obscenity statute (the so-called Comstock Law) and other legal battles, the Woodhull clique's fortunes had evaporated. With help from his friend George Harris, West made it back to London. He knew he could not stay there long, for as he wrote home, his British friends were "almost as poor as I am." Finally, throwing himself at the mercy of General R. C. Schenck, the American consul in London (and after lecturing him on how the pilgrims were the first American communists), West was lent the sum of eight pounds to purchase his ticket home. Engels later wrote Sorge that West's predicaments "amused us greatly."[60]

Sorge returned to America with the remains of the International in his steamer trunk. Entrusted with the minute books and seals of the party, Sorge was soon to be its general secretary, and the seat of the IWA was now to be in New York. Having achieved the purification of the International in both Europe and the United States, Marx and Sorge convinced themselves that the future of the eviscerated party was bright. Other insightful observers saw things more clearly. Sergei Andreyevich Podolinsky, a young Russian revolutionary who observed the proceedings of the Hague Congress, recognized immediately that Marx and Engels had chosen to fight to win, even though the fight itself would destroy the spoils of victory:

> In principle, though with concessions, Marx has won, but I am astonished that such an intelligent man as he could attach so much importance to the external side of victory when it was already clear from all facts that public opinion was inclined towards the other side. . . . He would have done better if he had yielded where, as he himself saw, he could only achieve a purely formal result in spite of all his endeavors. At least he would have left the stage with honour if he had remained with equal rights with the others, whereas now he is subjected to a shower of accusations, partly just.[61]

Podolinsky's observations were borne out by the rapid defections from the IWA that followed the Hague Congress. Even Cyrenus Osborne Ward, the only "Yankee" to attend the Tenth Ward Hotel's congress earlier that summer, and the only native American to be chosen by the Hague Congress to sit on the new General Council in New York, declined his appointment and denounced the entire congress as a "sham" that was orchestrated by a "ring" that violated the IWA's own federal principle of the autonomy of the section.[62]

KARL MARX never understood the Yankees or fully grasped the situation in America. Marx took his cues on America from Sorge, a man whom Podolinsky described as "plus marxiste que Marx" (more Marxist than Marx). Sorge's misunderstandings and slanders became Marx's own. Once he had determined that the Yankees were an impediment to the recruitment of trade unionists or Irish workers, Marx willfully overlooked the points of agreement between the Yankee's socialism and his own. It has been said that

Marxism was the culmination of one intellectual trend of the Enlightenment — the idea that social reality can be rationally analyzed as a science. Once armed with a proper understanding of society, Marx believed, the philosopher could formulate a strategy that, if acted upon, would move history from one point to the next. Assured of the correctness of their own myopic analysis of the American social context, Marx and Sorge believed that theirs was the only true path to socialist salvation. In the final analysis, reason ultimately failed them.[63]

To the Yankees, a priori social analysis was not a final blueprint for action but a guide to judge action incrementally as it was undertaken. By judging society, and their own actions against their Yankee code of morality — an inaccurate and variable yardstick of equality, justice, fairness, and truth — the Yankees adopted a more pragmatic approach. Lacking their unifying structures of reason, they could not understand Marx and Sorge's acts as anything but despotism and intolerance.

Had Marx been willing to understand the Yankees on their own terms, he might have found much upon which they could have agreed. Just days after the last gavel rapped the Hague Congress to a close, Marx traveled to Amsterdam and there delivered an address to the local section of the IWA. Before the small and adoring crowd, Marx defended the International against charges that it was a violent organization and, ironically, spoke up for the very republican principle that the Yankees held most dear. As one reporter noted, "The speaker defended the use of force when other means produce no result. Barricades are not necessary in North America because there the proletarians can, if they want, achieve victory through elections. The same applies to England and some other countries where the working class enjoys freedom of speech." This was an echo of the younger Marx speaking, the Marx who before the defeats of 1848 had seen democracy as a progressive force. This was the Marx with whom William West and the rest of Yankee International could have clasped hands, and whose ideas might have found fertile ground in republican America. But it was not to be.[64]

The Yankee International remained active for several years after suffering defeat at the Hague Congress. Though its members survived their long battle with their German American Marxist rivals, they emerged from this struggle a different organization. When William West arrived back in New York in the fall of 1872, he found the association he had so strenuously built up in tatters. The Spring Street Council could not attract enough members to its meetings to make its quorum. Boston's sections no longer met because, as the Boston labor press surmised, "the dissensions in London and New York have probably demoralized the movement here." Two of the Yankee International's most active leaders, John Elliot and Marie Huleck, resigned and left New York for points west. The Yankee's most famous members, Victoria Woodhull and Tennessee Claflin, were jailed and their newspaper shut down that November while they awaited trial on charges of publishing obscenities.[65]

In the face of these disasters the Spring Street Council showed signs of desperation. In the spring of 1873, the Yankees unanimously appointed the eccentric entrepreneur, Irish nationalist, and viciously racist Democrat George Francis Train to a seat on the Council. Long a gadfly on the margins of various reform movements, Train earned his popularity among reformers by virtue of his frequent and sizable donations. In 1867 he took up the cause of women's suffrage, supporting several projects of Susan B. Anthony and Elizabeth Cady Stanton. Later, Train underwrote the initial expenses of publishing Anthony's newspaper, *The Revolution*.[66] While the Yankee International was vigorous and growing, collaboration with a notorious figure like Train was out of the question. For example, in December of 1871, the Spring Street Federal Council received a letter from Train offering to speak at a mass demonstration and pointing out that after his fee they should net around nine hundred dollars. Train's offer was greeted with "much laughter" and quickly tabled. Two years later, however, after the Yankee International had suffered rejection by the Hague Congress and the precipitous decline of its membership and support in America, the Spring Street Yankees elected Train an honorary delegate to their Council. But Train apparently took no interest in this honor because he never came to a meeting.[67]

Philadelphia's Section 26 was but one branch of the International that survived the expulsion of the Spring Street Council without losing its radical momentum. Even though a few members were dropped from the rolls over the winter for nonpayment of dues, others continued to join, and the group made big plans for the future. A "committee on propaganda" was established to distribute throughout all the wards in the city short tracts of the principles of the IWA. Five thousand copies of "Papers for the People No. 1," a broadside that appealed to both "producers of wealth and you who have wealth that others have produced" to join the IWA and abolish "the systematized injustice" of a "system of society that gives to the masses excessive toil and excessive poverty and to the few leisure and wealth." Though the group was falling behind on the rent on its large meeting hall, for reasons of prestige they decided to keep it rather than move to smaller and cheaper quarters. The section even laid plans for hosting a world congress of the International during Philadelphia's Centennial Exposition commemorating the anniversary of the founding of the United States, which was to be held three years hence. Apparently, the distance of Philadelphia's radicals from the factional infighting in New York helped to preserve their optimism.[68]

But although Philadelphia's Yankee section retained some vitality and New York's sections persevered in spite of dwindling numbers and a lack of support from the city's labor movement, the Yankee International never recovered from the final rejection of the General Council and the International's Hague Congress. The Spring Street Council formally affiliated with the autonomous British Universal Federal Council, but the British body also languished. Though it limped along for another two years, occasionally rallying to again frighten the editors of the conservative press with the specter of the Paris Commune, the Yankee International, as a potential force in American politics and as a link connecting the American Left to older native American reform movements, was dead.

CHAPTER SEVEN

Race and Class in the Two Internationals

ROM THAT DAY in December 1871 when German American, Franco-American, and Yankee radicals nearly came to blows at the Tenth Ward Hotel until nearly four years later, there were two Internationals in the United States. One, Friedrich Sorge's "Tenth Ward Hotel" faction, was extraordinarily loyal to its intellectual and political leader, Karl Marx, and it became the institutional embodiment of Marxism in America and the foundation upon which the American Left was built. The other International, consisting of Yankees and their cosmopolitan allies who gathered at their hall on Spring Street, was the fleeting confluence of many streams of American radicalism. This hodgepodge of ideological remnants from a myriad of antebellum reform crusades was bound together by an egalitarian republicanism reinvigorated by a war of emancipation and the looming oppressions of industrial society.

Though it had but a brief independent existence, the Yankee International expressed the possibilities inherent in the rooting of socialist thought in the American reform tradition. Where it chose to struggle, what it struggled for, and whom it chose to recruit into its ranks, all expressed the values that it had inherited from this tradition. Some of the legacies handed down to it from the American reform tradition, such as the producer ethic and Free-Soil demands, meshed well with socialist principles and goals. But the Yankees' concern for republicanism and civil equality, both for women and racial minorities, departed from the direction that Marx, Sorge, and the German American International were pulling American socialism. In the measure of the distance between these two groups of radicals on such issues rested the future character of the American Left.

IN CONTRAST TO their public repudiation of women's political rights, German American Marxists never renounced their devotion to the principle of racial equality. Instead, the history of the immigrant Marxists' policies on race traced the rising and falling arc of concern drawn by the mainstream labor movement. German American radicals were in the forefront of racial tolerance before the war. In 1858, the Communist Club of New York expressed the common republican ideals of German Forty-Eighters and unanimously declared that they recognized "no distinction as to nationality or race, caste or status, color or sex." A decade later, when New York's communists organized under the banner of the Social Party, one of their seven principle demands was for the immediate repeal of "all laws in contravention to the perfect equality of men regardless of color, sex or religious belief." But as did their republican ideals in general, such sentiments faded in importance as the "scientific" strategies of Marxism took hold of New York's circle of German American radicals. For Marxism taught them that such ideals were just so many pretty wishes and that historical change was only brought about through hardheaded analysis and the class struggle that it directed. When Sorge and his comrades embraced the Marxist organizing strategies that placed their highest priority upon fostering trade unions among Irish and German workers, they soon came to believe that their principles of egalitarian internationalism conflicted with their goal of building and leading America's nascent trade union movement.

This contradiction between the socialists' racially egalitarian principles and the trade union movement did not become apparent in the early years of the International Workingmen's Association in America. Rather, for a brief time in the late 1860s, it seemed that the American trade union movement was itself on the verge of adopting an interracial organizing strategy. The National Labor Unions's overtures to black workers, the egalitarian pronouncements of labor reform conventions, and the labor presses' editorial support for the goal of an integrated labor movement, all combined to create the impression among many reformers that the traditionally ethnically, sexually, and racially exclusive labor movement had begun to open its doors to all workers. By delaying the time when it became obvious that the principles of racial brotherhood conflicted with the immediate goals of the growing trade union movement, the labor movement's brief flirtation with interracial organizing served to accommodate socialists to the trade union strategy. When, in the years after 1870, it became clear that the largest trade unions had rejected the idea of integrating the labor movement, Sorge and the other German American socialists followed suit and quietly turned their backs on the black worker.

Just as the ideology of American Marxism at this time was strained by the tension between ideals and tactics, America's trade unions struggled with a similar conflict between the "producer ethic" that had informed a wider working-class identity since colonial times, and the narrow, exclusionary practice that resulted from organizing along lines of skill and occupation. Whereas the older producerist tradition upheld politics as an important avenue for workingmen to protect their trades and communities, the newer breed of trade unionist, which was just beginning to make his appearance in the late 1860s, rejected broader political goals in favor of immediate economic ends. These ideological conflicts found expression in the great labor reform alliances, such as the eight-hour leagues, the labor reform parties, and the National Labor Union, that were formed between trade unions and traditional reform communities of abolitionists and feminists. Within these allied labor reform organizations the question of the role of African American and Chinese workers, and of women, demarcated the line between the older ideology of producerist labor reformers and the newer thought of exclusionist unionists.[1]

The victory of Union arms and the emancipation of the slaves brought the question of the status of the black worker to the fore of labor's agenda. Many of labor's most influential leaders — including William Sylvis, president of the Iron Molders' International Union, Richard Trevellick, president of the Ship Carpenters' Union, and Andrew Cameron, editor of the foremost labor paper of the day, the *Workingman's Advocate* — all attempted to reconcile the trade union movement with the traditional producerist ideologies of the antebellum era. Most importantly, these leaders attempted to convince the nascent trade union movement that the question of freed black workers could not be resolved by simply excluding them from trade unions.[2]

Andrew Cameron spoke for all of these labor reformers in the report he drafted on Negro labor for the National Labor Union's inaugural convention held in 1866. The war had irrevocably altered the position of the black worker, Cameron pointed out, and labor had to adjust to the new realities brought about by this fact. Citing the example of a recent strike of ship-caulkers in Boston that was broken by the importation of black caulkers from Virginia, Cameron warned that if black workers were not assimilated into the labor movement, they would surely become a source of weakness to it. Appealing to the producerist philosophy, Cameron reminded his "fellow toilers," "The interests of labor are one; . . . there should be no distinction of race or nationality. . . . There is only one dividing line — that which separates mankind into two great classes, the class that labors and the class that lives by other's labors." Finally, and perhaps most importantly, Cameron observed that the black population numbered over four million and that "a greater proportion of them labor with their hands than can be counted from among the same number of any other people on earth." Soon these millions of workers would wield the ballot, and since their voting strength "would be of incalculable value to the cause of labor," Cameron wondered, "can we afford to reject their proffered co-operation and make them enemies?" William Sylvis stated the same case even more bluntly before the New York State Workingmen's Assembly. "There is no concealing the fact that the time will come when the Negro will take possession of the shops," warned Sylvis, "if we do not take possession of the negro. If the workingmen of the white race do not conciliate the blacks, the black vote will be cast against them."[3]

However, such arguments were compelling only to those workers who shared these labor leaders' faith in political action and their willingness to view blacks as fellow producers and toilers. Sylvis, Cameron, and the others faced an uphill struggle against the prejudices of the average working man and the success of the exclusionary trade union model. Against the concerted effort of Sylvis, Trevellick, and even J. C. C. Whaley, president of the NLU, delegates from national trade bodies at the NLU's 1867 convention (especially the carpenters and the coachmakers) succeeded in tabling a proposal to organize a trade union among black workers. At this point the NLU was clearly split between a leadership that favored inclusion and a rank and file that viewed the African American worker as a threat that could be overcome through the usual trade union practices.[4]

Unable to pass a resolution affirming the goal of organizing black labor at the 1868 annual convention, president Whaley and Andrew Cameron appealed to black workers directly on behalf of the NLU's permanent executive committee, which they dominated. "We earnestly ask the cooperation of the whole people, white and black, male and female," they wrote, "to unite with and assist us . . . knowing, as we do, that the industrial prosperity of the nation interests alike all the people." This invitation came at a crucial time: in that same year African American workers assembled in many localities and states to consider ways of bettering their political and economic position. A few months after Whaley and Cameron issued their call to black workers, a general congress, also called the NLU, attracting over 160 black delegates, convened in Washington, D.C.[5]

Although black workers voiced many concerns and made many proposals at the their numerous conventions and less-formal gatherings in these years, the demand for an end to the pervasive practice of racial discrimination in employment was their most insistent plea. The question at the center of debate was how to overcome these racial barriers. Some believed that it was futile to demand inclusion in racist unions and hoped that either independent black labor organizations or a prosperous black cooperative movement could bypass these fraternities altogether. Others saw more clearly that as long as unions were organized by race, most avenues of economic advancement would remain blocked. In the end, the black NLU advocated that black workers pursue all these approaches simultaneously. Black workers were encouraged by their labor leaders to try to overcome their exclusion from white trade unions peacefully. But, believing that "although white mechanics may refuse you work with them . . . those who buy or employ labor, will be governed more by self-interest than by the power of Trades Unions," labor leaders also urged them to "negotiate with bankers and capitalists to furnish money in aid of the establishment of co-operative enterprises" and to form "separate associations" of trades to negotiate directly with employers.[6]

As a first step toward interracial organization, the black National Labor Union appointed nine black leaders to attend and demand recognition from the white National Labor Union convention held in Philadelphia in August 1869. The NLU convention cordially received the black delegates and adopted a resolution declaring that "the National Labor Union knows no north, no south, no east, no west, neither color nor sex, on the question of the rights of labor." But the white unionists of the NLU made it clear that the they were not interested in integration. No statement was made condemning the exclusion of black workers from white unions. Rather, the NLU compromised on a model of trade union segregation and called on black workers to form separate organizations.[7]

New York's German American Marxists followed the lead of the NLU and offered their support to New York's black workers in their efforts to organize unions. A few months after the Philadelphia congress of 1869, the IWA's Siegfried Meyer represented the General German Labor Union (the parent organization to Section 1 of the IWA) at a meeting of black workers held to nominate delegates to an upcoming black National Labor Convention. Going beyond the NLU's position, Meyer offered not only the GGLU's aid in forming black unions but, reportedly, also assistance in "obtaining admission to existing organizations." Within a few months a black union of some ninety members had been formed and with the help of the GGLU had gained admittance into the New York Workingmen's Union, the central council of New York's trade unions.[8]

Siegfried Meyer and his fellow German American radicals extended their hands to New York's black community during the brief time that the National Labor Union displayed interracial amity. Within the same year, however, the hopes of black workers that the labor movement might be persuaded to include them as equal members were dashed upon the rocks of prejudice and partisan politics. When the delegates to the National Labor Union met again in Cincinnati in 1870, the white majority refused to seat a prominent black delegate. Black NLU activist John M. Langston, who was inspector general of the Freedman's Bureau and dean of the law school of Howard University, was excluded on the grounds that he was an "office-holder" and a "politician" who "endeavored to use the colored laboring men in the interests of the Republican Party."[9]

Even if this rule were legitimate, it was clearly one unevenly applied: that same day, an even more prominent "politician," ex-congressman Samuel F. Cary of Ohio, was admitted to the convention "amid flattering applause." While Langston was but a political appointee, Cary had been elected to Congress in 1866 and, though gaining his seat as an independent, had an extremely consistent record of voting with the Democrats, who came to consider him one of their own. The handful of African American delegates present found Cary's enthusiastic reception all the more galling because Cary had shown himself especially hostile to black interests during his congressional career. Besides voting against Andrew Johnson's impeachment, Cary opposed both the Supplemental Reconstruction Act and the Fifteenth Amendment to the Constitution. Cary's quiet alliance with the Democrats soon broke into the open—his name was to be found on the Democratic ticket in 1875 as a candidate for lieutenant governor of Ohio. Allen Coffin, a printer and a delegate to the black NLU congress earlier that year, pointed out the hypocrisy of the situation and charged the white delegates with acting out of racial prejudice. "The real objection to Mr. Langston," railed Coffin, "was that the blood of Africa flowed in his veins!" [10]

The NLU's refusal to seat John Langston highlighted the fundamental gulf that separated white and black workers' views of politics. On one level there was the obvious political conflict between white workers, who generally supported the Democratic Party, and black workers, who were even more loyal to the Republicans. But on a deeper level, there was a serious misunderstanding between black workers and the labor reformers who rejected both established political parties, because they either favored an independent political course for workers or, like Sorge, rejected political action altogether. These white labor reformers could not understand that black workers' support for the Republican Party was the natural extension of their labor activities. Black workers clearly understood that their ability to rise economically depended upon the protection of their rights in civil society, especially the right to vote. The Republican Party, though increasingly dominated by Northern capitalists and merchants, was the only political force on the horizon that was willing and able to deliver such crucial legal reforms. As William F. Powell, one of New York's most important black spokesmen, observed, "What we most need (next to plenty of work) in New York, as well as in the Northern States, is the elective franchise. Figuratively speaking, it *lubricates* the corroded hinges upon which swings the portals of the temple of industry, comparatively closed against the colored man's right to labor, and which can only be opened by the *Talismanic* word of two syllables, viz: *The Ballot*." [11]

These essential political differences between black and white workers proved the downfall of the NLU's tentative attempts at forging an interracial movement of workers. One of the most debated topics at the 1870 congress was the question of forming an independent political party of workers. Black workers had already had a bitter preview of what an independent labor party might look like during the congressional tenure of Samuel Cary, the man who was known as "labor's congressman." They certainly would not cooperate with white workers to elect more copperheads in mechanics' garb. But the question of an independent labor party was especially disruptive to the coalition of black and white workers since the idea of a third party of labor was most popular among those very reform-minded leaders of the NLU who had shown the greatest courage in crossing the racial divide. Now black workers not only stood in opposition to the exclusionist trade union delegates but also found themselves at odds with their closest white allies. When the NLU congress voted decisively to found the National Labor Reform Party, what little reason black workers had to stay within the NLU evaporated. Though the NLU struggled through another four annual conventions, never again would a black delegate attend.[12]

With the collapse of the best attempt at interracial organization on a national level, those labor reformers favoring the organization of black workers were gradually supplanted by the trade unionists who represented a movement where policies of racial discrimination were nearly universal. Throughout the 1860s, of the thirty-two-odd national and local trade unions then in existence, not one admitted blacks. Just a few months after the adjournment of the NLU congress, the Cigarmakers International Union convened in Syracuse, New York, and upheld its restrictive constitutional clause that limited membership to "white practical cigar-maker[s]." The Carpenters and Joiners National Union went on record against the admission of blacks, following the lead of its New York local that had earlier inserted the word "white" into its constitution. In 1870, the International Typographical Union, one of the nation's largest trade associations, voted to allow local unions the option to exclude black workers. Similarly, at the Bricklayers National Union convention in January of 1871, some of the strongest opposition to the admission of black workers came from the two delegates from New York, and the bricklayers voted to allow locals the option to discriminate.[13]

After 1870, the National Labor Union lost much of its craft following and ceased to be representative of the trade union movement. And no one was more aware of this than those Marxists who pinned their millennial hopes on the growth and radicalization of trade unions. Friedrich Sorge reported to Marx in the spring of 1871 that "the National Labor Union is losing ground amongst the great National and International Trades Unions of this country. The Workingmen's Assembly of New York . . . The Cigarmakers International Union, the Bricklayers National Union etc. all refusing at their last conventions to appoint delegates to the next labor Congress in St. Louis."[14]

Over the next few years, with the collapse of the NLU's attempts to organize across racial lines, and its rejection by the increasingly prominent and powerful racist trade union movement, black workers retreated from labor activities to focus their energies on politics in a rearguard attempt to defend their tenuously held civil liberties. White workers, viewing the political activities of black workers through their distorted racial stereotypes, assumed that black support for the Republicans was corruptly driven by their rapacious leaders, sinecures, and whiskey. Such was the perspective of Friedrich

Sorge, who viewed black workers as being held in "the grip of the political suckers who kept them till now almost exclusively in the ranks of the so-called Republican Party." Sorge and other German American Marxists, already hostile to political action in theory, simply failed to understand that for black workers the Republican Party was but an extension of their bread-and-butter struggles. The cumulative effect of these trends was to cause the German American Marxists to abandon the cause of the black worker. After the General German Labor Union's offer of assistance to black workers in 1869, German American socialists never again reached out to the black community or seriously discussed their unique problems.[15]

Years later, when Friedrich Sorge wrote his history of the labor movement, he depicted black workers in a way that served to justify their exclusion from the mainstream labor movement. Calling African Americans a "naturally naive and credulous people," Sorge complained that they were easily mislead by "carpet baggers" and "their fanciful racial comrades" into crazy schemes such as migrating to Kansas. While praising the few examples of interracial organizing of the 1880s, Sorge painted the black man as a handy tool of the capitalists. Sorge explained that this was because the black man "had relatively fewer needs and required a longer apprentice and acclimatization period for raising their standard of living" than the poor white worker.[16]

While Sorge's German American "Tenth Ward Hotel" faction of the IWA sacrificed their Internationalist and egalitarian ideology to the practical necessities of recruiting Irish workers and established trade unions into the IWA, New York's Yankee Internationalists embraced the black worker. More importantly, many of New York's black workers eagerly accepted the Yankee's gesture. The city's African American community rallied around the Yankee International because only the Yankees recognized their identity as not only wage laborers but also a persecuted minority whose basic republican liberties needed to be defended.

Interracial cooperation within the Yankee International dated from the very beginnings of the Spring Street Council. Immediately upon organizing their own separate organization in the aftermath of Sorge's coup, the Yankee's Spring Street Council set about planning a demonstration to honor the memory of several heroes of the Paris Commune who had recently been executed for their revolutionary activities. Theodore Banks, one of the Yankee leaders of the Spring Street Council, made a special appeal to New York's black workers. Banks published the following notice in several of New York's largest dailies:

The New York City IWA parade in commemoration of the martyrs of the Paris Commune, with the Skidmore Guards at the head (North Wind Picture Archives)

> To the Editor . . . You would do justice to the International Working-men's Association by inserting in your paper that people of all nations, regardless of sex, color or religion, are cordially invited to join with us in our funeral procession on Sunday next, and to join with us in our sections and become members. I can assure them that, no matter how sensitive they may be in reference to religion or position in life, in the International Workingmen's Association alone can their conditions be fully respected. The poorer they are the warmer the reception will be, as the Internation-als consider man according to his moral worth and not to his wealth.[17]

The International's parade was made all the more appealing to New York's African Americans when it was first announced at a lecture given by Wendell Phillips, perhaps the most well-known white reformer in the black commu-nity.[18]

On December 17, 1871, the day of the parade, thousands gathered around the blocks from where the march was to commence. Parade marshals began organizing the participants into line. The first rank, traditionally reserved as a place of honor, was reserved for a company of black soldiers known as the Skidmore Guards. As one journalist explained, "This was, according to pre-vious arrangement and in order to show the indifference of the International

to every prejudice of color or caste or race." But the Yankee International's display of interracial brotherhood did not go unchallenged. As the marchers were directed to their places, the members of a military band hired for the occasion refused to march next to the black men. Theodore Banks, the chief marshal of the parade, was summoned, and according to the press accounts, when Banks "learned what had happened he grew very indignant, and told the band that the 'niggers' as they called them, were every bit as good as they were." When the band refused to back down, Banks arranged a compromise, pulling a number of fellow Internationals from the rear ranks to march between the band and the Skidmore Guards. Before a throng of spectators, estimated by some to have numbered as many as a quarter of a million, the Yankee IWA, with armed black men at their head, marched down Broadway. No clearer statement of the meaning of egalitarian "internationalism" could have been given in words. Sorge and the rest of the Tenth Ward Hotel faction, who complained that the parade was a sensational distraction for workers who only stood to lose a day's pay by participating, boycotted the march.[19]

Yankee radicals were not the only ones making a public statement that day. That the black Skidmore Guards participated at all itself constituted a political declaration that at least a portion of New York's black community perceived the Yankee International to be dedicated to the same political goals of liberty and civil rights that African Americans had struggled so long for. New York's African American militia companies were organized as part of the black community's ongoing struggle to achieve legitimacy, equality, and respect. Unlike the many black fraternal organizations, which were formed out of a need for the protection and development of the black community itself and were essentially internal to it, black military companies were by their nature public and outward-looking institutions. Their primary activity in peacetime was to parade for the public—all other activities, such as fund-raising, outfitting, and drilling, were just means to this end.

Militia parades, regardless of the occasion that they marked, were deeply layered with symbolic meaning. Nineteenth-century militias appealed to patriotic ideals and glorified themselves as the defenders of the republic. Such representations were all the more meaningful for African Americans, whose grip on citizenship was fresh and uncertain. In donning the military garb of the republican soldier, these black men connected themselves to a tradition that extended back to the American Revolution and in this way symbolically declared their right to full participation in the nation's polity. Their self-representation as soldiers highlighted the very qualities—discipline, order, and sobriety—that white racism had denied to them through its stereotype of the unruly, drunken, and undependable black man.[20]

New York's black militia leaders had a record of carefully choosing the occasions on which they would march in a way that would cultivate alliances with sympathetic whites. In the spring of 1871, a black militia company sparked a heated debate within the black community when they accepted the invitation of O'Donovan Roosa, the radical Fenian, to march in a parade celebrating the arrival of several well-known Irish leaders to New York. Marching with the Irish was bad enough in the eyes of many African Americans who remembered well the tragic days in 1863 when predominately Irish mobs rampaged through Manhattan lynching blacks and their white defenders. But worse still was the fact that the parade was organized by the Tammany Democratic Party, the sworn enemy of racial equality.

The thought of blacks marching in an Irish parade sowed just as much dissension among sachems as it did among black citizens. A resolution to extend an invitation to "our colored brethren" put to a meeting of Irish societies was "lost amid roars of laughter and cries of 'we want nothing to do with the Fifteenth Amendment.'" But the wily William Marcy Tweed, boss of New York's Democratic machine, thought he recognized a political opportunity to drive a crack into the solid black Republican vote and extended his personal invitation to the black men of the "Griffin Guards." In

NEW YORK CITY.—FIRST ANNUAL BALL OF THE SKIDMORE GUARD, A COLORED MILITARY ORGANIZATION, AT THE SEVENTH AVENUE GERMANIA ASSEMBLY ROOMS.

A formal ball of the Skidmore Guards, 1872 (North Wind Picture Archives)

the end, the participation of the black militiamen in the Fenian parade was a promising first step toward reconciling the two groups. At a dinner of Irishmen held the night after the parade, one enthusiastic son of Erin raised his glass and proposed a crude toast: "Ireland will now be free, for the Irish and the nagurs can whip the whole world!" Another Irish American published a poem celebrating this historic moment of reconciliation between races:

> "Och! for prejudice base there's no longer a place
> In my heart," loud cries generous Pat;
> "Be a man black as night, or than snow-drift more white.
> Be me sow! if I care aught for that."
> Division, too true, we've had oft cause to rue,
> 'Tis the cause of all suff'ring and wrong!
> Then let us unite, be we black, blue or white,
> for by union alone we grow strong . . . [21]

The other occasions that the black militias choose to mark also constituted a larger statement about their needs and aspirations. As would have been expected, they paraded on the Fourth of July and claimed their right to the revolutionary and republican heritage of America. Later, in the fall of 1871, a regiment of black troops unexpectedly fell into line among the thousands of white workers marching to demand the enforcement of New York's eight-hour law. A few months later a company of black soldiers appeared prominently in the IWA's march to commemorate the martyrs of the Paris Commune. This was but another comment in an ongoing series of political statements on the part of the most public of black institutions.[22]

Soon after the Commune martyrs' march, a few newspapers began to report that the International Workingmen's Association was forming sections composed of African Americans. Though no record of these sections has survived to the present day, their formation would have been consistent with the Spring Street Council's support for the political goals of New York's African American community. Its most public display of support came in March of 1872, when the Spring Street Council received an invitation from black citizens to join with them in marching to celebrate the passage of the Fifteenth Amendment to the Constitution. According to one reporter present at the Council's meeting, the invitation was "read and received with uproarious applause."[23]

Several weeks later, the largest demonstration of African Americans New York city had ever witnessed filled the streets in a mile-long parade. Along with dozens of black fraternal organizations, militia companies, and various dignitaries there appeared a lone knot of white faces carrying high their "familiar red banner of enormous dimensions" inscribed with the words "universal brotherhood and equality." These men and women were representatives of Yankee Section 35, a section based in the uptown wards where the majority of the African American population lived at the time. It was later reported that Section 35 included both black and white members.[24]

The Yankee International's support for the African American's struggle for equality was highlighted by the Equal Rights Convention of May 10, 1872, an event primarily organized by members of Sections 12 and 9. Indeed, it was reported later that "nine-tenths" of the delegates to the Yankee IWA's First Annual Congress were present at the Equal Rights Convention. For months prior to the convention, *Woodhull & Claflin's Weekly* carried the proposed Equal Rights Party's invitation for all people "regardless of race, sex, nationality or previous condition" to come to New York and take part in this "great and good work of reformation" to uphold "human equity" and "every human right." Of the several hundred delegates filling Apollo Hall, reporters noted, "all varieties of color and complexion" were represented. It was a member of the Yankee International, Moses Hull, who first nominated

Frederick Douglass as Victoria Woodhull's presidential running mate, and it was a member of Section 12 who demanded that another "gentleman of color be nominated in his stead," if Douglass declined their offer. Clearly, many Yankee Internationalists considered it of great importance that their already symbolic campaign should also encompass the symbol of the emancipated black struggling toward full equality.[25]

This statement was not lost on New York's black community. In June, the Equal Rights Party called a meeting at Cooper Union to ratify Woodhull's nomination and kick off her campaign. To the shock of many reporters and observers, several companies of black soldiers filed onto the stage in a show of support for the ticket. In the weeks after the Equal Rights Convention, Victoria Woodhull boasted that "several organizations of colored people have already given their adhesion to the new party." To what organizations she referred cannot be determined, though she may have been meant the companies of African American militia who, shortly after the convention nominated the ticket of Woodhull and Douglass, elected her sister, Tennessee, as their commander.[26]

Like many of her radical contemporaries and abolitionist forerunners, Woodhull's racial views were not unproblematic. While believing deeply in and consistently espousing the doctrine of equal political and civil rights regardless of color, Woodhull also believed in the existence of definite differences in the innate talents and abilities of peoples of different races. Her reform newspaper carried articles on "Stirpiculture," the system developed by the utopian socialist John Humphrey Noyes of "scientifically" pairing couples so as to gradually improve the human race. Later in life, Woodhull herself penned several pamphlets on the subject, including "The Scientific Propagation of the Human Race" and, in a more Spencerian vein, "The Rapid Multiplication of the Unfit." Even while standing tall for the equality of rights of all humanity in the Spring of 1872, Woodhull delivered her lecture "The Impending Revolution" to many audiences. One of her points in this speech was a quite egalitarian one—that America should be a center of liberty where people of all nations could seek refuge and over time coalesce into a "new race." But in elaborating this vision of America, Woodhull exposed some of its racist foundations. "Each race," she asserted, "is the distinct representative of some special and predominant characteristic, being weak in all others. The new race will combine all these different qualities in one grand character, and shall ultimately gather in all people of all races. Observe the merging of the black and white races. The white does not descend to the black, but the black gradually approaches the white."[27]

As was true of many antebellum social reformers, Woodhull did not entirely escape the pervasive racial stereotypes of her day. Woodhull's belief in racial difference coexisted with her egalitarian ideals of human brotherhood. Ultimately, to Woodhull and many other radicals who came out of the American reform tradition, a belief in the physical inequality of the races did not logically justify inequality in politics or society.

Like her more famous sister, Tennessee Claflin also publicly advocated the civil and social equality of African Americans. Both women believed in what would later be called in anarchistic circles the "propaganda of the deed," that is, that actions spoke far louder than words. Speaking out for women's rights at the frequent women's conventions was well and good, but Claflin and Woodhull held that the most effective way to further the status of women in society was to demonstrate their capabilities. It was this idea that underlaid the two women's venture on Wall Street, Victoria's campaign for President of the United States, and Tennessee's run for Congress and her bid to become the first female commander of a National Guard regiment in American history.

In 1871, the National Guard's white New York Ninth Regiment, nicknamed the "city guards," lost its commander, Colonel James Fisk, the well-known railroad tycoon, to an assassin's bullet. The post went unfilled for many months, and just before the Equal Rights Convention was due to meet, Tennessee Claflin offered her services to the regimental committee charged with finding a successor to Fisk. Acknowledging that her offer would "at first sight occasion incredulity as to my intentions," Claflin explained that "it has always been my desire to become actively connected with the service, and [I] have always gratified a passion I have for studying its rules and tactics, in which I am well versed." As to her qualifications, Tennessee was supremely confident: "There can be no objection to me, save that I am a woman. Permit me to remind those who urge it that Joan D' Arc was also a woman." [28]

The men of the Ninth Regiment had no interest in blazing a new trail for women's equality and never gave Tennessee Claflin's offer serious consideration. Soon after news of her rejection made the daily papers, Capt. Thomas J. Griffin, the controversial commander of the black militia company that had marched alongside Irish New Yorkers in honor of Fenian heroes, invited Claflin to run for the colonelcy of the newly organized black Eighty-fifth Regiment. This was no small offer. The Eighty-fifth regiment represented the fulfillment of a decade-long struggle on the part of black New Yorkers to win legal recognition of their equal right to serve in the militia. As early as 1851, at least three black militia companies were reported to be marching and drilling. In giving their units names such as the "Attucks Guards" and the "Free Soil Guards," these black New Yorkers clearly viewed soldiering as a political act that connected them to their revolutionary heritage (Crispus Attucks, a black worker, was shot by Redcoats in the Boston Massacre) and the demands for their future (free soil). From the beginning, the goal of these organizations had been to win state recognition and thereby gain legitimacy for their claims of citizenship, thus taking one significant step closer to social equality. However, such recognition was denied year after year, even after the outbreak of the Civil War.[29]

Soon after the war's first battles, black New Yorkers renewed their struggle to win the right to be soldiers. By the spring of 1861, black militia companies were renting private halls in which to march and practice their manual of arms. However, these early organizations were suppressed by the police. In July of 1861, leaders of the African American community formally offered New York's governor three regiments of black soldiers, but he refused them. For the next several years, then, hundreds of black men from New York traveled to Connecticut and Massachusetts, where they joined those states' black regiments.[30]

After the bloody assault upon New York's black residents that has passed down in history as the "draft riots" of 1863, those who had been struggling to raise a black unit gained the powerful support of the elite Union League Club. This influential ultranationalist organization of merchants and professionals provided funds for the outfitting of a new black regiment and used its influence to go over the head of the recalcitrant Governor Seymour and win approval of the regiment from Secretary of War Edwin M. Stanton himself. On March 5, 1864, New York's African Americans swelled with pride and victory as they watched the newly assembled Twentieth Regiment, a thousand black men in uniform, rifles in hand, parade down Broadway on their way to the front.[31]

With the passing of the wartime crisis, New York's black soldiers lost whatever toehold of acceptance and legitimacy their courage and sacrifice had won. Out of a total African American population, which stood around 12,000 in 1865, 877 black soldiers had died in the war. In other words, the black community sacrificed from one-quarter to one-third of their adult black males to defend the republic and crush slavery. In spite of this display of commitment and loyalty, the state of New York refused to grant legal status to black militia units after the war.[32]

Not until the spring of 1872 did the efforts to gain state sanction for black units pay off. That March, largely owing to the dedicated lobbying of "Captain Johnson," the state senate's black janitor, the governor signed a bill striking the word "white" from the state's militia code and provided for the organization of black regiments. Soon afterward, the various black companies around New York City combined into a single regiment, the Eighty-fifth, and applied for official status.[33]

Given the years of struggle that had culminated in the new militia code, and the tenuous status of the Eighty-fifth Regiment, whose pending incorporation into the National Guard represented a potentially major social and political victory for the black community, the decision to invite Tennessee Woodhull to assume its high-profile post of commander could not have been taken lightly. The daily press cynically interpreted the Eighty-fifth's invitation as a simple swap—new uniforms, drums, and muskets for the regiment in exchange for the colonel's title for the lady broker. Indeed, it was true that the Eighty-fifth struggled to properly uniform even a fraction of its men, and though their immediate material needs must have influenced their decision, the political symbolism of their choice of commander cannot be dismissed. A close reading of the few accounts of the regimental meeting where the question of nominating Claflin was put to a vote reveals that Claflin had earned the respect of New York's black community through her own actions, through her association with the Yankee International, and her participation in the recent Equal Rights Convention that had nominated Frederick Douglass for vice president.[34]

The Eighty-fifth Regiment met to consider the nomination of Tennessee Claflin as their commander at an old armory handed down to them by the white Eighth Regiment, complete with an unpaid gas bill of forty-five dollars. Consequently, the gas had been turned off and the meeting was held by the flickering light of coal-oil lamps. By eight o'clock, several hundred people had filled the dusty hall. Tennessee arrived with her sister and several other members of the Yankee International. She took her seat on the platform next to a number of the black officers, including Maj. William H. Carroll, the ranking officer who was nearing ninety years of age and had fought in the War of 1812, and Captain Andrew Parker, who had seen battle in both the Mexican-American War and the Civil War. Several of the companies and a drum corps then performed a short drill and paraded in front of the seated officers and invited guests.

When all the companies had completed their review, the meeting was called to order and the various company captains were called to the front to give their views on placing Claflin in command. Several captains, including the aged Major Carroll, came forward and pledged their support to Claflin. Captain Parker reportedly said in his speech that "he had worked hard to organize a colored regiment, and that he and his forty-two men were at the disposal of Miss Claflin that very night." Only one captain dissented. To a mixture of cheers and hisses, a "Captain Warfield" said that "he had been in five battles and would not be led by a woman."

Tennessee Claflin then gave a speech in which she attempted to connect her own struggle as a woman to gain her rights as a citizen and a professional to these battle-hardened black men's struggle for equality. "I have been the victim of despotism," she stated. "In Wall street they ask a year's rent in advance, then raise it $2,000. They refuse me lodgings in a hotel." When she undertook her bid for a colonelcy, Claflin continued, she "did not expect to get it, but only acted on principle . . . to show that woman can go to the front." She was espousing, of course, the same politics of example that her sister Victoria had pioneered with her candidacy for president and her brokerage business. But now that she was confronted with the prospect of actually being given the command of troops, Tennessee's purpose had shifted. Along with demonstrating the principle of gender equality, Tennessee claimed now to view the leadership of the regiment as a potentially revolutionary commitment. "I wish the command of a regiment," she told the attentive men before her, "because I know that now the working classes are asking for their rights, . . . despotism will oppress them and rivers of blood will flow." She vowed that when they were engaged in class war, and the metal began to fly, she would remain steadfastly at their front. The vote was called and Claflin won the command by a margin of three to one.[35]

With Tennessee Claflin's election to the command of the Eighty-fifth Regiment and Victoria Woodhull's run for the presidency on a ticket with Frederick Douglass, IWA's Section 12 had made greater strides toward bridging America's racial divide than had any radical movement since abolitionism. Claflin showed her commitment to her troops that summer when a number of her fellow soldiers arrived at her house to pick her up for the afternoon's drill. Claflin and her sister had suffered a rapid reversal of their fortunes that year and were at that time living in a boardinghouse. When the black men drove up in their carriage, the boardinghouse keeper warned Claflin that if she went off with those men she would turn her out. Claflin ignored her and rode off, only to find her belongings piled on the sidewalk when she returned.[36]

Woodhull and Claflin's schemes collapsed later that fall when they were prosecuted and imprisoned for violating the federal obscenity laws for printing the sensational story of the Reverend Henry Ward Beecher's affair with Rev. Theodore Tilton's wife. With the loss of their fortunes and their repression by the state, the sisters involvement with New York's African American community came to an end. The Yankee International never again had representatives so effective in establishing ties to the black community, though their pronouncements would continue to uphold the sisters' color-blind principles.

The Yankee International's support for black equality was not without cost. One of the few "Yankee" branches of the IWA south of the Mason-Dixon line tore itself apart over the question of racial equality. Section 44 was organized in Galveston, Texas, by John McMakin, a New York housepainter who was traveling through the West as an organizer for his national union. McMakin was a persuasive orator, and soon the meeting hall of Section 44 was packed with representatives of many of the city's trade unions. Within two months of its founding, Section 44 boasted some 200 members.[37]

Given the sensitivity of racial issues in a divided Southern city such as Galveston in the 1870s, it was perhaps inevitable that the race question would become the subject of discord within Section 44. Before its first month of meetings was over, a number of members had walked out rather than agree to a proposal to appoint a committee to visit a meeting of black workingmen and request their cooperation. In the debate over the issue, McMakin, the prime champion of the proposal, was reported to have "indulg[ed] in some personalities against his opponents" and they had flung back "some equally personal remarks." Though the resolution inviting the participation of the black workers passed, the questions of race and "social equality" were debated over and over again at their meetings. Amidst this climate of discord, McMakin returned to New York, and the forces in favor of social equality lost their most eloquent representative.[38]

Section 44's racial debate was fueled by the scattered news reports of New York's Yankee sections that trickled back to Galveston. On April 3, the *Galveston Daily News* reported that the black citizens of New York had invited the Internationals to join them in their Fifteenth Amendment celebration march. The next week the secretary of Section 44 received a circular from the Yankee Spring Street Council that condensed the IWA program into a mere ten points. The circular called for society to be reconstructed on an industrial basis and "to make industry alone a test of citizenship." It called for "complete political and social equality to all, without regard to nationality, sex or condition." This was apparently the last straw for many Galveston workers, who began to desert the IWA in droves. Within a few weeks the section fell moribund, and by June it was dead.[39]

Race may have been the death stroke of Internationalism in Texas, but it may have spurred recruitment efforts in other parts of the South. Long after the growth of the Yankee International had been stymied elsewhere in the country, an IWA activist by the name of Williams reported organizing seven sections across the South, especially in Virginia, over the course of a month. The key to his success appeared to be the maldistribution of land and the shortsightedness of "large landowners who could afford to give away half of their uncultivated acres and be richer for their generosity." It was these large plantations, the "bane of the South," as Williams called them, that "the Internationals of the South will use their endeavors to divide up." Though neither Williams nor anyone else at the meeting at which these developments were discussed characterized these new chapters of the IWA by race, given the egalitarian ideology of the Yankee IWA and these Southern sections' focus on the redistribution of plantation lands, it is not improbable that they may have included African Americans.[40]

Williams's Southern success was cause for a reevaluation of the membership recruitment strategies of the Yankee IWA. That autumn, the Spring Street socialists appointed six corresponding secretaries to manage the business of the IWA sections in various regions of the country, two of whose districts fell below the Mason-Dixon line: one secretary was appointed for Louisiana, Mississippi, and Alabama, and another was appointed for the Carolinas, Georgia, and Florida. Although this scheme soon proved to be a paper tiger, it reveals that the South, and possibly the recently emancipated African American community, figured prominently in the Council's plans to revive the fortunes of the IWA in English-speaking America.[41]

THE STATUS OF the African American worker was the most important racial question in the early years of Reconstruction. But beginning in 1870, this issue was quickly overshadowed in the minds of labor leaders and the socialists of the IWA by the question posed by the immigration of Chinese workers to the West and their first appearance east of the Mississippi in significant numbers. Labor's campaign against the Chinese gained strength for the next decade and culminated in the passage of the first racially based and most restrictive immigration laws in American history. Ultimately, labor's anti-Chinese campaign probably did more to cement its self-image of white-ness than did its flirtation with and rejection of the cooperation of black workers in the ill-fated NLU. The simple reason for this is that the exclusion of black workers from the trade union movement was so complete (with the great exception of the Knights of Labor) that black participation was hardly ever debated. The question of Chinese workers, however, never went away, partly because the law excluding them from the United States was subject to congressional renewal every ten years, and partly because the ideology of wages and "cheap men" that had become widespread in the Gilded Age singled them out.

Just as the demands of black workers for inclusion illicited sympathy from a few of labor movement's more egalitarian national leaders, the question of the status of the Chinese worker created a similar dilemma. Abolitionists and old-line reformers staunchly defended the equal right of the Chinese to immigrate to America and called upon the U.S. Congress to recognize them as citizens and voters. William Lloyd Garrison and Wendell Phillips op-posed attempts to restrict immigration along racial lines. Charles Sumner, the radical abolitionist senator who himself probably once enrolled in the International Workingmen's Association, led the way in 1870 in fighting for expunging all racially discriminatory provisions from the nation's naturaliza-tion laws. Sumner's staunchest ally in his crusade to make American citizen-ship color-blind was his fellow senator from Massachusetts, George Hoar, who was vilified in 1872 for swimming against the tide of journalistic slan-der and publicly declaring his "strong sympathy with the Internationale." In spite of the exertions of these two powerful men, Congress voted to add persons of African descent to their list of immigrants eligible for citizenship and explicitly denied the same right to the Chinese.[42]

As with the question of African Americans' inclusion into the labor move-ment, those within the International who most willingly adopted the racist slogans of the anti-Chinese campaign were those most devoted to the ideo-logical leadership of Karl Marx. Marx's historical materialism tended to strongly reinforce a European ethnocentrism that viewed Asia as a stagnant pool of human barbarism. Viewing Asians as naturally passive and submis-sive, locked in what Marx called their "hereditary stupidity," and incapable of organizing to overcome their total oppression by despots, Marx held Asia to be a region without history. Its only hope for progress was to be conquered and colonized, both politically and economically, by the West. In short, Marx's Internationalism when applied to Asia was hardly indistinguishable from European colonialism. When the American labor movement turned its attention to ridding itself of the competition of Chinese workers, Marx also warned of the importation of "Chinese rabble to depress wages." [43]

White labor's opposition to the Chinese was strongest in San Francisco, where the proportion of Chinese immigrants approached 10 percent of the population by the early 1870s. San Francisco was also the First International's greatest stronghold west of the Mississippi. A German American branch of the IWA was organized in San Francisco as early as 1868. By 1871, on any given week, a citizen of that city could listen to the proceedings of an International meeting in French, German, or English. Given that the issue of greatest concern to the labor movement of San Francisco was the presence of large numbers of Chinese workers, it was only a matter of time before the elements of the IWA who took their cues from the trade union movement would fall into line and support the anti-Chinese agitation. [44]

Eastern labor's opposition to the Chinese exploded in the summer of 1870 with the arrival from San Francisco of seventy-three Chinese men who had been contracted to work at a shoe factory in North Adams, Massachusetts. Mass protest meetings were held in several cities. New York's labor leaders, who were then beginning to organize an eight-hour movement that in a couple of years would culminate in the largest strike wave in American history, turned out en masse at Thompkins Square. Prominent among them were several future leaders of the Tenth Ward Hotel faction of the International Workingmen's Association. Haranguing the assembled crowds of workers, they condemned the forced association of Massachusetts workers with the "degraded labor of Asia." [45]

From this time on, Friedrich Sorge displayed an extraordinary interest in the movement against the Chinese. "In California," he reported to Marx in 1871, "some activity prevails in Workingmens circles engendered by the threatening increase of Chinese immigration encroaching upon the fields of Labor hitherto exploited by the white workingmen's population." In his monthly report to the General Council that October Sorge wrote: "In California the opposition against the imported Chinese finds vent on one side in a peaceable petition to Congress, on the other side in a violent attack on the Chinese." Eventually, Sorge showed his solidarity with his brethren in the San Francisco labor movement by agreeing to represent the German section of that city on the IWA's Central Committee. [46]

At their first annual congress after purging the Yankees from their midst, Sorge's Tenth Ward Hotel faction devoted much of its attention to the issue of the Chinese. In honor to their West Coast comrades, the convention chose Robert Blissert, the proxy delegate of a San Francisco section, president of the convention. Beneath their red banner inscribed with the words "Workingmen of all Countries Unite," the delegate representing San Francisco's Internationalists read his report:

> The white workingmen see and feel daily the effects of the Chinese labor in that State. We cannot only perceive how it affects us, but know assuredly that it will seriously affect the destiny of the working classes of this country. The Chinese have driven out of employment thousands of white men, women, girls and boys. . . . They are in all branches of the manufacturing business, and it is only a matter of time when they will monopolize all branches of industry; as it is impossible for white men to exist on the same amount and sort of food Chinamen seem to thrive upon.

California's Internationalists appealed to their Eastern comrades to do all they could to publicize the plight of the Western white worker and the grave threat posed to all white workers by the continued immigration of the Chinese. Their communication ended on a murderous note. "If Chinese emigration is not stopped," the message declared (according to one observer present at the meeting), "blood will yet flow in the streets of San Francisco on their account." The convention voted unanimously to "use [all] their endeavors to give all the publicity possible to the document." [47]

One reporter covering this Internationalist congress pointed out that "of all the delegates present . . . , not one was or is American born; all are Europeans — mostly Germans and Frenchman." Here, then, was a convention composed solely of immigrant workers voting to condemn the immigration of Chinese as a dire threat to America. [48]

After the convention adjourned, the drumbeat against the Chinese continued at the IWA meetings at the Tenth Ward Hotel. A report of one assembly a month later noted that a long report from a San Francisco section was read that was "almost entirely devoted to denunciations of the Chinese residents of California, for whom anything but fraternal feelings were expressed." At another Tenth Ward Hotel meeting that fall, members listened to more protests against the displacement of "white employees" from the laundry shops by "cheaper-paid Chinamen." [49]

In contrast to the Tenth Ward Hotel's hardening opposition to Chinese workers, the Yankee radicals of the Spring Street Council, whose roots extended deeply into the same liberal and egalitarian soil that produced Garrison, Phillips, Sumner, and Hoar, refused to go along with the labor movement's new burst of anti-Chinese nativism. These old-line American reformers viewed the Chinese as an oppressed racial minority and defended them according to the same republican principles that underlay the Reconstruction amendments to the Constitution. Victoria Woodhull repeatedly upheld the equal rights of Chinese, just as an immigrant from any other nation, to come to American shores and blasted those labor leaders who fomented the fears of Chinese competition among their followers. "The Chinese Question seems to us to have roused extravagant fears," Woodhull editorialized:

> The population of the country is forty millions. If the Chinese should come at the rate of five thousand a week, even that figure will nothing near equal the present ratio of the Irish and German immigration, and it would take a hundred and fifty years to import forty millions. . . . The economical idea of immigration is that every new comer is a producer; he directly contributes to the wealth of the community; he will not consume all that he produces. . . . As for any immediate influence of John Chinaman on the labor market and rate of wages that is an impossibility. The workingmen of New York protest against two or three hundred foreigners. What injury can accrue to them?[50]

When the U.S. Senate voted to deny citizenship to immigrant Chinese, Woodhull accused Republican senators of violating their principles of liberty and of performing the "Jump Jim Crow." To those senators who had fought for years on behalf of the freed black slaves but now denied those same rights to those of Asian heritage, Woodhull was uncompromising: "We want no re-establishment here of political slavery by the special friends of the negro."[51]

Section 26, the Yankee branch of the International in Philadelphia, devoted one of its evening meetings to the issue of the immigration of the Chinese worker. One member read a clipping from the London *Times* arguing that the migration of Chinese around the world was depressing wage rates in all the countries to which they came. In contrast to their German American rivals, whose Marxism proved a good deal less international than was claimed, Philadelphia's Yankee radicals concluded from this account not that the Chinese should be excluded or expelled but that the labor movement must redouble its efforts to organize workers without regard to national boundaries. Jacob Byrnes, a young man who was as active in the struggle for women's rights as he was in the IWA, argued that the immigration of the Chinese was "an argument in favor of the IWA and the affiliation of laborers all over the world." Proclaimed Byrnes: "Labor must either be organized on a world-wide basis or the destruction of the laborer would be sure as a necessary result of [competition], . . . hence the necessity of laborers of the world organizing for the benefit of all." [52]

A member of New York's Section 9, Leander Thompson, who had been elected president of the Yankee's first annual congress in July 1872, went so far as to publicly criticize the policy of trade unions and to endorse free immigration in a speech he gave under the auspices of the Cosmopolitan Conference, the lecture society established by members of the Yankee International. Thompson reportedly "ridiculed and denounced the fear of emigration, which some workingmen entertained and regretted the action of the trades unions on the subject." Taking a line of reasoning heretical to the labor movement of his day, Thompson declared his wish to "open wide the gates to the heathen" (and with a tinge of old-fashioned Yankee nativism, Thompson included the "priest-ridden Catholics" for good measure.) Moreover, Thompson continued, the "heathen" Chinese should be enfranchised and organized: "We want to place the ballot in their hands that they may assist us in overthrowing the great monopolies." [53]

Other well-known Yankee Internationalists took public stands on the issue. For example, Richard J. Hinton, leader of Section 23 in the District of Columbia, published several articles for the national magazine *The Galaxy* that supported unhindered Chinese immigration and condemned American intolerance toward the Chinese immigrants who had already settled in the States. At a time when mobs lynched Chinese Americans in the West and similar passions were just beginning to stir among workers in the East, Hinton wrote: "The [Chinese] emigration for the next ten or fifteen years, while it will be large, cannot possibly come faster than we can profitably absorb." [54] Stephen Pearl Andrews reportedly marched through the streets of Philadelphia on New Year's Day in 1871 bearing a huge banner upon which was pictured four men—one white, one black, one Native American, and one Chinese—clasped in friendship. On the reverse were the words: "Inasmuch as ye have not done it unto the least of these, my brethren, ye have not done it unto me; depart from me ye who work iniquity." Section 26's Damon Kilgore delivered a Wesleyan Academy alumni oration, "Caste, Suffrage, Labor, Temperance, Religion," in which he compared America's treatment of Chinese immigrants to its treatment of African Americans and Indians and assailed the "selfish and partial legislation which brands the Chinese immigrant alone as a Pariah among races." Kilgore also advocated a completely impartial immigration policy and called for dealing "with Chinese immigrants precisely as we do with other foreigners who leave their father-land to become part and parcel of The Great Republic." [55]

A similar stand on the Chinese question was adopted by the short-lived official Yankee Internationalist paper, *The Worker*, which was launched in 1873. In an article entitled "Don't Kill the Chinese," *The Worker* defended the equal rights of Chinese immigrants. Addressing workers directly, the paper expressed sympathy with men locked out by capitalists who employed Chinese workers to break strikes, and conceded that in such a situation it "was very natural that a feeling of indignation should run high." But, the Worker implored of its "Brother-Workmen," even though the displaced workers faced the prospect of slow starvation, even though they were being ground down by profit-hungry monopolists, and even though they could expect no justice from the law, "*don't kill the Chinese!*" Swimming against the tide of anti-Chinese labor sentiment, the *Worker* advocated a more far-sighted answer to the problem of the competition of Chinese workers:

> There is a much better thing to do with them: *Make Internationals of them*. Teach them as a first lesson, the American art of *striking*! Thro' them push the ranks of the International, even across the Pacific, to the extreme East itself, into the very heart of the Celestial Empire. The International must become universal, in order to fulfill its holy mission. The Human Race must become One Family of Peoples before we can have a true Social Order, Government by the sword and the cannon put an end to for ever.

Finally, the *Worker* appealed to the common humanity of all workers, regardless of whether they were white or Chinese: "For they, at all events, are innocent. They are, like yourselves, victims! We, the common people of all nations under the Sun, are all of us in one same boat; remember that, Brothers in toil, everywhere!" [56]

Just as the egalitarian stand of the Yankee Internationalists toward black workers proved the downfall of their affiliate in Galveston, Texas, so too their position on the Chinese cost them the support of the English-speaking IWA section in San Francisco. This section was the only group of Yankee radicals to join forces with Sorge's Tenth Ward Hotel faction immediately after the December coup, and its history reveals much about the contrasting views of the two Internationals and the ideological tensions that grew up between traditional American reformers and immigrant Marxists.

San Francisco's Yankee International grew out of Labor Union #1, an umbrella labor reform union affiliated with the National Labor Union. Like the other labor reform groups of its day, Labor Union #1 brought together trade unionists, labor radicals, and old-line, native-born reformers. Contrary to the custom of the city's other unions and labor organizations, Labor Union #1 held its meetings in the open, inviting all comers to its discussions and debates. Its interests, reflecting its diverse membership, were eclectic. Its evening meetings featured lectures on a variety of topics, from the Paris Commune and the International Workingmen's Association to currency theories and, what it termed, the "Chinese menace."[57]

In the summer of 1871, Labor Union #1 began debating its priorities and preparing for its first major public campaign. A mélange of resolutions, from proposals to reform land tenure, currency, interest, and taxation, to denunciations of stock speculation, militarism, and Chinese workers, were proposed by the organizers of the future English-speaking IWA in San Francisco. Of the sixteen resolutions, none was more debated than that calling for an end to the "importation of Coolie labor." No one supported the Chinese workers' right to free immigration, but the membership was divided between those who wanted to focus on the question of immigration alone and those who angrily felt that an anti-immigration policy did not go far enough to force those Chinese workers already in the country to leave. One man denounced the resolutions as "twaddle" and called for a committee to be appointed "to suggest a mode of getting rid of Chinamen." The future leader of San Francisco's English-speaking Internationals, Capt. J. N. Smith, defended his milder anti-immigration resolution by saying that it "embodied the spirit of the National Labor Platform"; but, in the end, Smith lost and the proposed resolutions were defeated.[58]

Like their Yankee comrades in the East, the Internationalists of Labor Union #1 displayed a great concern for women's rights. Indeed, the question of women's political equality in Labor Union #1 was one of the major issues that precipitated the splitting of the organization and the reformation of its dissenters as a section of the IWA. The issue arose when Labor Union #1 began a drive to petition Congress to abrogate the Burlingame Treaty with China (an accord that conferred "most favored nation status" on Chinese immigrants), a legal change that would end Chinese immigration to American shores and might also require the repatriation of resident Chinese. Captain Smith shocked the meeting attendees by moving that women be invited to sign the petition. The chairman gaveled Smith out of order and warned him not to introduce resolutions that "wasted the time of the Union frivolously." Smith shot back that he "was never so earnest in his life" and that women must be included because they "had even a more direct interest than men in the competition by which Chinamen were driving them out of employment." Smith's motion failed and another that he championed, expressing sympathy with the Paris Commune, was voted down to boot.[59]

Apparently, these issues were unnegotiable for Smith and other members of Labor Union #1, and they quit the union. They soon organized the first English-speaking section of the IWA on the Pacific Coast. At their inaugural meeting, which attracted some one hundred interested reformers, including many women, Captain Smith lectured on the aims and principles of the association. He described the International as dedicated to emancipating the working classes, to seizing political power through the ballot box, and to the ultimate "total destruction of class privileges." Seemingly unaware of the contradiction, Smith listed as another of the International's goals "the making of all persons entirely equal before the law" and went on to argue that "so long as Chinese or other labor had a tendency to degrade rather than elevate labor, so long would the Association legitimately be arraigned against it." Others, however, were not so blissfully heedless of this hypocrisy. D. S. Cutter, for example, pointedly asked "whether the association included the Celestials [i.e., Chinese]," a question that provoked a "lively debate." In the end, it was decided that they were not.[60]

Except for their position on the Chinese, there was little difference between the Yankee Internationalists of San Francisco and their counterparts on the East Coast. Both seemed dedicated to republican principles in their crusade to free the worker from wage slavery. Both trumpeted the cause of women's suffrage. Both were well stocked with Spiritualists. Yet, despite the great similarities in their memberships and outlooks, the Yankee Internationals of San Francisco did not affiliate with the Yankee Spring Street Council in New York. Instead it joined Sorge's German American–led Tenth Ward Hotel Council and chose Robert Blissert, one of the prominent speakers at the anti-Chinese rally the year before, as its representative.[61]

A few other scattered and ephemeral groups of Yankee Internationalists eventually joined up with Sorge's Tenth Ward Hotel Council. A section in St. Louis ordered its delegate in New York to abandon the Yankee council and apply for admission in Sorge's camp. In 1873, a Boston section sent their application to Sorge. But both of these sections had abandoned the sinking Yankee Internationalist ship after May 1872, when the London General Council's expulsion of Section 12 and repudiation of the Spring Street International was publicized. The San Francisco section was the only one to choose Sorge's organization when the fate of the Yankee International remained to be officially decided and the Spring Street Council was growing by leaps and bounds. Nothing explains the section's behavior except for the fact that both the Californians and the Tenth Ward Hotel Marxists shared a deep opposition to the Chinese.[62]

The same dynamic explains the actions of Cyrenus Osborne Ward, the only native-born Internationalist in New York to attend the first annual congress of Sorge's German American socialists. Ward made a brief appearance at the congress held in the summer of 1872 just long enough to make a "long speech against Chinese immigration, and the Chinamen both at home and abroad." His interest in the struggle against the Chinese proved a lasting one. In 1879, as a member of the IWA's descendent, the Socialist Labor Party, Ward delivered a public address entitled "The Appointing Power and the Socialists Cure (touching on Chinese, Prison, and other monopoly labor)." Like the Yankee radicals of San Francisco, Ward found the association of German American Marxists more hospitable to his views of the Chinese than the idealistic Yankees on the East Coast.[63]

Within the American International were two strongly opposed views and visions of political action, class, and race. Only one, however, survived the factional infighting of the First International and emerged as a vital force within the American labor movement. Though the rigorous and exclusionary brand of socialism exemplified by Friedrich Sorge and his fellow German American Marxists was the model that triumphed and left its lasting stamp upon future labor movements well into the twentieth century, the winds of history also carried along the distantly echoing voices of the more tolerant Yankee Internationalists.

CHAPTER EIGHT

The International, the Working Class, and the Trade Unions

HE CONCEPT OF the working class is at the heart of all movements that have claimed socialism as their goal. In Marxist theory the working class is the preordained agent of historic change and the living antithesis of capitalist social relationships. To less philosophically comprehensive and more ethically based varieties of socialism, the working class is the possessor of right—a moral force rather than a historic force, but a force all the same. For all the difference between the Marxist and moralist conceptions of the working class, in practice each is equally devoted to the empowerment, development, and progressive struggle of workers. From the perspective of what happens in the streets, all that really differs between the two approaches is the tactics each adopts.

Workers themselves often overlook or view as unimportant the underlying differences of philosophy and historical theory separating varieties of socialism. Such was the case for the International Workingmen's Association in America. Though the two wings of the American International conceived of the notion of the working class differently, both were fundamentally committed to empowering workers and defending their interests. Despite the bitter differences of principles, tactics, and priorities that separated the two IWA Councils, neither could be said to have to been more involved in labor issues than the other. Labor organizations and workers themselves did not concern themselves with the factional issues and ideological subtleties dividing the two standard-bearers of socialism in America. They tended instead to view them together, even after the split, as "the International." In the end, in spite of Marx and Sorge's belief that only by adopting the correct critical line could socialism make inroads into the American labor movement, American workers and labor leaders responded equally to the "purified" Marxist International and to its rival organization composed of its expelled Yankee elements: they rejected them both.

Neither the Yankee Spring Street International or that of the Marxist Tenth Ward Hotel succeeded in rallying many workers or labor organizations to their cause. The general lack of interest in socialism among America's trade unions disappointed but did not surprise Yankee socialists. Though they courted unions, aided strikers, and were constant supporters of the eight-hour movement, many Yankee radicals remained suspicious of labor unions because of their exclusivity and their failure to support the larger political demands of women and minorities. Because of their broad conception of the working class and their belief that reform could be pushed forward simultaneously on innumerable fronts, the Yankee International placed just as much significance in coming to the aid of fire victims in New York's Bowery as it did in providing material aid to striking silk workers. Unlike Sorge's Marxists, who conceived of trade unions as the fundamental expression of working-class self-activity and the linchpin of historical change, Yankee socialists brushed off their rejection by trade unions and continued to aid workers who were not represented by trade unions. The sting of rejection by trade unions caused the Tenth Ward Hotel Council to fall into yet another round of acrimonious ideological battles and splits. The same sting, however, did not seem to dispirit the Yankees, whose broad conceptions of change and of the working class seemed to have inoculated them against perceiving their own demise.

The failure of the Yankee International to attract significant trade union support can not be attributed to either its lack of effort or lack of commitment to working-class activism. The English-speaking sections of the International had from their inception maintained an active relationship with organized labor, and by the end of 1872 the remnants of the Yankee International were moving toward making trade unions the focus of their activities. With

the November elections behind them and the alliance of a spectrum of reformers and radicals that were forged in the Equal Rights Party in shambles,
the leaders of New York City's Yankee IWA pinned their hopes of reviving
the organization upon recruiting support from the city's trade unions. This
was not an entirely new idea—the Yankee's had been involved with the
Workingmen's Assembly for years, and some of the Spring Street Council's
leaders had been high profile leaders of the massive eight-hour strikes earlier
in the year—but given the flagging interest of reform allies such as Spiritualists and suffragists in the International, it represented a shift in direction. Yet
try as they might the Yankees' own broad idea of the working class, which
gave no conceptual priority to trade unions over other movements and needs
of workers, again and again brought them into conflict with the more parochial interests of trade unions. Yankee socialists devoted too much attention
to the ghetto dwellers, to women, and to the unemployed to make themselves useful to a trade union movement that was at that very time moving
toward business-oriented union practices and "pragmatic" labor principles.

For a time after the expulsion of the Spring Street Council from the
greater International it seemed as though trade unions were interested in
supporting or even joining the International. In December of 1872 a group
of silk weavers from Paterson, New Jersey, ventured across the Hudson to
attend a large gathering of New York City's Yankee socialists at International
Hall, where they told the story of their struggles with the silk barons and
Paterson's constabulary that served as the silk companies' private security
force. After reviewing the privations thousands of silk workers suffered in
their month-old strike to protest the slashing of their wages by a fifth and
the jailing of some of their union brothers on charges of conspiracy, some
of the members of the Spring Street Council could not contain their radical passions any longer. Citizen Halbert claimed the floor and declared,
"Those employers should be seized in the streets and hanged to the lampposts. . . . Citizens, let us band together and hang all such scoundrels who
thus ruthlessly starve you . . . band together at once and obtain that which is
your own." Halbert's rash outburst was splashed across the front page of the
World, forcing William West to dispatch a note to the editor clarifying that
Halbert's proposals were not shared by the Council as a whole, and even
commenting that he wondered if Halbert wasn't "desirous of martyrdom."[1]

Cooler heads prevailed, and no bosses were hung from lampposts in the
following weeks, and both the Spring Street and the Tenth Ward Hotel IWA
Councils sent aid to the Paterson unions. In turn, the Paterson silk weavers
credited the IWA with publicizing their struggle around the labor world

and declared themselves all Internationals, though they apparently did so in name only.[2]

In the wake of this victory, the Spring Street Council in New York considered ways of making membership in the IWA more appealing to workers. They considered instituting death and injury benefits, though these never seem to have materialized. They raised money to publish a new paper to replace the *Woodhull & Claflin's Weekly*, which they planned to call *The Striker*. Before the year was out, this renewed emphasis on attracting workers organizations appeared to be bearing fruit because the representatives of a half dozen trade unions began showing up at meetings of the Spring Street Council.[3]

As the Yankee International attempted to rebuild itself upon a foundation of trade unions, tensions arose between those who clung to a more eclectic agenda and those who were determined to keep the IWA in the straight and narrow path of the craftsman agenda. In the spring of 1873, these divisions came to a head when Victoria Woodhull was nominated to fill a vacancy on the Spring Street Council. Opposition to Woodhull came from the trade union delegates who worried that her presence would repel workingmen. They argued that "there was a great deal of prejudice among workingmen against the doctrines expounded by Woodhull, as generally the working people hold that the family bond is the most sacred thing to them upon the earth." When a bare majority voted Woodhull into office, two union leaders handed in their resignations. Upon hearing of the schism caused by her candidacy, Woodhull sent a message to the next meeting of the Council, thanking the Council for the great honor given her. However, Woodhull explained, she "would not unnecessarily compromise the principles or objects of the organization by introducing her own special mission." That was her last communication with the Yankee IWA.[4]

Throughout that spring and summer the Yankee International continued to attempt to win the support of New York's labor movement. William Hanson of Section 12 began giving a series of lectures entitled "The Philosophy of Strikes—their usefulness in the evolution of society."[5] The IWA also offered legal aid to unions. They proposed to arrange legal counsel for the workmen on public contract then laying tracks for the Harlem Railroad to challenge the legality of their being made to work long days. In what was a novel strategy for labor, the Yankee radicals offered to pursue a test case of New York's moribund eight-hour law before the courts. The Spring Street Council issued an invitation "to the officers and members of the union trade organizations in the city and state of New York" to meet in April and plan ways of forcing the enforcement of the state's eight-hour statute.[6]

At first, the IWA's initiative seemed to catch on among the city's unions. Delegates from the boxmakers', painters', coopers', carpenters', and engineers' unions responded to the Yankee's call and joined with the IWA to form the "Eight Hour Enforcement League." But it was not long before the Internationalists' universal vision of labor reform and the trade unionists' exclusive concern for their own members clashed. Particularly offensive to many of the union men was the speech of one of the Yankee Internationalists who very undiplomatically pointed out the faults of trade unions in general. His speech upheld the principles of Internationalism against self-interest. He was "not in sympathy with the small and individual organizations known as trades unions," he announced, "but believed in a union of all trades in one common body for the defence of a common cause." The problem with trade unions was that they had "for their purpose the cause of one particular branch of industry and that only were calculated to make the members narrow-minded." Indeed, much of the extreme unemployment in the city the previous winter, he regretted to say, "was attributable to the unions, which by their narrow ideas forbade the employment of any more than an established number of men." A leader of the painters' union countered that he had come to the meeting "under the impression that this was a labor organization, but if the movement was for everything under the sun, he considered that he had not business there." The IWA member who chaired the meeting, scrambling to head off the revolt of the labor leaders, assured them that the Internationals had only one concern—the eight-hour law. Indeed, he said, they were so "anxious that this eight hour question should be settled [that] . . . the Internationals were quite willing to step aside and allow the trade unions and the labor organizations to do it."[7]

In the end, the Yankee's labor initiative proved a victim of its own success. New York's trade unions flocked to it, and soon some sixteen trade unions were represented at the Eight Hour Enforcement League's meetings. But as the mix of delegates tipped the scales in favor of the trade unionists, the Internationalists were pushed aside. As soon as the meetings began to look more like a trade union coalition than an Internationalist front, the laboring men felt the need to make it clear to the press that they had "no connection with the Internationals, and that [they were] . . . not under the influence of that organization." True to their word, the Internationalist leaders of the organization announced at the next meeting that their work was now done and that, "owing to the prejudice entertained by some of the workingmen of America to the Federal Council of the Internationals," it was in the best interest of the organization that they tender their resignations.[8]

Despite the best efforts of the Spring Street Council to court labor, trade unions simply had no interest in socialism in the 1870s. When Section 9 took the lead in organizing eight-hour demonstrations in the summer of 1872, trade unionists objected to their bright red banners of the International, and one unionist explained that workers "would never sympathize with the murderers of the Archbishop of Paris." Fearing that the disgruntled trade union leaders would pull their men out of an upcoming eight-hour protest, the leaders of the Workingmen's Union prohibited IWA marchers from carrying their flags. But even after the IWA's Yankee leaders acquiesced in this flag ban, the leaders of the stonecutters' union and the house smiths bolted the city's Eight-Hour Convention, taking most of the other trade unions with them.[9]

In attempting to build alliances with New York's trade unions the International was swimming against the tide. Contrary to Marx and Sorge's emphasis on labor strategies and theories, American trade unionists had little interest in radicalism of any kind. James Mackintosh, a weaver by trade and a member of Philadelphia's Section 26 had what he called a "bitter experience" attempting to interest unionists in his city in the Spring Street Council's newspaper, *The Worker*. At one point the Spring Street Council invited several trade union delegates to attend one of their meetings to explain the objections their unions had against the IWA. At the meeting one of the delegates indicated quite plainly how union men perceived the organization. "Among the working people," he noted, "there was a prevailing impression that the Internationals were fanatics, opposed to all religions, and determined if possible to overturn society in general without substituting something better instead." And all along Sorge and his Marxists had argued that it was the presence of middle-class "bogus reformers" and a lack of revolutionary conviction within the Spring Street Council that kept the trade unions away.

There was more to labor's distrust of the International than merely the fear of an uncertain future or the more pointed belief of Catholic workers that the International was in the habit of stringing up priests. New York's trade unions had by this time begun a dramatic shift toward business methods and exclusionary tactics. Just a few years before, when New York's labor leaders were faced with a choice between the ambitious reformist agenda of the National Labor Union and the incremental but less risky strategy of the

"English" model of business unionism, they chose the latter. The idea of business unionism had one major advantage over all radical proposals for labor reform or revolutionary change; its emphasis on the closed shop and labor-market control promised to hold the line against the introduction of foreign and black workers. For many trade union members and for union leaders who stood to reap the gains of stable dues bases and the officers' salaries that dues provided, radicalism, because of its inclusiveness, carried more threat than promise.[10]

The Eight Hour Enforcement League was the high point of the Yankee International's relationship with New York's labor unions. Its expulsion from the trade union coalition did not noticeably dampen the spirits of the Yankee radicals. Rather than throwing up their hands because trade unions refused to accept a wider vision of social change, Yankee socialists redirected their campaign from the eight-hour day to municipal socialism. Within a week of their resignation from the Eight Hour Enforcement League, members of the Spring Street Council were addressing a large crowd at Cooper Union, demanding the municipal ownership of telegraph lines, urban transit lines, and gas systems. They were proclaiming as well that it was the government's responsibility to supply the public with "food, clothing and fuel . . . and as far as possible, with labor."[11]

The Spring Street Council continued to champion the cause of the worker and took up the cause of the unemployed, an issue that evoked little concern among established trade unions. In this their last public campaign, the Yankees combined their proposals for government ownership of industry and their concern for the victims of industrialism and demanded that the city provide work and relief to the unemployed.[12]

Throughout the summer of 1873 economic conditions steadily deteriorated. In September the massive bubble of speculative investments in railroads burst, throwing the nation into the worst depression of its history. As tens of thousands of workers were turned out of their jobs, with the annual miseries of winter approaching, the remnants of the IWA across the country swung into action to defend them. In several cities the crisis temporarily united the warring factions of the International in common action for the last time.

The onset of depression served to revive the International in Philadelphia, for example. Attendance had flagged so badly by August of 1873 that several meetings were canceled for lack of interest; and by September the Yankee socialists had decided to cease holding public meetings and use the money they would have spent for renting a hall to publish broadsides and tracts. But when, soon afterward, the New York stock market went bust and scores of businesses closed in Philadelphia, the Internationalists assumed the leadership of the cause for the unemployed. Prominent members of Section 26 led mass meetings that called upon the city council to provide work to the unemployed, and a labor committee, largely composed of Internationalists, was appointed to meet with city officials.

Several reform groups sympathetic to the International publicly allied themselves with the unemployed movement. The Pennsylvania Peace Society passed a resolution calling employment "freely offered by each department of government" to be "a wise and valuable peace measure," and the society's president, Lucretia Mott, as well as its vice president, Alfred H. Love, personally urged the gathering to use its influence to procure work for the unemployed. Philadelphia's First Association of Spiritualists held a "relief meeting" that attracted several hundred people and likewise demanded that the government employ workers and distribute aid to the needy.[13]

While the mayor expressed his support for the unemployed movement's goals, he claimed that he had no legal authority to employ workers or provide relief, so he advised the IWA delegation to petition the city council instead. The city council, in turn, refused to give them a hearing. After a week of this runaround, the leaders of the movement for public relief decided to call for a mass meeting in Independence Square, in spite of one member's fear that "a mass meeting would not give the people bread, but might result in blood, pressed to the wall as the working men now are."[14]

On the appointed day, Independence Square was filled with a large crowd of workers who listened to both German- and English-speaking orators "denounce the system which gives into the hands of the capitalist all the instruments of and means of employing labor," and demand that the city rent the mills and factories that were idle and allow the unemployed to run them. John Shedden of Section 26 told the crowd how the city council had refused to act and had claimed they had no legal authority to do anything but provide relief at the almshouse. "They further claimed," Shedden recalled, "that they had no precedent for such a course as the working men wished them to pursue, but," Shedden noted, "neither was there any precedent for the Declaration of Independence." To those in the press and pulpit who had advised workers to take whatever wage they could to get through the winter, Shedden retorted that no one had suggested that "capitalists should consent to work at lower rates of profit."[15]

In New York the IWA's unemployment campaign culminated in a series of mass meetings and an investigation into the conditions of the unemployed.

The largest of these rallies, held on December 12, filled Cooper Union to overflowing. To the approving cheers of thousands of desperate men and women, resolutions were passed calling for the city to provide work and declaring that those in need should take the initiative to supply themselves with shelter and whatever necessities of life they lacked and send the bills directly to the city treasurer. With intentional reference to the French Revolution, a "Committee of Public Safety" was appointed to represent the interests of the people "and, if need be, enforce them."[16]

These outpourings of distress from the thousands of men and women thrown into dire poverty found no sympathetic ears among the city's trade unions. Immediately following the Cooper Union rally the secretary of the Workingmen's Union of New York, the central organization of the city's trade unions, wrote to the *New York Herald*, curtly denouncing the movement: "I wish to state that there was not any member of the 'Workingman's Union' on the platform or outside stands as speaker or spectator. The Workingmen's Union does not sympathize with Communism in any of its phases; nor does it believe in clannish organizations, either German or French, whose avowed purpose is to subvert this government into a charity hospital for men too lazy to seek work."[17] Although some trades supported the unemployed movement, such as the painters, whose leaders were members of the Committee of Safety as well as longtime Internationals, and the Longshoremen, who in the best of times were but one rung above destitution, most shied away.[18] New York's United Order of Bricklayers were among them. It issued a statement to the press that it had no involvement with the International and condemned communist leaders "in the strongest language." New York's iron molders similarly attacked "Communists, Internationalists, and other social disturbers" who were determined to spread "social anarchy."[19] By early January virtually every trade union reportedly had repudiated the Committee of Safety and the unemployed movement, causing the *New York Times* editorialists to breath a sigh of relief. "The working men," they asserted, "have evinced a great deal of good sense in disclaiming all connection with those individuals who put themselves forward as their representatives . . . the so-called Committee of Public Safety."[20] Clearly, New York's trade unions were becoming increasingly distant from the masses of workers in the city whose livelihoods were not made relatively secure by their monopoly of a skill or membership in a trade union. And they didn't have sympathy for the ideals of socialism or the idealistic movements that claimed to speak for them, either.

Such pronouncements did not discourage Internationalists. Soon the movement of the unemployed took on a momentum of its own that frightened the powers and policy makers of the city. In a pattern reminiscent of the efforts made to prevent a march to commemorate the martyrs of the Paris Commune three years before, the police repeatedly denied the Committee of Public Safety permission to assemble and march. Revealingly, New York's police commissioners reportedly argued that the bona fide labor organizations had disclaimed all connection to the event's organizers and therefore the parade was not a workingmen's parade at all but a demonstration of "malcontents."[21] Ultimately, the logic of events led to the brutal police riot at Tompkins Square on January 13, 1874. As seven thousand men, women, and children assembled in the square to hear speeches demanding public relief for the unemployed, a massive force of police attacked, clubbing people indiscriminately. In the aftermath of the riot the nation's press and public opinion screamed out against communists with all the vitriol that had been flung against Paris's Communards and their American supporters years before.[22]

After the riot, New York's Spring Street Council simply faded away. A handful of the veterans of Yankee Sections 9 and 12 drifted into the various socialist formations that coalesced between the time of the effective death of the IWA in 1874 and the founding of the Socialist Labor Party in 1877. Many others simply pulled up their stakes, moved on, and pitched a new camp with others whose organizations seemed more active and vital at the time.

ACROSS TOWN the Tenth Ward Hotel's Marxists were discovering that labor unions were no more interested in their version of working-class liberation than they were in the Yankees' street organizing. Long freed from the distractions of its battle with the idealistic Yankees, the Tenth Ward Hotel's Marxists were free to implement their strategies and completely devote themselves to organizing workers into trade unions. In late 1872, the leaders of the Tenth Ward Hotel had sent out word to its affiliates that all their energies were to be devoted to "organize and nothing else but to organize the working people."[23] In keeping with this command, New York's Marxist leaders made a concerted effort to win over the State Workingmen's Assembly of New York. Concerned that their Yankee opponents had spread a false impression of the organization among labor leaders, a committee was sent to address the Workingmen's Assembly and plainly set out the labor principles upon which the "true" IWA stood. At the meeting, the Tenth Ward Hotel representatives proclaimed their complete devotion to the trade union cause, to its view that every wage increase was a step toward "the final emancipation of labor," and to its commitment to the self-emancipation of workers through "a combination of the men of labor." Strenuously disassociating themselves from the Yankee Spring Street group, the committeemen denounced all the follies of "universal freedom, free love, universal suffrage, and more such universalities" and encouraged the assembled labor leaders to throw off all the "bogus Reformers and small political quacks" who imposed such nonsense upon workingmen's organizations. But the trade union leaders of New York had just as little interest in Marxism, whatever its proclaimed commitment to their own organizations, as they had come to have for Yankee universal reform. In spite of the years of work the Tenth Ward Hotel Marxists put in the trenches of labor, from addressing untold numbers of meetings during the great eight-hour strike wave of 1872 to their ever-present willingness to fly to the aid of strikers throughout the area, the labor bosses tabled the address and went on with their usual business.[24]

Naturally, Sorge and other German Americans made greatest headway among their own countrymen. In his recollections of the First International, Sorge credits the IWA with influencing the growth of a number of trade unions, from miners in Pennsylvania to shoemakers in Massachusetts, but the only national union, the International Furniture Workers Union, that was founded for the most part by members of the Tenth Ward Council was composed chiefly of German immigrants. Of even greater significance was the part played by Internationalists in the organization of the Cigar Makers' International Union, a union that served as the cradle for some of the most notable American labor leaders, including Samuel Gompers and Adolph Strasser, and ultimately became the seedbed of the American Federation of Labor.[25] But in spite of their strenuous efforts and a few notable successes, Sorge and the other leaders of the Tenth Ward Hotel were powerless against the growing conservative nature of the very unions they had helped to erect; they watched as the unions they supported or had set in motion rejected their socialist ideology.

Sorge's cadres had great expectations that through the purification and disciplining of the International they would sharpen the class consciousness and militancy of the trade union movement and eventually assume its leadership. The vigor with which they executed their plans ultimately succeeded in reshaping the ideology and agenda of the Left and decisively influencing the direction of the mainstream labor movement in America. But theirs was an ironic success. Socialist parties, in spite of their efforts to court trade unions, remained isolated and embryonic throughout the century. Trade unions, even though they were led by men who had emerged from the inner ranks of Sorge's Marxists and whose ideology was forged in the factional furnace of New York's First International, turned out in the end to be politically conservative; and they finally shunned the socialists who had compromised so many of their Internationalist principles to woo them. Indeed, in an odd twist of fate, the Tenth Ward Hotel's hard-won antipolitical ideology boomeranged and became the substance of the labor movement's rationale for rejecting their socialist descendants.

In the fall of 1872, a new face began to appear among the small crowd of men who regularly attended the long meetings of Section 1 of the IWA — an English cigarmaker named Samuel Gompers. Gompers had been a keen observer of the International movement in New York for several years. He recalled in his memoirs having marched in the September 1871 eight-hour parade that was largely organized by elements of the Yankee International. Gompers witnessed the schism erupt between the Yankee socialists and Sorge's immigrant Marxists and marked it as one of the formative moments in his life.[26]

Gompers recalled the Yankee sections of the IWA as being "dominated by a brilliant group of faddists, reformers, and sensation-loving spirits." From his perspective such individuals as Victoria Woodhull were "pseudo-communists" who either "played with the labor movement" or used it as a "means to a career." When the Yankees were thrown out of the International by "the bona-fide trade unionists" of the Tenth Ward Hotel, Gompers learned an important lesson. "I was coming to an appreciation of the difference between revolutionary ideals and revolutionary tactics for securing them," he wrote. Through watching the internecine battles of the First International, Gompers developed the same bitter animosity to traditional American reform movements that Sorge's immigrant Marxists had displayed from the beginning. The lesson he learned from the experience, he later recalled, "burned itself into my memory so that I never forgot the principle in after years."[27]

Over time, Gompers was drawn more deeply into the inner circle of the immigrant Marxist milieu by Ferdinand Laurell, a fellow cigarmaker whom he met at the Lower East Side cigar factory where they both worked. Laurell was a longtime veteran of the Tenth Ward Hotel International and by the time he met Gompers was a delegate to the IWA's General Council that had only recently relocated from London to New York. Impressed by the earnestness and drive of the young English cigarmaker, Laurell took him under his wing and tutored him in the fundamentals of Marxism. Together they studied the *Communist Manifesto* — Laurell translating and interpreting it for Gompers from the original German, passage by passage. Laurell hammered into young Gompers the simple idea that trade unions were the only practical bulwark workers had against the viciousness of their employers and the vagaries of the economy. "Study your union card, Sam," Laurell sagely instructed his pupil, "and if the idea doesn't square with that, it ain't true." Gompers later recalled the impact those many hours studying Marx with Laurell had on him: "His kindly talks and warnings did more to shape my mind upon the labor movement than any other single influence." [28]

Gompers was eventually invited to attend meetings of a select "inner circle" of members of the International at the Tenth Ward Hotel. Calling themselves "Die Zehn Philosophen" (the ten philosophers), they would discuss and debate all night long. Gompers credited these discussions as forming the basis of his philosophy: "Long and earnestly we discussed plans, policies, and theories. Out of the chaos of radicalism and revolutionary phraseology we were seeking principles that would bring opportunities for better living to fellow-workers. . . . From this little group came the purpose and the initiative that finally resulted in the present American labor movement." [29]

If there ever was anything exceptional about the American labor movement compared to its counterparts in other industrial countries, it was the unique way in which the teleological underpinnings and revolutionary fervor of Marxism were deracinated and engrafted upon an essentially inward-looking and racially exclusive trade union movement. Samuel Gompers and his Internationalist colleague Adolph Strasser absorbed the passion, commitment, and historical materialism of their German American Marxist teachers but emerged the intellectual leaders of one the most politically conservative working-class movements of the nineteenth and twentieth centuries. From their close association with German American Marxists, who shunned the republican idealism of Yankee radicals as philosophically immature, politically undisciplined, and socially bourgeois, Gompers and Strasser learned to mistrust the rhetoric of egalitarianism and politics. They also acquired a thoroughgoing materialist view of society and history, though they stripped it of its millenarian expectations of a proletarian socialist revolution. Gompers and Strasser's lasting intellectual innovation was the decoupling of "historical" from "materialism." The intellectual system of historical materialism proved itself as readily adaptable to the American Federation of Labor's politics of industrial accommodation as it had been to Marx and Lenin's politics of worldwide social transformation. In the final analysis, the labor ideology of "pure and simple unionism," a conception that narrowed the horizons of the labor movement to improving wages, hours, and conditions of employment for its own members, originated out of Sorge and his Tenth Ward Hotel faction's collision with the American reform tradition and its refusal to adapt Marxism to American conditions.[30]

Gompers and Strasser's smooth transition from Internationalism to "pure and simple" exclusionary unionism is well illustrated by their actions as leaders of the Cigar Makers' International Union (CMIU) in the 1870s and 1880s. Gompers and Strasser began their labor careers by organizing cigarmakers who had been kept out of New York's cigarmakers' union by exclusionary codes and high dues. When Gompers and Strasser's union, CMIU Local 144, was still young and weak, the two favored an open-door policy that allowed cigarmakers of all nationalities and from both sexes into the union. At that time egalitarianism and trade unionism coincided as the trade was rapidly becoming dominated by thousands of recent immigrants, especially Bohemian women, whose extensive cigar-rolling experience posed a threat to the union men's monopoly over high-grade cigar manufacturing. As production had moved out from the factories and into the tenements of New York's Bohemian quarter, skilled cigarmakers lost their power to control the labor market through membership in their union. Deciding that their self-interest dictated that they organize everyone in the industry, for a time the cigarmakers became champions of industrial unionism in the cigar industry.[31]

This strategy was soon tested in the Great Cigarmakers Strike of 1877, when ten thousand cigarmakers of both sexes and all nationalities, from both factories and tenements, struck for the abolition of tenement outwork, but were defeated by the unity of the employers and the onset of winter. In the wake of the great strike the leadership and the membership of the union began to drift apart in two separate directions. Gompers and Strasser moved to reform the administration of the union and to implement more effective business methods. The majority of the rank and file, especially tenement outworkers, who were mostly women and now more disillusioned than ever with such trade union tactics, moved into the socialist camp and pinned their hopes for relief and redress on the success of their independent labor politicians.

Gompers and Strasser also looked to political action, but they had learned long before at the Tenth Ward Hotel to mistrust the ballot box and the "humbug" reformers who cherished it. Their goal was to protect the interests of the skilled hand-rollers who had elevated them to lead the cigarmakers' union, not to build an independent workers party. Instead of supporting their socialist membership they lobbied mainstream parties to pass a state anti-tenement labor bill, a law that would have driven the mostly female tenement workers out of the trade. Increasingly, the identities of skill, ethnicity, and sex that divided factory hand-rollers from tenement mold-rollers were themselves becoming involved in the question of independent socialist politics. Revealingly, Strasser began to characterize his union opponents as "tenement house scum," and Gompers copied a leaf from his old International tutors and accused those advocating socialist politics of being "utopians."[32]

Soon the principled gloves came off and Gompers and Strasser used the same methods to preserve their control over the CMIU that Sorge had employed against the Yankees in the International. When an insurgent socialist movement arose, demanded that the leadership of the union renounce association with mainstream politicians, and deposed Gompers of the presidency of Local 144 by electing his Bohemian socialist rival, Gompers ran off with the books and the treasury while Strasser worked behind the scenes to annul the election results. Predictably the insurgents withdrew and formed the Progressive Cigar Makers Union, whose membership soon outnumbered that of Local 144.[33]

The exodus of the tenement socialists gave Gompers and Strasser the freedom to further refine their business methods of administration and to attempt once again to build up the union through labor-market exclusion. Exclusion as a labor tactic became possible again due to the simple innovations of the union label and the consumer boycott. Pioneered by cigarmakers in California who had attempted to drive Chinese workers out of the industry in the 1860s, the union label promised to solve Strasser's "tenement scum" problem by putting indirect market pressure on employers to hire only union men. The first cigarmakers' union labels read: "The cigars herein contained are made by WHITE MEN. This label issued by authority of the Cigar Makers Association of the Pacific Coast." At a union meeting held in 1878, Gompers condemned the tenement house shops as "dens of filth," and Strasser compared the situation in New York to that in California, where the union label had allowed for "cigars made by white men" to be "distinguished from those made by the Chinese."

In 1880 the CMIU made the union label an effective national tool for preserving their control of the labor market, and Gompers and Strasser "reformed" Local 144 into a model of exclusive business unionism. Within a decade the CMIU had successfully remade itself into a formidable centralized union composed of a skilled segment of tobacco workers who jealously protected their labor-market niche against all other workers. Although about half of all cigarmakers in New York were female and another large proportion worked in tenement shops or occupied the lower rungs of the newly subdivided process of making cigars, neither of these groups was allowed into Gompers's cigarmakers' union.[34]

Samuel Gompers did not start out to be the defender of an aristocracy of skilled white labor, though his fetishistic view of trade unions ultimately took him there. Gompers, like the majority of the immigrant Marxists who surrounded him in his early years, adhered to the principle that workers should be organized regardless of their sex, race, or nationality. However, he too found that this belief conflicted with the higher principle that the trade union movement was the primary expression of class conflict and the only practical basis for social and political improvement. In the end, Gompers willingly bent his egalitarianism whenever the ideals of international brotherhood seemed to conflict with the growth and power of established trade unions.

As president of the American Federation of Labor, Gompers advocated organizing black workers, but his reasons for doing so were based on the best interests of white workers, not on a larger sense of working-class solidarity or humanitarian principle. His arguments in favor of the inclusion of blacks into the AFL followed the same line of reasoning that the committee charged with formulating policy for the old National Labor Union had employed in the 1860s, namely, that black workers posed a danger to the security of white workers and the best way for white workers to blunt this threat was to organize them into their own trade unions. "If we do not make friends of the colored men," said Gompers, "they will of necessity be justified in proving themselves our enemies."[35]

Whenever the issue came down to a choice between the strength of the union and the higher principle of racial brotherhood, Gompers never hesitated in his selection. In 1877 Gompers publicly advocated that any Chinese cigarmakers who were brought to New York by cigar manufacturers be met with "violent action." From the first convention of the Federation of Trades and Labor Unions, which Gompers helped organize in 1881 and at which he encouraged all members to "use their best efforts to get rid of the Chinese labor evil," into the twentieth century, when he published embarrassingly long examples of his racist spleen, including *Meat vs. Rice: American Manhood against Asiatic Coolieism: Which Shall Survive?*, Gompers personified the hypocrisy of the American labor movements attitude toward race.[36] As Gompers's AFL rose to lead the labor movement, it steadily abandoned women, ethnic minorities, African Americans, and all those whose unskilled work lent them little leverage over their employers.[37]

Such was one legacy of the Marxist tendency to conflate trade unions with the working class and to label radicals who demanded working-class inclusion, equality, and political rights as "petty bourgeois" opportunists. The expulsion of America's homespun radicals from the International may have had the long-range effect of separating the most powerful spokespersons for an inclusive vision of the American labor movement from the American Left, but it didn't remove them from other corners of the labor movement.

While the Marxist alumni of the Tenth Ward Hotel never gave up on their courtship of America's trade unions, their Yankee counterparts, rejected at every turn by the very organizations they were pledged to support, looked beyond trade unions to other means of organizing workers. Trade unions, in the eyes of many Internationalists, had become too exclusive, too particularistic in their demands, and too willing to accommodate themselves to capitalism in exchange for a slightly larger slice of the pie. Jacob Byrnes of Philadelphia's IWA, for one, refused all compromises with capitalism and set his sights "higher than strikes for wages." "If for instance we recognize wages," Byrnes argued, "we then recognize the Political economy which sanctions the wages system." Although Byrnes was one of the minority of professionals in Section 26, such complaints were not simply the product of middle-class privilege. Section 26's Thomas Phillips, a shoemaker who was himself an influential official in the shoemakers' union, the Knights of St. Crispin, had also become disillusioned with the narrowness of trade unions and even declared them to have "failed": "As a cure for the evils under which the working people suffer they are failures. This is true to a far greater extent than their friends think. The fundamental principles of Trades Unions are not calculated to emancipate labor."[38]

After the great unemployment protests they led had ended, Yankee Internationalists continued to support specific trade union struggles, but they devoted themselves to carrying the substance of their egalitarian and anticapitalistic crusade into a pair of new branches of the labor movement that also strove to transcend the wages system. Former Yankee socialists played leading roles in the development of two labor organizations that flourished in the 1870s but precipitously declined by the end of the 1880s. These two labor movements, the Knights of Labor and the lesser-known Sovereigns of Industry, a cooperative association modeled on the growing rural farm cooperative movement, constituted two of the largest labor movements of the nineteenth century and represented a dramatically contrasting model of labor organization to the American Federation of Labor. In both new organizations veterans of the Yankee IWA refused to compromise the principles of racial and gender equality for tactical gain.

From within these two groups former Yankee socialists left their mark on the history of the American labor movement. Both the Sovereigns and Knights eventually fell under the control of former Internationalists—official control in the case of the Sovereigns and de facto control in the case of the Knights. From their redoubts in the highest offices of the Knights' and the Sovereigns' unions, former Yankee Internationalists fought a rearguard battle against the rising power of the exclusivist trade union model and attempted to preserve a vision of a labor movement that encompassed all workers and combated the wages system.

The Knights of Labor was essentially an industrial union that attempted to organize all "producers," regardless of skill, race, or gender, into one large movement of workers, much as Industrial Workers of the World would a generation later. Although the origins of the Knights of Labor are remarkably well documented for what began as a secret, local organization that forbade its members even to utter its name in public, the debt the Knights of Labor owes the Yankee International has been entirely overlooked by its historians. Though the Knights was formally founded in 1869 by a half dozen Philadelphia garment cutters, it derived most of its ritual and ideology from an older secret labor fraternity, the "Brotherhood of the Union," that arose in Philadelphia a decade before the Civil War. Many members of the International Workingmen's Association were early members of the Brotherhood, including Section 9's John Commerford and Gilbert Vale.[39] The John Mills who appears on the roster of officers of the Industrial Brotherhood as the secretary of the "Progress Council" of Philadelphia is probably the same John Mills, a middle-aged tailor, who held the post of secretary for IWA Section 26 twenty years later. Another member of Section 26, Thomas Phillips, spoke up at a meeting of his section and revealed that "he belonged to a secret organization which had done more to indoctrinate men's minds than all the other open organizations put together in the U.S., . . . [though] he would not claim that the ideas of George Lipard [sic] were as clear as when he started the organization as the ideas are on the Labor Question at the present time."[40] Phillips was the first shoemaker to join the Knights, and he was charged with organizing his fellow tradesmen. He founded Assembly 64, a Knights of Labor trade body composed of his fellow shoemakers that soon grew to become the largest local in the Knights. With this feather in his cap and with his long experience as a correspondent and columnist in the labor press, Phillips was appointed to the Committee of Progress, the Knights' central body responsible for drafting and disseminating propaganda. Over the next year and half Phillips influenced the national ideology of the Knights from his propaganda desk, penning and publishing over four hundred articles explaining the principles and purpose of the Knights.[41]

Uriah Stephens, the man given credit for creating and nurturing the Knights of Labor, also had a deep connection to the IWA. Stephens was a native of New Jersey who studied for the Baptist ministry but was forced by necessity to give up the pulpit for the needle and become a tailor. In the 1860s Stephens traveled to Europe and made the acquaintance of J. George Eccarius, a fellow tailor, in London. Eccarius, a widely read and traveled German émigré who moved in the same radical circles as Marx and Engels, was a tremendous influence upon Stephens and is even reputed to have introduced him to the *Communist Manifesto*.[42]

Other former Internationalists moved into positions where they affected the policies and direction of the Knights. John T. Elliot, former general secretary of the Spring Street IWA, rose to a position of leadership within the Knights in Baltimore and was a delegate to the Knights' Grand Assembly in 1882. George Blair, a member of the Spring Street Council, joined the Knights when it first began organizing in New York in 1874. Within a decade he was elected chairman of the statewide Knights' committee. In 1880 the IWA's John Mills who kept the rich and detailed minutes of Section 26, served as secretary of the Knights of Labor's Eight Hour Delegation, a committee that included Albert Parsons, the man who would soon become one of labor history's most celebrated martyrs after the Haymarket bombing in Chicago. Victor Drury, the Internationalist who had close ties to Section 12 in New York, had organized the Yankee International in Boston, and had joined Section 26 after moving to Philadelphia, eventually became a leader of the General Executive Board of District Assembly 49, a Knights of Labor administrative unit. The unit, which governed all of New York City, was at times the most powerful force in the national union. Drury was the architect of the coalition of socialists and artisan traditionalists that became known as the "Home Club," a union within a union that played kingmaker of the Knights' national leadership.[43]

Like the Knights of Labor, the Sovereigns of Industry also attracted many former Yankee Internationalists to its ranks. But veterans of the Yankee

International not only contributed leadership to the Sovereigns of Industry, it also can claim a great deal of credit for the organization's conception. Throughout the English-language sections of the IWA there had been a strong current of support for the cooperative movement. Cooperation was a large and loaded term for Yankee socialists: it expressed both their anti-capitalistic ideals and a practical tactic for achieving them. Consumer cooperatives especially appealed to Yankee socialists because they were highly inclusive organizations that, unlike producer cooperatives that promised to improve the lives of only the cooperative's own workers, offered a general benefit to all workers, regardless of their skill, trade, sex, or color. In endorsing cooperation as an ideal, these native radicals were not hearkening back to the days of Fourierism and phalansteries but to hard-headed economic doctrine, battle-tested in the trenches of the working men of England.[44]

One of the most enthusiastic and active advocates of cooperation in the Yankee International was Maria Howland. Howland saw early in life the nature of industrial capitalism when she was working as a young girl in a Lowell textile factory. After several years at the power loom, Howland moved to New York City to pursue an acting career, but she found herself instead teaching at a school in Five Points, the most notorious slum in the city. Quickly rising through the pedagogical ranks, she became a principal by 1857, all the while drifting into more radical social circles. Around this time she moved into Stephen Pearl Andrews's urban commune with her first husband. She also became friends with Albert Brisbane, the famed father of Fourieristic socialism in America. Somewhere between the mill, the slum, and the commune, Howland became an ardent feminist and cooperative-minded socialist.[45]

After Howland spent several years in Europe, the wellsprings of her first marriage ran dry and her attention turned to a young Harvard graduate. True to her feminist free-love ideals, Marie Howland secured a divorce and moved with her new husband, Edward, to the bucolic orchardlands of southern New Jersey. Together they began their cooperative crusade by publicizing the writings of Jean Baptiste Godin, whose large industrial cooperative in Guise, France, Howland most likely toured when she lived in Europe. In April 1872, *Harper's New Monthly Magazine* published Edward Howland's description of the workings of Godin's so-called "Social Palace," which included Godin's extensive iron works, a "familistére," or apartment building, which housed over a thousand individuals, as well as theaters, parks, gardens, schools, and cooperative stores. Howland hailed Godin's social experiment as "the exit of society, from the cannibalistic competition of the present, to a higher form of civilization." Meanwhile, Marie translated Godin's principal work, *Social Solutions*, and carried the news of Godin's success to the Yankee socialists of Philadelphia.[46]

But Philadelphia's English-speaking radicals, though in the section perhaps most supportive of cooperative schemes within the American International, were not prepared to enshrine Godin's or anyone else's version of Fourierism in their program. Although the section offered to help Marie Howland publish her work-in-progress, "The Palace of Guise," they ultimately did not devote any money or time to this effort. Some were openly hostile to Godin's utopia. One member noted that cooperative communities most often failed and that "only those settlements glued together by religion like the Shakers seemed to succeed." Thomas Phillips pointed out that the "social palace" suffered from "a great fundamental error," namely, that it "was controlled by one man [Godin]." What working people needed, argued Phillips, was a "workingman's movement . . . without a Capitalist to lead them."[47] Phillips was well situated to criticize cooperative schemes with such authority. In 1862 he and a few fellow British immigrants founded a cooperative grocery store on the Rochdale plan in Philadelphia, and a few years later he wrote regularly for *Fincher's Trades' Review* as their resident expert on cooperation.[48]

Phillips was not the only English-speaking member of the IWA who had first-hand knowledge of the workings of cooperatives. Richard Josiah Hinton, secretary of Section 23 in Washington, D.C., traveled throughout England and Europe from 1868 to 1870, visiting cooperatives and dispatching his observations back to numerous American journals and newspapers. Hinton became a lifelong advocate of cooperatives, and he ultimately chaired the "colonization" commission of Eugene Debs's Social Democracy, a body charged with formulating plans for a cooperative colony in the Western United States.[49]

While the detailed utopian blueprints of Fourier or his disciples didn't sway the majority of Internationalists, the growth of pragmatic cooperative movements with less sweeping aims did. At its weekly meetings in the spring of 1873, Section 26 discussed "the Grange," a new society in the West that had reportedly fought the railroads in legislatures and courts and was actively organizing producer and consumer cooperatives among farmers. The Grange, formally known as the Patrons of Husbandry, was founded in 1866 by a clerk in the U.S. Department of Agriculture, Oliver Hudson Kelley, as a means of overcoming the atomization and isolation of rural life. It grew rapidly by incorporating existing rural clubs and societies, and within a decade it claimed three-quarters of a million members.[50]

Because the Grange accepted only farmers, few Internationalists became members in those early years, though Edward and Marie Howland were eligible for membership because they cultivated roses and fruit trees. Their home became the focal point of Grange organizing in the state. Edward eventually became president of the New Jersey state Grange, and Marie held the highest office a woman could, the "Ceres" of the state Grange. Both were sent as delegates to the Grange's national convention in St. Louis in 1874, where Marie shocked the men by joining them at their conference tables rather than taking a seat on the side benches reserved for "ladies." Though Edward and Marie Howland made their mark upon the Grange, it proved too conservative an organization to hold them. Complaining that it had become a "mere business caucus," they left the organization for the upstart radical cooperative movement the Sovereigns of Industry.[51]

Members of the old Spring Street Council in New York City caught the Grange fever as well and barged their way into an antimonopoly convention of politically restless officers of midwestern state farmers associations. J. B. Wolff, Joshua Ingalls, George W. Madox, and Theodore Banks were all eventually seated at the convention after being initially barred. They ultimately succeeded in pushing the convention's resolutions in a more stridently anticorporate direction.[52] Section 26 of the IWA wired its warm congratulations to the New York antimonopolists: "May your deliberations aid in a speedy deliverance of the people from the oppression of corporations and result in the distributors of wealth becoming the servants rather than the masters of the producers of wealth."[53] Here, then, years before the obvious marriage of Western agrarian protest and Eastern radicalism, the remnants of the Yankee International were attempting to form alliances with the antecedents of populism.[54]

By the summer of 1873, the Yankee Internationalists began discussing more concrete means of carrying forward their ideals of cooperation. Section 26 debated opening a cooperative store of its own as a practical step toward spreading anticapitalistic ideals. But they had no illusions that socialism would be ushered in across the counter of a cooperative store. Rather, these more pragmatic radicals were eager to do something that had practical effect, namely, moving their activities from the meeting halls to the streets. Isaac Rehn, the main proponent of the cooperative store idea, called his plan "educational" and advocated that they begin to "fight commerce with commerce — Hell with fire." For Rehn and the rest of the Philadelphia band, starting a cooperative store was merely "taking every club [they] could to belabor the present system." Even John Shedden, a member of Section 26 who was soon to become a leading force in the national cooperative movement, admitted that cooperation was not a panacea. When Victor Drury wrote to Shedden in 1877, criticizing cooperatives for rectifying but one-fifth of the exploitation of the worker, Shedden answered, "There must be a starting point . . . until man possesses all the elements, till society at large are possessor of all the elements, we should not have a harmonious whole, but while this may be . . . what is to be done now"? [55]

The men and women of Section 26 made their start in the fall of 1873 by transforming their organization from a section of the International into a chapter of the Patrons of Industry, an association that they were led to believe was the industrial counterpart to the agrarian Patrons of Husbandry. Though the organizers of the Patrons of Industry talked a good radical line, they began to look suspicious to Section 26 when they demanded that the new chapter purchase an official lodge seal, printed lodge books, an official gavel, member emblems, and other regalia that added up to the princely sum of fifty dollars. Victor Drury was sent to the headquarters in New York City to investigate and sent back the bad news that "I can only discover trickery — deception, humbug — I have been told LIES."

When Drury furthered his private inquiries into the men behind the Patrons of Industry, the Patrons' secretary granted them a charter and then abruptly revoked it a fortnight later. Apparently, Section 26 was rejected on the grounds that they were too radical. "We take not stock in Communism or Internationalists," the Patrons of Industry's secretary wrote to the section, "more than one of whom besides Drury were on your charter members list, and this would bring our principles and your practice at variance at once." This was a curious position for a labor organization whose organizers reportedly demanded "an equal division of wealth of the country" and called for workers to "rise en masse and force the Government and wealthy citizens, who are no better than harpies, to give it to them." [56]

Whether the Patrons of Industry was indeed just a scam, as Drury charged, will probably never be known. Nevertheless, fraudulent or not, the group probably succeeded in laying the groundwork for the rapid growth of the Sovereigns of Industry, an organization whose very name indicates some connection to the ephemeral Patrons who quickly passed into obscurity. Just a few weeks later, William H. Earle, a member of the Grange whose claim to agrarian status was a hobby fruit grove, resolved to form an organization for workingmen that would parallel the Grange. Reportedly, invitations were sent out to several dozen persons—the names of whom were probably gleaned from contacts already established by the Internationals, the Knights, and the Patrons of Industry—who might be interested in such a movement, and in early January of 1874 a founding meeting of the Sovereigns of Industry was held in Springfield, Massachusetts. Someone from Section 26 most likely attended that first meeting, for within that same month it had converted itself into Pioneer Council No. 1 of the Sovereigns.[57]

By March the Sovereigns had organized subsidiary councils in six states, an achievement that indicates that the group initially grew by picking up the pieces of earlier organizations. One of these was undoubtedly the International Workingmen's Association, since at least four of the six national deputies charged with organizing the Sovereigns outside of Massachusetts were former members of Yankee sections. For example, Thomas Phillips was particularly successful in spreading the cooperative ideal and later claimed to have personally organized five councils in Philadelphia alone, including the first one composed exclusively of women; Edward Howland was named one of the national officers; John Orvis, who had strong connections to the IWA, was the Sovereigns' full-time lecturer; and Edward Chamberlin, who was the author of its first official book-length history, had been a member of Boston's section of the IWA. Within a couple of years Thomas Phillips and John Shedden became coeditors of the association's national organ, the *Sovereigns of Industry Bulletin*. In 1878 Shedden was unanimously elected the Sovereigns' national president. That same year he had the unique experience of going to the White House and discussing the merits of cooperative industry with President Hayes.[58]

The rhetoric and principles of the Sovereigns were milder than those of the Yankee International, but they contained plenty of room for socialist maneuvering. At the core of the Sovereigns' ideology was the labor theory of value. One of the association's first circulars stated typically: "To the industrial classes the world is indebted for every dollar of its wealth." On top of this basic socialist principle the Sovereigns heaped blame upon the "capitalists," "middle men," and "aristocratic classes" who held "the surplus wealth of the country" and were "running the Government and ruling the country." Although pointed in their accusations, the Sovereigns were much duller in their plans of action. While they stated that "we institute the Order of the Sovereigns of Industry, for the purpose of overthrowing these evils" and they promised to do their "part towards the redemption of the world," in the same breath the Sovereigns consciously lowered their horizons and proclaimed simply that "the purpose of this organization to secure immediate benefits to its members by cheapening the cost of living." Such a program may not have rang with revolutionary fervor, but there was nothing there that a universally-minded Yankee socialist could object to. Even the Sovereigns' constitutional disclaimer, "We wage no war with persons or classes, but only with wrongs, discords and hardships, which have existed too long"—a sentiment boiled down for the masthead of the Sovereigns' national journal to "Capital and Labor—Friends, Not Enemies"—was not renouncing revolutionary aims but was making a higher claim that the capitalistic system transcends individual responsibility.[59]

For all the vague pronouncements of its charters and circulars, the Sovereigns of Industry stood upon one simple bedrock idea—that the inequalities and unjust arrangements of society could only be changed by workers who were educated, organized, and determined to affect them. Pennsylvania's Sovereigns issued a circular that began with the lines: the "proposition that the emancipation of the working people must come from the action of working people themselves, is too self-evident to need comment." The proclamation was lifted word for word from the preamble to the First International's constitution. The statement of purpose of one of the Sovereigns of Industry newspapers did not even mention the word "cooperation" but instead hammered home the message that "POWER LIES IN COMBINATION" and that workers "united, have all power, divided they are the servants of the money power and the toilers of corporate wealth." Cooperation, beyond its inherent value as an economic system antithetical to the logic of capitalism, was, just as importantly, simply the focal point for the organization of all workers, regardless of occupation, skill, ethnicity, sex, or race. All workers stood to benefit from cheaper goods; and from this practical advantage, a greater sense of solidarity and community of interest could grow and become a bastion of strength for future battles.[60]

Like the Yankee Internationalists before them, the Sovereigns were not terribly concerned with theorizing a detailed road map of what form those future struggles would take. In the grand tradition of American reform, the Sovereigns firmly believed that as long as their principles were true and just, their efforts unflagging, and their courage undaunted, then history would take care of itself. Marx's attempt at historical micromanagement in the First International would have struck the Sovereigns—just as it did the Yankee Internationalists—as a misguided sacrifice of principles to momentary advantage. Like American reformers before them the Sovereigns were willing to stand their ground and let the chips fall where they may. As Edwin

Chamberlin described in his book on the movement, the Sovereigns "are endeavoring solely to organize the industrial classes of the United States for future action," and "this action will not necessarily take place under the direction of the society, but may have a leadership outside of it. To educate the laborers into an harmonious and united movement, is the purpose of the society; but what that movement shall be, and in what manner it shall be undertaken, must be left to a future day to decide." [61]

Because the Sovereigns of Industry's program was, beyond its ethical underpinnings, a relatively empty vessel, it proved entirely compatible with the sort of state socialism that ran through the Yankee International. Edwin Chamberlin received journalistic praise from the Sovereign press for his book on the movement. The *State Sovereign* not only expressed its hope that Chamberlin's book would "find a welcome place at the fireside of every farmer and mechanic" but also chose for its lengthiest excerpt the book's advocacy of government ownership of the means of production, which included this passage: "The grandest and most successful works in all ages have been those which the government has accomplished, and there is no reason why it should not undertake the direction of industry than the direction of an army, the destroyer of industry." [62] The *State Sovereign*'s editors devoted the front spread of a number of issues of their short-lived journal to the socialistic writings of William G. H. Smart, and approvingly summarized his thesis: "His fundamental idea is . . . *the extension of the democratic principle of our government into the domain of wealth and industry*." The editors concluded that all "factories, workshops, and all the machinery of industry, and all the products of industry while undergoing the process of transfer and exchange, constitute the 'national wealth,' and should be placed under the immediate direction and control of officers appointed by the people in their collective capacity." [63]

Radicals fresh out of the Yankee International brought more than their socialist viewpoints to the Sovereigns' cooperative unions; they also carried along their advanced belief in the necessary equality of rights between men and women and white and black. While the Grange, the Sovereigns of Industry's rural cousin, drew a color bar across their association, the Sovereigns' constitution was uncompromising in its upholding of the "universal interests of humanity, and a philanthropy rising impartially above all distinctions of class, sex, creed, race or nationality" and its policy of making "no distinction as regards rights and privileges of membership . . . on account of sex, creed, race, or nationality." And former Internationalist leaders of the Sovereigns were willing to defend such rhetoric before a less equality-minded trade unionist audience.

As the Sovereigns of Industry's movement began to grow across the industrial Northeast in its second year, it was attacked by the *National Labor Tribune*, a labor journal tied more closely to trade unions than to the broader visions of labor reform. "The Sovereigns," claimed the *Tribune*'s editors, "do not make the protection and elevation of Labor's interest cardinal doctrine. . . . What good is cheap flour to a man who has no money to buy the flour with?" Keeping up the barrage in its next issue, the *Tribune* fired another accusation at the Sovereigns. It charged that its claim to be a union composed exclusively of workingmen was false because it had "professional men, and other non-producers; . . . it also has women in it, and yet it calls itself a secret order. What sort of security can it maintain where women are?"

Jacob S. Byrnes, "Deputy of the Order" and former member of IWA Section 26, responded to these attacks by explaining that Sovereigns, being wage earners themselves, were certainly for higher wages, but they went beyond the wage issue and "war with the whole wage-system," for "wages, whether high or low, alike rob the laborer and that upon that which wages take from labor, the wage payer lives, thrives and fattens into ease and luxury." Byrnes noted that cooperative purchasing was "but our first step" and that beyond that the Sovereigns hoped to use its consumer power to strengthen producer cooperatives and eventually replace "co-operation, production and exchange, for the present competitive system." Byrnes did little to soften the radical thrust of the Sovereigns' anticapitalism for his trade union readers, but when it came to defending the inclusion of women in the labor movement, Byrnes's passion rose to a new level: "Your reflections upon women in our order seems to me simply cruel. God help the workingwomen and children of Fall River, and other factories, if they are to be excluded from any labor organization that can afford them material or moral aid, of any kind or any degree. Yes! We have thousands of workingwomen in our order, and may it utterly perish when it excludes, without good and sufficient cause, the meanest or feeblest of them."[64]

Jacob Byrnes's passionate defense of the rights of women was but one typical example of how many former Yankee Internationalists distinguished themselves for their championing of racial and sexual equality. Thomas Phillips did so in all of the labor organizations in which he was active. During the Sovereigns' 1877 convention it was Phillips who sponsored a resolution to drop all fees for women so as to encourage them to join in great numbers and "infuse new life in the order." Phillips was an early opponent of exclusionary elements in the Knights of St. Crispins' union, and it was his Philadelphia shoemakers' union that organized the first local of workingwomen in the Knights of Labor. But of all the veterans of the First International, none left as remarkable a record of equal rights advocacy than did Victor Drury.[65]

Drury is an especially central figure to the history of the Knights of Labor. While Drury sat on the executive board of his section, District Assembly 49, it distinguished itself as one of the most advanced assemblies on the question of race in the Knights of Labor. Drury and his fellow New York radicals worked actively to open the Knights of Labor to men and women of all races. In 1886 Drury and other members of DA 49 plotted to use the upcoming Knights' convention, which was to be held in the segregated city of Richmond, Virginia, as an occasion to put the organization's own rhetoric of racial equality to the test.

Among the sixty delegates who traveled to the Richmond convention was the secretary-treasurer of DA 49, Frank Ferrell, a black machinist and an able socialist orator. Ferrell and his fellow New York delegates bravely flouted Richmond's strict racial segregation. Drury and the other delegates from DA 49 refused to sleep in a hotel that had denied a room to Ferrell, and the entire group moved to Harris Hall, a black boardinghouse, instead. Even more shocking to the whites of Richmond, when the men of DA 49 decided to take in a production of Hamlet, they escorted their friend Frank Ferrell to the whites-only section at the elite Mozart Academy of Music. Later in the week, Drury was invited to deliver a speech at a dinner party thrown in honor of the members of DA 49 by Richmond's appreciative black community.[66]

The following year Drury trespassed upon even more sensitive ground within the labor movement by encouraging the organization of Chinese workers. In 1887 Drury pushed DA 49 to grant a charter to a union of five hundred Chinese workers. Drury and Ferrell, who were in the minority in advocating that the Knights admit Chinese workers, argued that the "obliteration of lines of distinction in creed, color or nationality" were the first principles of labor organization.[67]

WITHIN the labor movement the Yankee International bequeathed an inheritance that upheld the antebellum radical's vision of universal reform and equality for all. They rejected the trade union tactic of winning a larger share of the capitalist pie by controlling access to labor markets and rejecting women and racial minorities from their membership rolls, and replaced it with a democratic and syndicalist strategy built as much around America's republican ideals and the public nexus of consumption as within the private space of the factory.

While the Yankee International's historic thrust was toward egalitarian and inclusive unionism, the legacy of Sorgean Internationalism veered off in the opposite direction. Samuel Gompers, Adolph Strasser, and P. J. McGuire, some of the most famous architects of the skill-, race-, and sex-defined trade union model, which became the basis of the modern American labor movement, cut their activist teeth at meetings of the Tenth Ward Hotel International. In this way the Marxist half of the American International served as the intermediary between Marx's revolutionary view of the trade union as the cradle of social transformation and the ideology of the American Federation of Labor, which retained Marx's view of unions as the vital vehicle of historic change but rejected revolutionary aims. It was not long before a bitter struggle ensued between the cheeks of this Janus-faced legacy of American Internationalism. This was a contest that at times pitted against each other the same opponents whose clash in 1871 had torn the IWA apart and ultimately left the prodigies of the same victors holding the field.

Between 1882 and 1886 the Knights of Labor and various trade unions wastefully competed with each other for jurisdictions, memberships, and contracts. In New York, a city that, as Samuel Gompers observed, became "the cradle of the modern American labor movement," the schism within Gompers's cigarmakers' union turned into a struggle between an emerging national federation of trade unions and the national Knights of Labor. At a time when Victor Drury's "Home Club" was at the apex of its power within the Knights, the Knights threw their support to Gompers's rivals, the "Progressive" cigarmakers' union, a union whose open membership policies, electoral socialism, and industrial organization were most compatible with its own inclusive ethos. As the disagreement dragged on, both the Knights-backed "Progressive" cigarmakers and the national trade federation–backed Cigarmakers International Union stooped to scabbing on each other's strikes, and each attempted to monopolize the use of its own unique cigar box label. Though these labor battles often seemed to be merely contests for power, on the whole they represented a deeper debate about the fundamental purpose and character of the labor movement, indeed, about the very nature of the future social terrain of American society.[68]

Similar conflicts in areas of the country where "dual unions" operated led to the entrenching of the ideological stands of both the Knights and the national trade unions. Ultimately, in 1886, the Knights of Labor took the precipitous step of demanding that the trade assemblies that had long functioned within the Knights' industrial structure either join in "mixed assemblies," that is, open up their membership to all workers regardless of their occupation, or leave. However, this step succeeded only in galvanizing the forces of exclusive trade unionism and provoking the organization of the American Federation of Labor. In 1886 a group of five leaders of national trade unions, including three former members of the Tenth Ward Hotel, issued a call for a conference to consider ways to protect their organizations from the "malicious work of an element who openly boast that 'trade unions must be destroyed.'" A month later it was at that convention that the AFL was born.[69]

The AFL quickly eclipsed the Knights and became the basis of labor organization for the next century. In its own attenuated and circuitous way the Yankee International, by incubating the leadership and influencing the inclusive and egalitarian ideology of the Knights, contributed to this outcome, as did its Marxist opponents, whose own meeting halls were, ironically, the training academies of the first generation of trade union bureaucrats.

Yankee Internationalists wrote a number of peculiar footnotes to the history of the labor movement in America. But because they are usually notes for battles lost, they have long been written out of a history of labor that has emphasized its progressive development over time. Yankee radicals, hoping to fight fire with fire and overturn capitalism by outcompeting it, built up the largest radical consumer cooperative movement in American history, only to witness it being consumed by its dynamic foe instead. In standing up for the principle that workers must organize as a class rather than along lines dictated by the capitalist division of labor or the social impositions of race and gender, Yankee radicals provoked a trade union backlash that ultimately led to the organization of the American Federation of Labor and laid the basis for the modern labor movement. Their historical legacy may be one of failure, but it is also one that spotlights the fact that the modern American labor movement did not only evolve from the antagonisms between workers and employers but was also the product of a clash of ideologies and strategies within the working class itself.

The Legacy of the Yankee International

B Y 1874 THE International was dead. Sorge's Section 1 was torn apart by squabbling over control of the party's newspaper, and his Marxist General Council attacked the Federal Council, which was controlled by a group of freethinking German Americans who espoused republican values and advocated political action. Still pursuing the goal of ideological purification, the General Council eventually suspended the Federal Council, though Dr. George Stiebling refused to surrender the Council's records and was duly expelled for his principled resistance. When the North American Federation of the IWA opened its second congress in the summer of 1874, Sorge resigned from the General Council and recommended that the organization suspend business for one year so as to regroup, which was, in effect, just an evasive way of accepting its demise. Most delegates insisted on clinging to the lingering aura of the International and allowed the body to molder for several more years before giving it a proper burial.[1]

Yankee socialists were less attached to the name and discarded it as they rushed forward to other reform fronts. When declining attendance and the insistent demands of what they termed "that most hideous of beings—a landlord" for the back rent on their hall reached the critical point, Philadelphia's Section 26 simply resolved to carry on its work under the rubric of other labor reform organizations. We can "employ our means as well to diffuse our principles" just as well by acting "discreetly," argued some members who advocated that the Internationals attempt to bend their purposes to the larger weekly workmen's meetings that were then being held at another hall. It was even suggested that the section meet just prior to the larger workingmen's meeting and use that caucus to prepare to "participate in the public meeting and thereby make our principles known." Such a strategy proved successful as former members of Section 26 soon came to dominate the committees and command the platforms of the unemployed workers' movement in Philadelphia.[2]

Other IWA veterans wandered into the swamp of monetary reform. Though currency and finance issues never ranked high on the IWA's list of concerns, they attracted several former socialists. Boston's venerable William B. Greene returned to promoting his monetary and banking schemes and moved closer to the ideology of anarchism, which was then being refined by his friend Ezra Heywood in the pages of *The Word*. Some members of Philadelphia's IWA became active greenbackers. Others retained the goal of socialist redistribution but advocated new means of achieving this end. John Wolff of Section 12 became secretary of the Graduated Tax Association of New York City, a group that viewed taxation as a "great equalizer of surplus products, and solution of the capital and labor controversy," and who advertised its organization in Spiritualist periodicals.[3] Elizabeth Daniels of Boston was also swept up in the graduated-tax enthusiasm, believing that the graduated tax would "arouse the working people to such a pitch of excitement as they have not reached in a long while, and be a principle means of freeing them."[4]

Other veterans of the Yankee IWA fanned out across the reform terrain carrying with them a mixture of the American reform tradition and Internationalist socialism. In this way they laid the seeds for a new generation of American radicals. Yankee Internationalists played an early and central role in the founding of the Sovereigns of Industry, a national cooperative association that ultimately enlisted and benefited tens of thousands of American workers. Experienced Internationalists also pioneered the doctrines of Christian socialism.[5] They were active in the Knights of Labor and opened its doors to women and attempted to do the same for the most abused minorities. They influenced the thinking of both Henry George and Edward Bellamy, two of the most famous American social critics of the latter half of the nineteenth century. But for all their remarkable achievements in the latter parts of their lives, they failed to make similar inroads into the ideology, movement culture, and tactics of the organized Left itself.

The failure of Yankee IWA veterans to gain leadership within socialist parties was not for lack of trying. Soon after the dissipation of New York's IWA a number of members of New York's Spring Street Council became active in the newly formed Social Democratic Workingmen's Party. A few former members of Section 12, such as George Madox, Leander Thompson, and William West, had pulled together a number of their old comrades and founded an English-speaking section of the Social Democratic Workingmen's Party (SDWP). A Yankee Internationalist stamp was evident on the platform of the SDWP, a portion of which called for the democratic reforms of the initiative and the recall—planks dear to the English-speaking sections of New York's IWA since the days of the New Democracy. Yet the influence of the old Yankee Internationalists proved fleeting.

It was not long before they discovered that their reform baggage was just as unwelcome in the newly founded socialist parties as it had been in the old. Soon the SDWP and other socialist groups moved to found a new unified socialist organization, the Socialist Labor Party. At the 1877 founding convention of the SLP, Thompson and Madox's credentials were rejected and their English-speaking section of the SDWP was suspended.[6] Over the opposition of the only female delegate in the hall, the SLP convention went on to pound out a set of resolutions, which reincorporated the old Workingmen's Party plank that Sorge had drafted a number of years before, condemning the movement for women's suffrage by arguing that "the emancipation of women will be accomplished with the emancipation of men, and the so-called women's rights question will be solved with the labor question." This formula that dismissed questions of civil and social equality by making them contingent upon the leveling of classes would bedevil the Left for the rest of the century. It would become the standard justification for the socialists' refusal to concern themselves with the particular oppressions of racial minorities. The SLP platform continued the Tenth Ward Hotel's campaign against the Chinese by condemning the "importation of Coolies under contract." Essentially, this tact was merely a more veiled way of courting workers agitated at the prospect of Chinese competition. Remarkably, the founding document of the SLP even omitted the customary phrase that declared their membership open to all regardless of race or religion, which had been a feature of nearly every socialist platform since the old Communist Club of the 1850s.[7]

In throwing out Thompson, Madox, and the other New York Yankees, the SLP threw out the Yankee reform legacy itself. The rejected radicals continued their reform efforts but without the institutional support of the organized Left. G. W. Madox went on to organize his own ephemeral "Congress of Humanity," which appealed to all "men, women, workers for perpetuity of civil liberty, equal rights and distributive justice" to unite a series of four principles including land and currency reform, workers ownership, and "control [of] the product," and called for the "inalienable right" of suffrage to be respected "without regard to race, condition, color or sex."[8] Madox, like many other former Yankee Internationalists, also joined the Knights of Labor and in the pages of its national journal continued to advocate his belief that the "great factors of in industry should be utilized by the whole people, through their governments, for the benefit of the whole."[9]

Eventually New York's plucky socialists pulled together a small English-speaking section of the SLP anyway. According to its membership rolls, William West, the Internationalist who by that time had nearly fifty years of radical experience in a succession of American reform movements, was among them. Next to the column where the secretary was to record the date on which his membership in the party began, he wrote, "Who can tell?" In spite of the years of purging from the membership those whose sympathies tended toward the republican tradition, the Yankee ghosts had not been entirely vanquished from this section. One of its first initiatives was to establish a library and reading room for the city's workers. The first volume donated to the collection was an edition of the writings of Thomas Paine.[10]

Only a few of the other veterans of the Yankee International remained fairly active in the official Marxist Left. Richard Josiah Hinton and Cyrenus Osborne Ward were two who seemed to carry around the stamp of their earliest reform experiences and attitudes throughout their lives. Ward, "a spare, sparsely-whiskered man with a prominent Adam's apple and a resonant voice," ran for lieutenant governor of New York on the SLP ticket in 1879. During the International's last official year of existence, Ward lived in a boardinghouse with a number of other "advanced thinkers," including George E. MacDonald, who was later to become the editor of the atheist's flagship journal, *The Truth Seeker*, and a "Mr. Brewster," who was an advocate of the "hollow globe theory." (Brewster believed that the interior of the earth was navigable through openings at either pole; and to illustrate his ideas he had constructed a three-foot globe complete with magnetized sailing ships.) Ward went on to research and write a landmark study of labor struggles and communism in the ancient world and their relationship to early Christianity.[11]

Richard Josiah Hinton also persevered within the Socialist Labor Party, emerging in 1886 as managing editor of the New York *Leader*, an English-language newspaper that the socialists had wrested out of the hands of Henry George's single-taxers. But Hinton's older reform commitments got him into trouble one last time when he was accused of campaigning for a Republican candidate in 1893, the same year he published a biography of John Brown. As a result, Hinton was thrown out of a socialist party for the second time in his life. It was not long afterward that Eugene Debs announced his newfound belief in socialist principles and strung together the Social Democracy from the pieces of his defunct American Railway Union. Hinton was soon given a column in the party organ, *The Social Democrat*, and was tapped to head the colonization commission, a committee whose charge was to find a suitable site for a cooperative colony in a sparsely settled Western state. Though he failed in his attempt, the latest in the long line of attempts to reform the world through frontier example that stretched back to John Winthrop's famed vision of making his colony the "city on a hill," Hinton eventually helped establish a cooperative colony in Washington State, where he passed his final years with his old friend from the IWA, Joshua King Ingalls.[12]

West, Ward, and a couple others aside, the SLP proved unattractive to New York's workers and those reformers whose vision was molded in older radical struggles. Soon reduced to seventeen members, the section was forced to appeal to English-speaking German American socialists to join them in order to prevent their section from dissolving altogether.

In the face of the SLP's obvious failure to make inroads among American workers, Augustus Henninger, one of the old German American Internationalists of the Tenth Ward Hotel, wrote to the president of the SLP with a critique of the party's platform. The time had come, argued Henninger, to quit courting trade unions by including in the platform special planks for their benefit: "The party has thus far made not gain among the trades union element on the strength of the said allusions, and it is not likely to make any such gain in the future on the strength of them. These people will not be dragged into the party by such means. The more we try to flatter and coax them, the more they will suspect us."[13] Henninger proposed that the SLP, thus freed from the old strategy of trying to "flatter" the trade unions into the party, expand its platform, including adding a plank for women's suffrage. Henninger's advice was not taken to heart, and the party never won a great following among native-born workers.

The outlook of the Yankee Internationalists who lost their connection to the organized American Left remained within the more racially egalitarian and "universal" tradition of American reform. Besides venturing into the Knights of Labor and helping found the Sovereigns of Industry, most members of Philadelphia's English-speaking Section 26, for example, moved into alliance with the Pennsylvania Women's Suffrage Association. However, their radicalism was too much for the more staid suffragists, and in 1876, seeing that the PWSA would not accommodate their "broader and more liberal views," the former Yankee Internationalists struck out on their own and formed a rival association. They even lured from the PWSA a number of former leaders of the Pennsylvania Anti-Slavery Association, most notably Edward M. Davis, Sarah Pugh, and Robert Purvis, and together they formed the Citizens' Suffrage Association. After Congress passed the Chinese Exclusion Act in 1882, the Citizens' Suffrage Association sent its "unqualified condemnation" of the popular law to the press.[14]

Yankee radicalism did not simply vanish because it was given no berth in the well-ruddered but largely empty ship of the American Left. American workers demonstrated time and time again throughout the nineteenth century that they were more animated by the easily understood cries of eighteenth-century republicanism than by the intellectual rigors of Marx. Henry George's "single tax" campaigners, Edward Bellamy's "nationalist" clubs, Christian socialists, cooperative unions, and many elements of the Populist movement each combined in its own unique way a hostility to industrialism, a limited vision of state socialism, and a devotion to political liberty. The number of Americans attracted to any one of these movements alone vastly outnumbered the combined ranks of all the fragments of the self-proclaimed socialist parties of the nineteenth century.[15]

Both George and Bellamy were to a significant degree inheritors of the Yankee International and the bridge between the American reform tradition and the twentieth century Left. In 1879 Henry George, the journalist-turned-economist, published a treatise that traced the source of social inequality to the increasing monopolization of land and that advocated a "single tax" on land that would confiscate and redistribute the unearned increase in landed property's value. Though such ideas had been around for quite some time, by the last third of the nineteenth century, George's master work, *Progress and Poverty*, became a sensation, reaching an estimated readership of three million and catapulting George to national fame. George's followers attempted to parlay his popularity into electoral power, and, in alliance with the Socialist Labor Party, they waged a spectacular campaign that came within a stone's throw of making George the mayor of New York City. Though the alliance of the single-taxers and the SLP barely lasted past election day, the campaign itself rejuvenated the SLP and temporarily gave the upper hand to the minority in the party who favored broad electoral strategies over trade union tactics.[16]

Many sources have been credited with influencing George's views, John Stuart Mill and Herbert Spencer being among the most often cited. But George appropriated much of his theory of the effect of land monopoly from a series of newspaper columns, entitled "The Land Question," written in 1871 by Edward T. Peters, an official with the Bureau of Statistics. Peters was an active member of the Yankee Section 23, and his views reflected one leading tendency among the land reform radicals in the International. Most likely, old radicals such as Lewis Masquerier and Joshua King Ingalls, who not only kept the land reform idea alive while they were active in the Yankee International but even expanded it to include other forms of capital, were instrumental in George's theoretical development.[17]

Edward Bellamy also achieved overnight fame with the publication of a book. Bellamy's novel *Looking Backward*, a utopian portrait of Boston as a cooperative commonwealth in the year 2000, became one of the century's three greatest selling novels and launched a renewed popular interest in socialism. After *Looking Backward*'s success in 1888, hundreds of "Nationalist" clubs espousing the a gradual electoral path of transforming the country into an egalitarian socialist republic sprang up across the country. Bellamy's republican socialism attracted the same sorts of radicals brought up in the American reform tradition as had the Yankee International before it. Boston's Nationalist Club, for example, included two surviving pillars of that city's antebellum reform crusades, Reverend Edward Everett Hale and Colonel Thomas Wentworth Higginson.[18]

Like Henry George, Edward Bellamy was influenced early in his adult life by the rise of the Yankee International. Raised in a parochial New England household, Bellamy had rarely traveled beyond his Massachusetts township before he took a position as a staff writer for the New York *Post* in January of 1871. Bellamy's year in New York coincided exactly with the period in which the Yankee IWA rose to prominence and staged its most public demonstrations. In New York, Bellamy was introduced to the founder of utopian socialism in America, Albert Brisbane. He also wrote articles for Theodore

Tilton's *Golden Age*, one of the most sympathetic papers to the International, on topics such as women's suffrage and on railroad disasters. Later, Bellamy would describe his time in New York as the part of his life when he left behind the small town, discovered the big city, and became a "nationalist."[19]

Bellamy's *Looking Backward* echoed not only the Yankee International's electoral socialism but its concern for the full social and economic equality of women as well. Not surprisingly, former Yankee Internationalists became active organizers of Bellamyite Nationalism throughout America. The spiritualist lecturer and former Yankee Internationalist Addie Ballou, for example, became a leader of the Nationalist movement in California. But though quite a few feminists and humanitarian radicals sneaked their way into the socialist movement through the back door of Nationalism, they no longer held the reins of the party or could aspire to being the rallying point of socialism in America as they had during the brief heyday of the Yankee International.[20]

Separated from its historical connection with the American reform tradition by Sorge and the immigrant Marxists, the institutional Left in America not only abandoned the issues of gender and racial equality given priority by the Yankee International, but also lost its potential reservoir of support among native-born radicals, the presence of which was briefly demonstrated by the rapid growth of the Yankee International in the winter of 1872–73. In 1888, as the isolation of the socialist movement from the mass of American workers became increasingly evident, a dissident "political" faction seized control of the SLP. But when this faction pressed its policy of "Americanizing" the party and bringing its message to a more representative cross section of workers, the party's old guard rebelled and swept the Americanizers out. The winnowing and suppression of discordant elements continued over the next decade until, by the early 1890s, the SLP's large national executive committee included only two men who spoke English. Ironically, even Frederick Engels eventually noted the corrosive effect of the SLP's sectarianism. "The Germans there have made a grievous mistake," he wrote to the young socialist reformer Florence Kelley, "when they tried in the face of a mighty and glorious movement not of their own creation, to make of their imported and not always understood theory a kind of *alleinseligmachendes* dogma [the one true path of salvation] and to keep aloof from any movement which did not accept that dogma." Kelley, a woman who would become one of the leaders of the Progressive movement, was herself expelled from the SLP in 1887 for criticizing the party's foreign isolation from American life.[21]

Through the dawn of the twentieth century, the American Left, remained dominated by the same dogmatic economism that Sorge and his comrades had pioneered. As a result, the Left followed a course of development parallel to that of the AFL and likewise tended to subsume "superstructural" issues of race, gender, and social equality beneath the "base" issue of class. In the long run, the institutional absence of the Yankee International's focus on the principles of republican liberty, civil rights, and human equality made it possible for the early American Left to abandon racial minorities and women.

This declension is abundantly illustrated by the early career of P. J. McGuire, who was originally introduced to the labor movement through the IWA and later become a leader of the Socialist Labor Party and the president of the International Carpenters and Joiners Union. McGuire initially joined Yankee Section 9, but over time he drifted into Sorge's camp. By 1873, like Samuel Gompers, he was to be found among the inner cadre, "Die Zehn Philosophen," of the International, hashing out the principles of the labor movement.[22]

Gompers and McGuire represent well the ironic twin legacies of Sorgean Marxism. The most important lesson both men took away from their education in the school of the International was that economic organization was the one true path to reform. Gompers, of course, went on to become the most articulate exponent of the antipolitical labor philosophy, which he termed "volunteerism," that basically was a restatement of the mature core of Sorgean Marxist ideology that eschewed all political activities except those "labor questions as may chance to be drawn into the arena of politics." The Tenth Ward Hotel faction in its convention of 1872 recognized only two issues that met this standard: the demand for laws mandating the eight-hour day and the legal exclusion of Chinese workers from the country. Such a view of politics proved immensely functional for a white trade union movement that successfully bridged the sectional nature of American politics by remaining silent on the questions of Jim Crow in the South and industrial segregation in the North. Because American industry was strongly segmented by race, sex, and ethnicity, looking to established trade unions to set the agenda for the entire working class only served to perpetuate existing inequalities.[23]

McGuire's trade union trajectory was similar to Gompers. In 1881 McGuire became head of the Amalgamated Carpenters and Joiners union, a weak and scattered national union, and built it into one of the strongest national trade bodies in the AFL, the United Brotherhood of Carpenters and Joiners (UBC). Like Gompers, McGuire concentrated on the "pure and simple" goals of unionism: wages, hours, and working conditions. He undermined the autonomy of locals and centralized finances and authority under the national executive council. Under McGuire's leadership, the UBC maintained a rhetorical commitment to racial equality and even protested the refusal of a restaurant to serve one of its token black delegates to its Fourth Annual Convention in Cincinnati. But although a handful of black locals were formed in the South, the UBC never wavered from its policy of allowing local unions to veto the granting of charters to black locals in their areas or barring African Americans from their union halls. McGuire's own requirement that there be just one UBC local per city further limited the chances of black membership in the union. From 1888 to 1892 the number of black locals in the UBC actually declined while the national union grew by leaps and bounds.[24]

Unlike Samuel Gompers, P. J. McGuire did not swear off electoral politics but tailored the Socialist Labor Party's political campaigns to the agenda of the white labor movement. Although McGuire did not accept the Sorgean theory of the bankruptcy of the ballot box, his efforts culminated in a defeat for the International socialist ideals of human brotherhood. Because McGuire believed that socialist political campaigns must express the interests of established labor unions and be rooted in their institutions, his political agenda did not stray too far from that of the white trade union movement. Perhaps the best illustration of this was the SLP's 1878 political campaign that sent McGuire stumping across America for the party with the rabidly racist, anti-Chinese demagogue Dennis Kearney. Kearney, the leader of San Francisco's "sandlot" mobs, frequently called for the lynching of Chinese. And his message to Eastern workingmen was a simple one — the Chinese must go.[25]

Kearney's call resonated throughout the party. The party paper, *The Socialist*, gave prominent attention to Kearney's travels and front-page coverage to a meeting organized by the Chicago branch where a series of "Kearney Resolutions" were approved. One of these read: "Resolved, That in answer to the California war-cry of 'The Chinese must go,' we echo the universal watchword of American workingmen: Not only the Chinese, but Chinese institutions must go." A new constitution was approved in California that disenfranchised all Chinese, prohibited Chinese from working in any public work or even for a corporation chartered by the state, and called for the legislature to pass laws banning future immigration. *The Socialist* noted that the laws smacked of "bigotry" but praised them nonetheless for dealing a blow to "this horde of barbarians" and for ending a "worse than Egyptian scourge that has been . . . pouring into the State."[26]

As the century wore on, the American Left's pro forma declarations on racial unity rang ever more hollow, and its actions grew progressively more tokenistic. By the turn of the century, when the socialist movement in America burgeoned, it was a party rife with contradictions; it ignored segregation in society at large and practiced it within its own affiliations. The Socialist Party accommodated Jim Crow practices in its Southern chapters by separating political and economic equality from what they called "social equality," or, in other words, common civil rights. Near the peak of their popularity and influence, the Left's long abandonment of racial minorities culminated in a resolution offered by leaders of the American Socialist Party at the 1907 Stuttgart Congress of the Second International that called for restrictions on the immigration of "inferior races."[27]

Nearly a century ago, in formulating the answer to his by now famous question, "Why is there no socialism in the United States?," Werner Sombart focused primarily upon those factors that were external to the articulation of Marxist ideology in America. Those who have followed in Sombart's footsteps have become equally ensnared in the same tangling web of his question. Historians of socialism have argued that the relative importance of American living standards, the consequences of immigration, religious and racial diversity, political liberalism, the two-party system, widespread suffrage, and outright repression are the causes for the relative weakness of American socialist movements. All of these factors share the premise of Sombart's original metaphor of the socialist ship running aground on "the shoals of roast beef and apple pie." With the notable exception of Daniel Bell, few historians have ventured to consider the internal dynamics and history of the American Left as a significant cause of its own marginalization.[28]

Compared with the socialist parties of other industrializing countries, the American Left that grew out of the Marxist tradition was uniquely removed from the intellectual and social traditions of this nation's indigenous radicalism. Yankee Internationalists were the link connecting such homegrown radicalism with Marxism and modern American socialism. When this link was broken, so was the chain of experience and ideology connecting the institutional Left to American history. By casting out the Yankee apostates from the party, Sorge took the first decisive step in creating a movement that, to paraphrase Daniel Bell, existed in American society but was not of it.

In 1875 Robert Schilling, the vice president of the national coopers' union, wondered, "How is it that the Social Democratic Party is composed almost entirely of men who have but lately arrived here from Germany, and that but very few of any other nationality take part in the organization?" Schilling was speaking from experience, not only as a trade union leader but as a native of Saxony who had been raised from a young age in the United States. Schilling answered his own question when he pointed to one of the main reasons for the weakness of socialism in America:

> Americans . . . are Republicans in the true sense of the word, and everything that smacks in the least of a curtailment of personal or individual liberty, is most obnoxious to them. They believe that every individual should be permitted to do what and how it pleases, as long as the rights and liberties of others are not injured or infringed upon. And this personal liberty must be surrendered and placed under the control of the State, under a government such as proposed by the social Democracy.[29]

The answer to this question, how to balance the republican tradition with the socialist program, was the key to creating and making successful a truly American version of socialism. Marx and Sorge had no interest in the question and chose to cynically dismiss such concerns as so much petty bourgeois humbug. No organization that existed prior the Socialist Party, which thrived after the turn of the century, made as much headway on this problem as the short-lived Yankee International. Combining its anticapitalism, a unique intellectual bequethment of Painite republicanism, Warrenite individualism, Garrisonian militancy, and Spiritualistic universality, the Yankee IWA produced a synthesis of republicanism and socialism—of rights and duties. This synthesis grew out of Warren and the land reformers' definition of the boundary of liberty in property—on the point at which one's own free control of property becomes destructive of others—and drew it squarely at the limit of one's own productive capabilities. What individuals produce for themselves, with their own labor power, is rightfully and absolutely theirs, they argued, but all private possession beyond that is exploitative, is a "monopoly" of the tools or land others require to sustain life, and is unjust and rightly the property of the community as a whole to use equally as the majoritarian process deems fit. Had this Yankee socialist ideology been allowed to become the face of American socialism, it would have rendered Schilling's complaints moot and perhaps even made American socialism far less exceptional than it once seemed.

A profound ideological reorientation affected the American Left as a whole as a result of the transformative collision of Marxism and traditional reform thought in America. As it happened within the First International, the greatest representatives of racial and sexual egalitarianism and of political republicanism were also those who were most identified with the professional class, and their liberal ideals themselves came to be dismissed as "bourgeois." Yankee Internationalists, reflecting their deep roots in a native republicanism that had deep suspicions of industrialism, saw no contradiction between their egalitarian and liberal ideals and their socialist goals. With equal fervor the men and women of the Yankee International could defend the memory of the Paris Commune, fight for the eight-hour day, uphold the political and social rights of women and racial minorities, call for state ownership of industry, and demand reform in the electoral structures of government. But as these Yankee radicals passed from being a native complement of immigrant Marxism to becoming American socialism's memory of the delusions and errors of bourgeois reformism, the goals of civil rights and political liberty were loosened from those of economic equality and social justice.

The Yankee's emphasis upon moral values and justice as the guiding lights to action, inherited from the age-old American radical tradition, enabled them to avoid the great pitfall of orthodox Marxism, namely, the teleological conception that social change and, therefore, party tactics were an all-or-nothing game. Yankee socialists never quite perceived that what underlay Sorge and Marx's machinations of the party was a fervently held and sincere belief that dialectical reasoning provided the theoretical key (and there was only one) to unlocking the door to the revolutionary future. Moreover, Marx and Sorge's fundamentally progressive view of history, their faith in the continual tendency of capitalism to undermine its own conditions of continued existence and, therefore, their expectation of its inevitable collapse, gave them a moral justification for their refusal to champion the very values, such as political and social equality, that they hoped socialism would one day make universal. Like generations of socialists that would come after them, Marx and Sorge rationalized inaction on issues of racial justice and women's rights on the grounds that these problems would simply fade away once the socialist stage of history was achieved. Skeptical Yankee radicals simply did not share such confidence in the future and feared that apocalypse rather than utopia lurked around the corner of history. Given the uncertainties of the future, to these homegrown socialists it was far better to live and struggle and uphold their fundamental principles against all compromise in the present.[30]

Although ultimately superseded by the Sorgean-Marxist prototype, the

Yankee International remained a ghostly presence within American radicalism for the next fifty years. Its racial and sexual egalitarianism would once again find a tenuous and brief expression within the Knights of Labor; some of its platform would be echoed through the century by America's homegrown radicals: the Populists, the Christian socialists, and Edward Bellamy's Nationalists. A century later, the Yankee International, by then forgotten under a deep pile of Old Left historiography that lauded Sorge's triumph over bourgeois sentimentalism, was reinvented by young campus radicals who, like the Spiritualists, long-hairs, free-lovers, and feminists who had circled around Victoria Woodhull, struggled against the institutions of capitalism both culturally and politically. The countercultural rebels of the New Left understood only vaguely that they were to the twentieth century what the Yankee International was to the nineteenth. These New Left radicals had to reinvent what had been lost because the two ends of this homegrown American radicalism had become separated by intrigue, infighting, and the amnesia of the victor's history.

ABBREVIATIONS USED IN NOTES

CC Corr.	Records of the Central Committee, Correspondence
GC Corr.	General Council Correspondence
GCM	*The General Council of the First International 1864–1866, Minutes*
IWAP	International Workingmen's Association Papers, State Historical Society of Wisconsin, Madison
MECW	*Karl Marx, Frederick Engels Collected Works*
NASS	*National Anti-Slavery Standard*
NLU	National Labor Union
Sec. 26 Corr.	Section 26 Correspondence
Sec. 26 MB	Section 26 Minute Book

INTRODUCTION

1. Guessing the true extent of the membership of the IWA is a difficult task. Morris Hillquit optimistically arrived at a total of 5,000 (*History of Socialism*, 197). Samuel Bernstein estimates there were fewer than 3,000 (*First International*, 65). In my own research I have identified by name nearly 400 members. As these 400 are drawn from fewer than a fifth of the number of sections claimed by the IWA (and assuming that these sections are representative of the rest), then perhaps 2,000 might be a reasonable estimate.

2. See Sally Miller, *Race, Ethnicity, and Gender*, 33–44, 97–117.

3. Paul Buhle and Mark Lause stand out for their pathbreaking reassessment of the character and significance of the English-speaking sections of the IWA. See Paul Buhle, *Marxism in the United States*; Lause, "American Radicals"; and Perrier, "Radicalisme américain et socialisme."

4. Goldberg, *American Radicals*, 2–3.

5. Ronald G. Walters, "Boundaries of Abolitionism," 8.

6. Salvatore, *Eugene V. Debs*, 150–51.

CHAPTER ONE

1. Samuel Bernstein, *First International*, 26; *GCM*, 1:97, 172–73; Ansley, *Columbia Encyclopedia*, 1454.

2. *GCM*, 2:72, 305.

3. Eric Foner, *Free Soil*, 20; Commons et al., *Documentary History*, 7:34. Greeley was an erratic supporter of every reform movement that drifted past him. Even his abo-

litionism ran hot and cold. In 1845, at the height of his Fourierism, Greeley declined to attend an antislavery convention in Cincinnati, writing, "You will readily understand, therefore, that, if I regard your enterprise with less absolute interest than you do, it is not that I deem Slavery a less but a greater evil. If I am less troubled concerning Slavery in Charleston and New Orleans, it is because I see so much Slavery in New-York, which appears to claim my first effort" (Mandel, *Labor Free and Slave*, 87).

Greeley did have one important contact in the world of European socialism. Through the 1850s his London correspondent was an obscure German refugee named Karl Marx. The political basis of their journalistic cooperation has been said to have lain in Greeley's antislavery editorial line, though Marx's columns ceased in 1862.

There is some confusion about the cause of Marx's break with Greeley's *Tribune*. Some have argued that Marx severed his ties to the *Tribune* because its editorial line began to advocate a negotiated peace settlement with the Confederacy by 1862. However, this was the year in which Greeley handed the editorial reigns to Sidney Howard Gay, a man best known for his abolitionist work and whose previous editorial job was managing the *National Anti-Slavery Standard*. Gay was hardly the man to soften the *Tribune*'s stand against slavery. Another less-cited source of tension was Greeley's cutting Marx's ten-dollar-a-week salary in half (see Hale, *Horace Greeley*, 154–55, and Stewart, *Holy Warriors*, 184).

4. Montgomery, *Beyond Equality*, 241, 318.

5. May, *Enlightenment in America*, pt. 3; Pessen, *Most Uncommon Jacksonians*, 103–11.

6. On the growth and ideology of land reform parties, see Zahler, *Eastern Working-men*, and Commons et al., *Documentary History*, 7:287–325.

7. Lause, "Unwashed Infidelity," 408–9; Pessen, *Most Uncommon Jacksonians*, 11, 97–99; Lause, "American Radicals," 57.

8. Schlensinger, *American as Reformer*, 12–15.

9. Lynd, *Intellectual Origins*, 27–29.

10. Loveland, "Evangelicalism and 'Immediate Emancipation,'" 172–88; Thomas, "Antislavery and Utopia," 246–48; Robertson, "Parker Pillsbury," 4.

11. Commager, *Theodore Parker*, 151–55; Veysey, *Perfectionists*, 11–13.

12. *Liberator*, Feb. 13, 1846.

13. David Brion Davis, *Antebellum Reform*, 1–3; Griffin, *Ferment of Reform*, 2–5; Walters, *American Reformers*; Ahlstrom, *A Religious History*, 637–38. For a sampling of abolitionist discussion of Spiritualism, see the following issues of the *Liberator*: Dec. 17, 1852; Apr. 15, 22, May 20, July 29, 1853; Jan. 1, 8, 29, Apr. 16, 23, Sep. 17, 1858; Apr. 29, Aug. 12, 1859; Aug. 24, 1860; May 24, Dec. 27, 1861; July 24, Aug. 7, Sep. 18, Oct. 2, 1863; Aug. 26, 1864.

14. McKivigan, *War against Proslavery*, 93–96; see also the excellent analysis of early Unitarianism and religious radicalism in Ruff, *"We Called Each Other Comrade."*

15. Perry, *Radical Abolitionism*, 9, 55–61; Fredrickson, *William Lloyd Garrison*, 49.

16. Buhle and Buhle, *Concise History of Woman Suffrage*, 96.

17. *Woodhull & Claflin's Weekly*, May 18, 25, 1872.

18. Buhle and Buhle, *Concise History of Woman Suffrage*, 94–95; Spurlock, *Free Love*, 70–71, 82–83, 91; Sears, *Sex Radicals*, 3–26.

19. Darnton, *Mesmerism*; Bednarowski, "Nineteenth-Century American Spiritualism," 72–74.

20. Braude, *Radical Spirits*; R. Laurence Moore, *In Search of White Crows*, and "Spiritualism and Science."

21. *Banner of Light*, Dec. 2, 1871.

22. Morita, "Modern Spiritualism," 71–78; Capron, *Modern Spiritualism*, 195, 335; Brown, "Spiritualism in Nineteenth-Century America," 134, 112.

23. Isaacs, "History of Nineteenth-Century American Spiritualism," 262–83.

24. Capron, *Modern Spiritualism*, 265–66.

25. Newton, *Educator*, 28–29.

26. MacDonald, *Fifty Years of Freethought*, 361–62; *Boston Investigator*, Feb. 7, 1872.

27. Braude, *Radical Spirits*, 2. For similarity in Spiritualist feminism in both the U.S. and Britain, see Owen, *Darkened Room*. Gerrit Smith is quoted in R. Laurence Moore, *In Search of White Crows*, 70. On Spiritualism and Fourierism, see Guarneri, *Utopian Alternative*, 349–53.

28. Levine, *Spirit of 1848*, 53.

29. *Liberator*, Jan. 1, 1831. In the same breath, Garrison goes on to express his respect for workers: "Labor is not dishonorable. The industrious artisan, in a government like ours, will always be held in better estimation than the wealthy idler." Schlüter, *Lincoln, Labor and Slavery*, 40–41; Rayback, "American Workingman," 152–63; Korngold, *Two Friends*, 62. For more on the New England Association, see Commons et al., *Documentary History*, 5:185–202.

30. *Liberator*, Jan. 28, 1831; Ansdell, "William Lloyd Garrison's Ambivalent Approach," 406.

31. Stewart, *Wendell Phillips*; Tappan, *Life of Arthur Tappan*; Walters, *Antislavery Appeal*, 116.

32. Gerteis, "Slavery and Hard Times," 320–21.

33. Eric Foner, *Politics and Ideology*, 60–61; Rayback, "American Workingman," 160–61; *Daily Unionist*, Feb. 1, 1854.

34. *Liberator*, Nov. 10, 1848; Lofton, "Abolition and Labor," 251.

35. Lofton, "Abolition and Labor," 253–61.

36. *New York Daily Tribune*, Mar. 25, 1845.

37. Friedrich Sorge, in his history of the labor movement, states that "abolitionists were . . . represented in large numbers" at this meeting. Foner and Chamberlin, *Friedrich A. Sorge's Labor Movement*, 72. A short history of the labor upheaval of the 1840s and the formation of the New England Workingmen's Association can be found in Ware, *Industrial Worker*, ch. 14; Garrison quoted in Rayback, "American Workingman," 153.

38. *Liberator*, June 20, 1845.

39. Ibid., July 4, 1845.

40. *New York Daily Tribune*, Oct. 18, 1845.

41. Kraditor, *Means and Ends*, 251. Kraditor argues that "when Garrisonian abolitionists favored advocacy of the claims of the free laborer they meant, of course, improvements in his condition, not change in his status" (ibid.). But this is not the point. The bulk of the labor movement, rooted as it was in artisanal republicanism, was not in favor of a change in his status, either. The status of labor was changing for the worse,

away from the ideal of artisanal independence—therefore the claims of labor carried a similar conservative cast. Indeed, the specific exhortation to "advocate the claims of free labor" was phrased in such a way as to ally the mass with labor reform, not to distinguish itself from it.

42. *Liberator*, Nov. 19, 1847.

43. Ibid., Feb. 13, 1852.

44. Lofton, "Abolition and Labor," 250; *American Workman*, June 5, 1869. Likewise, Stephen S. Foster, a Congregationalist minister and Garrisonian disciple, accused abolitionists of not being attentive to the needs of the laboring classes and called on abolitionists to work for "the elevation of the laboring classes to an equality with the capitalist, and the professions, in the enjoyment of social, civil, and religious rights and privileges" (Walters, *Antislavery Appeal*, 118).

45. Kraditor, *Means and Ends*, 267.

46. Lofton, "Abolition and Labor," 252.

47. Lydia Maria Child to Ellis Gray Loring and Louisa Gilman Loring, May 14, 1849, Child Papers, Ann Arbor, Mich.

48. Walters, *Antislavery Appeal*, 118. A brief biography of Wright can be found in Whitman, *American Reformers*, 907-8.

49. Huston, "Facing an Angry Labor," 209.

50. McKitrick, *Slavery Defended*, 14-15, 123-24.

51. Jenkins, *Pro-Slavery Thought*, 300.

52. *Liberator*, July 25, 1856. For the background of Fitzhugh's extensive correspondence with abolitionists, see Wish, *George Fitzhugh*, ch. 11.

53. *Liberator*, May 7, 1858.

54. William West to Wendell Phillips, Dec. 29, 1863, Phillips Papers, Cambridge, Mass.; Masquerier, *Sociology*, 126.

55. Stewart, *Wendell Phillips*, 250-51.

56. *NASS*, June 6, 1868.

57. Ibid., Sept. 25, 1869.

58. Ibid., June 5, 1869. The committee voted to replace the words "all abolitionists" with "all true Americans."

59. *NASS*, June 12, 1869.

60. Ibid., Nov. 27, 1869.

61. Ibid.

62. Montgomery, *Beyond Equality*, 123-24; *Fincher's Trades' Review*, May 12, 1866.

63. *NASS*, Feb. 20, 1869.

64. *American Workman*, May 28, 1870.

65. *Daily Evening Voice*, May 2, 1866. (It is also interesting to note that Garrison, perhaps out of long habit, still felt obligated to emphasize the greater and unique oppression of slaves.) David Montgomery first noted Garrison's participation in the eight-hour movement in *Beyond Equality*, 123-24.

66. *NASS*, Feb. 20, 1869.

67. *Independent*, Jan. 6, 1870. On Sylvis, see Grossman, *William Sylvis*; on the Boston *Daily Evening Voice*, see Philip Foner, "Labor Voice" and Roediger, "Racism, Reconstruction and the Labor Press."

68. *NASS*, June 16, 1866.

69. Ibid., July 18, 1868; A few biographical details of Mary Steward can be found in the *Labor Standard*, Mar. 3, 1878. On the American Social Science Association, see Haskell, *Emergence of Professional Social Science*, and Bernard and Bernard, *Origins of American Sociology*.

70. *NASS*, May 8, 29, 1869.

71. *Woodhull & Claflin's Weekly*, May 28, 1870; *Independent*, Apr. 21, 1870. Tilton's paper was not consistent in its endorsement of labor issues. At other times he endorsed the aging "Iron Law of Wages" theory: "Combinations of workingmen, trades' unions, and protective associations cannot successfully defy the great law of supply and demand" (*Independent*, Mar. 3, 1870).

72. See *NASS*, Oct. 20, 1866; Aug. 24, Oct 5, 1867; Mar. 21, Sept. 12, 1868; Jan. 1, Feb. 20, Apr. 17, May 8, 15, 29, June 5, July 31, Aug. 21, 28, Sept. 4, Oct. 9, 16, 23, 30, Nov. 6, 20, Dec. 4, 11, 18, 1869; Jan. 1, 15, 22, 1870.

73. Ibid., Mar. 7, 21, 1868; July 31, Aug. 21, Jan. 16, 1869.

74. Ibid., July 29, 1871.

75. *Independent*, Apr. 21, 1870.

76. *New York World*, May 10, 1871.

77. Mari Jo Buhle, "Woman's Culture."

78. Blair, *Clubwoman as Feminist*, 32–37.

79. New England Women's Club Papers, vol. 2, Nov. 30, 1868, Feb. 9, 1869, Schlesinger Library, Cambridge, Mass.; the Brussels Congress was covered in *Bee-hive*, Sept. 12, 19, 1868.

80. New England Women's Club Papers, vol. 2, Mar. 29, Apr. 12, 1869. Diary entry for Feb. 20, 1872, Harriet Hanson Robinson Papers, Schlesinger Library, Cambridge, Mass.

81. Balser, *Sisterhood and Solidarity*, 59; DuBois, *Feminism and Suffrage*, 110, 116–18, 121–25; Commons et al., *Documentary History*, 9:198; Kugler, "Trade Union Career of Susan B. Anthony," 90–100, and *From Ladies to Women*, 115–46; Barry, *Susan B. Anthony*, 210–18; Montgomery, *Beyond Equality*, 395–99.

82. *Revolution*, Feb. 3, 1870; *New York World*, May 7, 8, 9, 1871; *Revolution*, May 18, 1871.

83. *Woman's Journal*, Sept. 30, 1871; James, James, and Boyer, *Notable American Women*, 2:329–30.

84. DeSantis, "Belva Ann Lockwood," 42–49; Winner, *Belva A. Lockwood*, 19–20.

85. Curti, *Peace or War*, 74–81; DeBenedetti, *Peace Reform*, 60–61; Ziegler, *Advocates of Peace*, 177–81; *Philadelphia Monthly Tribune*, Nov. 1867.

86. *Bond of Peace*, Mar. 1871.

87. Roediger, "Ira Steward."

88. Morita, "Modern Spiritualism," 208–15; Reynolds, *George Lippard*, 85–86.

89. *Banner of Light*, quotes from Oct. 8, 1, Dec. 17, 1870; see also ibid., Feb. 19, Apr. 16, May 21, May 28, July 23, Nov. 5, Dec. 31, 1870; Jan. 14, 1871; *Religio-Philosophical Journal*, Jan. 15, 1870; copies of *The Optimist and Kingdom of Heaven* and its successor can be found at the Boston Public Library; *Workingman's Advocate*, July 8, 1871.

90. *Banner of Light*, Feb. 4, 1871; *American Spiritualist*, July 20, 1872.

91. *Boston Investigator*, Nov. 23, 1870; Ward, *New Idea*, 8.

CHAPTER TWO

1. *Bee-hive*, Oct. 1, 1864.

2. Lucraft is profiled in Bellamy and Saville, *Dictionary of Labour Biography*, 7:149-52. Katz, *Emancipation of Labor*, 2-3.

3. Mins, *Founding of the First International*, 4.

4. Quote from Marx's letter to Carl Klings, Oct. 4, 1864, in *MECW*, 42:4. See also Padover, *Karl Marx*, appendix xii.

5. Marx to Engels, Nov. 4, 1864, *MECW*, 42:15; Felix, *Marx as Politician*, 159-60; Collins and Abramsky, *Karl Marx and the British Working Class Movement*, 31-33; Padover, *Karl Marx*, 376-77. Padover describes Marx's London life before the founding of the IWA as "the politically isolated life of an unassimilated Continental refugee." On Eccarius, see Lessner, *Sixty Years*, 10.

6. Engels quoted in Stanley W. Moore, *Critique of Capitalist Democracy*, 107.

7. *GCM*, 1:38.

8. Mins, *Founding of the First International*, 64-65.

9. Ibid., 65. Marx is referring to the British socialist Robert Owen (1771-1858). See also Cole, *Life of Robert Owen*. *MECW*, 42:16-17.

10. Gouldner, *Two Marxisms*, 193-96; Tucker, *Marx and Engels Reader*, 595. The best single survey of Marx's relation to liberalism is Levin, *Marx, Engels and Liberal Democracy*.

11. Marx to Engels, Nov. 4, 1864, *MECW*, 42:17; *GCM*, 1:42.

12. Marx to Engels, Nov. 4, 1864, *MECW*, 42:17.

13. Ibid., 42:18.

14. Ibid.

15. Eccarius reporting for the *New York World*, Sept. 30, 1872.

16. For general treatments of Marx's early role in the IWA, see Collins and Abramsky, *Karl Marx and the British Working Class Movement*, ch. 3-4; Dutt, *Internationale*, ch. 2; and Felix, *Marx as Politician*, ch. 9. Corwin Edwards, in his study "The First International Workingmen's Association," identifies no less than six different ideological factions on the General Council at this time.

17. Engels to Marx, Nov. 7, 1864, *MECW*, 42:20.

18. Engels's and Marx's quotations can be found in *Karl Marx and Frederick Engels on Britain*, 491-93.

19. *GCM*, 1:50-51; Marx to Engels, Dec. 2, 1864, *MECW*, 42:49.

20. *GCM*, 1:53; *MECW*, 42:167-68. Lincoln responded through his ambassador to England, Charles Francis Adams, to the IWA's congratulations in a letter printed in *The Times* of London on Feb. 6, 1865. (Lincoln's response is reprinted in full in the *GCM*, 1:68-69.) Marx was delighted and wrote to Engels that it was "everything we could have asked for" from the "naive . . . old man" (Marx to Engels, Feb. 1, 1865, *MECW*, 42:73); on Marx's reformulation of this idea in *Das Kapital*, see *Capital*, 1939 edition,

329. Philip S. Foner maintains a more traditional view of Marx's thought on race and the Civil War in *American Socialism and Black Americans*, 32–33.

21. *GCM*, 1:119.

22. Ibid., 310–12.

23. Yorke, *Secret History*, 41.

24. *MECW*, 4:92–98, 101–2, 105, 194–95; Taylor, *Eve and the New Jerusalem*, 284. See also Draper and Lipow, "Marxist Women"; Royle, *Victorian Infidels*; and Barrow, *Independent Spirits*.

25. Engels to Weydemeyer, Nov. 24, 1864, Marx to Weydemeyer, Nov. 29, 1864, and Engels to Marx, Jan. 27, 1865, all in *MECW*, 42:39, 69; *GCM*, 1:383. For more on Weydemeyer, see Obermann, *Joseph Weydemeyer*.

26. Marx to Engels, Mar. 18, 1865, *MECW*, 42:135; Engels to Marx, May 3, 1865, ibid., 152.

27. Marx to Siegfried Meyer, Apr. 30, 1867, *MECW*, 42:367.

28. Hermann Meyer was from St. Louis and was a close associate of Joseph Weydemeyer. In 1867, when Weydemeyer took ill and lay upon his death bed, Meyer was his last companion and later cared for his widow, Louise. Later that year, Meyer traveled to London and sought out Marx, whom he had never met before, most likely at Weydemeyer's urging. Marx thought him "a fine active fellow. However, cooks slowly and somewhat boring." See Marx to Engels, c. May 22, 1867, *MECW*, 42:377.

29. Engels to Hermann Meyer, Oct. 18, 1867, *MECW*, 42:451–52.

30. *GCM*, 2:141–42; Foner and Chamberlin, *History of the Labor Movement*, 233.

31. Marx to Siegfried Meyer, July 4, 1868, *MECW*, 43:58.

32. Marx to Liebknecht, Nov. 21, 1865, *MECW*, 42:201–2; Felix, *Marx as Politician*, 165.

33. Lewis, *The Facts Concerning the Eight Condemned Leaders*.

34. *GCM*, 1:98, 101, 103–5.

35. Marx to Engels, June 24, 1865, *MECW*, 42:162; *GCM*, 1:106, 132, 187.

36. *GCM*, 1:131, 161.

37. Ibid., 172–73.

38. Fox's labors are well detailed in his annual report to the General Council, in *GCM*, 2:304–10. See also Grossman, *William Sylvis*, 224–25.

39. Commons et al., *Documentary History*, 9:333–36; Samuel Bernstein, *First International*, 28–29.

40. *GCM*, 2:162; *Bee-hive*, Sept. 28, 1867.

41. *GCM*, 2:165, 373; *Bee-hive*, Oct. 12, 1867.

42. *GCM*, 2:169.

43. Marx to Engels, Oct. 4, 1867, Nov. 30, 1867, *MECW*, 42:434–35, 485, 657–58; Collins and Abramsky, *Karl Marx and the British Working Class Movement*, 131.

44. Weir, " 'Here's to the Men Who Lose!,' " 531–32.

45. *GCM*, 2:165, 168, 373; Marx to Siegfried Meyer, Sept. 14, 1868, *MECW*, 43:97; Marx to Engels, Dec. 9, 1868, ibid., 177.

46. Marx to Engels, Oct. 4, 1867, *MECW*, 42:434; Collins and Abramsky, *Karl Marx and the British Working Class Movement*, 131.

47. Engels to Marx, Sept. 11, 1867, *MECW*, 42:422, 425, 428; Marx to Engels, Sept. 12, 1867, ibid., 434-35; Marx to Engels, Oct. 4, 1867, ibid., 655; Collins and Abramsky, *Karl Marx and the British Working Class Movement*, 130-31; Edwards, "First International Workingmen's Association," 115; *GCM*, 2:166.

48. Edwards, "First International Workingmen's Association," 114-15; *GCM*, 2:169. The strategic importance of the standing committee was well dramatized years before by Marx's own clever manipulation of it to outmaneuver his opponents and successfully enshrine his drafts of the IWA's rules and Inaugural Address as the foundation of the organization.

49. Marx to Siegfried Meyer and Vogt, Apr. 9, 1870, *MECW*, 43:471.

50. Marx to Engels, Nov. 14, 1864, *MECW*, 42:22.

51. Marx to Engels, Dec. 10, 1864, *MECW*, 42:54-55. After Fox moved to Vienna he wrote a conciliatory letter to Marx, and the two of them reached an amicable reproachment afterward (see *MECW*, 43:516, 532, 536, 538, 548). Fox was not the man of wealth that Marx made him out to be. When Fox died of pulmonary disease in 1869, he left his family in poverty. As soon as Marx learned of his death, he interceded on behalf of Fox's destitute family. He contacted Fox's wealthy mother, who had disowned her son because of his atheism and choice of wife, and threatened to take up public collections for her son's family if she did not contribute to their care (Marx to Engels, May 21, 1869, *MECW*, 43:285).

52. *GCM*, 2:180. Katz, *Emancipation of Labor*, 20.

53. *GCM*, 2:221. On August 18, 1868, the Council received a letter from William Jessup in New York stating that no letters from secretary Shaw ever reached him (*GCM*, 2:245).

54. *GCM*, 3:50.

55. Collins and Abramsky, *Karl Marx and the British Working Class Movement*, 131.

56. *GCM*, 3:98. Robert Shaw died of tuberculosis in January of 1870. Marx wrote an obituary for him praising him as "one of the most active members of the Council. A pure heart, iron character, passionate temperament, truly revolutionary intelligence, quite above any petty ambition or personal interest" (*GCM*, 3:408-9).

57. *GCM*, 3:36; *Bee-hive*, Oct. 3, 1868.

58. Marx to Vogt, Apr. 9, 1870, *MECW*, 43:475.

59. Marx to Meyer, Dec. 9, 1868, *MECW*, 43:177-78; Marx to Meyer and Vogt, Apr. 9, 1870, ibid., 472.

60. Applegarth said that he met Ward at a General Council meeting on Sept. 28, 1869 (*GCM*, 3:162-64); see also *National Cyclopedia of American Biography*, 13:112. For profiles of William Cremer, Robert Applegarth, and Benjamin Lucraft, see *Dictionary of Labor Biography*, 5:73-76, 2:16-22, 7:149-52, respectively; see also Humphrey, *Robert Applegarth*, and C. O. Ward to Mary Gunning, June 25, 1898, Ward Correspondence, Boston, Public Library.

61. Lause, "American Radicals," 55-80. On Martin Boon's activities, see *Dictionary of Labor Biography*, 9:9-16.

62. Marx to Meyer, Sept. 14, 1868, *MECW*, 43:97; Marx to Engels, Sept. 16, 1868, ibid., 101.

63. Marx to Meyer, Sept. 14, 1868, *MECW*, 43:97; Marx to Engels, Sept. 16, 1868, ibid., 101.

64. Marx to Meyer and Vogt, Oct. 28, 1868, *MECW*, 43:148.

65. Collins and Abramsky, *Karl Marx and the British Working Class Movement*, 264, 253, and appendix 1.

CHAPTER THREE

1. Foner and Chamberlin, *History of the Labor Movement*, 233, 413; Hillquit, *History of Socialism*, 153; Foner and Chamberlin, *Friedrich A. Sorge's Labor Movement*, 110, 153, 346 n. 104. In his *First International*, Samuel Bernstein scrambled the chronology of the IWA's coming to America. He places Sorge as the first agent of the International in America (27).

2. *GCM*, 2:142.

3. Foner and Chamberlin, *Friedrich A. Sorge's Labor Movement*, 155; *Social Party*; Nadel, *Little Germany*, 140–42.

4. Bernstein incorrectly claims that Drury and Izard submitted their banking scheme and International ideas before the 1867 congress of the NLU (*First International*, 27). In fact, they presented their proposals before the New York Workingmen's Union (see *Workingman's Advocate*, Nov. 2, 1867).

5. Nadel, *Little Germany*.

6. Thompson's occupation is given in the 1871 *New York City Directory*; on West, see *New York World*, Aug. 19, 1872, and Montgomery, *Beyond Equality*, 469. Allen's occupation was reported when he was arrested for carrying a red banner and marching without a permit (*New York Herald*, Nov. 10, 1871); Newberry advertised his dentistry practice in *Worker*, Feb. 2, 1873; for Esther Andrews, see obituary in clipping in "Anarchism — Stephen Pearl Andrews" vertical file, Labadie Collection, University of Michigan, Ann Arbor; Stern, *Pantarch*, pp. 99, 106; Gregory's obituary can be found in *Golden Age*, Dec. 23, 1871, and in the *New York Herald*, Jan. 3, 1872; I. B. Davis advertised his baths in *Woodhull & Claflin's Weekly*.

7. Lause, "American Radicals," 62–64.

8. Montgomery, *Beyond Equality*, 417. De Leon, *American as Anarchist*, 73; Herreshoff, *American Disciples*, 91.

9. Samuel Bernstein supports his view that the New Democrats were uninterested in socialism by quoting a passage from an address of the New Democracy, a passage that he claimed "uncovered the ultimate goal of the New Democracy": "In some way or other, in all countries, the people must learn to employ themselves on their own farms, in their own workshops, and they should exchange the products of their labor by agents of their own appointment, thus constituting a government 'deriving its just powers from the consent of the governed.'" But farther on in this same document, in a passage Bernstein did not care to quote, a very different view of the organization presents itself. In that portion of the address, the New Democracy's organizers, the same men that Montgomery sees as "anarchists," praise the resolutions of the recent IWA Congress at Basle, Switzerland: "We learn that resolutions favoring the abolition of private property in land were there

adopted. It is stated, also, that they want government to farm the land, to organize factories, and to become the controllers, or rather agents, of labor. This is all right." This was an odd position for a group uninterested in socialism to advocate. The resolutions to which the document referred were actually hard-fought victories of the Marxist over the anarchist factions at the Basle Congress and have been described as constituting "the victory of collectivism within the International." The true anarchists at Basle, led by Bakunin, opposed Marx's land reform plank and succeeded in preventing the congress from considering resolutions endorsing greater direct democracy through the referendum process, a measure that they saw as affirming the legitimacy of government. Instituting the referendum was at the top of the list of the New Democracy's priorities, a curious goal for a thoroughly anarchistic group of sentimentalists (*First International*, 106).

10. Commons et al., *History of Labour*, 2:210–11; Samuel Bernstein, *First International*, 107; Katz, *Emancipation of Labor*, 59, 60, 63.

11. Quote from Ward, *New Idea*; Martin, *Men against the State*, 18, 49; see also Warren, *Equitable Commerce*.

12. *New York World*, May 7, 1872.

13. *Woodhull & Claflin's Weekly*, Nov. 5, 1870.

14. Ibid., Nov. 12, 1870.

15. *Boston Investigator*, Aug. 16, 1871; Lause, "American Radicals," 77–78.

16. *Public Ledger*, Aug. 17, 1869.

17. Ward, *New Idea*, 12, 14.

18. *Woodhull & Claflin's Weekly*, Oct. 8, 1870.

19. See *New York World*, Oct. 10, 1869.

20. *Woodhull & Claflin's Weekly*, Nov. 12, 1870.

21. The classic treatment on Republican ideology remains Bailyn, Wood, and Pocock, *Machiavellian Moment*; on artisan republicanism, see Eric Foner, *Tom Paine*; for land reform ideology, see Zahler, *Eastern Workingmen*; on Loco-foco's and the workingmen's movement of the Jacksonian period, see Trimble, "Social Philosophy," and Wilentz, *Chants Democratic*; on Josiah Warren, see Martin, *Men against the State*.

22. See Huston, "American Revolutionaries"; Kasson, *Civilizing the Machine*.

23. *Report of the Committee of the Senate upon the Relations between Labor and Capital*, 2:949.

24. Preamble to the "Address and Provisional Rules of the Working Mens' International Association," reprinted in *GCM*, 1:288–91. *New York World*, Oct. 10, 1869, Jan. 20, 1870.

25. *New York World*, Oct. 30, 1869.

26. Ibid.

27. *Bee-hive*, Dec. 12, 1868; *GCM*, 3:292–98; Dutt, *Internationale*, 61; *New York World*, Oct. 10, 30, 1869.

28. *New York World*, Oct. 8, 22, Nov. 5, Dec. 3, 17, 31, 1869. On Albert Brisbane and the origins of Fourierism in America, see Guarneri, *Utopian Alternative*. On founding of Cosmopolitan Club, see *New York World*, Jan. 1, 1871, and *Workingman's Advocate*, Apr. 15, 1871.

29. Harrison, *Before the Socialists*, 215–30; Collins and Abramsky, *Karl Marx and the British Working Class Movement*, 164–65.

30. *New York World*, Jan. 20, 1870. Even Marx himself initially saw the Land and Labour League as a progressive step forward. A month before he took out his own membership card in the League, Marx wrote Engels in praise of its demand for the nationalization of the land, a position that he considered "a clean break with the bourgeoisie." Of course, Marx had in mind the utility of such demands in enlisting the British working class in the necessary task of breaking the power of the landed aristocracy—a historical requirement that was absent in America. But what was progressive for the English worker could also be conservative for the American. In the American context, these same demands would appear to Marx and his comrades as anachronistic at best (Marx to Engels, Oct. 30, 1869, *MECW*, 43:364).

31. Neither the General German Labor Union nor the New Democracy had yet formally applied to become a section of the International.

32. Commons's lists of delegates to the NLU congresses of 1866–70, published in *Documentary History*, vol. 9, are incomplete. They do not include delegates who were admitted to these congresses after the first day. A supplemental list of delegates can be found in the *New York World*, Aug. 18, 1869. Foner and Chamberlin mistakenly identify Sorge as the German Labor Union No. 5's delegate to the National Labor Union of 1869 (*Friedrich A. Sorge's Labor Movement*, 9, 346 n. 108).

33. Commons et al., *Documentary History*, 9:198; Kugler, "Trade Union Career of Susan B. Anthony," 90–100; DuBois, *Feminism and Suffrage*, 122–23; Balser, *Sisterhood and Solidarity*, 58–64; Foner and Rosenberg, *Women and the American Labor Movement*, 61–64.

34. For a detailed history of Anthony's Working Women's Association that places the accusation of "ratting" in its proper context, see DuBois, *Feminism and Suffrage*, ch. 5.

35. DuBois, *Feminism and Suffrage*, 158.

36. *Public Ledger*, Aug. 18, 1869; *New York World*, Aug. 18, 1869.

37. *Public Ledger*, Aug. 20, 1869; *New York World*, Aug. 20, 1869.

38. The roll-call vote was printed in the Philadelphia *Public Ledger*, Aug. 19, 1869, and in the *Report of Proceedings of the Eighteenth Annual Session of the International Typographical Union*, 52–53.

39. Foner and Chamberlin, *Friedrich Sorge's Labor Movement*, 157.

40. "To the National Labor Union of the United States," reprinted in *GCM*, 3:325, and *Workingman's Advocate*, Sept. 18, 1869.

41. *Revolution*, Oct. 28, 1869.

42. *Bee-hive*, Nov. 27, 1869; *GCM*, 3:352–53.

43. *GCM*, 3:197, 212, 215, 260; *MECW*, 43:375–76.

44. *GCM*, 3:259–60. A copy of the card can be found in the Miscellaneous International Workingmen's Association Materials, State Historical Society of Wisconsin, Madison. Lause, "American Radicals," 65–66.

45. Lause, "American Radicals," 66; *GCM*, 4:55, 63, 87; *MECW*, 44:57.

46. *Woodhull & Claflin's Weekly*, Oct. 21, 1870; *New York World*, Nov. 17, 20, 1870.

47. Samuel Bernstein, *First International*, 53–54; *New York World*, Oct. 3, 1870. The responsibilities of the central committee were spelled out in a letter to Marx from Friedrich Bolte and read at a meeting of the General Council (*GCM*, 4:95).

48. *GCM*, 4:95, 97.

49. Ibid., 81.

50. Sorge explained his position in his report to the General Council dated May 21, 1871, in CC Corr.

51. *GCM*, 4:85.

52. *MECW*, 44:101–2. Marx also advised New York's central committee to not allow individual sections to elect their own delegates, but to have them elected at an annual congress, thereby making it more difficult for "hostile" members to climb to the top (*GCM*, 4:108, 505).

CHAPTER FOUR

1. *New York World*, May 28, 1870; Katz, *Emancipation of Labor*, 31–35; *International Working Men's Association: Resolutions of the Congress of Geneva, 1866*, 14–15.

2. *Advocate of Peace*, Sept. 1870; *Bond of Peace*, Sept. 1870; IWA antiwar meeting coverage, *Bond of Peace*, Dec. 1870. The history of the Universal Peace Union is detailed in Brock, *Pacifism in the United States*, 923–32; for information on the membership of the UPU, see the various convention proceedings in *Bond of Peace*, June 1868, June and Dec. 1869, June, July, and Dec. 1870.

3. *Voice of Peace*, June 1872; Love Diaries, Dec. 7, 1871, Universal Peace Union Collection, Swarthmore College, Pa.

4. *Woodhull & Claflin's Weekly*, Sept. 3, 1870; Gregory quote from his obituary in *Golden Age*, Dec. 23, 1871; Ingalls, *Reminiscences*, 155–56.

5. *NASS*, Oct. 19, 1867.

6. Harrison's *Before the Socialists* pierces the oft-repeated assertion that it was Marx himself who organized the monster meeting at St. James Hall (for example, see Foner and Chamberlin, *History of the Labor Movement*, 1:316). Harrison was the first to carefully survey the contours of English workers' opinions of slavery, the war, Lincoln, and the Union. Contrary to what has been assumed by Foner and Chamberlin and others, it was not the most radical sectors of English labor who stood by the Union; rather, such support was primarily found among old, middle-class Chartists such as John Bright, and a rising generation of New Model trade unionists—skilled workers who, unlike more radical labor leaders of the time, did not allow their hatred of capitalism to spill over into a hatred for the industrial American North. The early IWA contained representatives of both elements. Harrison concludes, "it was in Britain, as in America, precisely the most militant and class-conscious leaders . . . who kept company with the slaveholders. It was not that they defended slavery, but that they detested the hypocrisy of its leading opponents" (*Before the Socialists*, 58–59).

7. *Liberator*, Jan. 30, 1863. The staunch opposition to slavery on the part of cotton workers was often noted by abolitionists. At about this same time, Richard Webb observed, "Your civil war and the cotton famine have caused an immensity of suffering throughout the British Islands. . . . Yet the very people who have been greater sufferers than any other portion of our population are those who have maintained the most persevering protest against any countenance being afforded to the slaveholders. I allude to the Lancashire operatives" (*NASS*, Feb. 14, 1863); *NASS*, Jan. 7, 1865; *GCM*, 1:50–54; Foner and Chamberlin, *Friedrich Sorge's Labor Movement*, 32–33.

8. Foner and Chamberlin, *History of the Labor Movement*, 1:317.

9. *NASS*, Oct. 31, 1868. The article was written by Richard Hinton, a Union soldier, civil engineer, and journalist who later became active in the American IWA.

10. *NASS*, Aug. 8, Sept. 11, Oct. 9, 1869. For other *NASS* letters and articles on the IWA, see Jan. 1, Sept. 3, 1870, and Sept. 9, 1871, issues.

11. Thompson, "Current Revolution," 121–30; *American Annual Cyclopedia*, 11:411–14.

12. See Samuel Bernstein, *Essays*, 169–82, and *First International*, 73–90.

13. *National Standard*, July 29, Aug. 5, 19, 1871; see also Linton's essay on Mazzini, ibid., July 1872. Linton also wrote an article on the Commune for the Boston *Radical*, a journal published by other veterans of the abolitionist crusade. For reports of the fate of Communards, see *National Standard*, Aug. 19, 26, Sept. 9, 16, 23, Oct. 7, Nov. 11, 18, 1871. For Edward King's poem, see *National Standard*, Aug. 26, 1871.

14. *National Standard*, Sept. 16, 1871.

15. *Workingman's Advocate*, Apr. 15, 1871; Powell, *Personal Reminiscences*, 202.

16. See the *Commonwealth*'s editorial of Apr. 20, 1871; Easton, *Hegel's First American Followers*, 153; Trachtenberg, *Karl Marx*, 83.

17. For biographical information on Moncure Conway, see d'Entremont, *Southern Emancipator*.

18. Conway, *Autobiography*, 2:221–24. For a history of the Peace and Freedom League and the Basle section of the IWA, see Katz, *Emancipation of Labor*, ch. 3.

19. *NASS*, Aug. 28, 1869. Conway's article went on to criticize communists who extended the principle of cooperative labor beyond workers to intellectuals and artists, whose talents would only be squandered thereby (like Hawthorne at Brook Farm, who found himself shoveling dung rather than writing stories). However, Conway was never critical of what he identified as the central institutions of working-class socialism — producer cooperatives, unions, worker's reading rooms and lyceums, parties, or cooperative housing.

20. *National Standard*, Dec. 7, 1871; see also the July 8 and Aug. 26, 1871, issues; Samuel Bernstein, *First International*, 79–83; Hofstadter, *American Political Tradition*, 208–9.

21. Parrington, *Main Currents*, 3:146; Samuel Bernstein, "American Labor."

22. The *Banner of Light* enjoyed a circulation of nearly 15,000 in 1871. See *American Newspaper Directory*, 63; *Banner of Light*, Apr. 29, July 15, 1871.

23. *Iconoclast*, Apr. 4, 1871.

24. Upon its inception, Susan B. Anthony's *Revolution* said of the *Golden Age*, "We heartily rejoice that the Woman Cause has been reinforced by so powerful an ally" (*Revolution*, Mar. 16, 1871). On Tilton, see Waller, *Reverend Beecher*, 38–44.

25. *Golden Age*, May 13, 27, 1871.

26. Ibid., June 17, 1871.

27. Ibid., June 3, 1871. See also, Oct. 14 and 21, 1871.

28. Ibid., Aug. 19, 1871; Jan. 13, 1872; Oct. 21, Dec. 9, 1871.

29. Ibid., Oct. 27, June 3, 1871.

30. Ibid., Dec. 9, 1871.

31. Ibid., Aug. 19, 1871.

32. In his eagerness to paint the Yankee Internationals as reformists who shrunk away from radical proposals, Samuel Bernstein, in *The First International*, erroneously claims that *Woodhull & Claflin's Weekly* vacillated in its opinion of the Paris Commune and ultimately accepted "at their face value the stories on the wicked government" propagated by the yellow press. To back up his claim, Bernstein cites two issues of the *Weekly* that, in fact, contain nothing but praise for the Commune. The August 26, 1871, issue, the first copy of the *Weekly* that Bernstein claims credits "the infamies fastened on" the Commune by the metropolitan press, contained but three references to the Commune. One was a brief mention of Thiers and the history of the conflict in Europe. Another was a brief editorial that criticized Theirs for being a "partisan of Rome" and for following a "reactionary policy." The last (the sort of stock filler that was used to even the columns on the page) was a quote by "Maccall," who criticized the Communards for not acting vigorously enough: "Whether the schemes of the Paris Commune were wise or unwise, whether the deeds of the insurgents were culpable or commendable, each Communist was giving the example which most of all in these craven days is needed: each Communist bounded with alacrity and joy to death for his convictions. . . . The fault of the Paris Commune was not in being too passionate, but in pondering and hesitating when it should have darted itself, a flame of passion, at wicked men and odious institutions."

Bernstein also holds up the September 30, 1871, issue as an example of Woodhull and Claflin's backsliding and criticism of the Commune along the lines of the mainstream press. In this issue, the full text of the General Council of the IWA's *Address on the War in France*, a spread-eagle defense of the Commune, was reprinted. (But Bernstein attempts to sweep this contradictory fact under his lumpy rug: "The fact that the . . . *Weekly* reprinted the General Council's *Address on the War in France* did not signify their approval of it.") On the same page, Woodhull and Claflin reported on the resolution of Section 12 of the New York IWA that supported the Commune and praised its many reforms as a model for other nations. In fact, *Woodhull & Claflin's Weekly* consistently and forcefully defended the Paris Commune and held up its reforms as an example for the world to follow. Jenny Marx's account of her experience under the Theirs government was printed in the Oct. 21, 1871, issue.

33. *New York World*, July 10, 1871.

34. *New York Herald*, Apr. 2, 1870.

35. *Investigator*, Apr. 3, 1872; see also Underhill, *Woman Who Ran for President*.

36. Andrews, *Love, Marriage*, 40; Spurlock, *Free Love*, ch. 4.

37. Stern, *Pantarch*.

38. On Theron Leland, see the *New York Times*, June 6, 1885; *Woodhull & Claflin's Weekly*, Dec. 16, 1871; Spurlock, *Free Love*, 111, 124; Wunderlich, *Low Living*; and MacDonald, *Fifty Years of Freethought*, 384–85; on Mary Leland, see Stoehr, *Free Love in America*, 432–33; and *New York Herald*, Nov. 4, 9, 1871.

39. *Pomeroy's Democrat*, Mar. 10, 1872; *American Spiritualist*, Aug. 8, 1872; MacKinley, *Pysche to the Nineteenth Century*, 4.

40. Clipping in Vertical File under "Anarchism—Andrews, Stephen Pearl," Labadie Collection, University of Michigan, Ann Arbor.

41. Some examples of Hume's many letters to the *NASS* can be seen in the follow-

ing issues: Aug. 24, 1867, Mar. 28, Apr. 25, May 2, 16, Sept. 12, 1868; Jan. 16, Aug. 28, Sept. 25, Oct. 9, 1869; Jan. 1, Apr. 9, Aug. 6, 27, Sept. 3, 10, June 17, July 22, 1870.

42. Stern, *Pantarch*; *Woodhull & Claflin's Weekly*, Dec. 9, 1871.

43. MacDonald, *Fifty Years of Freethought*, 384-85; Spurlock, *Free Love*, 111, 124.

44. *New York World*, Oct. 19, 1871; *Golden Age*, Jan. 27, 1872; *Woodhull & Claflin's Weekly*, Jan. 27, 1872; Tuttle and Peebles, *Yearbook of Spiritualism*, 229. On Boston's Working-Women's League, see *American Workman*, May 8, 1869. Daniels's participation in the New England Labor Reform League is noted in *American Workman*, June 5, 1869, *Banner of Light*, Feb. 6, 1870, *Woodhull & Claflin's Weekly*, May 6, 1871, Apr. 27, 1872, and *Revolution*, Jan. 13, 1870; for Daniels's testimony before Congress, see *Golden Age*, Jan. 27, 1872, and *New York Herald*, Jan. 11, 12, 1872.

45. Daniels described the Order of Equality and Justice during the American Labor Reform League Convention in New York (*New York World*, May 9, 1871).

46. *Boston Post*, Oct. 28, 1871; *New York World*, Oct. 19, 1871. Philbrick's membership in the IWA is noted in *New York World*, Oct. 19, 1871, and *Woodhull & Claflin's Weekly*, Sept. 23, 1871; her abolitionist ties are described in her obituary in the *Evening Transcript*, Oct. 12, 1891.

47. Martin, *Men against the State*, 81, 91-92, 120, 159; Bailie, *Josiah Warren*, 64, 78, 97.

48. Martin, *Men against the State*, 125-26, 133; *New York World*, Sept. 11, 1869; *Banner of Light*, Mar. 1, 1873.

49. "Biography of Rev. Moses Hull."

50. *New Thought*, July 30, 1887.

51. *Defense of the Paris Commune*.

52. *National Cyclopedia of American Biography*, 5:20-21; *Who Was Who*, 243; Lause, "American Radicals," 78.

53. *Official Historical Handbook*; Berlin, Reidy, and Rowland, *Freedom*, 335-36; Samuel Bernstein, *First International*, 31; Montgomery, *Beyond Equality*, 415-16.

54. A full membership list of Section 26 can be found in IWAP. On Kilgore's early activities, see *Liberator*, Nov. 11, 1854. He is noted as speaking at the Pennsylvania Anti-Slavery Society's Convention in 1869 in *NASS*, Nov. 27, 1869; Stout's eulogy is in Records of Section 26, Miscellany, IWAP.

55. Tuttle and Peebles, *Yearbook of Spiritualism*, 125; *Banner of Light*, Feb. 4, 1871; "What of the Future of Spiritualism?," *Banner of Light*, Nov. 11, 1871.

56. James, James, and Boyer, *Notable American Women*, 2:329-30.

57. Jacob Byrnes writings are printed in *Woodhull & Claflin's Weekly*, July 8, Aug. 29, 1871, and Feb. 17, 1872; Mary Byrnes letter is in *Woodhull & Claflin's Weekly*, Nov. 4, 1871; her argument with fellow Internationalists is found in Sec. 26 MB, Sept. 9, 1872, IWAP. For other women's rights activities of Section 26, see the minutes for July 1, Nov. 25, 1872, and Feb. 24, 1873.

58. *Golden Age*, Jan. 6, 1872.

59. *Woman's Journal*, Mar. 5, 26, 1870.

60. *Oneida Circular*, Aug. 29, 1870.

61. Cunningham, "Culture That Was Vineland," 197-200; *Oneida Circular*, Aug. 29, 1870; *Golden Age*, Feb. 17, 1872; report of Spiritualist convention, *Banner of Light*,

Sept. 3, 1870; The Women's Project of New Jersey, *Past and Promise*, 138-39, 198-99. On Vineland's origins, see also, Spann, *Brotherly Tomorrows*, 149-50. On the N.J. Suffrage Convention, see Stanton, Anthony, and Gage, *History of Woman Suffrage*, 479.

62. *Woodhull & Claflin's Weekly*, Sept. 30, 1871; *Golden Age*, Sept. 16, 1871.

63. On Dickenson, see *Woodhull & Claflin's Weekly*, Feb. 2, 1872. On Edwards, see MacDonald, *Fifty Years of Freethought*, 234; Sorge to Edwards, Sept. 20, 1871, CC Corr.

64. *Banner of Light*, Nov. 11, 1871.

65. Ibid., Sept. 21, 28, 1872.

66. On the response of some Spiritualists to Woodhull's election and program, see the following letters in the *Banner of Light*: J. K. Bailey, Nov. 25, 1871; Edmund S. Holbrook, Dec. 2, 1871; Mrs. E. C. H., Jan. 13, 1872; J. Wetherbee, Jan. 27, 1872; Emma Hardinge-Britten, Feb. 3, 1872; M. S. Townsend Hoadley, Feb. 10, 1872; E. S. Wheeler, Feb. 24, 1872; see also Hudson Tuttle in the *Religio-Philosophical Journal*, Dec. 16, 1871, and H. F. M. Brown in ibid., Mar. 9, 1872. Anna Middlebrook's quote is from *Banner of Light*, Mar. 30, 1872.

67. *Banner of Light*, Mar. 30, 1872.

68. *Woodhull & Claflin's Weekly*, Mar. 9, 1872.

69. *Workingman's Advocate*, Feb. 3, 1872.

70. Elliot to Rehn, n.d., IWA Corr., IWAP; MacDonald, *Fifty Years of Freethought*, 2:341.

71. *Woodhull & Claflin's Weekly*, Apr. 16, 1872.

72. Ibid., Jan. 27, 1872; *New York Herald*, Jan. 11, 1872.

73. *Woodhull & Claflin's Weekly*, Jan. 27, 1872.

74. Ibid.; *New York Herald*, Jan. 12, 1872.

75. *Woodhull & Claflin's Weekly*, Jan. 27, 1872; *New York Herald*, Jan. 12, 1872. The only representatives of the labor reform movement who spoke before the NWSA convention were members of the International Workingmen's Association.

76. *Golden Age*, Feb. 3, 1872.

77. DuBois, *Elizabeth Cady Stanton*, 104-5; Boydston, Kelley, and Margolis, *Limits of Sisterhood*, 188, 205-11. See also Hays, *Morning Star*, 229-40, and Elizabeth Cady Stanton's speech on labor, reprinted in DuBois, "On Labor and Free Love," 260-63.

78. *Golden Age*, Apr. 27, 1872.

79. *Woodhull & Claflin's Weekly*, May 18, 1872.

80. Barry, *Susan B. Anthony*, 244-45; DuBois, *Elizabeth Cady Stanton*, 105; Kugler, *From Ladies to Women*, 110; *Woodhull & Claflin's Weekly*, June 15, 1872; *Banner of Light*, June 1, 1872; *New York Herald*, May 10, 1872; *Present Age*, Dec. 23, 1871.

81. Barry, *Susan B. Anthony*, 246-47; *New York World*, May 11, 1872; Kugler, *From Ladies to Women*, 112; *New York World*, July 29, May 11, 12, 1872; *New York Sun*, May 11, 1872; *New York Herald*, May 11, 12, 1872; *Woodhull & Claflin's Weekly*, May 25, 1872.

82. Boydston, Kelley, and Margolis, *Limits of Sisterhood*, 210.

83. Sec. 26 MB, Dec. 23, 1872.

1. "Appeal to the Workingmen of America," May 19, 1872, Records of Central Committee, Broadsides, IWAP.

2. Sec. 26 MB, June 17, 1872.

3. "Appeal to the Workingmen of America," May 19, 1872, Records of Central Committee, Broadsides, IWAP. Examples of this class-based historical explanation are: Schlüter, *Die Internationale*; Quint, *Forging of American Socialism*, 10–11; Foner and Chamberlin, *History of the Labor Movement*, 415–16; Hillquit, *History of Socialism*, 179–81; and Commons et al., *Documentary History* 2:211–13.

4. Samuel Bernstein, in *First International*, 63, miscalculated the occupational composition of this section. He claims that sixteen members, "an influential minority," were "manufacturers or merchants." In fact, cross-checking the section's own records with the city directories and the census returns for 1870 reveals that only ten fell into this category. One of these whom I count as a merchant was described in the census as a "tailor-merchant" but described himself as a "tailor." See Records of Section 26, Membership Rolls, IWAP; *Philadelphia City Directory*; and *Federal Census*, 1870.

5. For a description of the instructions given to census enumerators, see Wright, *History and Growth of the United States Census*, 157. The best predictor of whether a member of the Philadelphia IWA was a member of the professions was not income, but gender. The Philadelphia branch of the International Workingmen's Association attracted more professional women than working-class women. Of ten women enrolled in Section 26, three were physicians, two were teachers, and one was a law student. Of the four blue-collar women, three were seamstresses and one worked as a housekeeper.

6. On West's occupation, see *New York World*, Aug. 12, 1872.

7. MacDonald, *Fifty Years of Freethought*, 1:222.

8. Marx to Siegfried Meyer, Apr. 9, 1870, MECW, 43:471; "Reminiscences of Theodor Cuno," in *Documents of the First International . . . Reports and Letters*, 625.

9. On S. Meyer's occupation, see Samuel Bernstein, *First International*, 27; on H. Meyer, see *MECW*, 43:687; on the proprietor of the 10th Ward Hotel, see Elliot to Rehn, Dec. 5, 1871, Records of Section 26, Corr., IWAP.

10. *Memorial Addresses, on the Life and Character of Edwin Martin Chamberlin.*

11. Sec. 26 MB, June 17, 1872, IWAP.

12. CC Corr., Report for Nov. 1871, IWAP. An example of this line of analysis is: Herreshoff, *American Disciples*, ch. 4. In essence, this is also the explanation of Samuel Bernstein, *First International*, ch. 7, and Montgomery, *Beyond Equality*, 418–21.

13. Elliot to Rehn, Jan. 1, 1872, IWAP.

14. Sec. 26 MB, Jan. 8, 1872, IWAP.

15. *Proceedings of the First Congress.*

16. *Worker*, Feb. 2, 1873.

17. *New York Herald*, Mar. 16, 1872; Sec. 26 MB, Oct. 30, 1871, May 6, 1872.

18. *Worker*, Feb. 1873.

19. Sec. 26 MB, June 3, 1872, IWAP; *Worker*, Feb. 2, 1873.

20. Sec. 26 MB, June 23, 1873, IWAP.

21. Ibid., Apr. 22, 1872.

22. Ibid., Oct. 21, 1872.

23. On Kinget, see *Toiler*, Oct. 10, 1874.

24. *Worker*, Jan. 26, 1873.

25. *New York World*, Oct. 22, Nov. 5, 1869.

26. Elliot to Rehn, Oct. 31, 1871, Sec. 26 Corr., IWAP.

27. "Notes on the Labor Question by an International," in *Workingman's Advocate*, Apr., 8, 1871.

28. *Workingman's Advocate*, June 1, 1872.

29. *New York Herald*, Mar. 16, 1872.

30. "Appeal of Section 12," in *Woodhull & Claflin's Weekly*, Sept. 23, 1871; *Woodhull & Claflin's Weekly*, Dec. 9, 1871; *Proceedings of the First Congress*.

31. *GCM*, 4:452; Marx to Engels, Nov. 4, 1864, *MECW*, 42:18.

32. *New York Herald*, Sept. 11, 1871.

33. *New York Times*, Dec. 16, 1871; "Constitution of the Federal Council of North America International Workingmen's Association," Sec. 26 MB, 42, IWAP.

34. "Appeal of Section 12," *Woodhull & Claflin's Weekly*, Sept. 23, 1871.

35. "Circular to all Sections," Dec. 1871, in Records of the Central Committee, Broadsides, IWAP.

36. "Address of the General Council," Oct. 20, 1872, Records of the Central Committee, Broadsides, IWAP; Foner and Chamberlin, *Friedrich A. Sorge's Labor Movement*, 109-10, 117, 119.

37. "Address of the General Council," Oct. 20, 1872, Records of the Central Committee, Broadsides, IWAP; *New York Herald*, June 21, 23, 24, 1872.

38. Foner and Chamberlin, *Friedrich A. Sorge's Labor Movement*, 3-4; Herreshoff, *American Disciples*, 57; Commons et al., *History of Labour*, 2:207; Wittke, *Refugees of Revolution*, 168-69. See also McMorrow, "Nineteenth Century German Political Immigrant." On the Communist Club, see Philip Foner, *American Socialism*, 27-31, and *Social Party*.

39. On the transformation of the Republican Party and the defeat of labor's legislative agenda, the standard work remains Montgomery, *Beyond Equality*. On the mire of New York politics, see Bridges, *City in the Republic*.

40. "Instructions for the Delegate of the General Council to the 6th General Congress," in Samuel Bernstein, *Papers of the General Council*, 103.

41. "Address and Annual Report," in Samuel Bernstein, *Papers of the General Council*, 106.

42. Sorge to Marx, July 15, 1872, *Documents of the First International . . . Reports and Letters*, 379.

43. Sorge to British Federation, May 9, 1873, in Samuel Bernstein, *Papers of the General Council*, p. 74.

44. Sec. 26 MB, June 17, 1872, IWAP.

45. Levin, *Marx, Engels and Liberal Democracy*, ch. 2. Cohen, "Marxism and Democracy," 6. There is much silliness in the writings on the relationship of Marx to liberalism and democracy. For example, A. Landy has this to say: "From the day of its birth as a scientific viewpoint of social development and as a practical party, Marxism . . .

inscribed democracy on its banner and allied itself with the democratic movements of Europe and the United States" (*Marxism and the Democratic Tradition*, 158).

46. *MECW*, 43:475.

47. Ibid., 474. Note that Marx sprinkled his original German text with the English words "poor whites" and "niggers." Earlier translators of Marx's letters to Americans were skittish about Marx's use of such epithets and sanitized his language. In, *Letters to Americans, 1848–1895*, 78, a collection translated by Leonard E. Mins and edited by Alexander Trachtenberg, the word "Negroes" is used in place of Marx's original term.

48. *MECW*, 43:476.

49. Sorge to the General Council, Aug. 23, 1871, CC Corr., IWAP.

50. See Engels's letter to Sigismund Borkheim, *MECW*, 44:329.

51. *New York World*, May 6, 1872.

52. Sec. 26 MB, Apr. 21, 1873, IWAP.

53. *New York World*, Nov. 27, 1871.

54. Mari Jo Buhle, *Women and American Socialism*, 12.

55. Ibid., 8–12.

56. On the "family wage," see Kessler-Harris, *Woman's Wage*, ch. 1; Central Committee Reports for Nov. 1871, Dec. 17, 1871, Jan. 1872, Jan. 21, 1872, CC Corr., IWAP.

57. *Woodhull & Claflin's Weekly*, Nov. 11, 1871.

58. *MECW*, 44:252.

59. Quote is from Foner and Chamberlin, *Friedrich A. Sorge's Labor Movement*, 163.

60. "Appeal of Section 12," *Woodhull & Claflin's Weekly*, Sept. 23, 1871; "Appeal to the Workingmen of America," May 19, 1872, Records of the Central Committee, Broadsides, IWAP.

CHAPTER SIX

1. Engels quote is found in Gerth, *First International*, xv. The best single source on the divisions within the International in Europe is Katz, *Emancipation of Labor*.

2. Sorge's "Report to the General Council for July," Aug. 6, 1871, CC Corr., IWAP; *MECW*, 44:217, 626.

3. This is also the reason that so little information could be found on the activities of this section.

4. *GCM*, 5:241–42, 528; Sorge to Hinton, Sept. 6, 18, 22, Oct. 4, 1871, CC Corr., IWAP; *MECW*, 44:217, 237, 627.

5. *Woodhull & Claflin's Weekly*, Aug. 19, 1871.

6. *New York Times*, July 31, Aug. 1, 17, 26, 1871.

7. *New York World*, Sept. 4, 1871; *Woodhull & Claflin's Weekly*, Sept. 16, 1871.

8. *Woodhull & Claflin's Weekly*, Sept. 16, Oct. 21, 1871.

9. CC Corr., Oct. 4, 12, 1871, IWAP.

10. *Woodhull & Claflin's Weekly*, Sept. 2, 23, 1871; *New York World*, Sept. 4, 1871.

11. While directing new sections to Sorge, the "Appeal" also included William West's address for those who wanted more information.

12. *Woodhull & Claflin's Weekly*, Sept. 23, 1871.

13. Ibid.

14. West to Sorge, Oct. 9, 1871, CC Corr., IWAP; *Woodhull & Claflin's Weekly*, Oct. 7, 14, 1871.

15. "Report to the General Council for September," Oct. 1, 1871, CC Corr., IWAP.

16. *Woodhull & Claflin's Weekly*, Nov. 4, 1871.

17. Ibid., Nov. 25, 18, 1871.

18. The vote totals in the Central Committee were reported in Sorge's "Report to the General Council for November," Dec. 17, 1871, CC Corr., IWAP; *New York World*, Nov. 6, 13, 1871; *Woodhull & Claflin's Weekly*, Nov. 18, 1871.

19. *Woodhull & Claflin's Weekly*, Dec. 2, 1871. "To the General Council of the IWA," Nov. 19, 1871, CC Corr.; "Report for November," Dec. 17, 1871, CC Corr.; Elliot to Rehn, Nov. 20, 1871, Sec. 26 Corr., all in IWAP.

20. *Woodhull & Claflin's Weekly*, Dec. 16, 1871.

21. Ibid., Dec. 2, 16, 1871.

22. For the text of the "Resolution on the Central Committee of the International's Sections," see *GCM*, 5:338, and *Woodhull & Claflin's Weekly*, Dec. 2, 1871.

23. Marx to Sorge, Nov. 6, 9, 1871, *MECW*, 44:236, 242; Marx to Sorge, Mar. 8, 1872, ibid., 334.

24. Marx to Liebknecht, Jan. 18, 1872, *MECW*, 44:298.

25. Sorge's "Report for November," Dec. 17, 1871, CC Corr., IWAP.

26. Samuel Bernstein, *First International*, 118; "The Blood-Red Flag," undated clipping in IWAP; *New York Herald*, Nov. 30, Dec. 4, 1871; *New York Sun*, Dec. 4, 1871; *Woodhull & Claflin's Weekly*, Dec. 16, 1871; *New York World*, Dec. 4, 1871; *New York Herald*, Nov. 30, 1871; Elliot to Rehn, Dec. 5, 1871, Sec. 26 Corr., IWAP.

27. Sorge's "Report for November," Dec. 17, 1871, CC Corr., IWAP. Philip Foner and Brewster Chamberlin scramble the chronology of these events, making it appear as though Sorge staged his coup and Marx suspended Section 12 only after Woodhull had convened her "Equal Rights Party" congress in May of 1872 and made the International the "laughing stock" of America (*Friedrich A. Sorge's Labor Movement*, 18–20). Clearly, this is a convenient way of making Sorge appear patient and tolerant of his Yankee allies and acting only as a last resort to save the International from being plunged into disrepute by Woodhull.

28. Sorge's "Report for November," Dec. 17, 1871, and "Report for January," n.d., CC Corr.; and Elliot to Rehn, Feb. 13, 1872, Sec. 26 Corr., all in IWAP.

29. Lilienthal's association with the Yankee Federal Council is reported in the *New York Herald*, Dec. 15, 1871; Paul Buhle, *Marxism in the United States*, 1–4; Bernstein, *First International*, 63.

30. *Woodhull & Claflin's Weekly*, Dec. 9, 23, 30, 1871; Jan. 6, 13, Feb. 24, 1872.

31. *GCM*, 5:91, 537, 109–10. Marx revealed in a letter to Sorge that his complaint arrived together with the one from the Counter-Committee, though only the one was read at the General Council meeting of Jan. 30, 1872 (see Marx to Sorge, Mar. 8, 1872, *MECW*, 44:334; *GCM*, 5:91). It was reported in a letter to the secretary of Section 26 that "Eccarius . . . informs us that our reports have never been introduced to the General Council. The trickery of these men has been discovered" (Elliot to Rehn, n.d.,

Sec. 26 Corr., IWAP). Marx admitted that the correspondence did not reach Eccarius at the meeting of May 11, 1872 (*GCM*, 5:189).

32. Section 12's "Appeal" appeared in *Woodhull & Claflin's Weekly*, Sept. 23, 1871. Marx's notes on the "American Split," are found in *MECW*, 23:636-43. This is only one of several of Marx's attempts to show that Section 12 had no conception of the proper aims of the International. In another section, Marx resorted to a gross omission to completely change the meaning of one of the statements West made in his response to the "Protest" of Section 1. Quoting West as saying that "Section 12 would also remonstrate against the vain assumption running all through the Protest under review, that the I.W.A. is an organization of the laboring classes," Marx left out the last dozen words in his sentence. What West really said was, "Section 12 would also remonstrate against the vain assumption running all through the Protest under review, that the I.W.A. is an organization of the laboring classes *which refuses, or at least does not invite, the cooperation of any other class.*"

33. West's original resolution is in *Woodhull & Claflin's Weekly*, Nov. 18, 1871. The disputed resolution is in the Oct. 21, 1871, issue. What the resolution on independent rights ultimately said was printed in *Woodhull & Claflin's Weekly*, May 4, 1872.

34. *GCM*, 5:120, 124-26.

35. Ibid., 410-13.

36. Marx to Sorge, Mar. 15, 1871, *MECW*, 44:341-42; *GCM*, 5:131, 168, 175. No leader of the First International in London has been more maligned in the history books than has Johann Georg Eccarius. Samuel Bernstein branded his actions "treasonable" and even heaped upon his shoulders responsibility for perpetuating the split in New York. While uncritically including every accusation made by Marx and Engels against Eccarius in their narratives, Bernstein and most other historians of the International are completely silent on the countercharges flung back against Marx and Engels. See, for example, Bernstein, *First International*, 124-25; Collins and Abramsky, *Karl Marx and the British Working Class Movement*, 250-51; and Katz, *Emancipation of Labor*, 122-23.

37. Marx to Eccarius, May 3, 1872, *MECW*, 44:363-64.

38. Ibid.; Engels to Liebknecht, May 27-28, 1872, *MECW*, 44:380-85.

39. *New York Herald*, Apr. 22, 1872; *New York World*, Apr. 22, 1872.

40. *New York World*, Apr. 16, 1872. *Ninth Census*, 3:797-823.

41. *Woodhull & Claflin's Weekly*, June 15, 1872.

42. Ibid., May 4, 1872.

43. *New York Herald*, May 20, Aug. 5, 1872.

44. *Woodhull & Claflin's Weekly*, May 11, 1872.

45. *New York Herald*, June 17, 1872.

46. Katz, *Emancipation of Labor*, 51-68, 96-112, 128-36; *Documents of the First International . . . Minutes*, xi-xvii; Samuel Bernstein, *First International*, 145-48.

47. Katz, *Emancipation of Labor*, 51-68, 96-112, 128-36; *Documents of the First International . . . Minutes*, xi-xvii; Samuel Bernstein, *First International*, 145-48; Marx to Sorge, June 21, 1872, *MECW*, 44:398.

48. Engels to Becker, Aug. 5, 1872, *MECW*, 44:419-20.

49. Ibid., 418; Sorge to Marx, July 15, 1872, 378; Sorge to Jung, Aug. 22, 1872, 470;

Speyer to Marx, Aug. 5, 1872, 419; Sorge to Marx, Aug. 6, 1872, 421; Hepner to Engels, Aug. 26, 1872, 484, all in *Documents of the First International . . . Letters*.

50. Sorge to Marx, July 15, 1872, *Documents of the First International . . . Letters*, 378. On Burton, see *New York World*, July 22, 1872.

51. *Woodhull & Claflin's Weekly*, Mar. 22, 1873; *GCM*, 5:280.

52. *Woodhull & Claflin's Weekly*, Mar. 22, 1873; *New York World*, Sept. 13, 1872.

53. Collins and Abramsky, *Karl Marx and the British Working Class Movement*, 260. Marx's oratory style was described by Theodor Cuno in his "Reminiscences," in *Documents of the First International . . . Reports and Letters*, 621; Gerth, *First International*, 194–95.

54. See Gerth, *First International*, 196, and *Documents of the First International . . . Reports and Letters*, 76.

55. *Documents of the First International . . . Reports and Letters*, 77; Engels has Sorge using the German word "negern" in his account. Gerth, *First International*, 49. Months earlier, Marx, in issuing his charges against Eccarius, presented virtually the same assessment of the working class in America: "The work of the Association did not concern the real Yankees so much as [it] did some of the other elements. The Yankees were instinctively speculators. The greatest labour interest in the States was Irish, next German, third the Negroes and fourth the Yankees themselves" (*GCM*, 5:206).

56. *Ninth Census*, 3:831–43; *Ninth Census. Compendium*, 376. In 1870 New York's proportion of workers in manufacturing was: native-born — 52,125; German — 43,287; Irish — 33,316. On immigrant New York, see Nadel, *Little Germany*.

57. Gerth, *First International*, 199. On Mottershead, see the letter of Jules Johannard to Hermann Jung, Sept. 4, 1872, *Documents of the First International . . . Reports and Letters*, 511–12.

58. On Law, see Bellamy and Saville, *Dictionary of Labour Biography*, 5:134–36; for Law's mandate, see *Documents of the First International . . . Minutes and Documents*, 313–14; on Zhukovsky, see Katz, *Emancipation of Labor*, 131.

59. Samuel Bernstein, *First International*, 155; Katz, *Emancipation of Labor*, 133.

60. West to Mills, Sept. 1872, Sec. 26 Corr., IWAP; *New York World*, Aug. 19, 1872; Engels to Cuno, Oct. 29, 1872, *MECW*, 44:442; clipping entitled "Impecuniousness and Generosity" in IWA Misc. Papers.

61. Podolinsky to Lavrov, Sept. 7, 1872, in *Documents of the First International . . . Reports and Letters*, 522.

62. Sorge to the GC, Dec. 22, 1872, GC Corr., IWAP.

63. Podolinsky to Lavrov, Sept. 5, 1872, in *Documents of the First International . . . Reports and Letters*, 517.

64. *Documents of the First International . . . Reports and Letters*, 637.

65. *New York Herald*, Aug. 19, 1872; *American Workman*, July 13, 1872; *New York World*, Aug. 19, Sept. 2, 9, 1872; Sachs, *"Terrible Siren,"* 178–82.

66. See DuBois, *Feminism and Suffrage*, 93–103.

67. *Woodhull & Claflin's Weekly*, Jan. 3, 1872; *New York Herald*, Mar. 31, 1873.

68. Sec. 26 MB, Dec. 9, 16, 1872, Apr. 4, 1873, IWAP.

CHAPTER SEVEN

1. Saxton, *Indispensable Enemy*, 41–44.

2. Bloch, "National Labor Union," 13–21; Matison, "Labor Movement"; Spero and Harris, *Black Worker*, 23–25. On Trevellick and Sylvis, see Montgomery, *Beyond Equality*, 222–29.

3. *Address of the National Labor Congress*. Spero and Harris, *Black Worker*, 23–24; Sylvis, *The Life, Speeches, Labors*, 77; Grossman, *William Sylvis*, ch. 10.

4. Commons et al., *Documentary History*, 9:185–88; Du Bois, *Black Reconstruction*, 355–56.

5. Matison, "Labor Movement," 437–38; Spero and Harris, *Black Worker*, 25–27; on the statewide black labor conventions, see Eric Foner, "Black Labor Conventions," 91–103.

6. See Foner and Lewis, *Black Worker*, 72, and Spero and Harris, *Black Worker*, 26–27.

7. Du Bois, *Black Reconstruction*, 356–57; Spero and Harris, *Black Worker*, 27; Commons et al., *Documentary History*, 9:239.

8. Philip Foner, *American Socialism*, 6; *Social Party*; *New York Times*, Nov. 12, 1869; Matison, "Labor Movement," 442–43.

9. Commons et al., *Documentary History*, 9:259–61. On John Langston, see *Biographical Directory of the American Congress*, 1262. Neither Lanston's autobiography (*From the Virginia Plantation*) nor the best biography of Langston (Cheek and Cheek, *John Mercer Langston*) details his labor activities.

10. Commons et al., *History of Labour*, 144–45. On S. F. Cary, see *Biographical Directory of the American Congress*, 714; *National Cyclopedia of American Biography*, 480; and Montgomery, *Beyond Equality*, 392–94 (though Montgomery strives too hard to paint Cary as friend of the freedman). On Cary's opposition to the Reconstruction Act, see *Congressional Globe*, 40th Congress, 2nd Session, 642, 647; for his vote against the Fifteenth Amendment, see *Congressional Globe*, 40th Congress, 3rd Session, 1564; on his reception at the NLU congress of 1870, see Commons et al., *Documentary History*, 9:259, and *Cincinnati Commercial*, Aug. 16, 1870.

11. W. E. B. Du Bois was the first to point out the connection between black workers' economic agenda and their political support for the Republican Party (*Black Reconstruction*, 359; *American Workman*, Jan. 29, 1870).

12. Spero and Harris, *Black Worker*, 29–31; Du Bois, *Black Reconstruction*, 359–67.

13. Bloch, "Labor and the Negro," 166; Matison, "Labor Movement," 444–45; *New York World*, Sept. 17, 1869; *NASS*, July 17, 1869; Spero and Harris, *Black Worker*, 20; Foner and Lewis, *Black Worker*, 277–78. In 1870, the carpenters relaxed their restrictive policy and allowed the formation of segregated black locals with the permission of existing white locals. In 1871, the cigarmakers struck the white worker clause from their constitution but continued to allow local unions to set their own membership policies. It has been pointed out that for all the variations on membership policy in these years, all told, very few black workers were organized into the labor movement during the 1870s (Wolfe, *Admission to American*, 114). See also Hill, "Race, Ethnicity."

14. Sorge to the General Council, Apr. 2, 1871, CC Corr., IWAP.

15. Ibid., June 1871.

16. Foner and Chamberlin, *Friedrich A. Sorge's Labor Movement*, 121, 177, 178.

17. *New York Herald*, *New York Sun*, Dec. 16, 1871.

18. *New York Sun*, Dec. 11, 1871.

19. *Golden Age*, Dec. 23, 1871; *New York Herald*, *New York Sun*, *New York Standard*, *New York World*, Dec. 18, 1871; *New York Sun*, Dec., 11, 1871.

20. On the public culture and symbolic meanings of volunteer militias in the nineteenth century, see Susan G. Davis, *Parades and Power*, 67–72.

21. *New York Sun*, Feb. 2, 7, 8, 10, Mar. 1, 1871. In the early 1870s, Tammany Hall attempted to gain support among the German American community in a juggling act in which it tried to put the racial issues of the Civil War to rest without endorsing the Fifteenth Amendment to the Constitution. Tweed's acceptance of black marchers in the Fenian parade should be seen in this context. See Iver Bernstein, *New York City Draft Riots*, 195–96, 217–18, 226–28.

22. *New York World*, Sept. 14, 1871; *Workingman's Advocate*, Sept. 23, 1871.

23. *New York Herald*, Mar. 25, 1872; *New York World*, Dec. 11, 1871.

24. *New York Herald*, Apr. 4, 1872. Six months later disagreements were reported to have broken out in Section 35 between its black and white members. Apparently, some of the white members recommended that the black members form their own separate sections (*New York World*, Sept. 16, 1872). (Note: This report mistakes Section 35 for a "French" section, probably because after the majority of Francophone sections split away from the Yankee Federal Council, some French-speaking Internationalists chose to join Yankee sections [*New York World*, Sept. 16, 1872].)

25. *New York World*, July 29, May 11, 12, 1872; *New York Sun*, May 11, 1872; *New York Herald*, May 11, 12, 1872; *Woodhull & Claflin's Weekly*, May 25, 1872; Kathleen Barry's *Susan B. Anthony* states that it was Isabella Beecher Hooker who "encouraged the convention to nominate Douglass" (246). However, all accounts I could find clearly indicate that Moses Hull placed Douglass's name in nomination for the ticket.

26. *Woodhull & Claflin's Weekly*, May 25, 1872; *New York World*, June 7, 1872; Sachs, *"Terrible Siren,"* 160–61; Johnston, *Mrs. Satan*, 148–49.

27. On the racial attitudes and actions of the radical abolitionists, see Pease and Pease, "Antislavery Ambivalence," 683–84; McPherson, "Brief for Equality"; and Allen and Allen, *Reluctant Reformers*, ch. 2; on stirpiculture, see *Woodhull & Claflin's Weekly*, Sept. 10, 17, Oct. 22, 28, Nov. 5, 1870; and "A Speech on the Impending Revolution," in *Woodhull & Claflin's Weekly*, Nov. 1, 1873, and reprinted in Stern, *Victoria Woodhull Reader*.

28. *Woodhull & Claflin's Weekly*, June 8, 1872; *New York Times*, May 16, 1872; *Boston Globe*, May 22, 1872.

29. Johnson, *African-American Soldiers*, 10–11.

30. Farley, *Underside of Reconstruction*, 18.

31. Ottley and Weatherby, *Negro in New York*, 121–24. See also Iver Bernstein, *New York City Draft Riots*, 65–68.

32. Rosenwaike, *Population History*, 44–45, 76–78.

33. *New York Herald*, Mar. 9, 1872.

34. See, for example, the editorial "A Question of Clothes," *New York Times*, June 16, 1872.

35. The two newspapers that carried accounts of the election of Claflin differed in their tally of the voting. The *Sun* put the count at 193 to 50, while the *Herald* counted 125 to 40 (*New York Sun*, June 14, 1872; *New York Herald*, June 14, 1872).

36. Sachs, *"Terrible Siren"*, 167; Johnston, *Mrs. Satan*, 148–49.

37. Reese, "Worker in Texas," 256–59; Philip Foner, *American Socialism*, 38–39; *Galveston Daily News*, Feb. 20, 28, Mar. 3, 1872.

38. *Galveston Daily News*, Mar. 3, Apr. 14, 1872; Reese, "Worker in Texas"; Philip Foner, *American Socialism*, 39.

39. *Galveston Daily News*, Apr. 3, 14, 1872; Reese, "Worker in Texas"; Philip Foner, *American Socialism*.

40. *Trades Journal and Financial Record*, Dec. 10, 1872; *New York Herald*, Dec. 2, 1872.

41. *New York Herald*, Oct. 21, 1872.

42. Foner and Rosenberg, *Racism, Dissent, and Asian Americans*, 41–42, 48–54, 89–90, 103–5; *New York Times*, Feb. 10, 1872; Daniels, *Asian America*, 43.

43. Locke, "Race and Ethnocentrism," 2–33; Horace B. Davis, "Nations, Colonies," 26–43; Weyl, *Karl Marx*, 118–24.

44. *GCM*, 3:50; 4:92, 166.

45. For details of the North Adams controversy, see Rudolph, "Chinamen in Yankeedom," 1–29; Stuart Creighton Miller, *Unwelcome Immigrant*, ch. 8; and Barth, *Bitter Strength*, 198–202. On the German American IWA and the 1870 anti-Chinese rally, see *New York World*, July 1, 1870, and Iver Bernstein, *New York City Draft Riots*, 226–27.

46. Sorge to the General Council, Aug. 6, 1871, Sorge to GC, "Report for the Month of October 1871," and Sorge to GC, Aug. 6, 1871, all in GC Corr., IWAP.

47. *New York Herald*, July 8, 1872.

48. *New York World*, July 7, 8, 9, 1872. In *The First International* Samuel Bernstein claims that the convention "left undefined its position on the question of Chinese labor, raised by a section in San Francisco. The delegates were content to reject slavery in any form, including indentured Chinese labor, and urged the enactment of legislation to prevent it" (143). In reality, the only question left unresolved was whether the Chinese should be forced onto boats heading back to China or whether Chinese blood should run in the streets of Western cities.

49. *New York World*, Aug. 5, Sept. 30, 1872.

50. *Woodhull & Claflin's Weekly*, July 2, 1870.

51. Ibid., Apr. 6, 1872.

52. Entry for Sept. 23, 1872, Sec. 26 MB, IWAP.

53. *New York Herald*, Mar. 31, 1873.

54. Hinton, "Talk With Mr. Burlingame," and "Race for Commercial Supremacy."

55. *Woodhull & Claflin's Weekly*, Jan. 27, 1872; Kilgore, *Questions of To-day*, 15–16.

56. *Worker*, Feb. 23, 1873.

57. Cross, *History of the Labor Movement*, 66–67; *Workingman's Advocate*, June 3, 1871.

58. *Workingman's Advocate*, July 15, 1871.

59. Ibid., Sept. 30, Oct. 27, 1871.

60. Ibid., Jan. 13–20, 1872; *Woodhull & Claflin's Weekly*, Dec. 16, 1871.

61. *Workingman's Advocate*, Apr. 27, May 11, 1872; clipping labeled "March 1872" in Misc. Clipping File, IWAP; Sorge to the GC, Jan. 21, 1872, CC Corr., IWAP.

62. Federal Council to the General Council, May 5, 1872, and Bolte to Chamberlin, Nov. 28, 1872, both in CC Corr., IWAP.

63. Ward missed the first day of the convention, at which a reporter noted that all the delegates were foreign-born, but he showed up on the second (*New York World*, July 8, 1872; Socialist Labor Party of America Records, New York City Section Minutes, State Historical Society of Wisconsin, Madison).

CHAPTER EIGHT

1. *New York World*, Dec. 16, 17, 1872; *Trades Journal and Financial Record*, Jan. 4, 1873.

2. IWA Central Committee Correspondence, n.d. (frame no. 150 on microfilm edition), IWAP; *New York Herald*, Dec. 16, 23, 1872.

3. *New York Herald*, Oct. 7, Dec. 16, 23, 30, 1872.

4. Ibid., Mar. 3, 10, 1873.

5. *Word*, Feb. 1873.

6. *New York Herald*, Apr. 18, 1873; Clipping of invitation is in Sec. 26 MB, IWAP, n.d.

7. *New York Herald*, Apr. 22, 23, 30, 1873.

8. Ibid., Apr. 30, May 4, 10, 1873.

9. *New York World*, July 17, 1872.

10. Costello, "New York City Labor Movement," 216–24.

11. *New York Herald*, May 18, 1873.

12. Samuel Bernstein, *First International*, 219–20.

13. *Public Ledger*, Nov. 13, 21, 1873.

14. Ibid., Nov. 17, 1873.

15. Ibid., Nov. 28, 1873.

16. *New York Herald*, Dec. 12, 1873; Samuel Bernstein, *First International*, 225–27.

17. *New York Herald*, Dec. 13, 1873.

18. *New York Times*, Jan. 18, 1874.

19. Gutman, "Thompkins Square 'Riot,' " 44–70.

20. *New York Times*, Jan. 22, 1874.

21. Ibid., Jan. 14, 1874.

22. Samuel Bernstein, *First International*, 233–40; Gutman, "Tompkins Square 'Riot,' " 44–70.

23. Samuel Bernstein, *First International*, 186.

24. Ibid., 188.

25. Foner and Chamberlin, *Friedrich A. Sorge's Labor Movement*, 161.

26. Theodore Cuno writes in "Reminiscences" that he first met Samuel Gompers at a Section 1 meeting in the Fall of 1872 (*Documents of the First International . . . Reports and Letters*, 625).

27. Gompers, *Seventy Years*, 1:55–57.

28. Kaufman, *Samuel Gompers*, ch. 2; Kaufman, *Making of a Union Leader*, 21–22; Gompers, *Seventy Years*, 1:70–75.

29. Gompers, *Seventy Years*, 1:87.

30. Gitelman, "Adolph Strasser," 71–83; Kaufman, *Samuel Gompers*.

31. Abbott, "Employment of Women," 1–25; Ware, *Labor Movement in the United States*, 258–62; Kaufman, *Making of a Union Leader*, 45–47.

32. Schneider, *Trade Unions and Community*, 101; Commons et al., *History of Labour*, 2:400.

33. Ware, *Labor Movement in the United States*, 261–65.

34. Saxton, *The Indispensable Enemy*, 73–77; *Making of a Union Leader*, 125; Cooper, *Once a Cigar Maker*, ch. 1.

35. Foner, *Organized Labor*, 66; Schneider, *Trade Unions and Community*, 95, 98; Weir, *Beyond Labor's Veil*, 257.

36. Kaufman, *Making of a Union Leader*, 114, 218, 230, 125; Gompers and Morrison, *Meat vs. Rice*.

37. On New York's cigarmakers, see Schneider, "New York Cigarmakers Strike," 325–52; Ware, *Labor Movement in the United States*, ch. 11.

38. Pioneer Council Correspondence, July 25, 1877, Sovereigns of Industry Papers, State Historical Society of Wisconsin, Madison; "Bills and Receipts, 1874–1879" folder, Box 2, IWAP.

39. Reynolds, *George Lippard*, 20.

40. Sec. 26 MB, Dec. 30, 1872, IWAP; George Lippard Papers, University of Pennsylvania, Philadelphia; see also Butterfield, "George Lippard."

41. Yearley, "Thomas Phillips," 167–96; "Biography of Thomas Phillips," in Thomas Phillips Papers, State Historical Society of Wisconsin, Madison; Yearley, *Britons in American Labor*, 277–80.

42. Yearley, *Britons in American Labor*, 277; Commons et al., *History of Labour*, 2:197n.

43. On Blair, see *Report of the Committee of the Senate upon the Relations between Labor and Capital*, 2:44–45; on Elliot, see Laurie, *Artisans into Workers*, 190; on Mills, see *Journal of United Labor*, May 15, 1880; on Drury, see Weir, *Beyond Labor's Veil*, 43, and " 'Here's to the Men Who Lose!,' " 530–56.

44. See Gurney, "Higher State of Civilization," 542–47. See also Archer, "Cooperative Ideal," 252–58. Commons et al., *History of Labour*, 2:173. See also the Sovereigns of Industry Papers, State Historical Society of Wisconsin, Madison.

45. Guarneri, *Utopian Alternative*, 396–97. See also Stern, *Pantarch*, and Wunderlich, *Low Living*. On Maria Howland, see Robert Fogarty's introduction to Marie Howland, *The Familistére*; Fogarty, *All Things New*, 124–26, and *Dictionary*, 55–56; and Spann, *Brotherly Tomorrows*, 165–72.

46. *Harper's New Monthly Magazine*, Apr. 1872, 701–16; Godin, *Social Solutions*.

47. Sec. 26 MB, Dec. 23, 1872, Apr. 14, 1873, Dec. 30, 1872, IWAP.

48. Yearley, *Britons in American Labor*, 208–11.

49. *Official Historical Handbook*.

50. Nordin, *Rich Harvest*, 3–30.

51. Marti, *Women of the Grange*, 38–39; *New York Times*, Feb. 5, 1874.

52. *New York Times*, May 7–8, 1873; Unger, *Greenback Era*, 288.

53. Sec. 26 MB, May 19, 1873, IWAP.

54. For more on the marriage of Eastern radicalism and Western populism, see Destler, "Western Radicalism."

55. Sec. 26 MB, June 9, 1873, IWAP; Sovereigns of Industry, Pioneer Council Correspondence, Feb. 7, 1877, State Historical Society of Wisconsin, Madison.

56. Sovereigns of Industry, Pioneer Council Correspondence, Nov. 24, 1873, Dec. 4, 5, 6, 20, 1874, State Historical Society of Wisconsin, Madison; *New York Times*, Dec. 25, 1873.

57. *Equity*, Oct. 1874, 53; "Roll of Members," Sovereigns of Industry, Pioneer Council, Papers, Box 1, State Historical Society of Wisconsin, Madison.

58. *New York Times*, Feb. 1, 1874; Yearley, "Thomas Phillips," 186–87; Sovereigns of Industry, Pioneer Council Correspondence, Mar. 28, 1877, Apr. 10, 1878, State Historical Society of Wisconsin, Madison; *Constitution of the Order of the Sovereigns of Industry: Revised*; Montgomery, *Beyond Equality*, 414; Chamberlin, *Sovereigns of Industry*.

59. "To the Industrial Classes," a Sovereigns of Industry organizing circular reprinted in the *New York Times*, Feb. 1, 1874; "Our Principles," *State Sovereign*, Apr. 1875; *Constitution of the Order of the Sovereigns of Industry*. The Sovereigns' boilerplate statements about the unity of capital and labor have been often misinterpreted as evidence of their procapitalism. John Shedden, president of the Sovereigns of Industry in 1876, made this clear: "One of the great errors in thought that those [commercial and money] interests have been instilling into the popular mind is that capital and labor are one in interest" (*Bulletin of the Sovereigns of Industry*, Sept. 1876).

60. Circular from the State Council of Pennsylvania, n.d., Sovereigns of Industry, Pioneer Council Papers, Box 2, State Historical Society of Wisconsin, Madison; *State Sovereign*, July 1875.

61. Chamberlin, *Sovereigns of Industry*, 152.

62. Ibid., 81; *State Sovereign*, July 1875.

63. *State Sovereign*, July 1875.

64. *National Labor Tribune*, Oct. 9, 23, 1875.

65. Sovereigns of Industry, Pioneer Council Correspondence, Mar. 28, 1877, State Historical Society of Wisconsin, Madison.

66. Philip Foner, *American Socialism*, 64–67; Rachleff, *Black Labor*, 171–78.

67. Weir, " 'Here's to the Men Who Lose!,' " 556.

68. Gompers, *Seventy Years*, 1:61.

69. Ware, *The Labor Movement*, 280–81.

EPILOGUE

1. Samuel Bernstein, *First International*, 258–63.

2. Sec. 26 MB, Sept. 29, 1873, IWAP.

3. *American Spiritualist*, May 11, 1872.

4. *Word*, Feb. 1873.

5. Among the founders of Boston's Bellamyite Nationalist Club were Edward D. Linton and E. M. Chamberlin, men who had also chartered the first English-speaking section of the IWA (Reinders, "T. Wharton Collens," 58).

6. *Socialist Labor Party Platform*; *New York World*, Dec. 27, 30, 1877; *New York Sun*, Dec. 27, 28, 29, 30, 1877.

7. *Socialist Labor Party Platform*.

8. Maddox to Van Patten, Mar. 1880, Executive Committee Correspondence, 1878–84, Socialist Labor Party of America Records, State Historical Society of Wisconsin, Madison.

9. *Journal of United Labor*, Aug. 15, 1880.

10. Ledger and entry in Minutebook for Nov. 13, 1878, New York City American Section Minutes, Socialist Labor Party of America Records, State Historical Society of Wisconsin, Madison.

11. MacDonald, *Fifty Years of Freethought*, 1:150–51; Ward, *History of the Ancient Working People*.

12. Quint, *Forging of American Socialism*, 44, 304; *Official Historical Handbook*.

13. Henninger to Van Patten, Nov. 23, 1879, National Executive Committee Correspondence, Socialist Labor Party of America Records, State Historical Society of Wisconsin, Madison.

14. Entries for Apr. 1882 and May 1883, Minutebooks, Citizens Suffrage Association of Philadelphia Papers, State Historical Society of Wisconsin, Madison.

15. Destler, *American Radicalism*, 78–82.

16. Bell, "Background and Development of Marxian Socialism," 240–41; Lens, *Radicalism in America*, 176–77.

17. Dorfman, *Economic Mind*, 3:35, 146–47; Peters's series ran in the *Workingman's Advocate* between April and July of 1871.

18. Mann, *Yankee Reformers*, 15.

19. Morgan, *Edward Bellamy*, 370–71; Bowman, *Year 2000*, 38–39.

20. Mari Jo Buhle, *Women and American Socialism*, 78–79; Braude, *Radical Spirits*, 198.

21. Herreshoff, "Daniel DeLeon," 206; Perrier, "Socialists and the Working Class," 488; Trachtenberg, *Karl Marx*, 166; Sklar, *Florence Kelley*, 128–29.

22. Lyon, "World of P. J. McGuire," 18.

23. Commons et al., *History of Labour*, 2:218–19; *New York World*, July 8, 1872.

24. Galenson, *United Brotherhood*, 38–39, 54, 64; Horowitz, *Structure and Government*, 66; Foner, *Organized Labor*, 45.

25. Lyons, "World of P. J. McGuire," 112–14; *National Socialist*, Sept. 7, Aug. 17, 31, 1878.

26. *Socialist*, May 24, 31, 1879.

27. R. Laurence Moore, "Flawed Fraternity," 1–17; Sally Miller, "Socialist Party"; Kraditor, *Radical Persuasion*, 154–83; see also Sally Miller, *Race, Ethnicity, and Gender*.

28. See Laslett and Lipset, *Failure of a Dream?*, a collection of recent writings on the Sombart question.

29. *Cooper's Journal*, June 1875.

30. On comparative socialistic views of electoral possibilities, see Przeworski and Sprague, *Paper Stones*, 22–28; on prevailing Gilded Age fears of the future, see Painter, *Standing at Armageddon*.

BIBLIOGRAPHY

MANUSCRIPT MATERIALS

Ann Arbor, Mich.
  Clemete Library, University of Michigan
    Lydia Maria Child Papers
  Labadie Collection, University of Michigan
    John F. Bray Papers
    Ezra Heywood Papers
    Agnes Inglis Files
    Benjamin R. Tucker Papers
    Josiah Warren Papers
Boston, Mass.
  Boston Public Library
    Cyrenus Osborn Ward Papers
    Victoria Woodhull Papers
Cambridge, Mass.
  Crawford Blagden Collection, Houghton Library, Harvard University
    Wendell Phillips Papers
  Schlesinger Library, Radcliffe College
    New England Women's Club Papers
    Leonora O'Reilly Papers
    Harriet Hanson Robinson Papers
Carbondale, Ill.
  Morris Library, Southern Illinois University
    Victoria Woodhull-Martin Papers
Madison, Wisc.
  State Historical Society of Wisconsin
    American Bureau of Industrial Research Collection
    Stephen Pearl Andrews Papers
    Citizens Suffrage Association of Philadelphia Papers
    International Workingmen's Association Papers
    Knights of Labor Papers
    Thomas Phillips Papers
    Socialist Labor Party of America Records
    Sovereigns of Industry, Pioneer Council, Papers
    Ira Steward Papers

Philadelphia, Pa.
   University of Pennsylvania
      George Lippard Papers
Swarthmore, Pa.
   Swarthmore College
      Universal Peace Union Collection
Topeka, Kans.
   Kansas State Historical Society
      Richard Josiah Hinton Papers
Worcester, Mass.
   American Antiquarian Society
   George Lippard Papers

NEWSPAPERS

The Advocate of Peace (Philadelphia)
The American Spiritualist (Cleveland)
American Workman (Boston)
Banner of Light (Boston)
The Bee-hive (London, England)
Bond of Peace (Philadelphia)
The Boston Globe
The Boston Investigator
Boston Post
The Bulletin of the Sovereigns of Industry (Worcester, Mass.)
Cincinnati Commercial
Commonwealth (Boston)
Congressional Globe (Washington, D.C.)
Cooper's Journal (Cleveland, Ohio)
Daily Evening Voice (Boston)
Daily Unionist (Cincinnati)
Equity (Boston)
Evening Transcript (Boston)
Fincher's Trades' Review (Philadelphia)
Galveston Daily News
The Golden Age (New York)
Harper's New Monthly Magazine (New York)
The Iconoclast (Washington, D.C.)
Independent (New York)
Journal of United Labor (Philadelphia)
Labor Standard (New York)
Liberator (Boston)
National Anti-Slavery Standard (New York)
National Labor Tribune (Pittsburgh)
National Socialist (Cincinnati)

The National Standard (New York)
New Thought (Des Moines, Iowa)
New York Daily Tribune
New York Herald
New York Standard
New York Star
New York Sun
New York Times
New York World
Oneida Circular (Oneida, New York)
The Optimist and Kingdom of Heaven (Berlin Heights, Ohio)
Philadelphia Monthly Tribune
Pomeroy's Democrat (New York)
The Present Age (Chicago)
Public Ledger (Philadelphia)
The Radical (Boston)
Religio-Philosophical Journal (Chicago)
The Revolution (New York)
The Socialist (Chicago)
The State Sovereign (Boston)
The Toiler (New York)
The Trades Journal and Financial Record (Boston)
Trade Union or Scientific Socialist (Berlin Heights, Ohio)
The Voice of Peace
Weekly Voice (Boston)
Woman's Journal (Boston)
Woodhull & Claflin's Weekly (New York)
The Word (Princeton, Massachusetts)
The Worker (New York)
Workingman's Advocate (Chicago)

CONSTITUTIONS, PROCEEDINGS, PUBLISHED DOCUMENTS

Address of the National Labor Congress to the Workingmen of the U.S. Chicago: Hazlitt & Quinton, 1867.
Constitution of the Order of the Sovereigns of Industry. Worcester, Mass.: West & Lee Game Printing Co., 1875.
Constitution of the Order of the Sovereigns of Industry: Revised and Adopted at a Special Session of the National Council, Held at Springfield, Mass., March 5th, 6th and 7th, 1874. N.p.: Edward R. Fiske & Co. 1874.
Defense of the Paris Commune: Address of the General Council of "The International" to the Working-Men of Europe and America. Washington, D.C.: n.p., 1871.
Documents of the First International: The Hague Congress of the First International, September 2–7, 1872, Minutes and Documents. Moscow: Progress Publishers, 1978.

Documents of the First International: The Hague Congress of the First International,
September 2–7, 1872: Reports and Letters. Moscow: Progress Publishers, 1978.
The General Council of the First International, 1864–1866: Minutes. 5 vols. Moscow:
Progress Publishers, 1962–68.
The International Working Men's Association: Resolutions of the Congress of Geneva,
1866, and the Congress of Brussels, 1868. London: Westminster Printing Co., n.d.
Memorial Addresses, on the Life and Character of Edwin Martin Chamberlin. . . .
Boston: Committee of Arrangements, 1892.
Ninth Census. Compendium. Washington, D.C.: Government Printing Office, 1872.
Ninth Census. Volume 3. The Statistics of the Population of the United States . . . .
Washington, D.C.: Government Printing Office, 1872.
Official Historical Handbook of the Independent Order of the Knights of Labor. Jersey
City, N.J.: A. Datz, 1898 (in Knights of Labor Papers, State Historical Society of
Wisconsin, US MSS 5A, Box 1).
Philadelphia City Directory. Philadelphia: J. Gopsill, 1871.
Proceedings of the First Congress of the American International Workingmen's
Association Held in Philadelphia, Pa., July 9 and 10, 1872. New York: The Federal
Council, 1872.
Report of Proceedings of the Eighteenth Annual Session of the International
Typographical Union, Held in Cincinnati, Ohio, June 6, 7, 8, 9, and 10, 1870.
Philadelphia: n.p., 1870.
Report of the Committee of the Senate upon the Relations between Labor and Capital.
3 vols. Washington, D.C.: Government Printing Office, 1885.
Socialist Labor Party Platform, Constitution, and Resolutions Adopted at the National
Congress . . . Held at Newark, N.J., Dec. 26–31, 1877. Cincinnati: n.p., 1878.
Social Party: Constitution and Plan of Organization. New York: "Printed in the Office
of the Solidarity," 1868.
Trow's New York City Directory. New York: Trow Directory, Printing and Bookbinding
Co., 1871.

ARTICLES, UNPUBLISHED PAPERS

Abbott, Edith. "Employment of Women in Industries: Cigarmaking—Its History and
Present Tendencies." *Journal of Political Economy* (Jan. 1907): 1–25.
Ansdell, Douglass, B. A. "William Lloyd Garrison's Ambivalent Approach to Labour
Reform." *Journal of American Studies* 24:3 (Dec. 1990): 402–7.
Archer, Julian. "The Cooperative Ideal in the Socialist Thought of the First
International in France." In *Proceedings of the Seventh Annual Meeting of the*
Western Society for French History, edited by Joyce Duncan Falk, 252–58. Santa
Barbara: ABC-Clio Inc., 1981.
Bell, Daniel. "The Background and Development of Marxian Socialism in the United
States." In *Socialism and American Life*, edited by Donald Drew Egbert and Stow
Persons, 213–406. Princeton, N.J.: Princeton University Press, 1952.
Bernstein, Samuel. "American Labor and the Paris Commune." *Science and Society* 15
(Spring 1951), 144–62.

"Biography of Rev. Moses Hull." *The Psychic Era*, March 1902.

Bloch, Herman D. "Labor and the Negro, 1866–1910." *Journal of Negro History* 50:3 (July 1965): 163–84.

———. "The National Labor Union and Black Workers." *The Journal of Ethnic Studies* 50:3 (Spring 1973): 13–21.

Brooks, Frank H. "Ideology, Strategy, and Organization: Dyer Lum and the American Anarchist Movement." *Labor History* 34:1 (Winter 1993): 57–83.

Buhle, Mari Jo. "Woman's Culture and Politics in the Gilded Age." Unpublished paper delivered at the Historical Dimensions of Women's Culture Conference, Boston College, April 23, 1983. A copy of this paper is held by the Schlesinger Library, Radcliffe College.

Butterfield, Roger. "George Lippard and His Secret Brotherhood." *The Pennsylvania Magazine of History and Biography* 74:3 (July 1955): 284–307.

Cohen, Robert S. "Marxism and Democracy." In *Marxism and Democracy: A Symposium*, edited by Herbert Aptheker, 1–17. New York: Humanities Press, 1965.

Cunningham, Edward. "The Culture That Was Vineland." *The Vineland Historical Magazine* 26 (Apr. 1941): 197–200.

Davis, Horace B. "Nations, Colonies, and Social Classes: The Position of Marx and Engels." *Science and Society* 29:1 (Winter 1965): 26–43.

DeSantis, Vincent P. "Belva Ann Lockwood." *Timeline* (Dec. 1987–Jan. 1988): 42–49.

Destler, Chester McArthur. "Western Radicalism, 1865–1901: Concepts and Origins." *Mississippi Valley Historical Review* 31 (December 1944): 335–68.

Douglass, Dorothy W. "Ira Steward on Consumption and Unemployment." *Journal of Political Economy* 40:4 (Aug. 1932): 532–43.

Draper, Hal, and Anne G. Lipow. "Marxist Women Versus Bourgeois Feminism." In *The Socialist Register, 1976*, edited by Ralph Milliband and John Saville, 179–226. London: Merlin Press, 1976.

DuBois, Ellen, ed. "On Labor and Free Love: Two Unpublished Speeches of Elizabeth Cady Stanton." *Signs* 1:1 (Autumn 1975): 260–63.

Foner, Eric. "Black Labor Conventions during Reconstruction." In *Culture, Gender, Race, and U.S. Labor History*, edited by Ronald C. Kent, Sara Markham, David R. Roediger, and Herbert Shapiro, 91–103. Westport, Conn.: Greenwood Press, 1993.

Foner, Philip. "A Labor Voice for Black Equality: The Boston *Daily Evening Voice*, 1864–1867." *Science and Society* 38 (Fall 1974): 304–25.

Gerteis, Louis S. "Slavery and Hard Times: Morality and Utility in American Antislavery Reform." *Civil War History* 29:4 (Dec. 1983): 316–31.

Gitelman, H. M. "Adolph Strasser and the Origins of Pure and Simple Unionism." *Labor History* 6:1 (Winter 1965): 71–83.

Glickstein, Jonathan. "Poverty Is Not Slavery: American Abolitionists and the Competitive Labor Market." In *Antislavery Reconsidered: New Perspectives on the Abolitionists*, edited by Lewis Perry and Michael Fellman, 195–218. Baton Rouge: Louisiana State University Press, 1979.

Gurney, Peter. " 'A Higher State of Civilization and Happiness': Internationalism in the British Co-operative Movement between c. 1869–1918." In *Internationalism in the Labour Movement, 1830–1940*, edited by Frits van Holthoon and Marcel van der Linden, 2:542–64. Leiden, Netherlands: E. J. Brill, 1988.

Gutman, Herbert. "The Tompkins Square 'Riot' in New York City on January 13, 1874: Re-examination of Its Causes and Its Aftermath." *Labor History* 6:1 (Winter 1965): 44–70.

Herreshoff, David. "Daniel DeLeon: The Rise of Marxist Politics." In *American Radicals: Some Problems and Personalities*, edited by Harvey Goldberg, 199–215. New York: Monthly Review Press, 1957.

Hill, Herbert. "Race, Ethnicity and Organized Labor: The Opposition to Affirmative Action." *New Politics* 1:2 (Winter 1987): 31–82.

Hinton, Richard J. "The Race for Commercial Supremacy in Asia." *The Galaxy* 8:2 (Aug. 1869): 180–94.

———. "A Talk With Mr. Burlingame About China." *The Galaxy* 6:5 (Nov. 1868): 613–23.

Huston, James L. "The American Revolutionaries, the Political Economy of Aristocracy, and the American Concept of the Distribution of Wealth, 1765–1900." *American Historical Review* 99:4 (Oct. 1993): 1079–105.

———. "Facing an Angry Labor: The American Public Interprets the Shoemakers Strike of 1860." *Civil War History* 28:3 (Sept. 1982): 197–212.

Kugler, Israel. "The Trade Union Career of Susan B. Anthony." *Labor History* 2:1 (Winter 1961), 90–100.

Kuritz, Hyman. "Ira Steward and the Eight Hour Day." *Science and Society* 20 (Spring 1956): 118–34.

Lause, Mark A. "The American Radicals and Organized Marxism: The Initial Experience, 1869–1874." *Labor History* 33:1 (Spring 1992): 55–80.

———. " 'The Unwashed Infidelity': Thomas Paine and Early New York Labor History." *Labor History* 27 (Summer 1986): 385–409.

Lofton, Williston H. "Abolition and Labor." *Journal of Negro History* 33:3 (July 1948): 249–53.

Loveland, Anne C. "Evangelicalism and 'Immediate Emancipation' in American Antislavery Thought." *Journal of Southern History* 32 (May 1966): 172–88.

McPherson, James. "A Brief for Equality: The Abolitionist Reply to the Racist Myth, 1860–1865." In *The Antislavery Vanguard*, edited by Martin Duberman, 156–77. Princeton, N.J.: Princeton University Press, 1965.

Matison, Sumner Eliot. "The Labor Movement and the Negro During Reconstruction." *Journal of Negro History* 32:4 (Oct. 1948): 426–68.

Messer-Kruse, Timothy. "Chinese Exclusion and the Eight-Hour Day: Ira Steward and the Political Economy of Cheap Labor." Paper delivered at the Pullman Centennial Conference, Indiana State University, Terre Haute, Sept. 23, 1994.

Miller, Sally. "The Socialist Party and the Negro, 1901–1920." *Journal of Negro History* 56:3 (July 1971): 220–29.

Moore, R. Laurence. "Flawed Fraternity — American Socialist Response to the Negro, 1901–1912." *The Historian* 32:1 (Nov. 1969): 1–18.

———. "Spiritualism and Science: Reflections on the First Decade of Spirit Rappings." *American Quarterly* 24 (Oct. 1972): 474–500.

Pease, William H., and Jane H. Pease. "Antislavery Ambivalence: Immediatism, Expediancy, Race." *American Quarterly* 37:4 (Winter 1965): 682-95.

Perrier, Hubert. "Radicalisme américain et socialisme: les sections 'autonomistes' de la Premiére Internationale aux etats-unis." In *Why Is There No Socialism in the United States?*, edited by Jean Heffer and Jeanine Rouet, 193-207. Paris: Editions de L'École des Hautes Études en Sciences Sociales, 1988.

———. "The Socialists and the Working Class in New York: 1890-1896." *Labor History* 22:4 (Fall 1981): 488-511.

Rayback, Joseph. "The American Workingman and the Antislavery Crusade." *Journal of Economic History* 3, no. 4 (Nov. 1943): 152-63.

Reinders, Robert C. "T. Wharton Collens and the Christian Labor Union." *Labor History* 8:1 (Winter 1967): 53-70.

Roediger, David. "Ira Steward and the Anti-Slavery Origins of American Eight Hour Theory." *Labor History* 27:3 (Summer 1986): 410-26.

———. "Racism, Reconstruction and the Labor Press: The Rise and Fall of the *St. Louis Daily Press*, 1864-1866." *Science and Society* 42 (Summer 1978): 156-77.

Rudolph, Frederick. "Chinamen in Yankeedom: Anti-Unionism in Massachusetts in 1870." *American Historical Review* 53 (Oct. 1947): 1-29.

Schneider, Dorothee. "The New York Cigarmakers Strike of 1877." *Labor History* 26:1 (Winter 1985): 325-52.

Shapiro, Herbert. "Labor and Antislavery: Reflections on the Literature." *Nature, Society and Thought* 2:4 (1989): 471-90.

Thomas, John L. "Antislavery and Utopia." In *The Antislavery Vanguard: New Essays on the Abolitionists*, edited by Martin Duberman, 240-69. Princeton, N.J.: Princeton University Press, 1965.

Thompson, Robert. "A Current Revolution." *The Penn Monthly* (Apr. 1870): 121-30.

Trimble, William. "The Social Philosophy of the Loco-Foco Democracy." *American Journal of Sociology* 26:6 (May 1921): 705-15.

Walters, Ronald G. "The Boundaries of Abolitionism." In *Antislavery Reconsidered: New Perspectives on the Abolitionists*, edited by Lewis Perry and Michael Fellman, 3-23. Baton Rouge: Louisiana State University Press, 1979.

Weir, Robert. " 'Here's to the Men Who Lose!': The Hidden Career of Victor Drury." *Labor History* 36:4 (Fall 1995): 530-56.

Yearley, Clifton K., Jr. "Thomas Phillips, A Yorkshire Shoemaker in Philadelphia." *Pennsylvania Magazine of History and Biography* 79:2 (Apr. 1955): 167-96.

BOOKS, DISSERTATIONS

Ahlstrom, Sidney E. *A Religious History of the American People*. New Haven, Conn.: Yale University Press, 1972.

Allen, Robert L., and Pamela P. Allen. *Reluctant Reformers: Racism and Social Reform Movements in the United States*. Washington, D.C.: Howard University Press, 1983.

The American Annual Cyclopedia and Register of Important Events of the Year 1871. New York: D. Appleton & Co., 1872.

American Newspaper Directory. New York: Geo. P. Rowell & Co., 1871.

Andrews, Stephen Pearl. *Love, Marriage, and Divorce and the Sovereignty of the Individual.* 1853. Reprint, New York: Source Books, 1972.

Ansley, Clark F., ed. *The Columbia Encyclopedia.* New York: Columbia University Press, 1935.

Bailie, William. *Josiah Warren: The First American Anarchist.* 1906. Reprint, New York: Arno Press, 1972.

Bailyn, Bernard, Gordon Wood, and J. G. A. Pocock. *The Machiavellian Moment: Florentine Political Thought and the Atlantic Republican Tradition.* Princeton, N.J.: Princeton University Press, 1975.

Balser, Diane. *Sisterhood and Solidarity: Feminism and Labor in Modern Times.* Boston: South End Press, 1987.

Barnes, Gilbert Hobbs. *The Antislavery Impulse, 1830–1844.* New York: Harcourt, Brace & World, Inc., 1933.

Barrow, Loogie. *Independent Spirits: Spiritualism and English Plebians, 1850–1910.* Boston: Routledge & Kegan Paul, 1986.

Barry, Kathleen. *Susan B. Anthony: A Biography of a Singular Feminist.* New York: New York University Press, 1988.

Barth, Gunter. *Bitter Strength: A History of the Chinese in the United States, 1850–1870.* Cambridge, Mass.: Harvard University Press, 1964.

Bednarowski, Mary Farrell. "Nineteenth-Century American Spiritualism: An Attempt at a Scientific Religion." Ph.D. diss., University of Minnesota, 1973.

Bellamy, Joyce M., and John Saville, eds. *Dictionary of Labour Biography.* 7 vols. London: Macmillan, 1972–84.

Berlin, Ira, Joseph P. Reidy, and Leslie S. Rowland, eds. *Freedom: A Documentary History of Emancipation, 1861–1867,* Series 2. New York: Cambridge University Press, 1982.

Bernard, Luther, and Jessie Bernard. *Origins of American Sociology: The Social Science Movement in the United States.* New York: T. Y. Crowell, 1943.

Bernstein, Iver. *The New York City Draft Riots: Their Significance for American Society and Politics in the Age of the Civil War.* New York: Oxford University Press, 1990.

Bernstein, Samuel. *Essays in Political and Intellectual History.* New York: Paine-Whitman Publishers, 1955.

———. *The First International in America.* New York: A. M. Kelley, 1962.

———, ed. *Papers of the General Council of the International Workingmen's Association, New York, 1872–1876.* Milano: Feltrinelli Editore, 1961.

Biographical Directory of the American Congress, 1774–1971. Washington, D.C.: Government Printing Office, 1971.

Blair, Karen J. *The Clubwoman as Feminist: True Womanhood Redefined, 1868–1914.* New York: Holmes & Meier Publishers, 1980.

Bowman, Sylvia E. *The Year 2000: A Critical Biography of Edward Bellamy.* New York: Bowman Associates, 1958.

Boydston, Jeanne, Mary Kelley, and Anne Margolis, eds. *The Limits of Sisterhood: The Beecher Sisters on Women's Rights and Women's Sphere.* Chapel Hill: University of North Carolina Press, 1988.

Braude, Ann. *Radical Spirits: Spiritualism and Women's Rights in Nineteenth Century America*. Boston: Beacon Press, 1989.

Bridges, Amy. *A City in the Republic: Antebellum New York and the Origins of Machine Politics*. New York: Cambridge University Press, 1984.

Brock, Peter. *Pacifism in the United States: From the Colonial Era to the First World War*. Princeton, N.J.: Princeton University Press, 1968.

Brown, Burton Gates, Jr. "Spiritualism in Nineteenth-Century America." Ph.D. diss., Boston University, 1972.

Buhle, Mari Jo. *Women and American Socialism, 1780–1920*. Urbana: University of Illinois Press, 1981.

Buhle, Mari Jo, and Paul Buhle, eds. *Concise History of Woman Suffrage: Selections from the Classic Work of Stanton, Anthony, Gage, and Harper*. Urbana: University of Illinois Press, 1978.

Buhle, Paul. *Marxism in the United States: Remapping the History of the American Left*. London: Verso Press, 1987.

Capron, E. W. *Modern Spiritualism: Its Facts and Fanaticisms, Its Consistencies and Contradictions*. 1855. Reprint, New York: Arno Press, 1976.

Chamberlin, Edwin M. *The Sovereigns of Industry*. 1875. Reprint, Westport, Conn.: Hyperion Press, 1976.

Cheek, William, and Aimee Lee Cheek. *John Mercer Langston and the Fight for Black Freedom, 1829–1865*. Urbana: University of Illinois Press, 1989.

Cole, G. D. H. *The Life of Robert Owen*. 1930. Reprint, Hamden, Conn.: Archon Books, 1966.

Collins, Henry, and Chimen Abramsky. *Karl Marx and the British Working Class Movement: Years of the First International*. New York: Macmillan & Co., 1965.

Commager, Henry Steele. *Theodore Parker*. New York: Little Brown & Co., 1936.

Commons, John R., Ulrich B. Phillips, Eugene A. Gilmore, Helen L. Sumner, and John B. Andrews, eds. *A Documentary History of American Industrial Society*. 11 vols. Cleveland: The A. H. Clark Co., 1910–11.

Commons, John R., David J. Saposs, Helen L. Sumner, E. B. Mittelman, H. E. Hoagland, John B. Andrews, and Selig Perlman. *History of Labour in the United States*. 4 vols. New York: Macmillan Co., 1918–35.

Conway, Moncure Daniel. *Autobiography: Memories and Experiences*. 2 vols. New York: Negro University Press, 1902.

Cooper, Patricia A. *Once a Cigar Maker: Men, Women and Work Culture in American Cigar Factories, 1900–1919*. Urbana: University of Illinois Press, 1987.

Costello, Lawrence. "The New York City Labor Movement, 1861-1873." Ph.D. diss., Columbia University, 1967.

Cross, Ira. *History of the Labor Movement in California*. Berkeley: University of California Press, 1935.

Cunliffe, Marcus. *Chattel Slavery and Wage Slavery: The Anglo-American Context, 1830–1860*. Athens: University of Georgia Press, 1979.

Curti, Merle Eugene. *Peace or War: The American Struggle, 1636–1936*. New York: W. W. Norton, 1936.

Daniels, Roger. *Asian America: Chinese and Japanese in the United States Since 1850*. Seattle: University of Washington Press, 1988.

Darnton, Robert. *Mesmerism and the End of the Enlightenment in France*. Cambridge, Mass.: Harvard University Press, 1968.

Davis, David Brion, ed. *Antebellum Reform*. New York: Harper & Row, 1967.

Davis, Susan G. *Parades and Power: Street Theatre in Nineteenth Century Philadelphia*. Philadelphia: Temple University Press, 1986.

DeBenedetti, Charles. *The Peace Reform in American History*. Bloomington: Indiana University Press, 1980.

De Leon, David. *The American as Anarchist: Reflections on Indigenous Radicalism*. Baltimore: Johns Hopkins University Press, 1978.

d'Entremont, John. *Southern Emancipator: Moncure Conway, The American Years, 1832–1865*. New York: Oxford University Press, 1987.

Destler, Chester McArthur. *American Radicalism, 1865–1901*. 1946. Reprint, Chicago: Quadrangle Books, 1966.

Dorfman, Joseph. *The Economic Mind in American Civilization*. 5 vols. New York: Viking Press, 1946–59.

DuBois, Ellen Carol. *Feminism and Suffrage: The Emergence of an Independent Women's Movement in America, 1848–1869*. Ithaca, N.Y.: Cornell University Press, 1978.

―――, ed. *Elizabeth Cady Stanton, Susan B. Anthony: Correspondence, Writings, Speeches*. New York: Shocken Books, 1981.

Du Bois, W. E. B. *Black Reconstruction in America*. 1935. Reprint, New York: Atheneum, 1969.

Dutt, R. Palme. *The Internationale*. London: Lawrence & Wishard Ltd., 1964.

Easton, Lloyd D. *Hegel's First American Followers: The Ohio Hegelians: John B. Stallo, Peter Kaufmann, Moncure Conway, and August Willich, with Key Writings*. Athens: Ohio University Press, 1966.

Edwards, Corwin D. "The First International Workingmen's Association." Ph.D. diss., Cornell University, 1928.

Farley, Ena L. *The Underside of Reconstruction New York: The Struggle over the Issue of Black Equality*. New York: Garland Publishing, 1993.

Felix, David. *Marx as Politician*. Carbondale: Southern Illinois University Press, 1983.

Fogarty, Robert S. *All Things New: American Communes and Utopian Movements, 1860–1914*. Chicago: University of Chicago Press, 1990.

―――. *Dictionary of American Communal and Utopian History*. Westport, Conn.: Greenwood Press, 1980.

Foner, Eric. *Free Soil, Free Labor, Free Men: The Ideology of the Republican Party before the Civil War*. New York: Oxford University Press, 1970.

―――. *Politics and Ideology in the Age of the Civil War*. New York: Oxford University Press, 1980.

―――. *Tom Paine and Revolutionary America*. New York: Oxford University Press, 1976.

Foner, Philip S. *American Socialism and Black Americans: From the Age of Jackson to World War II*. Westport, Conn.: Greenwood Press, 1977.

————. *History of the Labor Movement in the United States: From Colonial Times to the Founding of the American Federation of Labor.* Vol. 1 of *History of the Labor Movement in the United States.* New York: International Publishers, 1947.

————. *Organized Labor and the Black Worker, 1619–1973.* New York: Praeger, 1974.

Foner, Philip S., and Brewster Chamberlin, eds. *Friedrich A. Sorge's Labor Movement in the United States.* Westport, Conn.: Greenwood Press, 1977.

Foner, Philip S., and Ronald L. Lewis, eds. *The Black Worker during the Era of the National Labor Union.* Philadelphia: Temple University Press, 1978.

Foner, Philip S., and Daniel Rosenberg, eds. *Racism, Dissent, and Asian Americans from 1850 to the Present: A Documentary History.* Westport, Conn.: Greenwood Press, 1993.

————. *Women and the American Labor Movement: From the First Trade Unions to the Present.* New York: Free Press, 1979.

Frederickson, George M. *William Lloyd Garrison.* Englewood Cliffs, N.J.: Prentice-Hall, Inc., 1968.

Galenson, Walter. *The United Brotherhood of Carpenters: The First Hundred Years.* Cambridge, Mass.: Harvard University Press, 1983.

Gerteis, Louis S. *Morality and Utility in American Antislavery Reform.* Chapel Hill: University of North Carolina Press, 1987.

Gerth, Hans, ed. *The First International: Minutes of the Hague Congress of 1872.* Madison: University of Wisconsin Press, 1958.

Glickstein, Jonathan. *Conceptions of Free Labor in Antebellum America.* New Haven, Conn.: Yale University Press, 1991.

Godin, Jean Baptiste André. *Social Solutions.* Translated by Marie Howland. New York: J. W. Lovell Co., 1887.

Goldberg, Harvey, ed. *American Radicals: Some Problems and Personalities.* New York: Monthly Review Press, 1957.

Gompers, Samuel. *Seventy Years of Life and Labor.* 2 vols. 1925. Reprint, New York: E. P. Dutton & Co., 1943.

Gompers, Samuel, and Frank Morrison. *Meat vs. Rice: American Manhood against Asiatic Coolieism: Which Shall Survive?* Washington, D.C.: American Federation of Labor, 1902.

Goodell, William. *Slavery and Anti-Slavery: A History of the Great Struggle in Both Hemispheres, with a View of the Slavery Question in the United States.* 1852. Reprint, New York: Negro Universities Press, 1968.

Goodheart, Lawrence B. *Abolitionist, Actuary, Atheist: Elizur Wright and the Reform Impulse.* Kent, Ohio: Kent State University Press, 1990.

Gouldner, Alvin W. *The Two Marxisms: Contradictions and Anomolies in the Development of Theory.* New York: Seabury Press, 1980.

Griffin, C. S. *The Ferment of Reform, 1830–1860.* New York: Thomas Y. Crowell, 1967.

Grossman, Jonathan. *William Sylvis, Pioneer of American Labor: A Study of the Labor Movement during the Era of the Civil War.* New York: Columbia University Press, 1945.

Guarneri, Carl J. *The Utopian Alternative: Fourierism in Nineteenth Century America.* Ithaca, N.Y.: Cornell University Press, 1991.

Hale, William Harlan. *Horace Greeley: Voice of the People*. New York: Harper & Bros., 1950.

Harrison, Royden. *Before the Socialists: Studies in Labour and Politics, 1861–1881*. London: Routledge & Kegan Paul, 1965.

Haskell, Thomas. *The Emergence of Professional Social Science: The American Social Science Association and the Nineteenth-Century Crisis of Authority*. Urbana: University of Illinois Press, 1977.

Hays, Elinor Rice. *Morning Star: A Biography of Lucy Stone, 1818–1893*. New York: Octagon Books, 1978.

Herreshoff, David. *American Disciples of Marx: From the Age of Jackson to the Progressive Era*. Detroit: Wayne State University Press, 1967.

Hillquit, Morris. *History of Socialism in the United States*. 1903. Reprint, New York: Funk & Wagnalls Co., 1910.

Hofstadter, Richard. *The American Political Tradition and the Men Who Made It*. 1948. Reprint, New York: Vintage Books, 1974.

Horowitz, Morris A. *The Structure and Government of the Carpenters' Union*. New York: John Wiley & Sons, 1962.

Howland, Edward, ed. *Social Solutions*. New York: John W. Lovell Co., 1886.

Howland, Marie. *The Familistère*. Philadelphia: Porcupine Press, 1975. Reprint of *Papa's Own Girl*. New York: John B. Jewett, 1874.

Humphrey, A. W. *Robert Applegarth: Trade Unionist, Educationist, Reformer*. Manchester, England: National Labour Press Ltd., 1913.

Ingalls, Joshua King. *Reminiscences of an Octogenarian*. Elmira, N.Y.: Gazett Company, 1897.

Isaacs, Ernest J. "A History of Nineteenth-Century American Spiritualism as a Religious and Social Movement." Ph.D. diss., University of Wisconsin, 1975.

James, Edward T., Janet W. James, and Paul S. Boyer, eds. *Notable American Women, 1607–1950: A Biographical Dictionary*. 3 vols. Cambridge, Mass.: Belknap Press, 1971.

Jenkins, William Sumner. *Pro-Slavery Thought in the Old South*. Chapel Hill: University of North Carolina Press, 1935.

Johnson, Charles, Jr. *African-American Soldiers in the National Guard: Recruitment and Deployment during Peacetime and War*. Westport, Conn.: Greenwood Press, 1992.

Johnston, Johanna. *Mrs. Satan: The Incredible Saga of Victoria C. Woodhull*. New York: G. P. Putnam's Sons, 1967.

Karl Marx and Frederick Engels on Britain. Moscow: Foreign Languages Publishing House, 1953.

Karl Marx, Frederick Engels Collected Works. New York: International Publishers, 1987.

Kasson, John F. *Civilizing the Machine: Technology and Republican Values in America, 1776–1900*. Philadelphia: Grossman Publishers, 1976.

Katz, Henryk. *The Emancipation of Labor: A History of the First International*. Westport, Conn: Greenwood Press, 1992.

Kaufman, Stuart, ed. *The Making of a Union Leader, 1850–1886*. Vol. 1 of *The Samuel Gompers Papers*. Urbana: University of Illinois Press, 1986.

———. *Samuel Gompers and the Origins of the American Federation of Labor, 1848–1896*. Westport, Conn.: Greenwood Press, 1973.

Kessler-Harris, Alice. *A Woman's Wage: Historical Meanings and Social Consequences*. Lexington: University Press of Kentucky, 1990.

Kilgore, Damon Y. *The Questions of To-day, Caste, Suffrage, Labor, Temperance, Religion: An Oration Delivered before the Wesleyan Academy Alumni Association at Wilbraham, Mass., June 29, 1870*. New York: Hurd & Houghton, 1870.

Korngold, Ralph. *Two Friends of Man: The Story of William Lloyd Garrison and Wendell Phillips and Their Relationship with Abraham Lincoln*. Boston: Little, Brown & Co., 1950.

Kraditor, Aileen. *Means and Ends in American Abolitionism: Garrison and His Critics on Strategy and Tactics*. New York: Pantheon Books, 1969.

———. *The Radical Persuasion, 1890–1917: Aspects of the Intellectual History and the Historiography of Three American Radical Organizations*. Baton Rouge: Louisiana State University Press, 1981.

Kugler, Israel. *From Ladies to Women: The Organized Struggle for Woman's Rights in the Reconstruction Era*. Westport, Conn.: Greenwood Press, 1987.

Landy, A. *Marxism and the Democratic Tradition*. New York: International Publishers, 1946.

Langston, John M. *From the Virginia Plantation to the National Capitol*. Hartford, Conn.: American Publishing Company, 1894.

Laslett, John, and Seymour Martin Lipset. *Failure of a Dream?: Essays in the History of American Socialism*. Garden City, N.Y.: Anchor Press, 1974.

Laurie, Bruce. *Artisans into Workers: Labor in Nineteenth- Century America*. New York: Noonday Press, 1989.

Lens, Sidney. *Radicalism in America*. New York: Thomas Crowell, 1969.

Lessner, Frederick. *Sixty Years in the Social-Democratic Movement . . . Recollections of an Old Communist*. London: The Twentieth Century Press, 1907.

Levin, Michael. *Marx, Engels and Liberal Democracy*. New York: St. Martin's Press, 1989.

Levine, Bruce. *The Spirit of 1848: German Immigrants, Labor Conflict, and the Coming of the Civil War*. Urbana: University of Illinois Press, 1992.

Lewis, Leon. *The Facts Concerning the Eight Condemned Leaders*. Greenport, N.Y.: n.p., 1887.

Locke, Rovan George. "Race and Ethnocentrism in Karl Marx's World View: Some Third World Perspectives." Ph.D. diss., University of Michigan, 1978.

Lynd, Staughton. *Intellectual Origins of American Radicalism*. New York: Pantheon Books, 1968.

Lyon, David Nicholas. "The World of P. J. McGuire: A Study of the American Labor Movement, 1870–1890." Ph.D. diss., University of Minnesota, 1972.

MacDonald, George E. *Fifty Years of Freethought*. New York: The Truth Seeker Company, 1929.

MacKinley, Francis Rose. *Psyche to the Nineteenth Century: A Chant of Love and Freedom*. N.p., n.d.

McKitrick, Eric L., ed. *Slavery Defended: The Views of the Old South*. Englewood Cliffs, N.J.: Prentice-Hall, Inc., 1963.

McKivigan, John R. *The War against Proslavery Religion: Abolitionism and the Northern Churches, 1830–1865*. Ithaca, N.Y.: Cornell University Press, 1984.

McMorrow, Mary E. "The Nineteenth Century German Political Immigrant and the Construction of American Culture and Thought." Ph.D. diss., New School for Social Research, 1982.

McNeill, George E., ed. *The Labor Movement: The Problem of To-Day*. Boston: A. M. Bridgman & Co., 1887.

Mandel, Bernard. *Labor Free and Slave: Workingmen and the Anti-Slavery Movement in the United States*. New York: Associated Authors, 1955.

Mann, Arthur. *Yankee Reformers in the Urban Age*. Cambridge, Mass.: The Belknap Press of Harvard University, 1954.

Marti, Donald B. *Women of the Grange: Mutuality and Sisterhood in Rural America, 1866–1920*. Westport, Conn.: Greenwood Press, 1991.

Martin, James J. *Men against the State: The Expositors of Individualist Anarchism*. New York: Libertarian Book Club, 1957.

Marx, Karl. *Capital*. New York: International Publishers, 1939.

Masquerier, Lewis. *Sociology or the Reconstruction of Society . . . . 1877*. Reprint, Westport, Conn.: Greenwood Press, 1970.

May, Henry F. *The Enlightenment in America*. New York: Oxford University Press, 1976.

Miller, Sally M., ed., *Race, Ethnicity, and Gender in Early Twentieth-Century American Socialism*. New York: Garland Press, 1996.

Miller, Stuart Creighton. *The Unwelcome Immigrant: The American Image of the Chinese, 1785–1882*. Berkeley: University of California Press, 1969.

Mins, L. E., ed. *Founding of the First International: A Documentary Record*. New York: International Publishers, 1937.

Montgomery, David. *Beyond Equality: Labor and the Radical Republicans, 1862–1872*. 1967. Reprint, Urbana: University of Illinois Press, 1981.

Moore, R. Laurence. *In Search of White Crows: Spiritualism, Parapsychology, and American Culture*. New York: Oxford University Press, 1977.

Moore, Stanley W. *The Critique of Capitalist Democracy: An Introduction to the Theory of the State in Marx, Engels, and Lenin*. New York: Paine-Whitman Publishers, 1957.

Morgan, Arthur E. *Edward Bellamy*. New York: Columbia University Press, 1944.

Morita, Sally Jean. "Modern Spiritualism and Reform in America." Ph.D. diss., University of Oregon, 1995.

Nadel, Stanley. *Little Germany: Ethnicity, Religion, and Class in New York City, 1845–1880*. Urbana: University of Illinois Press, 1990.

National Cyclopedia of American Biography. New York: James T. White & Co., 1907.

Newton, A. E., ed. *The Educator: Being Suggestions, Theoretical and Practical,*

Designed to Promote Man-Culture and Integral Reform. Boston: Office of Practical Spiritualists, 1857.

Nordin, D. Sven. *Rich Harvest: A History of the Grange, 1867–1900*. Jackson: University of Mississippi, 1974.

Obermann, Karl. *Joseph Weydemeyer: Pioneer of American Socialism*. New York: International Publishers, 1947.

Ottley, Roi, and William J. Weatherby, eds., *The Negro in New York: An Informal Social History*. Dobbs Ferry, N.Y.: New York Public Library, Oceana Publications, Inc., 1967.

Owen, Alex. *The Darkened Room: Women, Power, and Spiritualism in Late Nineteenth-Century England*. London: Virago Press, 1989.

Padover, Saul. *Karl Marx: An Intimate Biography*. New York: McGraw Hill Book Co., 1978.

Painter, Nell Irvin. *Standing at Armageddon: The United States, 1877–1919*. New York: W. W. Norton, 1989.

Parker, Theodore. *Speeches, Addresses, and Occasional Sermons*. Boston: Ticknor and Fields, 1860.

Parrington, Vernon. *Main Currents in American Thought*. New York: Harcourt, Brace & Co., 1930.

Perry, Lewis. *Radical Abolitionism: Anarchy and Government of God in Antislavery Thought*. Ithaca, N.Y.: Cornell University Press, 1973.

Pessen, Edward. *Most Uncommon Jacksonians: The Radical Leaders of the Early Labor Movement*. Albany: SUNY Press, 1967.

Powell, Aaron M. *Personal Reminiscences of the Anti-Slavery and Other Reforms and Reformers*. Plainfield, N.J.: A. R. Powell, 1899.

Przeworski, Adam, and John Sprague. *Paper Stones: A History of Electoral Socialism*. Chicago: University of Chicago Press, 1986.

Quint, Howard H. *The Forging of American Socialism: Origins of the Modern Movement*. Indianapolis: The Bobbs-Merrill Company, 1953.

Rachleff, Peter J. *Black Labor in the South: Richmond, Virginia, 1865–1890*. Philadelphia: Temple University Press, 1984.

Reese, James V. "The Worker in Texas, 1821–1876." Ph.D. diss., University of Texas, 1964.

Reynolds, David S. *George Lippard*. Boston: Twayne Publishers, 1982.

Robertson, Stacy Marie. "Parker Pillsbury, Anti-Slavery Apostle: Gender and Religion in Nineteenth-Century U.S. Radicalism." Ph.D. diss., University of California at Santa Barbara, 1994.

Roediger, David R. *The Wages of Whiteness: Race and the Making of the American Working Class*. New York: Verso Press, 1991.

Rosenwaike, Ira. *Population History of New York City*. Syracuse: Syracuse University Press, 1972.

Royle, E. *Victorian Infidels: The Origins of the British Secularist Movement, 1791–1866*. Manchester, England: University of Manchester Press, 1974.

Ruff, Allen. *"We Called Each Other Comrade": Charles H. Kerr & Company, Radical Publishers*. Urbana: University of Illinois Press, 1997.

Sachs, Emanie. *"The Terrible Siren," Victoria Woodhull, 1838–1927*. New York: Harper & Brothers, 1928.

Salvatore, Nick. *Eugene V. Debs: Citizen and Socialist*. Urbana: University of Illinois Press, 1982.

Saxton, Alexander. *The Indispensable Enemy: Labor and the Anti-Chinese Movement in California*. Berkeley: University of California Press, 1971.

———. *The Rise and Fall of the White Republic: Class Politics and Mass Culture in Nineteenth-Century America*. New York: Verso Press, 1990.

Schlensinger, Arthur M. *The American as Reformer*. Cambridge, Mass.: Harvard University Press, 1950. Reprint, New York: Atheneum Press, 1968.

Schlüter, Herman. *Die Anfange der deutschen Arbeiterbewegung in Amerika*. 1907. Reprint, New York: P. Lang, 1984.

———. *Die Internationale in Amerika*. Chicago: Sozialistischen Partei der Vereinington Staaten, 190-?.

———. *Lincoln, Labor and Slavery: A Chapter from the Social History of America*. New York: Socialist Literature Company, 1913.

Schneider, Dorothee. *Trade Unions and Community: The German Working Class in New York City, 1870–1900*. Urbana: University of Illinois Press, 1994.

Sears, Hal S. *The Sex Radicals: Free Love in High Victorian America*. Lawrence: Regents Press of Kansas, 1977.

Sklar, Kathryn Kish. *Florence Kelley and the Nation's Work: The Rise of Women's Political Culture, 1830–1900*. New Haven, Conn.: Yale University Press, 1995.

Spann, Edward K. *Brotherly Tomorrows: Movements for a Cooperative Society in America, 1820–1920*. New York: Columbia University Press, 1989.

Spero, Sterling D., and Abram L. Harris. *The Black Worker: The Negro and the Labor Movement*. 1931. Reprint, Port Washington, N.Y.: Kennikat Press, 1966.

Spurlock, John C. *Free Love: Marriage and Middle-Class Radicalism in America, 1825–1860*. New York: New York University Press, 1988.

Stanton, Elizabeth C., Susan B. Anthony, and Matilda Joslyn Gage, eds. *History of Woman Suffrage*. 1887. Reprint, New York: Arno Press, 1969.

Stern, Madeleine B. *The Pantarch: A Biography of Stephen Pearl Andrews*. Austin: University of Texas Press, 1968.

———, ed. *The Victoria Woodhull Reader*. Weston, Mass.: M & S Press, 1974.

Stewart, James Brewer. *Holy Warriors: The Abolitionists and American Slavery*. New York: Hill & Wang, 1976.

———. *Wendell Phillips: Liberty's Hero*. Baton Rouge: Louisiana State University Press, 1986.

Stoehr, Taylor. *Free Love in America*. New York: AMS Press, 1979.

Sylvis, James C. *The Life, Speeches, Labors and Essays of William H. Sylvis*. Philadelphia: Claxton, Remesna nd Haffelfinger, 1872.

Takaki, Ronald T. *Race and Culture in Nineteenth-Century America*. New York: Knopf, 1979.

Tappan, Lewis. *The Life of Arthur Tappan*. New York: Hurd and Houghton, 1870.

Taylor, Barbara. *Eve and the New Jerusalem*. New York: Pantheon Books, 1983.

Thomas, John L. *The Liberator: William Lloyd Garrison, a Biography*. Boston: Little, Brown & Co., 1963.

Trachtenberg, Alexander, ed. *Karl Marx and Frederick Engels: Letters to Americans, 1848-1895*. New York: International Publishers, 1953.

Tucker, Robert C., ed. *The Marx and Engels Reader*. New York: W. W. Norton & Co., 1972.

Tuttle, Hudson, and J. M. Peebles. *The Yearbook of Spiritualism for 1871*. Boston: William White & Co., 1871.

Underhill, Lois Beachy. *The Woman Who Ran for President: The Many Lives of Victoria Woodhull*. Bridghampton, New York: Bridge Works Publishing Co., 1995.

Unger, Irwin. *The Greenback Era: A Social and Political History of American Finance*. Princeton, N.J.: Princeton University Press, 1964.

Veysey, Laurence, ed., *The Perfectionists: Radical Social Thought in the North, 1865-1860*. New York: John Wiley & Sons, 1973.

Waller, Altina L. *Reverend Beecher and Mrs. Tilton: Sex and Class in Victorian America*. Amherst: University of Massachusetts Press, 1982.

Walters, Ronald. *American Reformers, 1815-1860*. New York: Hill & Wang, 1978.

———. *The Antislavery Appeal: American Abolitionism after 1830*. Baltimore: Johns Hopkins University Press, 1976.

Ward, Cyrenus Osborne. *A History of the Ancient Working People, from the Earliest Known Period to the Adoption of Christianity* . . . . Washington, D.C.: Press of the Craftsman, 1889.

———. *The New Idea: Universal Co-operation and Theories of Future Government*. New York: The Cosmopolitan Publishing Company, 1870.

Ware, Norman. *The Industrial Worker, 1840-1860*. 1924. Reprint, Chicago: Quadrangle Books, 1964.

———. *The Labor Movement in the United States, 1860-1895: A Study in Democracy*. New York: D. Appleton & Co., 1929.

Warren, Josiah. *Equitable Commerce*. 1852. Reprint, New York: Burt Franklin, 1967.

Weir, Robert E. *Beyond Labor's Veil: The Culture of the Knights of Labor*. University Park: Pennsylvania State University Press, 1996.

Weiss, John. *Life and Correspondence of Theodore Parker*. New York: D. Appleton & Co., 1864.

Weyl, Nathaniel. *Karl Marx: Racist*. New Rochelle, N.Y.: Arlington House, 1979.

Whitman, Alden, ed. *American Reformers*. New York: H. W. Wilson Co., 1985.

Who Was Who in America: Historical Volume, 1607-1896. Chicago: Marquis Press, 1963.

Wilentz, Sean. *Chants Democratic: New York City and the Rise of the American Working Class, 1788-1850*. New York: Oxford University Press, 1984.

Winner, Julia H. *Belva A. Lockwood*. Lockport, N.Y.: Niagara County Historical Society, 1969.

Wish, Harvey. *George Fitzhugh: Propagandist of the Old South*. Gloucester, Mass.: Peter Smith, 1962.

Wittke, Carl. *Refugees of Revolution: The German Forty-Eighters in America*. Westport, Conn.: Greenwood Press, 1952.

Wolfe, F. E. *Admission to American Trade Unions*. Baltimore: Johns Hopkins Press, 1912.

The Women's Project of New Jersey. *Past and Promise: Lives of New Jersey Women*. Metuchen, N.J.: Scarecrow Press, 1990.

Wright, Carroll D. *The History and Growth of the United States Census*. Washington, D.C.: Government Printing Office, 1900.

Wunderlich, Roger. *Low Living and High Thinking at Modern Times, New York*. Syracuse: Syracuse University Press, 1992.

Yearley, Clifton K., Jr. *Britons in American Labor: A History of the Influence of the United Kingdom Immigrants on American Labor*. Westport, Conn.: Greenwood Press, 1957.

Yorke, Onslow. *Secret History of "The International" Workingmen's Association*. London: Strahan & Co., 1872.

Zahler, Helene. *Eastern Workingmen and National Land Policy, 1829–1862*. New York: Columbia University Press, 1941.

Ziegler, Valarie H. *The Advocates of Peace in Antebellum America*. Bloomington: Indiana University Press, 1992.

General German Labor Union (GGLU), 73, 85, 88, 90, 133, 192, 195

George, Henry, 249, 251, 252–53

Gibson, C. W., 61

Godin, Jean Baptiste, 236–37

Goldberg, Harvey, 4

The Golden Age, 7, 104

Gompers, Samuel, 227–32, 245, 255

Goodloe, Daniel R., 24

Graduated Tax Association of New York City, 248

Grant, Ulysses S., 34

Greeley, Horace, 6–7, 21, 118, 261 (n. 3)

Greene, William Batchelder, 114, 248

Gregory, J. W., 74, 96

Grew, Mary, 30, 117

Griffin, Thomas J., 202

Grosse, Edward, 166

Halbert, John, 219

Hale, Edward Everett, 32, 253

Hales, John, 182; and women's rights, 57; and Yankee IWA rift, 170, 174–75, 181

Hammond, John Henry, 25

Hanson, William, 220

Harmonial Benevolent Association, 16

Harris, George, 67, 179, 182

Hayes, Rutherford B., 240

Henninger, Augustus, 251

Hepner, Adolph, 178

Herreshoff, David, 75

Heywood, Ezra, 32, 248

Hillquit, Morris, 129

Hinton, Richard Josiah: attends meeting of IWA General Council, 62; George Odger and, 67, 70; biography, 115, 237; and IWA Section 23, 158–59; Chinese issue and, 212; post-IWA activities, 250–51

Hoar, George, 99, 208

Hooker, Isabella Beecher, 13, 123, 125–26, 284 (n. 25)

Howe, Julia Ward, 37

Howland, Edward, 236–37, 239, 240

Howland, Maria, 236–38, 239

Hubert, Françoise Jean Baptiste, 165

Huleck, Marie, 63, 185

Hull, Moses, 114, 200

Hull's Crucible, 7, 121

Hume, Robert, 70, 89–90; founding IWA Section 9, 95; abolitionism and, 112

The Independent (New York): views of trade unions, 33; and eight-hour demand, 34; and labor reform, 36; views of the Paris Commune, 104–5

Industrial congresses, 21–23

Industrial Workers of the World, 234

Ingalls, Joshua King: spiritualism and, 41, 96; and founding of IWA Section 9, 95; portrait of, 97; in Sovereigns of Industry, 238; last years, 251, 253

International Furniture Workers Union, 227

International League of Peace and Liberty. *See* League of Peace and Freedom

International Typographical Union, 194

International Workingmen's Association (IWA): accusations against, 1; immigration to America, 6–7, 58–63, 66–67, 72–74, 89–90, 94, 182–83; Brussels Congress (1868), 37, 69, 84; founding meeting of, 45–48; constitution of, 49–53, 83–84; London Conference (1871), 56; Geneva Conference (1866), 60, 63, 95; Lausanne Conference (1867), 61, 63, 97; Hague Congress (1872), 69, 157, 172, 177–86; and international pacifism, 95; Basle Congress (1869), 100; Chicago sections, 121; Section 40 (Baltimore), 121; Marx's strategy for, 149–51, 182, 188, 218; Section 2 (New York), 165; French American sections, 165–66; Section 13 (New York), 170; Section 35 (New York), 200, 284 (n. 24); Section 44 (Galveston, Texas), 206–7; San Francisco sections, 209–10, 213–15;

demise of, 247. *See also* Yankee International

—Central Committee (U.S.), 2, 209; founding of, 91; letter to Lincoln, 99; Yankee IWA sections and, 153, 158, 159–69

—General Council: constitutional committee of, 49–53; republicanism in, 54–56; and woman's rights question, 57, 153; American corresponding secretary, 58, 60, 66; standing committee, 64–65; American views of, 82–85, 174–76; and Land and Labour League, 84–85; and New Democracy, 88–90; Yankee IWA and, 158–59, 166–77, 179; exile to America, 182–83

—German American sections: views of Yankee sections, 2, 90–93, 128–29, 131–33; and Forty-Eighters, 18; founding of, 58–60, 72–73; women's rights and, 87–88, 152–54; membership of, 131; Marxism of, 133–34, 183–84; anti-republican thought of, 140, 143–46, 154–56; centralizing tactics of, 146–47, 162–63; African Americans and, 151–52, 180–81, 188–89, 191–95, 197, 232; trade unions and, 151–52, 194, 217–18, 226–30; anti-Chinese movement and, 209–10, 249, 285 (n. 48); Die Zehn Philosophen, 229, 255; legacy of, 245–46

—Section 1 (New York): women's rights and, 152–53; and Yankee IWA, 164, 169, 173, 178; African Americans and, 192; Samuel Gompers and, 228–29; demise of, 247

—Section 9 (New York): founding of, 94–95; membership of, 131; protest to IWA General Council, 173–74; and trade unions, 222, 255

—Section 12 (New York), founding of, 106–7; free love and, 110–11; American reformers and, 112; membership of, 131, 178; ideology of, 134, 141–42; *Westfield* disaster resolution of, 160–

61; "Appeal" of, 162–65; Central Committee and, 166; Marx's view of, 171–72; Eccarius's defense of, 172–73; IWA Hague Congress and, 178, 179, 182; race and, 201, 205; trade unions and, 220; socialist legacy, 249;

—Section 20 (Boston): founding of, 112; membership of, 112–14

—Section 23 (Washington, D.C.): membership of, 114–15, 131, 253; rift with Central Committee, 158–59

—Section 26 (Philadelphia), 39, 185–86; and the UPU, 96; membership of, 115–17, 130–31, 277 (n. 5); debate on eight-hour day, 132; ideology of, 134, 136; and Chinese question, 211; unemployed campaign, 223–24; legacy of, 234–35, 237–40; demise of, 248

—Section 27 (Vineland, New Jersey), founding of, 117–19; women's rights and, 141–42, 153

—Spring Street Federal Council: formation of, 169; growth and decline of, 170, 175–76, 184–85, 215; General Council and, 172–76; George Francis Train and, 185; recruitment of African Americans, 195–97, 200, 206–7; and Chinese question, 210–13; and trade unions, 218–23; unemployed campaign, 223–26; socialist legacy, 249

—Tenth Ward Hotel Provisional Federal Council, 73, 133, 183, 187; formation of, 166, 168; membership of, 169–70; strategy, 195; anti-Chinese movement and, 209–10, 249, 255; and trade unions, 217–18, 226–28, 245, 251, 255

Irish Americans, 6; Marx's strategy for, 149–52, 180–81; German American IWA and, 161–62, 168–69, 180–81; African Americans and, 198–99

Iron Molder's International Union, 189

Izard, 63, 74

Jefferson, Thomas, 8, 72, 75, 77, 80, 81

Jessup, William, 61, 63, 74

Kearney, Dennis, 256–57
Kelley, Florence, 254
Kelley, Oliver H., 237
Kilgore, Damon, 30–31, 115, 212–13
Kinget, Theodore, 139
Knights of Labor, 233, 234–35, 244–46, 248, 250
Knights of St. Crispin, 233
Kuhn, Conrad, 88

Labor Reform, 189; abolitionists and, 18–25, 26–27, 30–33, 106; feminists and, 36–39, 86–88; pacifists and, 39–41; spiritualists and, 41–42, 112–13; Yankee IWA and, 112–13; racial controversy, 189–94. *See also* National Labor Union
Labor Reform League. *See* American Labor Reform League
Labor Unions. *See* Trade Unions
Lafort, Henri, 47
Land and Labour League (London), 84, 179, 271 (n. 30)
Land reform: and abolitionists, 28, 30; transatlantic connections, 67, 84–85; New Democracy and, 72, 75, 80; IWA and, 95, 131, 135, 253, 258
Langston, John M., 192
Laurell, Ferdinand, 228
Law, Harriet, 181–82
Lawrence, Matthew, 65
League of Peace and Freedom (LPF), 52, 67, 95, 102, 115
Leavitt, Joshua, 19
Leland, Mary, 111, 142
Leland, Theron, 112
Le Lubez, 51, 52
Lessner, Friedrich, 66
Lewis, Dio, 32
Lewis, Leon, 60–61
Liberty Party, 19
Liebknecht, Wilhelm, 60, 173
Lincoln, Abraham, 54–55, 98, 145, 266 (n. 20)
Linton, Edward D., 88, 113–14

Linton, W. J., 101, 104
Lippard, George, 41, 234
Livermore, Mary, 37
Locke, John, 76, 80, 141
Lockwood, Belva, 39, 115
Love, Alfred H., 41, 96, 224
Lucraft, Benjamin, 47, 67, 95

MacDonald, George E., 17, 250
McGuire, P. J., 245, 255–56
MacKinley, Francis Rose, 111
Mackintosh, James, 137, 222
McLean, Charles, 86
McMakin, John, 206
McNeill, George, 32
Madox, George W., 238, 249, 250
Marx, Karl: manipulation of IWA General Council, 48–56, 60, 63, 65–67, 170–73, 177–78; views of African Americans, 55, 150, 279 (n. 47); Eccarius and, 63, 67–70; role in purge of Yankee IWA, 92, 157–58, 167, 170–86, 280 (n. 31), 281 (n. 32); Declaration of Principles, 135; anti-idealism of, 142, 154; antirepublicanism of, 148–49, 258–59, 278 (n. 45); strategy for IWA, 149–51, 182, 188, 218; views of women's rights, 152–53, 179; Communist Manifesto, 170; rivalry with Bakunin, 177–78; intellectual hubris of, 183–84; views of Chinese, 208–9
Marxism, 217; alienation from American reform tradition, 2, 3, 45–46, 133, 254–55, 257–60; immigration to U.S., 18; informs German American IWA, 73, 188, 228–29; adapted to business unionism, 229–30, 232–33, 245–46, 255
Masquerier, Lewis, 43–44, 78–79, 253
Massachusetts Anti-Slavery Society, 22–23, 28
Metcalf, Kate, 114
Meyer, Hermann, 131, 267 (n. 28)
Meyer, Siegfried, 66, 69, 72, 85, 88, 91, 92, 131, 150, 192

Middlebrook, Anna, 120
Millot, Theodore, 166, 169
Mills, John, 234, 235
Modern Times, New York, 110, 112, 113
Monopoly, monopolists, 136–37
Montgomery, David, 75, 130
Morton, Marcus, 21
Mott, Lucretia, 224
Mottershead, Thomas, 181
Mutualism, 76–77. *See also* Sovereignty, individual

National Anti-Slavery Society. *See* Reform League
National Anti-Slavery Standard (*NASS*), 37; views of the IWA, 7, 24, 67; views of emancipation, 29–30; debate over discontinuation, 31; on eight-hour demand, 33; and trade union discrimination, 34–35; change of name, 35; and English labor abolitionism, 98–100; and the Paris Commune, 101
Nationalist movement, 252–54
National Labor Reform Party, 193–94
National Labor Union, 222; Congress of 1869, 35; African Americans and, 35, 188–94; female delegates, 38, 86–88; IWA and, 61–63, 66, 79, 85–89; black NLU, 191
National Liberal League, 17
National Woman Suffrage Association (NWSA), 2, 86; IWA and, 121–27
Newberry, Edward, 74; testimony before Senate, 81–82
New Democracy: founding of, 71–72, 74–75, 110; significance of, 72; historiography of, 75, 78; ideology of, 75–82, 249; interpretation of IWA principles, 82–85, 88–90; activities, 84; and German American Marxists, 91–93; and Section 9, 94–95; and Section 12, 107
New England Anti-Slavery Society, 23–24, 30
New England Association of Farmers, Mechanics, and other Workingmen.

See New England Workingmen's Association
New England Labor Reform League, 24, 113; spiritualism and, 42
New England Women's Club, 37
New England Workingmen's Association, 18, 20–21, 23
New Jersey State Association of Spiritualists and Friends of Progress, 119
New York Anti-Slavery Society, 24
New York Draft Riot of 1863, 198, 203
New York Labor League, 91
New York Social Reform Club, 84, 85. *See also* New Democracy
New York State Workingmen's Assembly, 61, 190, 219, 226–27
New York Workingmen's Union, 192, 222, 225
Nicholson, William, 162, 168
Noyes, John Humphrey, 201

Odger, George: founding of the IWA and, 46, 52; and women's rights, 57; ouster as president of IWA, 63; Richard Hinton and, 67; and American Civil War, 99–100
Order of Equality and Justice, 113
Orsini, Cesare, 6, 27, 61, 71, 90
Orsini, Felice, 6, 26–27
Orvis, A., 176
Orvis, John, 240
Owen, Robert, 21, 57, 76

Pacifism: and labor reform, 39–41; the IWA and, 41, 95–96, 115
Paine, Thomas, 8, 9, 121, 250, 258
Panic of 1837, 19, 20
Paris Commune (1871), 1, 100–106, 175, 177, 186, 214, 226, 259, 274 (n. 32)
Parker, Andrew, 204, 205
Parker, Theodore, 21
Parsons, Albert, 235
Paterson, New Jersey, 219–20
Patrons of Industry, 239–40
Pennsylvania Anti-Slavery Society, 252

working class and, 98–100. *See also* Abolitionism

Smart, William G. H., 242

Smith, Adam, 76

Smith, Gerrit, 17, 31

Smith, J. N., 214

Social Democracy, 237, 251

Social Democratic Workingmen's Party, 249

Socialiste (New York, N.Y.), 170

Socialist Labor Party (SLP), 249–52, 253, 254, 255

Socialist Party, 3, 155, 257, 258

Social Party (New York, N.Y.), 73, 145, 188

Social Science Association of Boston, 33, 97

Sombart, Werner, 257

Sorge, Friedrich, 2, 18, 69, 85; joins the IWA, 59–60, 73; Yankee International and, 90–93, 118, 127, 157–70, 173, 180, 181; biography, 131, 145; antirepublican views, 140, 143–46, 154–56, 188; centralizing tactics of, 146–47, 162–63; strategies for IWA, 150–52, 180–81; views of women's rights, 152–54, 249; purge of Yankee IWA, 164–70, 173; at IWA Hague Congress, 178, 180; racial views, 180, 181, 188–89, 194–95, 259; assumes secretariat of IWA, 182, 183; and the NLU, 194; anti-Chinese work of, 209–10; legacy of, 245, 246, 254, 255, 257–60

Sovereigns of Industry, 233, 238, 240–44, 248, 288 (n. 59)

Sovereignty, individual, 76, 77–78, 80–81

Spear, John Murray, 16

Speyer, Carl, 151, 178

Spiritualism: Yankee IWA and, 7, 96, 112, 114, 115–16, 118–21, 175, 180, 215; "Rochester rappings," 13; origins of, 13–15; "science" of, 15; growth of, 15–16; reform beliefs of, 16–17; labor reform and, 41–42; views of the Paris Commune, 103–4

Spring Street Federal Council. *See* International Workingmen's Association: Spring Street Federal Council; Yankee International

Stanton, Edwin M., 203

Stanton, Elizabeth Cady, 13, 17; and labor reform, 38; and NLU controversy, 86; IWA and, 117, 123–26; and George Francis Train, 185

Stephens, James, 6

Stephens, Uriah, 235

Steward, Ira, 31, 33, 41

Steward, Mary, 33

Stiebling, George, 166, 247

Stirpiculture, 201

Stone, Lucy, 37

Stout, John, 115, 132

Strasser, Adolph, 227, 229–31, 245

The Striker (New York), 220

Suffrage. *See* Women's Rights

Sumner, Charles, 6–7, 90, 208

Swedenborg, Emanuel, 14

Sylvis, William, 33, 61, 88, 189–90

Tammany Hall, 33, 145, 198, 284 (n. 21)

Tappan brothers (Arthur and Lewis), 18

Tenth Ward Hotel Council. *See* International Workingmen's Association: German American sections; International Workingmen's Association: Tenth Ward Hotel Provisional Federal Council

Thompson, Leander, 249, 250; as president of New Democracy, 74; IWA Section 9 and, 95; and immigration issue, 212

Tilton, Theodore, 34, 104–6, 112, 123, 206, 254, 265 (n. 71)

Tompkins Square Riot, 226

Trade unions: abolitionist views of, 32, 106; women's rights and, 38–39, 86–88, 243; racial policies of, 87, 189–94, 231–33; and German American Marxists, 92, 151–52, 188, 217–18, 226–28; and Yankee IWA, 218–26,